Gender Diversity Disclosure Regulation

MÜNSTERANER SCHRIFTEN ZUR INTERNATIONALEN UNTERNEHMENSRECHNUNG

Herausgegeben von Peter Kajüter

Band 24

Lennart Prinz

Gender Diversity Disclosure Regulation

Empirical Evidence from Germany

PETER LANG
Berlin · Bruxelles · Chennai · Lausanne · New York · Oxford

Bibliographic Information published by the Deutsche Nationalbibliothek
The Deutsche Nationalbibliothek lists this publication in the Deutsche Nationalbibliografie; detailed bibliographic data is available in the internet at http://dnb.d-nb.de.

Library of Congress Cataloging-in-Publication Data
A CIP catalog record for this book has been applied for at the Library of Congress.

Zugl.: Münster, Univ., Diss., 2025

DE-19
ISSN 1868-7687
ISBN 978-3-631-94089-1 (Print)
ISBN 978-3-631-94107-2 (ePDF)
ISBN 978-3-631-94108-9 (ePUB)
DOI 10.3726/b23078

Published by Peter Lang GmbH, Berlin, Germany

info@peterlang.com

www.peterlang.com

Contact for General Product Safety Regulation (GPSR): gpsr@peterlang.com

Preface

In recent years, growing societal and political concern about the underrepresentation of women in corporate leadership has prompted regulators to promote gender diversity across different corporate hierarchy levels. However, regulators face the challenge of designing effective regulations without unduly interfering with companies' decision-making freedom in personnel matters. One novel approach, gender diversity disclosure regulation (GDDR), aims to increase transparency and foster public pressure, encouraging companies to appoint more women to management positions. While GDDR has already been implemented by regulators, empirical research on this regulatory approach remains scarce.

In this study, Lennart Prinz investigates the disclosure practice and development in corporate gender diversity, determinants of GDDR efficacy, and potentially unintended consequences on the financial reporting quality of companies. The empirical analysis is based on a sample of 214 German companies that are affected by GDDR between 2015 and 2021.

The first sub-study shows that the disclosure practices vary across the regulated companies. Surprisingly, a considerable share of the analyzed reports do not or not fully comply with the disclosure requirements. However, the results reveal a steady increase in gender diversity on corporate boards. Nevertheless, the increase in gender diversity varies across different company sizes, legal form or listing status. Therefore, Lennart Prinz deals with the determinants of GDDR efficacy. The results of multivariate panel regression models indicate that public pressure, listing status, companies' gender diversity reporting practice before the implementation of the GDDR and hierarchy-specific determinants are associated with GDDR efficacy. Moreover, the third sub-study investigates the potentially unintended consequences of GDDR. Lennart Prinz shows that companies which considerably increase gender diversity on the supervisory board in response to high public pressure during the sample period exhibit weaker financial reporting quality. Thus, the results indicate that increased gender diversity in the context of GDDR may be accompanied by consequences beyond the intention of regulators.

The empirical study of Lennart Prinz provides remarkable insights into the regulatory efficacy of GDDR and contributes to literature on targeted transparency regulations. The results shed light on the diversity in the disclosure practice, the determinants of GDDR efficacy and indicate that changes in board compositions may entail unintended consequences. The findings of this study are useful for regulators, users and preparers of gender diversity reports, auditors, and enforcement institutions.

Against the backdrop of increased political and public awareness on corporate gender diversity and the valuable contribution of the findings, I wish that Lennart Prinz's work receives the attention by academia and practice it deserves.

Münster, 31.05.2025 Prof. Dr. Peter Kajüter

Contents overview

Contents

List of figures

List of tables

List of abbreviations

.com	Commercial (Top-Level Domain)
.de	Deutschland (Top-Level Domain)
.eu	European Union (Top Level Domain)
.org	Organizations (Top-Level Domain)
Adj.	Adjusted
AG(s)	Aktiengesellschaft(en) (corporation(s) in Germany)
AGG	Allgemeines Gleichbehandlungsgesetz (German General Equal Treatment Act)
AktG	Aktiengesetz (German Stock corporation Act)
Approx.	Approximately
BaFin	Bundesanstalt für Finanzdienstleistungsaufsicht (German enforcement institution)
BCGC	Berlin Center of Corporate Governance
BGBl.	Bundesgesetzblatt (Federal Law Gazette)
Big 4 auditor	Label for the four largest auditors worldwide (Deloitte, EY, KPMG, PwC)
BMEL	Bundesministerium für Ernährung und Landwirtschaft (Federal Ministry of Food and Agriculture)
BMFSFJ	Bundesministerium für Familie, Senioren, Frauen und Jugend (Federal Ministry for Family Affairs, Senior Citizens, Women and Youth)
BMJ	Bundesministerium der Justiz (formerly Bundesministerium der Justiz und für Verbraucherschutz) (Federal Ministry of Justice)
BDA	Bund Deutscher Arbeitgeber (trade association in Germany)
BDI	Bundesverband der Deutschen Industrie e.V. (trade association in Germany)
BR	Bundesrat
BT	Bundestag
BT-Drs.	Bundestagsdrucksache (Bundestag printed matter)
BvD Dafne	Bureau van Dijk Dafne database

Bündnis 90/Die GRÜNEN	Green Party (Party in Germany)
CA	Current assets
CACC	Current accruals
CDU	Christian Democratic Union (German party)
CEO	Chief Executive Officer
Cf.	Confer
CFO	Cash flows from operating activities
CL	Current liabilities
C. p.	Ceteris paribus
CSR	Corporate social responsibility
CSRD	Corporate Sustainability Reporting Directive
CSR-RUG	CSR-Richtlinie-Umsetzungsgesetz (German Act on the implementation of Directive 2014/95/EU)
CSU	Christian Social Union (German party)
DACC	Discretionary accruals
DAX	Deutscher Aktienindex
Dep	Depreciation expenses
DIC	Deutsche Immobilien Chancen (DIC Asset AG (German company))
DIHK	Deutscher Industrie- und Handelskammertag
DIP	Dokumentations- und Informationssystem für Parlamentsmaterialien
DIW	Deutsches Institut der Wirtschaftsforschung (German Institute for Economic Research)
Djb	Deutscher Juristinnenbund (German Women Lawyers Association)
Dpa	Deutsche Presse-Agentur (German Press Agency)
Dr.	Doctor
DRS	Deutscher Rechnungslegungs Standard
DrittelbG	Drittelbeteiligungsgesetz (German Act of One-Third Participation)

EBEI	Earnings before extraordinary items
EC	European Community
Ed.	Editor
E.g.	Exempli gratia (for example)
Eds.	Editors
EEG	European Econcomic Community
EG	Eingetragene Genossenschaft (German corporation)
EGAktG	Einführungsgesetz zum Aktiengesetz (German Introductory Act of the Stock Corporation Act)
ESRS	European Sustainability Reporting Standards
Et al.	Et alii, aliae, alia
EU	European Union
E.V.	Eingetragener Verein (registered association)
EY	Ernst & Young
FDP	Free Democratic Party (German party)
Fes	Friedrich-Ebert-Stiftung
FidAR e.V.	Frauen in die Aufsichtsräte e.V.
Frequ.	Frequency
FüPoG I	Führungspositionengesetz (German Act on Equal Participation of Women and Men in Leadership Positions in the Private and the Public Sector)
FüPoG II	Zweites Führungspositionengesetz (German Act to Supplement and Amend Regulations for the Equal Participation of Women in Leadership Positions in the Private and Public Sector)
GCGC	German Corporate Governance Code
GDDR	Gender Diversity Disclosure Regulation(s)
GEA	Gesellschaft für Entstaubungsanlagen (GEA Group AG (German company))
GG	Grundgesetz (Basic Law for the Federal Republic of Germany)
GmbH(s)	Gesellschaft(en) mit beschränkter Haftung (corporation(s) in Germany)

GmbH & Co. KG	Gesellschaft mit beschränkter Haftung & Compagnie Kommanditgesellschaft (corporation in Germany)
GmbHG	Gesetz betreffend die Gesellschaften mit beschränkter Haftung (German Law on Limited Liability Companies)
H	Hypothesis
HGB	Handelsgesetzbuch (German Commercial Code)
Html	Hypertext markup language
Http	Hypertext transfer protocol
Https	Hypertext transfer protocol secure
I.c.w.	In connection with
I.e.	Id est (that is)
IFRS	International Financial Reporting Standard(s)
KPMG	KPMG International (formerly "Klynveld, Peat, Marwick and Goerdeler")
KGaA(s)	Kommanditgesellschaft(en) auf Aktien (corporation in Germany)
Lit.	Littera
Max	Maximum
MDAX	Mid-Cap-DAX
Min	Minimum
MitbestG	Mitbestimmungsgesetz (German Co-Determination Act)
MontanMitbestG	Montanmitbestimmungsgesetz (German Iron and Steel Co-Determination Act)
MontanMitbestGErgG	Montan-Mitbestimmungsgesetzergänzungsgesetz (German Supplementary Act to the Iron and Steel Co-Determination Act)
MSc	Master of Science
N.a.	No author
N/a	Not applicable

NACE	Nomenclature statistique des activités économiques dans la Communauté européenne
NFRD	Non-Financial Reporting Directive
NGO(s)	Nongovernmental organization(s)
No.	Number
OLS	Ordinary least squares
P.	Page
PACC	Predicted accruals
Para.	Paragraph
Pdf	Portable document format
Pp.	Pages
PPE	Property, plant and equipment
Prof.	Professor
PwC	PricewaterhouseCoopers International Limited
RESET	Regression specification error test
RegE	Regierungsentwurf (Government draft)
Rev	Sales revenue
Rev.	Revision
RGBl.	Reichsgesetzblatt (National Law Gazette)
Rn.	Randnummer(n)
ROA	Return on assets
RQ	Research question
SAP	Systemanalyse Programmentwicklung (SAP SE (German company))
SDAX	Small-Cap-DAX
SE	Societas Europaea (European company)
SEs	Societates Europaeae (European companies)

SEAG	SE-Ausführungsgesetz (German Act Implementing Council Regulation (EC) No. 2157/2001 of October 8, 2001 on the Statute for European Company (SE))
Sent.	Sentence(s)
SIC	Standard industry classification
SPD	Social Democratic Party (German party)
SSOAR	Social Science Open Access Repository
SSRN	Social Science Research Network
STD	Short-term debt
Std. dev.	Standard deviation
TA	Total assets
TACC	Total accruals
TecDAX	Technology-DAX
UK/U.K.	United Kingdom
UmsG	Umsetzungsgesetz
URL	Uniform resource locator
US/U.S.	United States
VRA	Volta River Authority
VdU	Verband Deutscher Unternehmerinnen (trade association in Germany)
VIF	Variance inflation factor
Vol.	Volume
Vs.	Versus
VSUD	Vereinigung Schweizerischer Unternehmen in Deutschland (trade association in Germany)
VVaG	Versicherungsverein auf Gegenseitigkeit (German Insurance Corporation)
Wabco	Westinghouse Air Brake Company (Wabco Holding GmbH (German company))
Westf.	Westfalen (region in Germany)

Www	World wide web
ZDH	Zentralverband des Deutschen Handwerks (trade association in Germany)

List of symbols

β	Regression coefficient
ε	Error term
τ_b	Kendall's Tau-b coefficient
i	Item in the company index
N (n)	Number of observations
p	Probability (significance level)
Q25	25% percentile
Q75	75% percentile
R^2	Regression coefficient of determination
F	F-value of the F-Test
t	Item in the Period Index
x	Independent variable
y	Dependent variable
*	Significance level
&	And
€	Euro
#	Number
%	Percent
Σ	Sum
(+)	Expected positive direction of the association between an independent variable and the dependent variable
(-)	Expected negative direction of the association between an independent variable and the dependent variable
Δ	Delta (change in a variable)
>	Larger
<	Smaller
§	Paragraph

1 Introduction

1.1 Motivation and research questions

The social role of men and women is continuously changing. In the last six decades, the proportion of women in the labor force has increased constantly all over the world (*Goldin* (2014), pp. 1091–1092; *Hayghe* (1999), pp. 41–42). In many industrial countries, women's educational attainment exceeds that of men (*Singh et al.* (2008), p. 53; *Stevenson/Wolfers* (2009), p. 215). However, women are more often part-time employed or paid less for the same work (*Arulampalam et al.* (2007), p. 166). Moreover, studies indicate that women are less likely to advance to the top of companies' hierarchy (*Cotter et al.* (2001), pp. 669–671). This phenomenon is especially evident on corporate boards, as the proportion of women in management positions remains disproportionately low (*Labelle et al.* (2015), p. 339; *Terjesen et al.* (2015), p. 234). The **underrepresentation of women in management positions** is also particularly apparent in Germany. For instance, in 2019, 46.6% of all employees in Germany were female (*Statistische Bundesamt* (2024)). In striking contrast, women accounted for only 9.3% of the executive boards of Germany's 160 largest listed companies (*Kirsch/Wrohlich* (2020b), p. 35). As a result of this large discrepancy, public debates are increasingly focused on why women are underrepresented in leadership positions and on why companies do not recruit more women to their supervisory and executive boards.

On the one hand, companies should strive to raise the proportion of women in management positions, as an increasing number of studies suggest positive impacts of gender-diverse corporate boards on corporate governance (*Abbott et al.* (2012), p. 607; *Adams/Ferreira* (2009), pp. 296–298; *García Lara et al.* (2017), p. 660; *Gull et al.* (2018), pp. 259–260; *Krishnan/Parsons* (2008), pp. 71–72; *Lai et al.* (2017), p. 19; *Srinidhi et al.* (2011), p. 1638). For example, studies indicate that female board members are more likely to attend board meetings (*Adams/Ferreira* (2009), pp. 296–297), enhance earnings quality (*Srinidhi et al.* (2011), p. 1638), and contribute to higher audit quality (*Lai et al.* (2017), p. 1708). However, other research finds no or even negative relationships between board gender diversity and corporate governance quality (*García Lara et al.* (2022), p. 11) or corporate financial performance (e.g., *Chapple/Humphrey* (2014), pp. 715–722; *Gregory-Smith et al.* (2014), pp. F119–F120; *Joecks et al.* (2013), pp. 67–69). Overall, the body of literature examining this relationship is inconclusive and the positive impact of increased gender diversity in top management positions is doubtful (for overviews, see: *Adams et al.* (2015); *Kirsch* (2018); *Post/Byron* (2015)). The sluggish increase of female supervisory and executive board members reflects **companies' skepticism about potential benefits of gender-diverse corporate boards** (*Gregorič et al.* (2017), p. 271; *Mensi-Klarbach et al.* (2021), p. 577).

On the other hand, another research stream indicates that there may also be **structural and cultural barriers** for women, such as the popular glass ceiling effect.[1] Companies often prioritize continuity to benefit from retaining board members' expertise. Since incumbents of corporate boards are predominantly male, they could be interested in preventing a

[1] The glass ceiling effect implies that gender-based disadvantages (or other) make it less likely to rise to the top of a (corporate) hierarchy. For a more detailed consideration, cf. *Cotter et al.* (2001), pp. 655–656.

change in the existing institutionalized practices of nominating board members (*Gregorič et al.* (2017), p. 268). Many companies are controlled by individuals with demographically similar characteristics, the same attitudes, social values, and ways of thinking (*Perrault* (2015), p. 154; *Westphal/Stern* (2006), pp. 174–175). This group of current board members, often dubbed the old elite[2], prefers to fill vacant board positions with candidates familiar with their social circles and networks (*Useem/Karabel* (1986), p. 188; *Westphal/Zajac* (1995), pp. 75–77). Hence, the established and institutionalized selection process can impede female board representation. If the external, societal pressure to overcome these structures is insufficient, a change in the appointment behavior of board members is improbable (*Mensi-Klarbach et al.* (2021), p. 580). Besides that, there may be other obstacles (e.g., the unavailability of sufficient qualified female candidates for corporate boards) to an increase in female board participation (*Gregorič et al.* (2017), p. 274).

Due to society's increasing awareness of gender diversity issues, the structural inequality of women has become more prominent (*Mensi-Klarbach et al.* (2017), pp. 1–2). Breaking through existing structural disparities and promoting more participation of women on corporate boards have increasingly become subjects of political and social debate in recent years (*European Commission* (2020); *Ferreira* (2015), pp. 108–111; *World Economic Forum* (2022)). In Europe, regulators strive to address the inequality of women in the working world (*Seierstad et al.* (2017b), p. 289). Already in 2003, Norway was the first European country to enact a law to force companies to increase the involvement of women in corporate management (*Seierstad/Huse* (2017), pp. 11–13). In subsequent years, many other countries have followed Norway's pioneering role and enacted comparable gender diversity regulations (for overviews, see: *Mensi-Klarbach/Seierstad* (2020), pp. 620–621; *Terjesen et al.* (2015), pp. 235–237)). Regulators are confronted with the **dilemma** of achieving their political objectives of promoting corporate gender diversity without interfering unduly with corporate decision-making freedom in appointment processes (*Labelle et al.* (2015), p. 341). To remedy this issue, regulators have various options that differ in severity to promote gender equality in companies (*Klettner et al.* (2016), p. 397).

One way to shape corporate behavior is to impose **mandatory gender quotas** to raise the presence of women on corporate boards. Regulated companies must abide by legal requirements, notwithstanding of specific conditions. In the case of non-compliance, companies can be sanctioned sharply (such sanctions can vary from warnings over fines to, in further consequence, forced dissolution (*Kirsch* (2018), p. 351)). In this way, regulators force companies to increase the number of women in the desired positions by statutory regulation. These "coercive regulations" have high expected efficacy, as companies are forced to comply with the regulations (*Sojo et al.* (2016), p. 527). However, this type of regulation represents a substantial interference in corporate decision-making authority, and thus, companies' expected resistance is high (*Doldor* (2016), pp. 157–161). While coercive regulations achieve the intended objective of forcing companies to recruit more women into management positions, unintended effects can arise. For example, state-imposed

[2] This study uses the term "old elite" to label those corporate board members who are the majority in terms of age, nationality and gender (similar, *Gregorič et al.* (2017), p. 268).

gender quotas can trigger the phenomenon of token women[3]. Although the required proportion of women is reached, the objective of women's equal participation may not be realized.

To avoid such rigid regulatory interventions, regulators can aim to shape corporate behavior indirectly. Instead of enacting mandatory quotas for the participation of women on corporate boards, regulators can implement **mandatory disclosure requirements**. Such disclosure requirements do not oblige companies to achieve prescribed quotas but to disclose the current proportion of women at one or various management levels. Regulators also have several options for designing and customizing these gender diversity disclosure requirements. To sensitize companies to the issue of gender diversity, regulators can oblige them to specify and publish self-set targets for the participation of women in management positions. The publication of self-set targets increases public transparency and the commitment character of the gender diversity targets. If companies miss their own targets, they could face public pressure from stakeholders (*Weil et al.* (2013), pp. 1410–1411). This mechanism enables the regulator to influence companies' behavior indirectly without imposing mandatory gender quotas. *Fung et al.* (2007) characterize this type of regulation as "targeted transparency" (*Fung et al.* (2007), p. xiii) because the objective is to shape the behavior of companies indirectly in a targeted manner through a higher degree of transparency. Is a targeted transparency regulation applied in the context of gender diversity, it is a **gender diversity disclosure regulation** (GDDR).

> *"Men and women shall have equal rights. The state shall promote the actual implementation of equal rights for women and men and take steps to eliminate disadvantages that now exist."*
>
> *(Basic Law for the Federal Republic of Germany (GG), Article 3 (2), (1949))*

As efforts to promote corporate gender diversity through recommendations in a national corporate governance code failed to achieve the intended results, calls for mandatory regulations intensified (*Heidemann et al.* (2013), p. 507). In 2015, Germany passed the "Act on Equal Participation of Women and Men in Leadership Positions in the Private and the Public Sector" (Führungspositionengesetz (FüPoG I); (BGBl. 2015 I no. 17, pp. 642–662)) to facilitate more gender-equitable representation on management level in the corporate sector. As the law combines two types of regulations, the German regulator chose a unique approach. Besides a mandatory gender quota for supervisory boards of some particular publicly listed companies[4], FüPoG I implements a **GDDR on different corporate hierarchy levels**. Companies are obliged to disclose self-set targets for the participation of women on the supervisory board, the executive board, and the first two management levels below the executive board. The political discussion during the legislative process of FüPoG I was heated and highly controversial (*Deutscher BT/BR – DIP* (2015b), pp. 7914–7934). In addition to general doubt about the appropriateness of regulatory intervention, there were disagreements about the efficacy of GDDR (*Deutscher BT/BR – DIP* (2015c),

[3] Since corporate boards have often only one female member or a small minority of women, this group is designated as "token women". For a more differentiated definition, cf. *Kanter* (1977b), pp. 965–966.

[4] Companies that are listed on the regulated market of a German stock exchange and parity co-determined are subject to a mandatory gender quota on the supervisory board. These companies have to appoint a supervisory board consisting of at least 30% female and male board members.

pp. 8741–8746). Despite the evaluation of FüPoG I indicated an overall increase in the proportion of women on corporate boards two years after the law was implemented (*Deutscher BT/BR – DIP* (2020c), BT-Drs. 19/24615, p. 35), the regulator revised the regulation of FüPoG I and some areas of the GDDR were exacerbated and reinforced as coercive regulations.

The fact that GDDR do not force companies to increase gender diversity raises the question whether the presence of women on corporate hierarchy levels increased after the implementation of the GDDR. Although regulation affects many companies and its effectiveness is questionable, descriptive studies focus on certain large, mostly publicly listed companies and predominantly examine the impact on supervisory and executive boards (e.g., *FidAR e.V.* (2021); *Kirsch/Wrohlich* (2021b)). Therefore, it is important to assess whether **differences in the development of female participation on different corporate hierarchy levels** occur to understand whether GDDR efficacy varies depending on the targeted hierarchy level. Moreover, the GDDR grants regulated companies in some reporting obligations "*very broad scope for discretion*"[5] (*BT-Drs.* 18/4227, p. 21). However, descriptive studies that analyze the impact of the GDDR beyond corporate boards do not provide detailed insights into companies' disclosure practices (e.g., *Deutscher BT/BR – DIP* (2023b), BT-Drs. 20/9850). Since GDDR rely on increased transparency, disclosure of information is crucial (*Weil et al.* (2006), p. 157). Disclosure required by the GDDR enables stakeholders to assess whether companies' intention to promote female participation aligns with their expectations. Thus, variation in the **disclosure practice** may influence the level of public pressure, which may result in varying regulatory efficacy. By investigating the disclosure practices of companies subject to the GDDR, this study provides evidence of companies' disclosure practices in the context of this novel type of gender diversity regulation.

The effectiveness of GDDR is questionable because they do not oblige companies to increase the participation of women in management positions. This raises the question of **which determinants are associated with GDDR efficacy**. Surprisingly, no empirical study has yet investigated what determines whether companies increase corporate gender diversity after the implementation of a GDDR. In this vein, the presumed regulatory mechanisms of targeted transparency regulation suggest that public pressure affects the efficacy of regulations (*Hombach/Sellhorn* (2019), pp. 151–152). Thus, companies' visibility in society may influence the level of public pressure companies face. Moreover, companies might align their behavior with companies in similar environments (e.g., similar capital market orientation) to prevent reputational damage if they do not meet cultural or societal expectations (*DiMaggio/Powell* (1983)). Thus, similar environments may also influence GDDR efficacy. Furthermore, companies' internal structures may determine how they shape corporate gender diversity while affected by a GDDR. For example, companies that voluntarily address gender diversity issues on corporate boards in advance of the GDDR may react differently to the implementation of a GDDR. Since these companies disclose gender diversity targets beforehand, they might be less affected by the mandatory reporting requirements of the GDDR. Moreover, the composition of upper corporate hierarchy

[5] Note that the quotation is translated from German into English.

levels may determine the appointment of members on lower corporate hierarchy levels. For example, more gender-diverse upper management levels may employ more female candidates at lower management levels (*Gould et al.*, p. 932).

In addition to the intended objective of promoting gender equality, further (potentially unintended) consequences of GDDR (e.g., through changes in board composition) remain unclear. The monitoring function of corporate boards is an important corporate governance control mechanism which depends on the experiences and qualifications of corporate board members (*Campbell/Mínguez-Vera* (2008), p. 436). Principal-agent theory suggests that companies appoint an optimal composition of board members to ensure the proper monitoring of the company (*Labelle et al.* (2015), p. 342). A central task of corporate boards is to monitor management decisions and ensure sound financial reporting quality (*García Lara et al.* (2022), pp. 1–2). In order to mitigate information asymmetries between investors and companies and to ensure the smooth functioning of capital markets, the quality of financial reporting is of crucial importance (*Biddle/Hilary* (2006), p. 964; *Healy/Wahlen* (1999), p. 365). In this light, some empirical studies indicate that female board members contribute to enhanced monitoring abilities in settings without gender diversity regulations (e.g., *Lai et al.* (2017), p. 1681; *Srinidhi et al.* (2011), p. 1632)). However, in the context of mandatory gender quotas, prior research finds negative impacts of increased board gender diversity on companies' financial reporting quality (*García Lara et al.* (2022), p. 11). However, contrary to mandatory gender quotas, GDDR do not oblige companies to increase board gender diversity. Instead, GDDR aim to increase gender diversity indirectly through public pressure. Nevertheless, increasing board gender diversity in response to public pressure might result in a non-optimal composition of corporate boards. This leads to the question of whether the implementation of **GDDR is associated with companies' financial reporting quality** and, consequently, the functioning of capital markets. This research gap is a critical problem because regulators cannot assess the consequences that come along with implementing GDDR.

Addressing the research gaps mentioned above, the following **four research questions** (RQ) can be derived for this study. First, the study at hand sheds light on the disclosure practices of companies affected by the GDDR. Therefore, companies' disclosure of self-set gender diversity targets is analyzed for each corporate hierarchy level. Moreover, the study investigates whether GDDR shape the proportion of women in management positions. Therefore, the change in the proportion of women on supervisory boards, executive boards, and the first two management levels below the executive board are examined at the time of the regulation's implementation and six years thereafter.

RQ1a Do GDDR shape the proportion of women in management positions?

RQ1b How do reporting practices differ across companies affected by GDDR?

Second, the study analyzes possible **determinants of GDDR efficacy**. It is anticipated that the development in the proportion of women in management positions varies among companies subject to GDDR. Therefore, it is crucial to identify and investigate these determinants to understand the conditions under which GDDR are effective.

RQ2 What determinants are associated with the efficacy of GDDR?

Third, the study investigates whether the implementation of GDDR shapes the monitoring abilities of corporate boards and is thus associated with companies' financial reporting quality. Identifying **potential consequences** is important to understand which unintended consequences GDDR may cause beyond the intended promotion of increased gender diversity.

RQ3 Are GDDR associated with companies' financial reporting quality?

Accordingly, this study is composed of **three sub-studies**. Figure 1-1 summarizes the relationship between the three sub-studies.

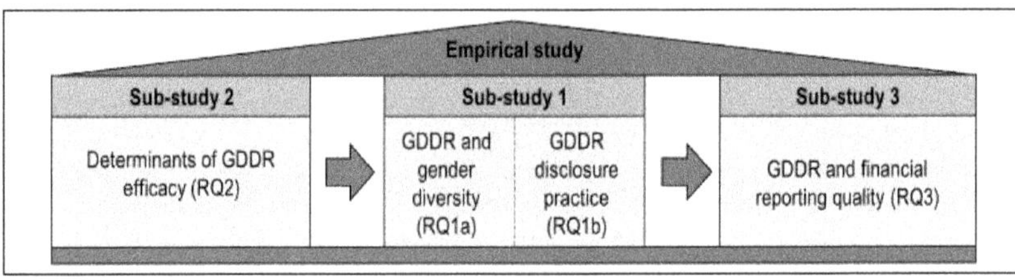

Figure 1-1: Research fields of the study

The need for extensive research on the efficacy and consequences of GDDR is supported by calls for further research on targeted transparency regulations (*Hombach/Sellhorn* (2019), pp. 163–165; *Weil et al.* (2013), p. 1411). To answer the research questions, the **German regulatory environment** is particularly promising for several reasons. First, in contrast to other countries that often have enacted mandatory gender quotas, the German regulator established a law to foster the participation of women on corporate boards mainly through GDDR. Second, unlike most gender diversity regulations, the extent of FüPoG I is not limited to the top hierarchy level of companies. Therefore, the German gender diversity regulation is appropriate for identifying differences in GDDR efficacy between different corporate hierarchy levels. Third, Germany's FüPoG I has been in force long enough to evaluate its efficacy. Fourth, a considerable proportion of companies is subject to the law because all German co-determined and listed companies, approximately 3.500 in total, are affected (*Deutscher BT/BR – DIP* (2020c), BT-Drs. 19/24615, p. 46). Thus, FüPoG I applies to publicly listed and private companies. This allows to compare the increase in gender diversity in the context of GDDR between both types of companies. Fifth, German companies are very experienced in preparing and publishing information on corporate governance issues, as regulated companies have to report corporate governance information for several years (e.g., in 2002, the German Corporate Governance Code (GCGC) was adopted to improve transparency of corporate management and requires companies to report corresponding information within the corporate governance statement).[6]

This study contributes to literature and practice in several ways. As the study concentrates primarily on a regulatory perspective, it particularly yields implications for (inter-)national regulators. The results of the empirical analysis enable regulators to assess whether GDDR shape corporate gender diversity. In particular, with regard to the enactment of comparable laws in other countries or other applications, it supports political decision-makers in finding a suitable regulatory approach. Moreover, a deeper understanding of the determinants helps regulators to design and enact gender diversity regulations that target specified companies more precisely. The study also helps regulators to increase their capacity to anticipate potential unintended consequences of GDDR. Additionally, the study provides **implications** for users of corporate disclosures, preparers, auditors, and enforcement institutions by enhancing the understanding of the impact of GDDR. For instance, users of corporate disclosures may benefit from the findings by becoming more critical in evaluating companies' reporting practices. Preparers can gain an understanding of the potential consequences associated with the implementation of GDDR. Moreover, auditors and enforcement institutions might identify deficiencies in disclosure practices that the study uncovers, aiding in more effective enforcement.

Furthermore, answering the research questions also **contributes to literature threefold**. First, it adds to the descriptive studies that examine the development of female participation in management positions and reporting practices after the GDDR came into force. The study is the first to thoroughly investigate whether the GDDR shapes gender diversity on (the two) management levels below corporate boards and analyze the disclosure practices of companies in detail. Second, the study contributes to the body of literature that investigates the effectiveness of gender diversity regulations. Since empirical research focuses on voluntary policies or mandatory gender quotas, this study provides insights into the so far unique German regulatory approach that combines two types of regulations. Lastly, the findings of this study contribute to the literature by analyzing the consequences of increased board gender diversity in the context of gender diversity regulations. Understanding which potential consequences arise from GDDR is important because it enhances the awareness of potential unintended effects these regulations may cause.

1.2 Scientific positioning

Science is a systematic process aimed at the detection, formulation, and resolution of problems (*Lingnau* (1995), p. 124), with the overarching goal of **advancing and accumulating knowledge** (*Fülbier* (2004), p. 267). Distinct from belief or intuition, science requires the verification and justification of claims, ensuring that evidence substantiates knowledge (*Kornmeier* (2007), p. 4). The philosophy of science investigates the approaches and objectives of science that facilitate the acquisition and validation of knowledge

[6] For detailed information on the GCGC and reporting on corporate governance issues, refer to section 2.2.3.4.

(*Kornmeier* (2007), p. 8). Thus, the philosophy of science can be regarded as a form of meta-science (*Fülbier* (2004), p. 266).

Science can follow different research objectives. *Schweitzer* (1978) differentiates between **four science objectives**, with one or more of them being germane (*Schweitzer* (1978), pp. 3–9). First, descriptive science aims to systematically document and characterize occurring phenomena. Second, explanative objectives surpass descriptive science by offering explanations for causal relationships. Third, pragmatic science uses these causal relationships to improve predictions and decision-making, thereby further expanding research objectives. Finally, science can specify normative objectives by utilizing theoretical knowledge to provide desired targets or recommendations.

The study at hand follows **three research objectives**. First, this study focuses on the descriptive research objective by offering detailed insights into the development of corporate gender diversity after the implementation of GDDR. Second, empirical testing of hypotheses derived from theory provides explanations for the determinants and consequences of GDDR, thereby addressing an explanative objective. Finally, based on the testing of various hypotheses, the study provides implications for regulators, users of disclosure, preparers, auditors, and enforcement institutions in the context of GDDR. Hence, the study at hand also follows a pragmatic objective.

In the field of business economics research, two dominant epistemological approaches prevail in achieving research objectives (*Fülbier* (2004), p. 268; *Raffée/Abel* (1979), p. 3). On the one hand, **constructivism** posits that knowledge is created through argumentation, allowing for conclusions or trend statements to be derived based on theoretical considerations and arguments through deduction (*Kornmeier* (2007), p. 40). However, knowledge gained from deductive argumentation is not incontrovertible due to human fallibility (*Lorenzen* (1974), pp. 113–118). Thus, knowledge derived from constructivism is never regarded as an absolute or ultimate truth (*Fülbier* (2004), p. 269).

On the other hand, **critical rationalism**, rooted in the work of *Popper* (1934), relies on the recognition of the inherent fallibility of human knowledge (*Kornmeier* (2007), pp. 40–41). Critical rationalists suggest that knowledge is inherently temporary due to the possibility of falsification (*Kornmeier* (2007), p. 41; *Lingnau* (1995), p. 124). *Popper* (2005) argues that this is an opportunity instead of a drawback, as it allows for continuous learning and approximation of the truth through the process of falsifying knowledge (*Popper* (2005), pp. 16–19). The methodology of critical rationalism involves developing hypotheses to explain observable phenomena, empirically testing these hypotheses, and discarding those that are falsified (*Fülbier* (2004), p. 268; *Kornmeier* (2007), p. 42). This iterative process leads to the formation of temporarily valid hypotheses or theories until they are falsified (*Bartel* (1990), p. 58).

Despite the **dominance of critical rationalism** in current business research, the relevance of constructivism should not be underestimated (*Fülbier* (2004), p. 269). Solely depending on critical rationalism may be problematic due to the inherent limitations of empirical research (*Frank* (2003), p. 283). Thus, integrating both approaches can provide a more comprehensive framework for understanding and advancing knowledge in business economics. For instance, regarding corporate gender diversity reporting, empirical research may analyze how a gender diversity regulation shapes corporate gender diversity. On the other hand, researchers can deduct valuable recommendations to support the development of appropriate and effective gender diversity regulations. This study follows the paradigm of critical rationalism to gain insights and new knowledge about GDDR. To this end, it derives hypotheses from theory to investigate determinants and consequences of the implementation of GDDR. These hypotheses are tested in order to discard those that are falsified.

Based on the chosen research approach, selecting a **research strategy** that aligns with the objectives of the study is essential. In business economics, three primary research strategies are commonly employed: the conceptual, the analytical, and the empirical research strategy (*Grochla* (1978), p. 71).

A **conceptual research** strategy focuses on understanding complex phenomena through logical reasoning (*Grochla* (1978), pp. 72–78). This approach is grounded in plausibility and involves mentally constructing and simulating specific aspects of reality, enabling researchers to generate implications for both theory and practice. Although the definitional or descriptive statements derived from conceptual research often have a hypothetical nature, they are not subjected to empirical validation (*Grochla* (1978), p. 72).

An **analytical research** strategy focuses on investigating specific problems and employing abstract models rather than attempting to fully capture the complexity of real-world phenomena (*Grochla* (1978), p. 85). This approach is characterized by its aim to support decision-making, acknowledging that it does not fully represent reality.

An **empirical research** strategy is centered on testing hypotheses and theories against reality, aiming either to validate or refute them (*Grochla* (1978), pp. 78–85). Empirical researchers make statements about reality that can be descriptive or explanatory (*Grochla* (1978), p. 78). Explanatory statements focus on uncovering causal relationships between variables (*Grochla* (1978), pp. 79–80). The findings of this strategy can be compared with theoretical expectations to contribute to theory development. The study at hand refers to an empirical research strategy for two reasons. First, the evaluation of the disclosure practice of companies subject to GDDR aims to provide detailed insights that contribute to the empirical evidence on GDDR. Hence, it is a descriptive empirical analysis. Second, the analyses of the determinants and consequences of GDDR intend to gain insights into relationships in the context of GDDR.

1.3 Study outline

The study is structured into eight chapters. The outline is displayed in Figure 1-1. The **first chapter** motivates the topic, highlights its relevance, and presents the research questions. It also delineates the scientific research strategy to explain the employed research approach.

The **second chapter** starts with the conceptual foundation of the study at hand. Different types of gender diversity regulations and regulatory mechanisms of GDDR are explained to create an understanding of regulators' possibilities to promote corporate gender diversity. Thereafter, the German gender diversity regulation is discussed in detail to emphasize the particularities of the regulatory approaches in Germany, as this regulatory environment grounds the legal and regulatory basis for the empirical analysis.

The **third chapter** reviews the research streams in the area of GDDR. First, descriptive studies of how GDDR shape corporate gender diversity are presented. Since prior research has not yet investigated GDDR in terms of inferential statistics, this chapter further discusses qualitative and quantitative literature on different gender diversity regulations. Moreover, the chapter presents literature on the consequences of increased board gender diversity on financial reporting quality. Lastly, based on the summarized main findings and limitations of prior studies, a significant research gap is identified.

The **fourth chapter** introduces the relevant theories and derives the hypotheses of this study. The theoretical foundation includes principal-agent theory and different system-oriented theories (legitimacy theory, stakeholder theory, institutional theory, and resource dependence theory) to provide sound theoretical reasoning for analyzing GDDR. Against the backdrop of these theories, hypotheses for the three sub-studies are derived.

The **fifth chapter** delineates the empirical results for the first sub-study, i.e., how GDDR shape corporate gender diversity and how companies disclose required information. First, the chapter describes the research design and sample selection. Afterward, it presents the empirical results, starting with describing the used sample to generate an overall understanding of the sample characteristics. Subsequently, it elucidates the overall compliance with the reporting requirements introduced by FüPoG I to provide first insights into the disclosure practice. To analyze how GDDR shape corporate gender diversity, the development of the proportion of women on the supervisory and executive board, as well as at the first two management levels below the executive board, are investigated. Then, the chapter compares the disclosure practices of companies for the gender diversity target setting on all hierarchy levels affected by GDDR. The chapter concludes with a discussion of the results.

The **sixth chapter** empirically analyzes the determinants associated with GDDR efficacy by employing multivariate panel regression models. First, it describes the applied statistical method, introduces the variables used in the empirical models, and highlights the necessity of two subsamples. Second, the determinants of GDDR efficacy on the supervisory and executive board are reported. For each subsample, the chapter presents the descriptive results for the independent variables, the results of a correlation analysis, the results of the multivariate panel regressions, and the results of robustness tests and sensitivity analyses. Initially, the results of each subsample are discussed separately before the findings of both sub-studies are compared to generate a broader understanding of the determinants of GDDR efficacy.

The **seventh chapter** analyzes the relationship between increased gender diversity on the supervisory board and financial reporting quality. For this purpose, two different identification strategies are explained. Thereafter, the chapter describes the variables used in the multivariate panel regression and gives reasons for the selected sample. The empirical results are presented similarly to the determinants analysis (chapter 6). The results of descriptive statistics follow the results of the correlation analysis, the multivariate panel regression, the robustness tests, and sensitivity analyses. Finally, the chapter concludes with a discussion of the results.

Lastly, the **eighth chapter** summarizes the main findings, discusses limitations, and highlights the implications derived for regulators, users of disclosure, preparers, auditors, and enforcement institutions. The study ends by outlining avenues for future research.

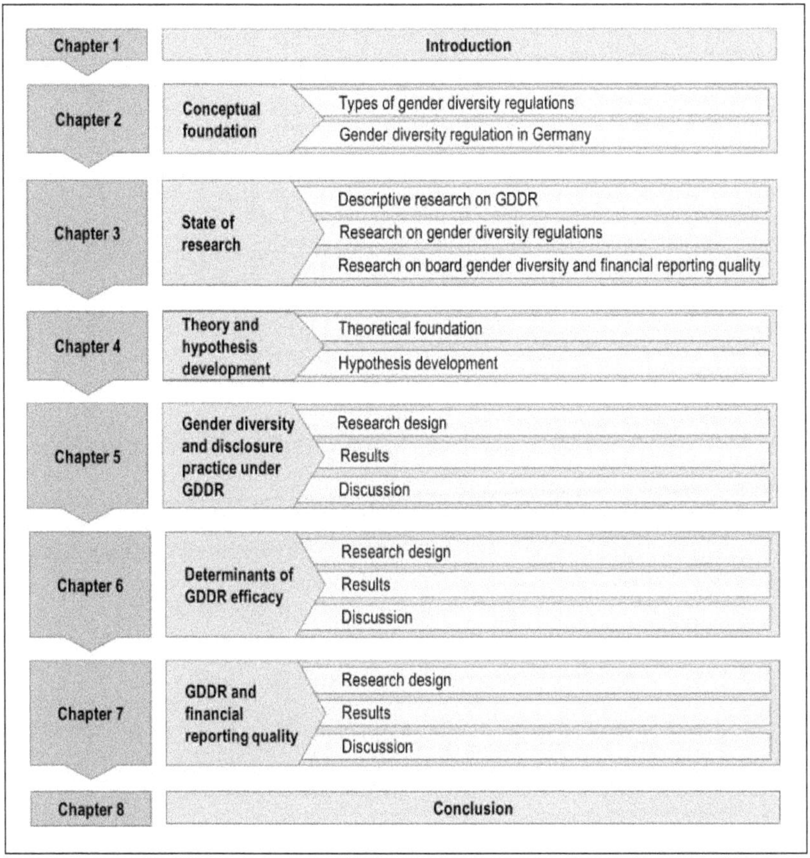

Figure 1-2: Study outline

2 Conceptual foundation

This chapter presents the conceptual foundation of regulatory approaches designed to influence corporate gender diversity in an intended manner. Section 2.1 examines the regulatory tools available to regulators for shaping corporate behavior, outlines the theoretical framework of targeted transparency regulations, and explains the regulatory mechanisms of GDDR. Based on that, section 2.2 elucidates the gender diversity regulation in Germany. Finally, section 2.3 concludes with a summary.

2.1 Types of gender diversity regulations

2.1.1 Regulatory landscape

Regulators have various means to influence, steer, and control the behavior of organizations in their interests to achieve political or economic objectives (*Davies* (1999), pp. 18–20). Companies are frequently subject to regulatory intervention owing to their size and societal meaning (*Leuz* (2010), pp. 232–233). To this end, companies are frequently subject to regulatory interventions that aim to foster gender diversity to address societal or ethical issues. However, regulators have a **bunch of different regulatory tools** at their disposal to achieve their objectives in an intended way (*Labelle et al.* (2015), p. 341; *Sojo et al.* (2016), p. 520). Besides the type of legal anchoring, regulatory tools aiming to increase corporate gender diversity differ in strictness and progressiveness (*Mensi-Klarbach/Seierstad* (2020), pp. 619–621). Figure 2-1 illustrates the continuum of different approaches for promoting corporate gender diversity, ranging from non-regulatory actions to soft laws and, ultimately, to hard laws in the form of coercive regulations. Given that the approaches vary in both expected efficacy and the expected resistance from companies, this section elucidates the approaches that can be applied to shape corporate gender diversity.

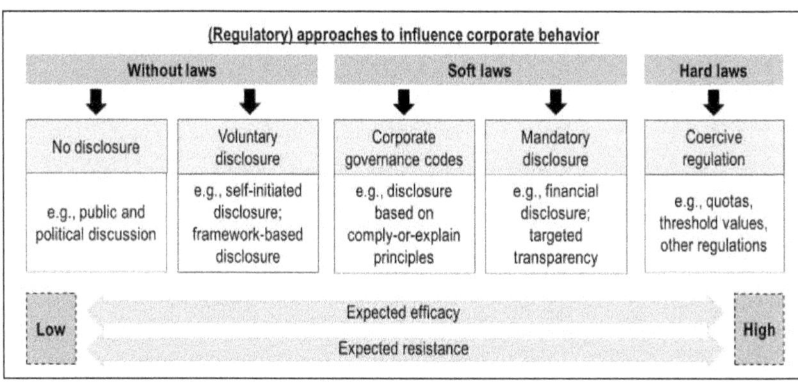

Figure 2-1: Regulatory approaches to influence corporate behavior

Public and political discussion

Public and political discussion presents an opportunity to influence corporate gender diversity before legal requirements are enacted. Around the world, regulators identify male-dominated corporate boards as a concern for ethical and societal reasons (e.g., *Gregorič et al.* (2017), p. 267; *Labelle et al.* (2015), p. 339). Therefore, the underrepresentation of women on corporate boards has gained increasing attention in society and among regulators (*Seierstad* et al. (2017a), p. 1; *Terjesen et al.* (2009), p. 321). In the spirit of equal rights, regulators aim to increase the proportion of women and encourage companies to appoint more gender-diverse corporate boards (*Kogut et al.* (2014), p. 891). However, enacting laws or stipulating regulations is a lengthy and protracted political process (e.g., *Kirsch* (2017), pp. 214–218). Moreover, the authority to legislate and enact binding policies is limited to governments or other powerful regulators (e.g., securities regulators). By contrast, **public or political discussion can be initiated by actors without legislative authorities**.

Since gender diversity is a societal concern, a broad range of actors, including media and private associations, encourage the process of fostering corporate gender diversity (*Seierstad et al.* (2017b), p. 295). As an initial step of intervention, **public and political discussion** can raise companies' awareness of gender diversity issues on corporate boards. Even in the absence of direct regulatory intervention, public and political discussions pave the way for further regulatory actions (e.g., *Seierstad/Huse* (2017), p. 17). Political parties and other actors, beyond legislative bodies, can initiate a discourse on gender diversity issues. In doing so, NGOs, trade unions, media, and other interest groups can draw attention to grievances in terms of gender diversity (*Abbott/Snidal* (2000), pp. 450–453). Through public and political discussions, these actors address concerns, debate various positions, and enhance societal awareness (e.g., *Gabaldon/Giménez* (2017), p. 57). Additionally, companies and industry representatives can engage in these discussions to emphasize the economic sector's interests.

As soon as an initial unstructured public debate reaches political parties and is discussed in official bodies (e.g., national parliaments), public attention (e.g., through increased media coverage) rises (*Seierstad et al.* (2017b), p. 302). Due to these parliamentary discussions, companies may **fear the potential initiation of legislative processes** that could lead to coercive regulations to foster gender-diverse corporate boards. To avoid such far-reaching regulations that may conflict with their interests, companies can employ various strategies. On the one hand, companies or industry representatives might attempt to influence the discussion by presenting their perspectives or running campaigns. They can attempt to shape the political debate in their favor and evade stricter regulatory interventions. On the other hand, companies can align with societal and political demands for gender-diverse corporate boards and commit to increasing the proportion of female board members. By demonstrating their commitment, companies can prove their dedication to improving gender diversity. This can encourage political actors to avoid imposing coercive regulations, believing that companies will meet these objectives voluntarily.

In summary, however, public and political discussion is **not a regulatory intervention** by nature. However, these debates highlight political and societal demands and often serve as a starting point for further regulatory actions. Due to their non-binding nature and inherent vagueness, resistance from companies is expected to be low. Conversely, the expected efficacy of these debates is also limited because they lack direct and binding regulations.

Voluntary disclosure

Corporate voluntary disclosure regarding gender diversity is a commonly practiced approach (*Klettner et al.* (2016), p. 395). Basically, corporate voluntary disclosure is defined as "*information primarily outside of the financial statements that are not explicitly required by accounting rules or standards*" (*Boesso/Kumar* (2007), p. 270). This type of disclosure aims at a broader group of stakeholders beyond shareholders (*Meek et al.* (1995), p. 557). Voluntary disclosure can be divided into two types: self-initiated voluntary disclosure and framework-based voluntary disclosure (*Healy/Serafeim* (2020), pp. 113–114). **Self-initiated voluntary disclosure** refers to instances where companies independently choose to disclose gender diversity information. Without regulatory mandates, companies may publish information (e.g., about their actual board gender diversity or gender diversity strategies) to gain benefits (e.g., if they are a forerunner in fostering female participation) and signal their values (e.g., to stakeholder groups sensitive to social objectives) (*Eng/Mak* (2003), p. 326).[7] Conversely, companies with lower levels of female participation in top management positions may avoid disclosing such information to prevent reputational damage.

A more institutionalized form of voluntary reporting is **framework-based voluntary disclosure** (e.g., by sustainability reporting frameworks). Although these frameworks do not obligate companies to disclose information, they provide a framework that recommends reporting specific gender diversity information (*Aguilera/Cuervo-Cazurra* (2009), pp. 376–377). Unlike self-initiated voluntary reporting, reporting frameworks can create indirect pressure on companies to adhere to these recommendations, particularly when competitors or industry peers adopt these frameworks (*Healy/Serafeim* (2020), p. 124).[8] To avoid reputational damage and meet stakeholders' information needs, companies with lower levels of gender diversity are also incentivized to report voluntarily (section 4.1.2.3). As a result, overall transparency tends to increase, enabling stakeholders and the broader public to assess the gender diversity of a wider range of companies. However, the information is not mandatory, and companies still have the option to choose whether or not to disclose it.

Disclosure based on corporate governance codes

A stricter form of gender diversity reporting is anchoring recommendations in law. These types of regulatory policies, for example, require certain companies to apply a **national corporate governance code** (for the example of Germany, see section 2.2.2). Such corporate governance codes frequently include provisions for disclosing corporate gender diversity information (*Mateos de Cabo et al.* (2022), pp. 703–704). However, corporate governance codes do not compel companies to comply with recommendations. Instead, they use the so-called "comply-or-explain" approach, which allows companies to decide whether to adhere to gender diversity recommendations (e.g., *Aguilera/Cuervo-Cazurra*

---

[7] For example, *Healy/Serafeim* (2020) investigate the effects of voluntary, self-regulatory, and mandatory disclosure of company's payment to foreign governments in the oil and gas industry. They argue that voluntary disclosure of companies causes potential benefits (e.g. lower cost of capital) and costs (e.g., political costs) for companies (*Healy/Serafeim* (2020), p. 111).

[8] For a similar argument regarding voluntary reporting in the oil and gas industry aimed at reducing corruption, cf. *Healy/Serafeim* (2020).

(2009), p. 382; *Cromme* (2005), p. 363). If companies choose not to follow the recommendations, they must provide reasons for non-compliance and explain their decision. Nevertheless, this does not create an obligation to disclose gender diversity information or to increase board gender diversity. However, companies may use such policies to gain benefits or to address pressure to comply with the recommendations (*Cuomo et al.* (2016), p. 223).

The efficacy of a non-mandatory disclosure regime in promoting corporate gender diversity is questioned by many regulators (*Mensi-Klarbach et al.* (2021), p. 577). Since the disclosure of information or compliance with recommendations remains non-binding and there are **no legal sanctions for non-compliance**, the expected efficacy of voluntary disclosure or disclosure based on national corporate governance codes is limited. However, resistance from companies to adopting such voluntary regulatory tools is expected to be low. Nonetheless, given the concern about potentially stricter regulatory interventions, voluntary recommendations on gender diversity can be seen as an attempt to avoid the imposition of mandatory gender quotas (*Henning* (2011), p. 52).

Mandatory disclosure

In contrast to voluntary disclosure, mandatory disclosure follows a binding approach. Mandatory disclosure regulations can be divided into two subtypes: those aimed at ensuring the smooth functioning of capital markets (financial disclosure regulations) and those intended to influence corporate behavior in a socially desired manner (targeted transparency regulations). Targeted transparency regulations can be applied to foster corporate gender diversity. Given their different objectives, corporate **financial disclosure regulations vary significantly from targeted transparency regulations** (*Hombach/Sellhorn* (2019), p. 141).

First, the intended objectives of financial disclosure regulations and targeted transparency regulations differ.[9] Financial disclosure regulations primarily aim to foster financial transparency and, thereby, ensure the functioning of capital markets. Based on financial data, market participants (e.g., investors or other capital providers) can assess a company's financial performance and stability. Consequently, financial disclosure reduces information asymmetries between different market participants as well as between shareholders and managers (*Fung et al.* (2007), p. 82). This reduction in asymmetries, in turn, supports the accurate valuation of companies, which is crucial for the efficient allocation of resources in the economy (*Hombach/Sellhorn* (2019), p. 141). In line with this objective, certain companies in regulated markets within the EU must prepare and disclose consolidated financial statements in accordance with IFRS (EU Regulation No. 1606/2002).[10] However, in contrast to financial disclosure regulations, the objectives of targeted transparency regulation aiming at increased gender diversity extend beyond facilitating efficient capital markets (*Hombach/Sellhorn* (2019), p. 141). Targeted transparency regulations seek to mandate "*information in standardized formats to reduce specific risks, […] to fully consider social costs*

[9] Here and in the following, cf. *Hombach/Sellhorn* (2019), p. 141.

[10] This regulation is also mentioned by *Hombach/Sellhorn* (2019) to provide an example for a mandatory financial disclosure regulation that aimed to ensure financial transparency and thereby functioning of capital markets.

associated with a product, or to improve provision of public goods and services" (*Weil et al.* (2013), p. 1410). Accordingly, by introducing targeted transparency regulations to foster corporate gender diversity, regulators pursue **objectives beyond the traditional goal** of ensuring functional capital markets, instead focusing on incorporating social perceptions.

Second, there are significant differences between financial disclosure and targeted transparency regulations concerning the **intended audience** (*Fülbier/Sellhorn* (2023), pp. 1101–1102). In contrast to financial disclosure regulations, targeted transparency regulations do not primarily serve investors but cater to a broader range of stakeholders due to their often social or ethical objectives (e.g., increased board gender diversity) (*Fülbier/Sellhorn* (2023), pp. 1101–1102). Particularly, non-investor stakeholders and the interested public, who are more concerned with social or ethical issues, are empowered by this information to exert pressure on companies and incentivize socially desirable behavior (*Hombach/Sellhorn* (2019), p. 138).

In the context of corporate gender diversity, targeted transparency regulations require companies to publish specific gender diversity information (*Sojo et al.* (2016), p. 520). Such regulations can be codified by securities regulators in mandatory reporting standards (e.g., IFRS) or by governments in national laws (*Hombach/Sellhorn* (2019), p. 138). Consequently, certain companies are subject to these targeted transparency regulations and must report on specified gender diversity topics. Unlike voluntary disclosure, targeted transparency regulations, as a subtype of mandatory disclosure regulation, **impose sanctions** on companies that fail to comply (*Bainbridge* (2000), p. 1052). For example, these sanctions can include financial penalties or the refusal of the audit opinion.

However, targeted transparency regulations do not cause increased female presence on corporate boards by law as these regulations **do not compel companies to achieve a predefined objective** (*Hess* (2008), p. 453). Instead, similar to framework-based voluntary disclosure or disclosure based on corporate governance codes, this regulatory approach relies also on increased transparency and on "*the power of information rather than on enforcement of rules*" (*Weil et al.* (2013), p. 1410). By mandating the publication of required information, companies with lower levels of gender diversity cannot avoid disclosing relevant details to stakeholders. As a result, targeted transparency regulations contribute to a more comprehensive reporting landscape that provides society and stakeholders with insights into corporate gender diversity (*Hess* (2008), pp. 457–458; *Weil et al.* (2006), p. 157). Resistance from companies to the introduction of regulations with mandatory requirements is expected to be higher than the introduction of disclosure policies relying on comply-or-explain principles (*Abbott/Snidal* (2000), p. 423). However, due to the described advantages (e.g., required transparency), stricter disclosure regulations also promise higher efficacy (*Weil et al.* (2006), pp. 165–167).

Coercive regulations

The strictest form of regulatory intervention is coercive regulation. A commonly used type of so-called "*command-and-control regulations*" (*Dhir* (2015), p. 98) in the context of gender diversity is **mandatory gender quotas** (e.g., *Klettner et al.* (2016), p. 395; *Kogut et al.* (2014), p. 891). A quota is defined as "*a percentage target that mandates a proportional representation of a particular group*" (*Kogut et al.* (2014), p. 892). Regarding gender diversity, the definition implies that a gender quota targets an increase of an underrepresented group. Therefore, mandatory gender quotas are not solely designed to enhance female presence on corporate boards but also to achieve a specified degree of gender diversity in terms of male and female board members (*Sojo et al.* (2016), p. 520).

Regulators define the scope of targeted hierarchy levels subject to a mandatory gender quota (e.g., commonly corporate boards). Companies affected by the mandatory gender quota **must achieve the specified degree of gender diversity** within a predefined period of time. Consequently, these companies must adjust their management structures or replace managers to comply with the legal requirements (*García Lara et al.* (2022), p. 13; *Terjesen/Sealy* (2016), p. 48). In the event of non-compliance, regulators can impose sanctions on companies. The severity of these sanctions varies depending on the regulatory design of the mandatory gender quota. Sanctions can range from minor, symbolic penalties (e.g., provisional appointment) to financial penalties (e.g., fines) and even to far-reaching sanctions (e.g., delisting of the company).[11] Mandatory gender quotas are considered highly effective because companies are legally obligated to comply (*Arndt/Wrohlich* (2019), p. 340). However, while companies might consider not appointing more gender-diverse corporate boards when facing financial penalties, this is less likely when the potential consequences include more severe outcomes such as delisting.

Although mandatory gender quotas are considered highly effective in promoting gender diversity (*Arndt/Wrohlich* (2019), p. 340), such regulations considerably encroach on **companies' decision-making freedom** (*Mensi-Klarbach et al.* (2021), p. 581). Companies subject to mandatory gender quotas must appoint members to corporate bodies not only based on their individual knowledge, experience, or skills but also with consideration of their gender. Since the composition of top management levels crucially affects company performance (e.g., *Ferrari et al.* (2022); *Miller/Triana* (2009)), companies have strong interests in making optimal candidate choices (*Boone et al.* (2007), pp. 67–68). Consequently, resistance to the introduction of mandatory gender quotas is expected to be high (*Arndt/Wrohlich* (2019), p. 338; *Gregorič et al.* (2017), p. 268; *Hughes et al.* (2017), p. 332). Some companies therefore make considerable efforts to avoid such regulations (e.g., by changing organizational form (*Bøhren/Staubo* (2014)). Thus, legislating mandatory gender quotas to promote gender diversity is a subject of controversial debate worldwide (*Labelle et al.* (2015), p. 340; *Terjesen/Sealy* (2016), p. 24). On the one hand, regulators believe in the effectiveness of mandatory gender quotas in ensuring increased gender diversity. On the other hand, interference with corporate decision-making processes is viewed with skepticism from economic and legal perspectives (e.g., *Mensi-Klarbach et al.* (2017), p. 2).

In summary, regulators need to balance political, societal, and corporate interests to design and legislate effective and widely accepted regulatory approaches (*Labelle et al.* (2015), p. 340). The approaches to shape corporate behavior described, which aim to foster gender diversity on corporate boards or at lower management levels, **vary in their expected efficacy and the level of expected resistance from companies**. Mandatory gender

[11] For an overview of sanctions in the context of mandatory gender quotas in Europe, cf. *Arndt/Wrohlich* (2019). For more detailed information on specific regulatory designs applied in European countries, cf. *Mensi-Klarbach/Seierstad* (2020).

quotas, due to their legally binding nature, are referred to as *"hard laws"* (*Abbott/Snidal* (2000), p. 421; *Zenou et al.* (2017), p. 119). In contrast, disclosure regulations that do not compel companies to change their behavior rely more on self-regulation and are often labeled as *"soft laws"* (*Abbott/Snidal* (2000), p. 422; *Klettner et al.* (2016), p. 395). Soft and hard laws are viewed as *"two poles on a continuum of enforceability"* (*Mensi-Klarbach/Seierstad* (2020), p. 617). While hard laws, such as mandatory gender quotas, inherently increase the representation of the underrepresented gender, the mechanisms that determine the efficacy of soft laws, such as targeted transparency regulations, are more complex (*Hess* (2008), p. 450; *Hombach/Sellhorn* (2019), p. 139). As regulators increasingly rely on the power of information to address social or ethical issues (*Dhir* (2015), p. 97; *Estlund* (2011), p. 354), they need to understand the factors that influence the efficacy (*Klettner et al.* (2016), p. 415). The following section explores the mechanisms of targeted transparency regulations aimed at shaping corporate behavior in a socially intended manner.

2.1.2 Targeted transparency regulations

As mentioned in the previous section, targeted transparency regulations rely on the power of transparency. Generally, this regulatory tool can be applied both within and outside the corporate context, each with distinct characteristics and mechanisms.[12] To analyze targeted transparency regulations as a **specific type of mandatory disclosure** in the corporate context, it is essential to grasp the basic regulatory mechanisms underlying these regulations. Therefore, this section explains the theoretical regulatory mechanisms, provides a vivid example of targeted transparency regulations in the corporate context, and discusses the mechanisms of gender diversity regulation through targeted transparency in detail.

Basic regulatory mechanism

Targeted transparency regulations require the *"disclosure of specific factual information"* (*Fung et al.* (2007), p. XIII) and are designed to achieve specific objectives that extend beyond mere information dissemination (*Fung et al.* (2007), p. 13). The objectives of **targeted transparency regulations** often stem from new scientific insights into public risks or ethical and societal concerns, aiming to enhance public awareness (*Weil et al.* (2013), p. 1410). Specifically, they seek to influence individual or organizational behavior and encourage economic actors to modify their actions in a desired manner (*Andreicovici et al.* (2018); *Meijer* (2013), p. 401).[13] In contrast to coercive regulations, targeted transparency regulations rely on mechanisms of increased transparency rather than imposing behavioral changes by law, making it more *"light-handed"* (*Choudhury* (2016), p. 205) approach.

As targeted transparency regulations do not legally mandate behavioral changes by individuals or organizations, their effectiveness remains uncertain (e.g., *Meijer* (2013),

---

12 Mandatory disclosure regulations outside the corporate context aim to promote general openness (e.g., transparent reporting of election results to support democratic principles) or to address critical situations (e.g., warning systems prior to volcanic eruptions to inform the public of imminent dangers). This study focuses on targeted transparency regulations as a specific type of mandatory disclosure regulations within the corporate context and, therefore, does not examine non-corporate applications in detail.

13 For a variety of examples of targeted transparency regulations issued in the US, cf. *Fung et al.* (2007), pp. 21–23.

p. 398). Nonetheless, regulators depend on the presumed efficacy of these regulatory tools to achieve desired outcomes. Therefore, understanding the underlying causal mechanisms of targeted transparency regulations is essential (*Fülbier/Sellhorn* (2023), p. 1101; *Hombach/Sellhorn* (2019), p. 164). To elucidate how targeted transparency regulations operate, *Fung et al.* (2007) developed a **theoretical framework** that explains the underlying action cycle (*Fung et al.* (2007), pp. 53–54). This framework is versatile and can be applied not only to corporate settings but also to public policies in general (*Hombach/Sellhorn* (2019), p. 151). Fundamentally, the concept by *Fung et al.* (2007) integrates perspectives from both information disclosers and users.[14]

Figure 2-2 illustrates the action cycle of targeted transparency regulations and delineates the **causal chain**, which can be divided into five distinct steps:

1. **Initial disclosure:** The subject of a targeted transparency regulation is mandated to disclose specific information.
2. **Evaluation by users:** Information users assess the disclosed information in light of their individual expectations and evaluate the behavior and actions of the discloser accordingly.
3. **Incorporation and behavioral change:** Users integrate the information into their decision-making processes and modify their behavior and actions within the context of their interactions with the discloser.
4. **Anticipation or evaluation by disclosers:** Disclosers either anticipate changes in users' behavior or assess these changes after they occur.
5. **Adjustment by disclosers:** Based on the observed or anticipated user responses, disclosers adjust their behavior to align with users' perceptions. Subsequently, disclosers must publish information about their updated behavior, thus initiating a new cycle of action.

[14] Here and in the following, cf. *Fung et al.* (2007), pp. 54–70.

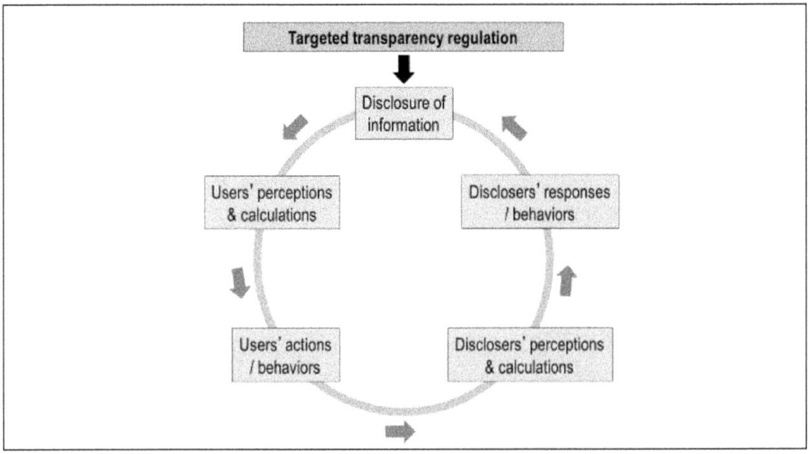

Figure 2-2: Targeted transparency action cycle
(based on *Fung et al.* (2007), p. 54)

Based on the causal chain described, it is possible to distinguish between changes in the discloser's behavior that result from anticipating the users' expectations and those that occur in response to actual changes in the users' actions (*Hombach/Sellhorn* (2019), p. 150). Consequently, targeted transparency regulations can yield intended effects both before the information is initially disclosed and as a result of the increased transparency in subsequent periods. This distinction highlights the **dual pathways** through which transparency regulations can influence behavior: preemptive adjustments by the discloser, motivated by the anticipation of user expectations, and reactive changes following observable user behavior. Both pathways contribute to the overall efficacy of targeted transparency as a regulatory tool.

An **illustrative example** of the theoretical functioning of targeted transparency regulations is animal welfare labeling.[15] Regulators mandate the inclusion of specific labels on packages of raw meat (e.g., pork or beef) that indicate the form of animal husbandry.[16] This targeted transparency regulation aims to improve the conditions under which livestock are raised, thereby enhancing animal welfare and enabling consumers to make informed purchasing decisions (e.g., *BMEL* (2023)).

In contrast to regulations that impose legal requirements to enhance animal husbandry conditions directly, animal welfare labels seek to influence these conditions through **public pressure exerted by consumers**. The regulator (e.g., the government) mandates that

[15] For additional examples of the use of targeted transparency regulation in a broader context, cf. *Fung et al.* (2007), pp. 84–85.

[16] The German Federal Government has enacted such a regulation (Animal Husbandry Labeling Act) in 2023 (*BT-Drs.* 20/6498). The law requires the labeling of raw pork products and shall be extended to other livestock types in the future (*BMEL* (2023)). The law stipulates a five-level categorization of husbandry conditions, which must be uniformly labelled on the front of the packaging.

livestock farmers or distributing companies (referred to as "disclosers" in *Fung et al.* (2007)) disclose the animal husbandry conditions on the front packaging of their products (first step). Consumers (referred to as "users" in *Fung et al.* (2007)) then assess the level of animal welfare represented by the label (second step). This information can influence consumers' current or future purchasing decisions. Suppose a product does not meet consumers' expectations or preferences regarding husbandry conditions (e.g., lack of natural light or cramped stables), they may decide to refrain from purchasing the product (third step). Farmers and distributors may anticipate potential negative sales revenue effects resulting from a low animal welfare score on their products. If they do not anticipate these effects beforehand, they can evaluate the impact after the implementation of the animal welfare label (fourth step). Based on this assessment and the potential risk of declining sales revenues, farmers may improve the husbandry conditions of their livestock to achieve a higher animal welfare rating. Consequently, the animal welfare label affects the behavior of food producers and prompts changes in their practices. The causal chain concludes with the updated animal welfare label and recommences with a new cycle (fifth step).

However, under certain conditions, the causal chain of targeted transparency regulations can be disrupted, leading to outcomes that **fail to achieve the intended objectives**. Firstly, if the information provided under the targeted transparency regulation does not enhance users' information set or is not utilized in their decision-making, the regulation may fail to induce the desired effect (*Fung et al.* (2007), p. 51). For instance, in the context of animal welfare labels, consumers might notice the labels but still base their purchasing decisions predominantly on factors such as taste or price. In such cases, the regulation will not exert public pressure through reduced sales, thereby failing to incentivize farmers to improve husbandry conditions. Consequently, the regulation's objective is not achieved. Secondly, some regulations may effect a change in individual or organizational behavior, but not in a manner aligned with the regulations' intent (*Fung et al.* (2007), p. 53). For example, with animal welfare labels, consumers may avoid purchasing raw meat with poor husbandry ratings, reducing the consumption of low-quality raw meat. However, they might substitute this with convenience foods containing processed, low-quality meat to fulfill their nutritional needs. Since animal welfare labels are typically mandatory only for unprocessed, raw meat, they do not provide transparency regarding the conditions of processed meat. Thus, while the regulation might alter consumer behavior, it may fail to improve overall animal welfare conditions. For regulators, it is crucial to design and implement well-targeted and precisely directed regulations to avoid ineffective or misleading outcomes based on targeted transparency mechanisms.

In summary, regulators can employ targeted transparency regulations to influence individual or organizational behavior in an intended manner without resorting to coercive measures. These regulations foster a form of **self-regulation through enhanced transparency**. However, in a corporate context, targeted transparency regulations address ethical or societal issues and often trigger more complex causal mechanisms and multifactorial reactions within regulated companies. Given the broad audience and the instability of long-term contractual relationships between companies and their stakeholders[17], the uncertainty associated with targeted transparency regulations is heightened (*Fülbier/Sellhorn* (2023), pp. 1102–1103). GDDR is a vivid example of such a regulation.

Gender diversity regulation through targeted transparency

In countries around the world, the underrepresentation of women on corporate boards is increasingly recognized as an issue concerning the equal participation of women and men in the workforce. To promote gender diversity on corporate boards without resorting to coercive regulations, such as mandatory gender quotas, regulators have adopted the approach of targeted transparency. This approach allows regulators to address this societal concern through a more light-handed regulatory approach that respects companies' decision-making authority in determining the composition of their corporate hierarchy levels. In this study, a gender diversity regulation through targeted transparency is referred to as **GDDR**.

Under GDDR, companies are required to transparently disclose specific information regarding the gender composition of various corporate hierarchy levels. In addition to reporting the gender distribution across different levels, this disclosure may – depending on the design of GDDR – include additional details such as self-set targets or explanations of the company's diversity strategy. The primary **objective of GDDR is to provide consistent and meaningful information** about gender diversity within a company, thereby informing a broad audience of interested stakeholders.

As noted by *Fung et al.* (2007), the efficacy of targeted transparency regulations relies on various factors that ensure the proper functioning of the action cycle. Given the specific context of corporate environments, *Hombach/Sellhorn* (2019) adapted the action cycle framework originally developed by *Fung et al.* (2007), expanding it to account for corporate-specific agents (*Hombach/Sellhorn* (2019), p. 151). Based on the principles of this modified action cycle (Figure 2-3), the **underlying causal chain of GDDR** can be elucidated.

Initially, a regulator introduces a GDDR that mandates certain companies to disclose information related to corporate gender diversity. According to the framework developed by *Hombach/Sellhorn* (2019), GDDR can influence outcomes through **two distinct information channels**. It is important to note that these internal and external information channels are not mutually exclusive and may operate concurrently.[18]

---

17 For example of eroding stability of long-term contractual relationships in a corporate setting, cf. *Fülbier/Sellhorn* (2023), p. 1102.

18 Note that the following explanations are based on the framework developed by *Hombach/Sellhorn* (2019). To date, the study at hand is the first that systematically describes the regulatory mechanisms of targeted transparency in the context of GDDR.

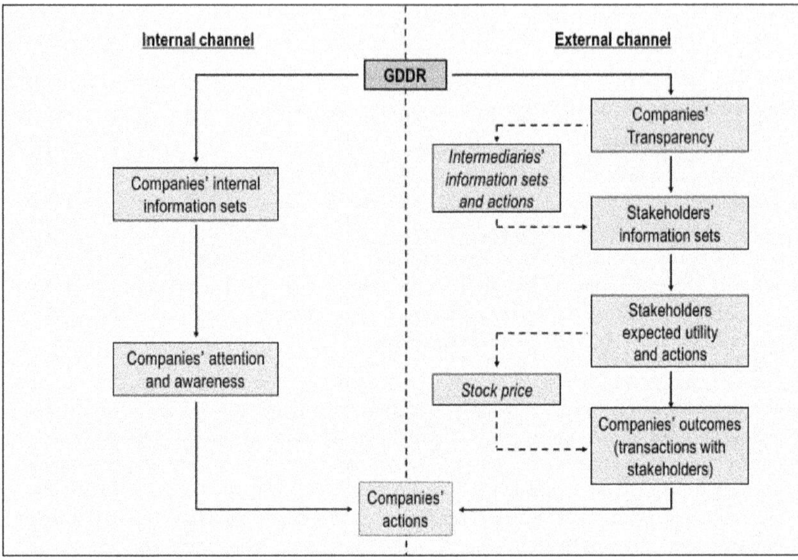

Figure 2-3: GDDR causal chain
(based on *Hombach/Sellhorn* (2019), p. 151)

GDDR aim to impact both the quantity and quality of gender diversity information collected and disclosed. This information, as mandated by GDDR, may also enhance **companies' internal information sets**. Consequently, companies gain a deeper understanding of their gender diversity metrics, potentially leading to greater awareness of related issues. With this improved knowledge, companies might adjust their practices regarding gender-balanced appointments at the management level. Regarding the internal information channel, GDDR influence corporate gender diversity by requiring companies to gather and maintain information on gender diversity within the organization. This approach does not rely on external transparency or stakeholder engagement but on the mechanism of improved decision-making informed by better internal data. However, the effectiveness of this internal pathway assumes that the behavioral changes encouraged by GDDR align with the companies' interests. Therefore, despite enhanced internal information sets, companies may not alter their appointment practices unless they perceive additional benefits.

The **external information channel** involves more complex mechanisms due to the indirect regulatory approach. Firstly, starting with the introduction of a GDDR, companies' external transparency is increased. Initially, with the implementation of GDDR, companies' external transparency increases as information regarding the gender-diverse composition of corporate hierarchy levels is publicly available. This consistent and transparent disclosure of gender diversity information improves the quantity and quality of available data.

Some stakeholders (e.g., professional investors or political parties) can independently perceive and evaluate the information published under GDDR. These stakeholders can **directly assess the gender diversity data** disclosed by companies, thereby enhancing their information sets with novel, standardized details that were previously inaccessible. Conversely, other stakeholders (e.g., employees or customers), who may lack the necessary knowledge, experience, or time, depend on information intermediaries. These **information intermediaries** (e.g., media or labor unions) evaluate the disclosures under GDDR and present the information in a condensed, more accessible format (e.g., newspaper articles or newsletters). Consequently, these information intermediaries are crucial in disseminating gender diversity information to a broader audience. As a result, even less-experienced stakeholders benefit from improved information sets through the intermediaries' preparation and presentation.

Based on their improved knowledge, stakeholders **assess companies' performance** in terms of gender diversity and align the information with their individual preferences and expectations. Consequently, stakeholders can incorporate the information provided in response to GDDR into their interactions with the company. For instance, if a company fails to promote gender diversity at corporate hierarchy levels, it may disappoint stakeholders (e.g., employees or customers) who value equal participation of women and men due to ethical or societal beliefs. As a result, these stakeholders may alter their behavior toward the company. Non-investor stakeholders, therefore, have the power to sanction companies that do not meet their gender diversity expectations (e.g., by restricting access to capital or boycotting products).

The altered behavior of stakeholders leads to changes in their interactions with the company, potentially **affecting the company's outcomes**. Non-investor stakeholders can directly influence the company's financial outcomes. For example, customers might boycott products or services to sanction the company for not meeting their expectations. This, in turn, could lead to a decrease in sales, directly impacting company's financial performance. Indirect effects on the company's outcomes are also possible. For instance, significant non-investor stakeholders, such as employees, might restrict or deny access to the resources they provide, making it difficult for the company to attract and retain qualified employees, indirectly affecting its overall performance.

If non-investor stakeholders' sanctions prove to be effective, companies are compelled to reassess their current behavior and take action to **align with stakeholder expectations** concerning corporate gender diversity. By proactively aligning their practices with these expectations, companies can avoid potential negative impacts on their outcomes. If companies fail to anticipate these adverse effects, they can still adjust their strategies afterward to mitigate any negative consequences and lessen the impact of stakeholder sanctions.

In addition to the influence of non-investor stakeholders, investors can also indirectly affect company's actions as part of GDDR's causal chain. Investors may anticipate or evaluate changes in non-investor behavior that impact company's outcomes. As they incorporate this information, the **company's stock price** may be affected, adding further pressure on the company to meet stakeholder expectations regarding gender diversity.

In summary, GDDR, as a specific form of targeted transparency regulations, rely on a complex causal chain that involves regulators, companies, and stakeholders. From an internal perspective, the implementation of a GDDR requires companies to collect and analyze gender diversity data, enhancing their understanding of gender imbalances. However, compared to other targeted transparency regulations (e.g., carbon footprints reported under CSR-related targeted transparency regulations), the internal channel may be less significant as companies are typically well aware of the composition of their corporate boards. Nevertheless, GDDRs' standardized and comprehensive reporting requirements further enhance corporate awareness regarding gender diversity in top management positions. From an external perspective, GDDR address a particularly controversial topic, with stakeholder interests in gender diversity on corporate boards often diverging. Some stakeholders are directly invested in promoting gender diversity, while others, especially those with financial interests, may only value increased gender diversity if it positively impacts financial performance. There is also a third group of stakeholders who may not be interested in gender diversity at all. Overall, given the contentious and heated political and social debates surrounding this issue, **GDDR operate within a complex regulatory environment** influenced by a multitude of factors.

2.2 Regulatory environment in Germany

2.2.1 Corporate governance system

In order to understand the regulations regarding gender diversity on corporate boards in Germany, it is essential to recognize the particularities of the **German corporate governance system.**[19] The corporate governance systems in most developed countries are based on an Anglo-American unitary system (*Aguilera/Jackson* (2003), p. 461). In contrast, the board structure in Germany follows a dualistic corporate governance system (*Du Plessis et al.* (2017), p. 8). The one-tier system involves a single body (board of directors) composed of both executive and non-executive directors. The executive directors manage the daily and operational business of the company, while the non-executive directors oversee the board's activities. However, in daily operations, there is often no clear distinction between executive and non-executive directors (*Du Plessis et al.* (2017), p. 8).

In contrast to the Anglo-American (one-tier) board structure, German corporate governance is traditionally grounded on a dualistic (two-tier) system.[20] Accordingly, the allocation of decision-making power within the company differs between the two systems. Rather than concentrating management and supervision within a single board, the two-tier system separates these functions into distinct administrative bodies, ensuring both organizational and personnel separation, as individuals may not serve on both the executive and supervisory board simultaneously. Figure 2-4 illustrates the differences between a one-tier and a two-tier board structure.

---

[19] For detailed information on accounting and business economics tradition in Germany, cf. *Busse von Colbe/Fülbier* (2013), pp. 39–68.

[20] Besides Germany many European continental countries apply the dualistic system (e.g., Austria, Denmark, Sweden, and Finland), cf. *Du Plessis et al.* (2017), p. 8.

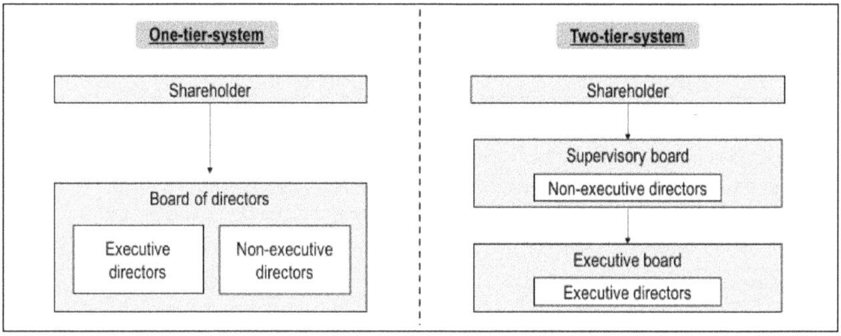

Figure 2-4: Comparison between one-tier and two-tier corporate governance systems (based on *Schumann et al.* (2024), p. 142)

On the one hand, the supervisory board consists of the non-executive directors. Its primary purpose is to oversee and monitor the actions of the executive directors (section 111 (1) Aktiengesetz (AktG)); also, *Habersack* (2019a), Rn. 1). Additionally, the **supervisory board** provides strategic guidance to the executive board without actively influencing the company's management decisions (*Gerum et al.* (2007), pp. 203–204). A key responsibility of the supervisory board in its monitoring role is the auditing of financial statements and management reports (section 171 (1) AktG). Thus, the supervisory board is of central importance and responsibility in ensuring the legal compliance of corporate financial reports (*Du Plessis/Saenger* (2017b), p. 148).

On the other hand, the **executive board**, composed of executive directors, is responsible for strategic decision-making and overseeing operational activities. The primary responsibility of the executive board is to manage the corporation (section 76 (1) AktG; *Du Plessis/Saenger* (2017a), p. 84). While the specific tasks are not legally defined, they encompass a wide range of responsibilities inherent to operational management, depending on the nature of the business (*Spindler* (2019), Rn. 16). A fundamental task of the executive board is to prepare the corporate financial statements and the management reports (section 264 Handelsgesetzbuch (HGB)). For instance, members of the executive board may exercise discretion in applying accounting standards (e.g., choice of depreciation methods) to manage the company's earnings (*Schipper* (1989), pp. 92–93).

In Germany, certain corporate types, such as the KGaA and the SE, operate under specific governance structures that diverge from the typical two-tier system. The KGaA combines elements of both a limited liability company and a stock corporation. KGaAs consists of at least one individual or entity with unlimited liability (section 278 (1) AktG), which manage the corporation (section 278 (2) AktG). In contrast to stock corporations (i.e., AGs), a KGaA has no executive board (section 278 (3) AktG). As the supervisory board does not appoint the general partners, this setup does not follow the characteristics of the typical two-tier system (*Grunewald/Müller* (2023a), Rn. 5). However, in many other respects, the supervisory board of a KGaA has the same rights and obligations as in the stock corporation (*Kallmeyer* (1983), 66–75).

The SE, an EU-based corporate form, offers companies flexibility to choose a one-tier or two-tier governance structure, depending on their preferences and operational needs (*Grunewald/Müller* (2023b), Rn. 3). If the two-tier structure is chosen, it resembles the German model, with distinct supervisory and executive boards (*Sandrock* (2017), p. 282). However, if the one-tier structure is selected, the SE operates similarly to an Anglo-American board, with both executive and non-executive directors serving on a single board that combines management and oversight functions (*Koch* (2023), Rn. 17). Thus, the KGaA and SE structures represent alternatives within German corporate governance that diverge from the traditional two-tier system.

Size of the supervisory board

Stock corporations (e.g., Aktiengesellschaft) and private limited liability corporations (e.g., GmbH) with more than 500 employees are legally required to establish a supervisory board (section 23 (5) AktG and section 52 (1) Gesetz betreffend die Gesellschaften mit beschränkter Haftung (GmbHG); also, *Habersack* (2019b), Rn 5).[21] The number of supervisory board members is determined by the size of the company (section 95 AktG). The supervisory board must consist of at least three members but can be expanded through by-laws (section 95 sent. 2 AktG). Depending on the company's share capital, the maximum number of supervisory board members is restricted and is capped at 21 members (*Habersack* (2019b), Rn. 13). Due to the recognition of employee participation in the German corporate governance system, the requirements of **co-determination laws** must also be taken into account (section 95 sent. 3 and 4 AktG). Limited liability companies with more than 500 but less than 2,000 employees are subject to German Act of One-Third Participation (Drittelbeteiligungsgesetz (DrittelbG)) (section 1 DrittelbG i.c.w. section 1 (1) and (3) MitbestG)[22]. For these companies, the number of supervisory board members must be divisible by three to ensure the required co-determination (section 95 sent. 3 AktG). Limited liability companies with more than 2,000 employees are subject to the MitbestG, which mandates that half of the supervisory board members are employee representatives (section 7 (1) MitbestG). For these parity co-determined companies, the number of supervisory board members is determined by the number of employees and increases with the size of the company. Companies with more than 20,000 employees can appoint a maximum of 20 board members (section 76 (1) MitbestG).

[21] The regulations on the composition of the supervisory board for private limited liability corporations are determined by the provisions of the AktG (section 52 (1) GmbHG). Accordingly, no differentiation is made between the different legal types of company in the following.

[22] Note that, for historical reasons, there are special laws on employee co-determination for companies in the iron and steel industry. Therefore, the provisions of the Iron and Steel Co-Determination Act Montan-Mitbestimmungsgesetz (MontanMitbestG)) and the German Supplementary Act to the Iron and Steel Co-Determination Act (Montan-Mitbestimmungsgesetzergänzungsgesetz (MontanMitbestG-ErgG)) apply to these companies. For reasons of clarity, no reference is made to these regulations in this study.

Composition of the supervisory board

For companies outside the scope of a co-determination act, the supervisory board is composed entirely of shareholder representatives[23] (section 96 (1) AktG). The shareholder representatives are directly elected by the Annual General Meeting (section 101 (1) AktG) unless there are differing appointment rights (section 101 (2) AktG). In co-determined companies, the supervisory board is proportionally constituted of **shareholder and employee representatives**, as required by the applicable co-determination act (section 96 (1) AktG).

In the case of **parity co-determination**, employee representatives are elected directly or indirectly by the employees (section 9 MitbestG). For companies with not more than 8,000 employees, representatives are elected directly; in larger companies with more than 8,000 employees, they are elected by employee delegates (*Habersack* (2019c), Rn. 8). According to section 7 (2) MitbestG, the composition of employee representatives, including the proportion of trade union members, depends on the size of the supervisory board. Although the MitbestG mandates parity on the supervisory board, the appointment of the chairperson is reserved for a shareholder representative (sections 27 (1) and (2), 29 (2) and (3) and 31 (4) MitbestG). For both operational and constitutional reasons, the chairperson of the supervisory board is granted a second vote (*Habersack* (2019c), Rn. 9), thereby providing a slight advantage to shareholders.

In companies subject to **one-third employee participation**, the election of employee representatives to the supervisory board is conducted directly (section 5 DrittelbG). In contrast to MitbestG, indirect election by delegates is not permitted (*Habersack* (2019c), Rn. 23). In accordance with section 6 of DrittelbG, nominations for employee representatives come from the works councils and employees. As in parity co-determined companies, the supervisory board is chaired by a shareholder representative who has a second vote to resolve stalemates and ensure the board's effective functioning.

Size and composition of the executive board

The executive board is a **mandatory body** of the company, consisting exclusively of natural persons (section 76 (3) AktG). The regulations governing the number of executive board members are less restrictive than those applicable to the supervisory board. According to section 76 (2) sent. 1 AktG, the executive board must consist of at least one person. However, companies with a share capital exceeding three million Euros are required to have an executive board composed of at least two members (section 76 (2) sent. 2 AktG). However, companies can stipulate a smaller size by by-laws. Members of the executive board are appointed by the supervisory board (section 84 (1) AktG). Section 84 (1) sent. 1 and 2 AktG limit the maximum term of office for executive board members to five years. However, reappointment is not restricted by law, allowing companies significant discretion regarding the size and composition of the executive board (*Spindler* (2019), Rn. 117).

---

[23] The function of shareholder representatives in two-tier corporate governance systems is formally comparable to the governance function of outside directors in one-tier systems (*Bozhinov et al.* (2021), p. 1326; *Fauver/Fuerst* (2006), p. 675).

In contrast to stock corporations, German law does not mandate an executive board for private limited liability companies (e.g., GmbHs). Instead, corporate management in these companies is the responsibility of **managing directors**, whose role is analogous to that of an executive board.[24] Similar to stock corporations, the management of private limited liability companies must consist of one or more persons (section 6 (1) GmbHG). According to section 6 (2) sent. 1 and 2 GmbHG, only natural persons who do not meet any legally specified exclusion criteria may be appointed as managing directors. If the company is required to establish a supervisory board, this board is responsible for appointing the managing directors.

2.2.2 German Corporate Governance Code

To strengthen corporate governance systems and increase both transparency and accountability, the introduction of corporate governance codes has become a widespread approach (*Cuomo et al.* (2016), p. 222). Following the example of various European neighbors[25], starting with the UK in 1992, Germany adopted the **GCGC** in 2002 (*Cromme* (2005), p. 364; *Kaspereit et al.* (2017), p. 166; *Wilsing* (2012), p. 292). This code was adopted by a government commission appointed by the Federal Ministry of Justice and aims to enhance transparency and increase investor confidence in German corporate governance mechanisms by providing "*principles, recommendations and suggestions*" (*GCGC* (2022), p. 2) for good and responsible corporate governance (*Kaspereit et al.* (2017), p. 168; *Werder et al.* (2005), p. 178). The GCGC is continually updated and amended in response to evolving corporate governance demands (*Fink/Kajüter* (2021b), p. 379; *Kaspereit et al.* (2017), p. 166).

The GCGC is based on self-regulatory mechanisms and, therefore, does not impose mandatory rules (*Cromme* (2005), p. 364). Companies are required to disclose annually whether they comply with the GCGC's recommendations (*Cromme* (2005), p. 364; *Werder et al.* (2005), p. 178). Although the **GCGC is not legally binding** by definition (*Goette* (2019), Rn. 22), section 161 (1) AktG mandates that listed corporations declare their conformity with the code on an annual basis, using the comply-or-explain approach (*GCGC* (2022), p. 2). This so-called "declaration pursuant to section 161 AktG" is part of the corporate governance statement (section 2.2.3.4) and must be published on the company's website (section 161 (2) AktG. Consequently, listed companies are obliged to address the GCGC's recommendations. Moreover, a high degree of transparency is ensured through mandatory disclosure (*Goette* (2019), Rn. 1).). Previously, the GCGC required companies to publish an explicit corporate governance report (e.g., *GCGC* (2010), p. 10). In its current version, however, the GCGC no longer mandates a corporate governance report but instead refers to the annual publication in the corporate governance statement (*GCGC* (2022), principle 23). This change in the reporting requirements aims to avoid duplicative reports that could reduce the clarity and comprehensibility of corporate governance reporting (*Fink/Kajüter* (2021b), p. 368). Furthermore, the mandatory declaration exerts pressure on listed companies to comply with the GCGC's recommendations in order to avoid reputational

---

[24] Due to the analogous roles of managing directors in private companies and executive board members in public companies, this study uses the term executive board members to refer to both corporate bodies.

[25] For an overview and timeline about the introduction of European Corporate Governance Codes, cf. *Mensi-Klarbach et al.* (2017), pp. 5–7.

damage (*Goette* (2019), Rn. 34; *Werder et al.* (2011), p. 501). This indirect external pressure results in a broad application of the recommendations.[26]

In 2010, the GCGC was amended to include **recommendations on gender diversity** for the composition of supervisory boards, executive boards, and management positions for the first time (*Heidemann et al.* (2013), p. 489). The GCGC recommended that companies "*respect diversity and, in particular, aim for an appropriate consideration of women*" (*GCGC* (2010), section 5.1.2) on the executive board and in management positions (*GCGC* (2010), pp. 6–9). Furthermore, supervisory boards were encouraged to "*specify concrete objectives*" (*GCGC* (2010), section 5.4.1) that "*stipulate an appropriate degree of female representation*" (*GCGC* (2010), section 5.4.1). These recommendations were intended to increase the proportion of women at various levels of corporate hierarchy (*Heidemann et al.* (2013), p. 495). However, the term "*appropriate degree*" (*GCGC* (2010), section 5.4.1) regarding the proportion of women on supervisory or executive boards was not defined in detail (*Krieger* (2012), p. 210). Consequently, companies had considerable discretion in interpreting this requirement and deciding what constitutes an appropriate level of female representation. For example, this resulted in a heterogeneous interpretation of an appropriate proportion of women on supervisory boards among DAX companies and additionally to target achievement periods (*Werder/Böhme* (2011b), p. 1350).

The GCGC's recommendations on the gender-diverse composition of corporate boards for listed companies can be **classified as soft law** (section 2.1.1). Since these recommendations are not legally binding, their application – and thus an increase in corporate gender diversity – remains voluntary. Nevertheless, due to the implicit pressure to justify their decisions, companies risk negative consequences and reputational damage if they choose not to comply (e.g., *Krieger* (2012), p. 217).

However, if corporate governance codes fail to achieve the desired outcomes, regulators can introduce **more stringent regulatory measures** to enhance gender diversity on corporate boards (*Goette* (2019), Rn. 18, see also section 2.1.1). The German Government intensified efforts to promote corporate gender diversity by enacting a gender diversity law. The next section details the legislative process and regulatory requirements of FüPoG I.

2.2.3 FüPoG I

2.2.3.1 Legislative process

In the lead-up to a mandatory gender diversity regulation in Germany, various interest groups with diverse agendas actively engaged in the public debate. Critical actors possess the ability to influence legislative processes and shape regulatory decisions to align with their interests (*Seierstad et al.* (2017b), p. 306). To understand Germany's gender diversity regulation development aimed at increasing the representation of women on corporate

[26] The Berlin Center of Corporate Governance (BCCG) in Germany regularly examines the acceptance and implementation of the GCGC (*Werder et al.* (2003), (2004); *Werder/Talaulicar* (2005), (2006), (2007), (2008), (2009), (2010); *Werder/Böhme* (2011b), (2011a); *Werder/Bartz* (2012), (2013), (2014); *Werder/Turkali* (2015); *Werder/Danilov* (2018); *Werder et al.* (2021). The BCCG starts to analyze the reporting practice in 2003 and the latest examination is from 2021.

boards, it is essential to consider the agendas of these key actors. Additionally, the heated discussions that characterized the legislative process and the underlying **political and regulatory motivations** must be considered. Therefore, this section explores the public debate and the legislative process from the outset, providing a detailed overview of the positions and influences of important actors involved.

Until FüPoG I came into force, Germany experienced a prolonged and controversial debate surrounding the legislative process (*Teigen* (2012), p. 132). Initially, gender diversity efforts were based on **voluntary participation by companies**. In 1998, the governing Social Democratic Party (SPD) and Green Party (Bündnis 90/Die GRÜNEN) expressed in their coalition agreement a commitment to promoting women's equal participation in the private sector through "*binding rules*" (*SPD and Bündnis 90/Die GRÜNEN* (1998)).[27] However, the specific regulatory tools or political instruments to achieve this objective were not detailed. In 2000, aiming to further gender equality, the Federal Minister for Women's Affairs proposed a concept for an Equal Opportunities Act for the private sector. An expert commission developed a draft bill based on this concept (*Alemann* (2008), p. 2645; *n.a.* (2001), p. 5). Nonetheless, due to strong opposition from business associations, the draft was never presented to the Bundestag[28] (*Pfarr* (2001), pp. 5–6). Instead of enacting a hard law (e.g., a mandatory gender quota on the supervisory board), a less restrictive approach emerged. In 2001, leading industry associations and the German government developed and signed a voluntary agreement[29] to promote equal opportunities for men and women in the private sector (*Pfarr* (2001), p. 6; *Seierstad et al.* (2017b), p. 296). As this agreement was merely a declaration of intent without legal obligations regarding gender equality on corporate boards, it faced criticism from political parties, women's associations, and labor unions for its lack of impact (*Kirsch* (2017), p. 215; *Pfarr* (2001), p. 6). Over time, this voluntary approach was deemed ineffective in achieving meaningful progress in women's participation in management positions (*Kirsch* (2017), p. 215; *Seierstad et al.* (2017b), p. 296).

In the early 2000s, discussions on gender equality gained further momentum, leading to the enactment of the General Equal Treatment Act (Allgemeines Gleichbehandlungsgesetz (AGG)) in 2006. On the occasion of this law, **efforts to establish more binding regulations** or a mandatory quota for the participation of women and men on corporate boards increased. Despite repeated attempts by the Green Party to introduce a mandatory quota in 2007 and 2009, these efforts were unsuccessful (*BT-Drs.* 16/5279, pp. 1–2; *BT-Drs.* 16/12108, pp. 1–2). However, in 2009, the governing coalition of the Christian Democratic Union (CDU)/Christian Social Union (CSU) and Free Democratic Party

---

27 For the following description of the legislative process in Germany refer also to *Kirsch* (2017), pp. 215–218.

28 The Bundestag (Federal Parliament) is Germany's primary legislative body, elected directly by the citizens, and responsible for passing federal laws and electing the Chancellor.

29 The so-called "Vereinbarung der Bundesregierung und der Spitzenverbände der deutschen Wirtschaft zur Förderung der Chancengleichheit von Frauen und Männern in der Privatwirtschaft" was signed by Bund Deutscher Arbeitgeber (BDA), Bundesverband der Deutschen Industrie e.V. (BDI), Deutscher Industrie- und Handelskammertag (DIHK) and Zentralverband des Deutschen Handwerks (ZDH). For the complete declaration, cf. *Pfarr* (2001), pp. 145–148.

(FDP) formally enshrined the plan to achieve a "*substantial increase*"[30] (*CDU/CSU and FDP* (2009), p. 74) in female representation on executive and supervisory boards, as well as in management positions across both private and public sectors. The strategy focused on "*binding reporting duties and transparent voluntary commitments*"[31] (*CDU/CSU and FDP* (2009), p. 74) to encourage companies to improve gender diversity through increased transparency rather than imposing mandatory quotas.

In 2010, initiatives to increase female representation on German corporate boards emerged without mandating gender quotas. The **GCGC introduced recommendations** for the "*appropriate consideration of women*" (*GCGC* (2010), section 4.1.2). Concurrently, major German companies began setting and publicly sharing individual targets for women in top management positions (e.g., Deutsche Telekom AG) (*Sattelberger* (2011), pp. 429–435). These individual endeavors led to a collective stance by DAX companies in 2011 (*Kirsch* (2017), p. 216). The companies report the proportion of women in management positions and disclose self-set targets for future increases (*BMFSFJ* (2011a)). Proponents of a mandatory quota law argued that voluntary disclosure was merely motivated by preventing more restrictive regulations (*Groll* (2011)). However, the companies did not establish binding rules for gender diversity on executive and supervisory boards (*BMFSFJ* (2011a)).

In addition to the political debate and business associations' interests, women's associations advocated for a mandatory quota law. In 2011, six leading women's associations, with support from female parliament members, published the "Berliner Declaration" (*Kirsch* (2017), p. 216). This petition called for a 30% gender quota for supervisory boards (*Berliner Erklärung* (2024)). Additionally, **women's associations** aimed to influence public debate through various actions. A private initiative attended over 300 shareholders' meetings of major German companies to critically observe personnel decisions and supervisory board elections (*djb* (2024); also *Kirsch* (2017), p. 217). These efforts sought to increase non-governmental pressure by raising public awareness.

Due to the implementation of mandatory gender quotas in many European countries[32], the political discussion in Germany gained further traction. The **debate on a mandatory gender quota** for supervisory boards was controversial and characterized by disagreement (*Seierstad et al.* (2017b), p. 296). Within political parties, there was often no consensus on gender equality strategies. This disunity is particularly evident in the discussion within the CDU in 2011. Federal Minister of Labor and Social Affairs, Ursula von der Leyen (CDU), signatory of the "Berliner Declaration", advocated for a 30% gender quota on supervisory boards. In contrast, Minister for Family Affairs, Kristina Schröder (CDU), opposed a mandatory quota law for various reasons (e.g., *Gathmann/Teevs* (2011); also *Kirsch* (2017), p. 217), proposing the idea of a "*flexi quota*"[33] instead (*BMFSFJ* (2011b); also *Kirsch* (2017), p. 217). This **modification of a mandatory gender quota** obliges companies to self-set

30 Note that the quotation is translated from German into English.

31 Note that the quotation is translated from German into English.

32 For an overview on the implemented mandatory gender quotas in Europe, cf. *Arndt/Wrohlich* (2019). For detailed information on the designs of mandatory gender quotas implemented in Europe and their regulatory background, cf. *Gabaldon et al.* (2017), pp. 240–253.

33 Note that the quotation is translated from German into English.

and disclose individual targets for the participation of women on corporate boards. The controversy within the CDU highlighted differing views on regulatory approaches to gender equality.

After the federal elections in 2013, the CDU/CSU and SPD coalition included a plan for a mandatory gender quota in the coalition agreement (*CDU/CSU and SPD* (2013), p. 72). On June 20, 2014, the first bill for mandatory regulation of the proportion of women in management positions (**FüPoG I**) was published (*BMJ* (2014a)). The bill combined two regulatory approaches: a mandatory gender quota of 30% for supervisory boards of certain large companies and a "*flexi quota*" for a broader range of companies, relying on the disclosure of self-set targets for more public visibility. The bill also targeted the executive board and the first two management levels below. Business associations once again criticized the proposal for a mandatory gender quota (*dpa* (2014)).

Almost simultaneously, on June 25, 2014, the opposition party Bündnis 90/Die GRÜNEN submitted an alternative bill to the Bundestag (*BT-Drs.* 18/1878, pp. 1–24). In contrast to the government's bill, their bill included a mandatory gender quota of 40% on supervisory boards. Similar to the pre-existing proposal, it also featured a "*flexi quota*" for the lower corporate management levels but foresees a broader application of a mandatory gender quota. This intensified the controversial debate between government and opposition parties over **appropriate regulatory designs** and the scope of companies (*Deutscher BT/BR – DIP* (2014), pp. 4195–4209).

The significant **political and public interest** in the legislative process was evident from the numerous statements on the second draft bill (*BMJ* (2014c)). The responsible ministry received 17 statements from various organizations and associations (*BMFSFJ* (2017)). Most business associations strongly opposed a mandatory quota (e.g., *BDA/BDI* (2014); *VdU* (2014)), while women's associations argued that the proposed regulations were not far-reaching enough (e.g., *Deutscher Frauenrat* (2014); *FidAR e.V.* (2014a)). Additionally, company representatives particularly opposed the mandatory gender quota (e.g., *BDA/BDI* (2014); *VSUD* (2014)), aligning with the expectation that companies would resist coercive regulations (section 2.1.1).

After a third revision of the draft bill (*BMJ* (2014b)), the CDU/CSU and SPD coalition agreed on a government draft bill on December 10, 2014. The bill was passed by a large majority on March 6, 2015 (*Deutscher BT/BR – DIP* (2015c), p. 8761) and approved by the Bundesrat[34] on March 27, 2015 (*Deutscher BT/BR – DIP* (2015a), p. 102). **FüPoG I** was published on April 30, 2015, and came into force on May 1, 2015. The next section discusses the regulatory requirements of FüPoG I in detail.

---

[34] The Bundesrat (Federal Council) is the constitutional body representing Germany's federal states at the national level. It participates in the legislative process by reviewing and approving legislation passed by the Bundestag.

2.2.3.2 Mandatory gender quota

Scope

FüPoG I is an omnibus law that amends several existing provisions, including the HGB, AktG, MitbestG, DrittelbG, and further related acts.[35] FüPoG I introduces **two regulatory approaches**: a mandatory gender quota on supervisory boards and a GDDR for executive boards and lower management levels.[36] FüPoG I differentiates two groups of companies, as the mandatory gender quota on supervisory boards applies solely to a specified scope of companies:

1. companies that are listed <u>and</u> parity co-determined, and
2. companies that are <u>either</u> listed <u>or</u> co-determined.

A company is considered "**listed**" within the meaning of FüPoG I if its shares are listed on a regulated market of a German stock exchange, as legally defined in section 3 (2) AktG. This means the market is supervised by state-recognized authorities, operates regularly, and is directly or indirectly accessible to the public.[37] By contrast, companies listed on an open market of German stock exchanges are not subject to the provision, as an open market is not considered a regulated market of section 3 (2) AktG.

Companies are considered "**parity co-determined**" within the meaning of FüPoG I, settled in section 96 (2) sent. 1 AktG, if they are obliged under the MitbestG, the MontanMitbestG, or the MontanMitbestGErgG to constitute a supervisory board with equal participation of employees and shareholders representatives. The same applies to companies resulting from cross-border mergers, cross-border changes of legal form, or cross-border divisions subject to co-determination (section 96 (3) AktG). In addition, the provisions applicable to the AG also apply to the KGaA (section 278 (3) AktG). The mandatory quota also expands to SEs, listed on the stock exchange and subject to parity co-determination in the supervisory board (section 17 (2) SE-Ausführungsgesetz (SEAG)). In essence, the mandatory gender quota of 30% applies to AGs and KGaAs with more than 2,000 employees and SEs with equally co-determined supervisory boards (*Kirsch* (2017), p. 219). When FüPoG I was passed, about 108 companies were affected by the mandatory gender quota (*BT-Drs.* 18/4227, p. 11).

Figure 2-5 illustrates the groups of companies that are subject to the mandatory gender quota on the supervisory board as per FüPoG I.

---

[35] As the legislator continuously adapts legal provisions for companies, these laws are subject to constant change. With the enactment of FüPoG II in 2021, the provisions of FüPoG I were also affected. Therefore, the references to legal provisions in this section (section 2.2.3) pertain to the version of the laws prior to the amendment on August 12, 2021.

[36] Besides the provisions for the private sector, FüPoG I also includes regulations for gender-diverse appointments to leadership positions in the public sector. Since the study at hand focuses on the private sector, the regulations for the public sector will not be discussed further.

[37] Only the listing on the stock exchange is decisive in this respect. The regulator does not specify that the shares of the company must be listed in Germany. Theoretically, companies that are headquartered in Germany and are listed on a foreign stock exchange are also be affected by FüPoG I, cf. *Teichmann/Rüb* (2015).

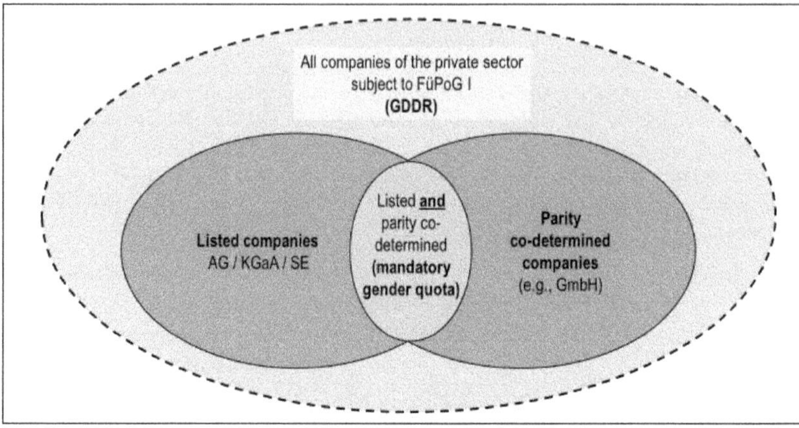

Figure 2-5: Companies subject to FüPoG I
(based on *Deutscher BT/BR – DIP* (2017b), BT-Drs. 18/13333, p. 48)

Mandatory gender quota on supervisory boards

According to section 96 (2) sent. 1 AktG, only **listed and co-determined companies** are required to compose their supervisory board of at least 30% women and 30% men. This mandatory gender quota applies to the supervisory board as an overall body (section 96 (2) sent. 2 AktG). However, the law allows both shareholder and employee representatives to object to the overall fulfillment (section 96 (2) sent. 3 AktG). Individual supervisory board members cannot declare this objection, as it must be voted on within a group of representatives (*Herb* (2015), p. 964; *Teichmann/Rüb* (2015), p. 899; *Wasmann/Rothenburg* (2015), p. 292). With the right of objection of the shareholder and employee representatives, FüPoG I implicitly creates new legal bodies within the supervisory board (*Teichmann/Rüb* (2015), p. 899) that can pass legally effective resolutions (*Herb* (2015), p. 965; *Teichmann/Rüb* (2015), p. 899). In case of disagreement regarding the overall fulfillment, both shareholder and employee representatives must separately achieve the gender quota of 30% (*Fink/Schmidt* (2015), p. 2157). In all cases, companies must mathematically adjust the gender ratios upwards or downwards to the whole number of persons (section 96 (2) sent. 4 AktG), which can lead to different results when considering the representative groups separately compared to the overall assessment.[38]

The mandatory gender quota applies to new elections from January 1, 2016 (section 25 (2) sent. 1 Einführungsgesetz zum Aktiengesetz (EGAktG)). Suppose the number of new positions to be elected on the supervisory board is insufficient to achieve the mandatory

[38] For a supervisory board consisting of 16 persons, at least five representatives of the underrepresented gender (rounded up from 4.8) would have to be represented in the case of overall fulfillment. On the other hand, in the case of separate fulfillment, four representatives are sufficient, as only two representatives are required per representative group (rounded down from 2.4), cf. *BT-Drs.* 18/3784, p. 120; *Teichmann/Rüb* (2015), p. 899.

proportion of women and men, a member with the underrepresented gender must be appointed (section 25 (2) sent. 2 EGAktG). All existing **mandates remained valid until their regular expiry** (section 25 (2) sent. 3 EGAktG).

Sanction of non-compliance

An election that does not comply with the mandatory gender quota will result in invalidity (section 96 (2) sent. 5 AktG). In such cases, the vacant position on the supervisory board remained unseated (section 96 (2) and (3) AktG). This sanction is known as the "***empty chair***"[39] (*BT-Drs.* 18/4227, p. 11). The invalidity of the election and the vacancy on the supervisory board can have far-reaching consequences.[40] Generally, the supervisory board retains a quorum (*Herb* (2015), p. 966). However, until the position is filled in accordance with FüPoG I, the parity of votes on the supervisory board may be disrupted (*Rotsch/Weninger* (2015), 301). Since neither representative party is interested in underrepresentation on the supervisory board, this sanction intends to have a behavioral steering function (*BT-Drs.* 18/3784, p. 122). Nevertheless, this statutory sanction can also lead to further legal uncertainties and insecurities (*Habersack* (2019c), Rn. 54; *Herb* (2015), pp. 966–967). In addition to the mandatory gender quota, which is classified as hard law and includes strict sanctions (section 2.1.1), FüPoG I includes provisions relying on a softer regulatory design. The following section introduces the GDDR provisions applicable to all companies subject to FüPoG I.

2.2.3.3 GDDR

Scope

In addition to the mandatory gender quota, FüPoG I introduced several further requirements based on the principles of targeted transparency. It mandates **listed or co-determined companies** to set targets for the proportion of women on the supervisory board, the executive board, and the first two management levels below the executive board (sections 111 (5) sent. 1, 76 (4) sent. 1 AktG). Accordingly, disclosure requirements of the GDDR apply to AG, KGaA, GmbH, SE, eG, and VVaG legal forms (*Herb* (2015), p. 968; *Rotsch/Weninger* (2015), 302). Under certain conditions, the legal form of GmbH & Co. KG can also be subject to section 289f (2) no. 4 HGB (*Fink/Kajüter* (2021b), p. 370).

The term "**listed**" is defined identically for the provisions of the GDDR compared to the group subject to the mandatory gender quota. In contrast to the mandatory gender quota, the GDDR applies to "**co-determined**" companies. Thus, the GDDR affects not only companies that are subject to co-determination on a parity basis but also companies that are subject to DrittelbG (sections 76 (4), 96 (2) and (3), 111 (5) AktG, sections 36, 52 (2) GmbHG). Companies already affected by the mandatory gender quota (see section 2.2.3.2) are also subject to the GDDR. However, for listed and parity co-determined companies,

[39] Note that the quotation is translated from German into English.

[40] An exploration of additional legal implications (e.g., in accordance to company law) extends beyond the scope of this study. For information on the consequences resulting from a nullity of the election resolution, cf. *Habersack* (2019c), Rn. 53.

the GDDR provisions apply only to the executive board and the two management levels below.

Figure 2-6 illustrates the scope for the GDDR according to FüPoG I.

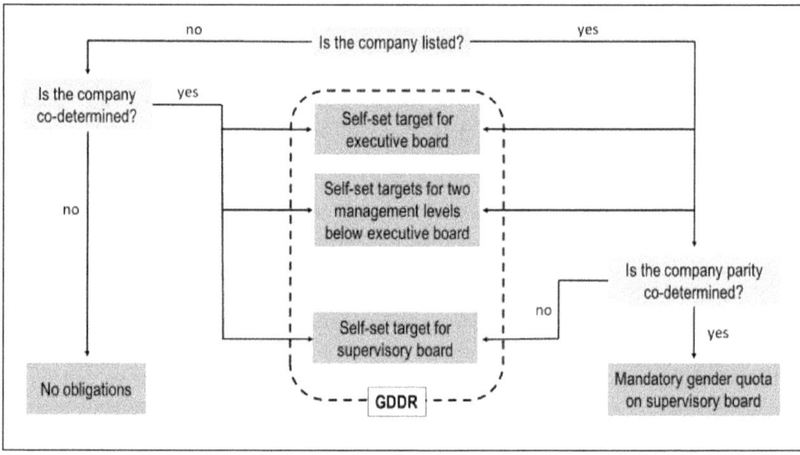

Figure 2-6: Decision tree on the scope of GDDR and mandatory gender quota under FüPoG I (based on *Fink/Schmidt* (2015), p. 2159)

In summary, the disclosure requirements of the GDDR apply to both listed and private companies across various legal forms (e.g., AG, KGaA, GmbH, SE, eG, and VVaG) (*Herb* (2015), p. 968; *Rotsch/Weninger* (2015), 302). Due to the broader application require-ments, the **GDDR affects considerably more companies than the mandatory gender quota**. Estimates of the exact number of companies within the scope differed noticeably. Estimates of companies subject to FüPoG I (including the mandatory gender quota and GDDR) ranged from 2,500 to 3,500 at the time of its enactment (*Bayer/Hoffmann* (2015), p. R5; *BDA/BDI* (2014), p. 15; *Wasmann/Rothenburg* (2015), p. 294).

Definition of management levels

In contrast to supervisory boards and executive boards, "management levels" are not legally codified organs. FüPoG I does not contain a definition of management levels (e.g., *Kajüter* (2020), Rn. 32), thus it is **open to interpretation** (*Herb* (2015), p. 968; *Teichmann/Rüb* (2015), p. 902). However, the government's explanatory memorandum provides a more detailed description of management levels. Thus, management levels refer to the hierarchical levels established in the company below the executive board, which are "*equal to each other but subordinate to a common management*" (*BT-Drs.* 18/3784, p. 119; also, *Kajüter* (2020), Rn. 32).[41] Due to the plural form in the government's explanatory memorandum, the prevailing opinion is that targets should be set independently for each management level (*Herb* (2015), p. 968; *Frombolzer/Simons* (2015), pp. 463–464; *Winter et al.* (2015), p. 1331).

[41] For a detailed discussion of the term "management level", cf. *Frombolzer/Simons* (2015), pp. 462–464.

Since there are no binding rules in general concerning the structure of corporate organizations, the legislator acknowledges that FüPoG I offers a "*very broad scope for discretion*"[42] (*BT-Drs.* 18/4227, p. 21) in defining targets on management levels. Smaller companies or companies with flat organizational structures that have only one hierarchical level below the executive board need to specify only one self-set target (*BT-Drs.* 18/3784, p. 119; *Herb* (2015), p. 969; *Rotsch/Weninger* (2015), pp. 304–305). While not legally required, explaining the definition of management levels can enhance understanding of the scope of the self-set targets (*Kajüter* (2020), Rn. 32).

In addition to the delimitation of the hierarchical level, companies also face the question of whether they can define the self-set target for the entire corporation. Companies must set targets for each subsidiary individually, not for the entire corporation (*BT-Drs.* 18/4227, p. 21). Thus, each subsidiary subject to the provisions of FüPoG I must set individual targets for the proportion of women on the first two management levels (*Herb* (2015), p. 969; *Wasmann/Rothenburg* (2015), p. 294). In addition, leeway exists on whether management levels within a company are to be limited to national employees or are to be interpreted internationally. Generally, it can be assumed that the **provisions of FüPoG I aim at national employees**, and therefore, a target is to be set for the national employees (*Hohenstatt et al.* (2014), p. 2224). Nevertheless, the leeway granted by the legislator and the complex structures of multinational laws also suggests that an international definition is permissible (*BT-Drs.* 18/4227, pp. 21–22; *Herb* (2015), p. 969; *Rotsch/Weninger* (2015), p. 304).

Responsibility for targets and target achievement periods

The supervisory board is required to set targets and target achievement periods for the proportion of women for both the **supervisory and the executive board** (section 111 (5) sent. 1 and 6 AktG). The supervisory board defines these targets by resolution (*BT-Drs.* 18/3784, p. 124). Although the supervisory board cannot influence the election of employee representatives and can only propose candidates for shareholder representatives, the literature assumes that the target applies to all representatives on the supervisory board (*Herb* (2015), p. 968). Furthermore, the law does not specify whether the supervisory board must set an overall target or if separate targets for shareholder and employee representatives are permitted. The leeway for setting targets mentioned in the explanatory memorandum supports this right of choice (*Fromholzer/Simons* (2015), p. 462; *Herb* (2015), p. 968). Nevertheless, companies subject to the mandatory gender quota of 30% on the supervisory board are not required to set additional targets for the proportion of women on this hierarchy level (section 111 (5) sent. 5 AktG).

Specific rules apply to **GmbHs** subject to DrittelbG for setting targets for the executive board (*Rotsch/Weninger* (2015), pp. 302–303). The shareholders' meeting, which has the authority to appoint the executive board (section 52 (2) sent. 1 GmbHG), is responsible for defining and implementing these targets. On the contrary, for GmbHs subject to parity co-determination, the supervisory board remains responsible for target setting (section 52 (2) sent. 2 GmbHG). A further exception to the target setting for the executive board occurs

[42] Note that the quotation is translated from German into English.

for KGaAs (*Fromholzer/Simons* (2015), p. 459). The supervisory board of **KGaAs** cannot set targets for the managing directors as there is no executive board with personnel authority to appoint them (*BT-Drs.* 18/4227, p. 22). In these cases, therefore, there is no obligation for the supervisory board to set a target (section 278 (3) AktG).

The **executive board** sets targets and target achievement periods for the first two management levels below the executive board (section 176 (4) AktG). These targets are defined collectively by the entire executive board and cannot be delegated to a single executive board member (e.g., *Herb* (2015), p. 968).

All targets and target achievement periods on the various hierarchy levels had to be determined by June 30, 2015 (section 25 (1) sent. 1 EGAktG). This **first target achievement period** could not exceed June 30, 2017 (section 25 (1) sent. 1 and 2 EGAktG). All subsequent target achievement periods may not be longer than five years (sections 111 (5) sent. 4, 76 (4) sent. 4 AktG). However, it is permissible to set shorter target achievement periods from the outset (*Fromholzer/Simons* (2015), p. 464; *Herb* (2015), p. 970). FüPoG I does not specify if companies are bound by the defined target achievement period or if they can set new targets before the period expires (*Fromholzer/Simons* (2015), p. 464). However, neither the law nor the explanatory memorandum indicates that such an approach is not permissible. On the contrary, it may be desirable for transparency to adjust an unreasonable achievement period in a timely manner to provide valid information about the company's actual gender diversity targets (*Fromholzer/Simons* (2015), p. 464). However, consistently setting new target achievement periods before the current one expires could lead to a lack of transparency, preventing a clear evaluation of the targets in the context of FüPoG I. Nevertheless, the legislator expects companies to set short target achievement periods to make their efforts visible due to public pressure (*BT-Drs.* 18/3784, p. 119).

Targets for supervisory boards, executive boards, and management levels

In contrast to the mandatory gender quota regulation of 30% on the supervisory board, **FüPoG I does not set fixed quantitative specifications for self-set targets** for the supervisory board, executive board, and management levels (*Rotsch/Weninger* (2015), p. 303; *Teichmann/Rüb* (2015), p. 902). Moreover, the provisions for self-set targets are explicitly required only for the proportion of women, not for both genders, even if women are already in the majority in the respective group (*Herb* (2015), p. 968). Generally, companies are widely unrestricted in setting targets for the participation of women at the respective hierarchy level (*Kajüter* (2020), Rn. 29-31). However, if the proportion of women is less than 30% when the target is set, the target may not be lower than the current proportion (section 111 (5) sent. 2 AktG). This "**prohibition of deterioration**" prevents companies from setting targets that would reduce women's representation (*BT-Drs.* 18/3784, p. 123; *Kajüter* (2020), Rn. 30). However, under certain conditions, "*extreme statements*"[43] (*BT-Drs.* 18/3784, p. 123) are also conceivable as targets for the proportion of women. Generally, a target of zero (i.e., 0%) is permissible if no women have previously been employed at the relevant hierarchy level (*Wasmann/Rothenburg* (2015), p. 295). Although this does not aim to increase the proportion of women, it does not target a decrease, thus complying with FüPoG I

---

[43] Note that the quotation is translated from German into English.

(*Fromholzer/Simons* (2015), p. 461). In other scenarios (e.g., with hierarchy levels consisting of a small number of employees), a target of 100% can also be feasible. Especially for executive boards of smaller companies, which often consist of one or two persons, targets of 0% or 100% may frequently prevail (*BT-Drs.* 18/3784, p. 123).

The government's explanatory memorandum implies an initial determination of the proportion of women at the respective management level (*BT-Drs.* 18/3784, p. 119). The corporate body responsible for determining the status quo is the one that sets the target for the respective hierarchy level (*Fromholzer/Simons* (2015), pp. 460–461). However, the law does not precisely define how to quantify the self-set targets. The government's explanatory memorandum states that the determination of target levels will "*typically consist of a percentage*"[44] (*BT-Drs.* 18/3784, p. 119), though this is not obligatory. The prevailing opinion states that the target must be **numerical and sufficiently specific**, so exclusively qualitative targets are not permissible (*Fromholzer/Simons* (2015), p. 462; *Schulz/Ruf* (2015), p. 1161; *Seibt* (2015), Rn 47). Thus, companies can measure the proportion of women as a percentage or in absolute numbers. However, non-standardized practices could reduce comparability and transparency intended by the law. Since the mechanisms of GDDR rely on the power of transparency (section 2.1.2), disclosing gender diversity information is essential to encourage public pressure. Therefore, the next section discusses disclosure requirements that provide information on corporate gender diversity and ensure transparency.

2.2.3.4 Publication requirements

Since the provisions of FüPoG I, except for the mandatory gender quota on supervisory boards, are based on the **principle of targeted transparency** (section 2.1.2), the disclosure of information is crucial. Companies must disclose their performance, targets, and achievements for gender diversity at each hierarchy level in their corporate reports. FüPoG I requires companies to include this information in the corporate governance statement, which is part of the annual management report.

Management report

In addition to the annual financial statements, certain companies must prepare and publish a management report according to sections 289-289f i.c.w. 315, 315a-315d HGB. The management report is a **separate information instrument** and extends the financial statements with additional, typically qualitative and prognostic, information (*Fink/Kajüter* (2021a), p. 3). The obligation to prepare a management report is codified by the regulations of the HGB.[45]

According to section 264 (1) HGB, companies that are classified as medium-sized or large corporations, as defined in section 267 (2) and (3) HGB, must publish a management report. Small corporations within the meaning of section 267 (1) HGB and the smallest corporations within the meaning of section 267a (1) HGB (section 267a (2) HGB) are

---

[44] Note that the quotation is translated from German into English.

[45] In addition, there are some special laws that regulate the obligation to prepare a management report in special cases. For more information, cf. *Fink/Kajüter* (2021a), pp. 10–13.

exempt from the obligation to prepare a management report. However, if these corporations are capital market-oriented within the meaning of section 264d HGB, they are considered as large (section 267 (3) sent. 2 HGB) and are therefore required to publish a management report (*Fink/Kajüter* (2021a), p. 10).

A company can be exempted from the obligation to prepare a management report under certain conditions. If a company is a **subsidiary** and meets the cumulative conditions in section 264 (3) HGB, it can be exempt from preparing a management report (*Fink/Kajüter* (2021a), pp. 10–11). These subsidiaries are integrated into the **group management report** of the parent company and do not prepare a separate management report (*Fink/Kajüter* (2021a), p. 11).[46]

Furthermore, parent companies may also be exempt from the obligation to prepare a management report if they are included in the **consolidated financial statements** and group management report of an EU-based parent company prepared according to EU directives (section 291 HGB). For parent companies based outside the EU, equivalent reporting to the group management report is sufficient (section 292 (1) HGB).

Corporate governance statement

The corporate governance statement is part of the management report (sections 289f i.c.w. 315d HGB). However, which **companies required to disclose a corporate governance statement is not uniformly defined,** as it varies depending on the requirements of different laws and guidelines (*Kajüter* (2020), Rn. 6). According to section 289f (1) and (3) HGB, only stock corporations listed on the stock exchange, public partly limited partnerships listed on the stock exchange, and some other specific types of stock corporations must include a corporate governance statement in their management report, which constitutes a separate section of the management report. Additionally, companies subject to FüPoG I, which mandates these companies to report targets and target achievement periods for the participation of women in corporate hierarchy levels, also have to publish a corporate governance statement (*Kajüter* (2020), Rn. 10).

The legislator grants companies a choice between **two disclosure options** (*Fink/Kajüter* (2021b), pp. 373–374). Instead of including the corporate governance statement in the management report, companies can opt to publish the statement separately on the company's website (section 289f (1) sent. 2 HGB, also *Kajüter* (2020), Rn. 13). In the event of a separate publication, a reference to the corporate governance statement must be included in the management report (section 289f (1) sent. 3 HGB). The timing of the corporate governance statement's publication on the company's website must coincide with when it would have appeared as part of the management report (*Fromholzer/Simons* (2015), p. 465; *Kajüter* (2020), Rn. 15).

The components of the corporate governance statement are codified in section 289f (2) HGB. The corporate governance statement includes (DRS 20.K227):

---

[46] The requirements for group management reporting according to section 315 HGB are specified in Deutscher Rechnungslegungs Standard (DRS) No. 20 (DRS 20.1). A corresponding application of this standard to the management report according to section 289 HGB is recommended (DRS 20.2).

- the declaration pursuant to section 161 HGB (section 289f (2) no. 1 HGB),
- a reference to the disclosures in the remuneration report (section 289f (2) no. 1a HGB),
- information about the governance practices (section 289f (2) no. 2 HGB),
- a description of the operating methods of the executive board and the supervisory board (section 289f (2) no. 3 HGB),
- information on the diversity policy related to the composition of the representative body and the supervisory board (section 289f (2) no. 6 HGB), and
- **information on gender diversity** in accordance with the provisions of FüPoG I (sections 289f (2) no. 4 and 5, 289f (4) HGB).

According to sections 289f (2) no. 4 and 289f (4) HGB, companies must state whether the defined targets set in accordance with FüPoG I have been achieved during the relevant period and, if not, provide the reasons.[47] **Companies subject to the mandatory gender quota** on the supervisory board must also provide information on whether the specified minimum quota has been met in the relevant period and, if not, provide the reasons (section 289f (2) no. 5 HGB). Moreover, companies not obliged to draw up a management report must disclose the information required by FüPoG I in a separate statement on the company's website (section 289f (4) sent. 2 and 3 HGB).

Although section 289f HGB defines the scope and structure of the corporate governance statement, there is still some **discretionary leeway** regarding content. Sections 289f (2) no. 4 and 5, 289f (4) HGB only require companies to disclose whether self-set targets have been achieved and, if not, provide reasons. The legislator does not mandate justification for the definition of the self-set targets or target achievement periods (*Fink/Kajüter* (2021b), p. 395). Moreover, there is no obligation to quantify the extent of target achievement or shortfall. A brief verbal statement – even without precise percentage values – is sufficient (*Fink/Kajüter* (2021b), p. 395). Consequently, report recipients cannot assess whether self-set targets are marginally or significantly met or missed. Furthermore, the disclosure requirements do not mandate interim reporting on the target achievement status before the end of the target achievement period (*BT-Drs.* 18/4227, p. 26). However, for long-term target periods, annual information on actual target achievement may be beneficial to show progress (*Kajüter* (2020), Rn. 33). In the context of GDDR, it seems reasonable to evaluate and state actual target achievement annually to provide transparent and decision-useful information (section 2.1.2). Nevertheless, short-term fluctuations in the proportion of women (e.g., due to vacant positions) should not give misleading impressions regarding the self-set targets. For transparent communication, companies should report precise figures on the proportion of women at respective levels (*Fromholzer/Simons* (2015), p. 464).

Additionally, companies are not required to explain the **definition of management levels** and the included group of persons in detail. However, as the legislator has granted some leeway in defining management levels (see section 2.2.3.4), it is difficult for report recipients of the corporate governance statement to compare gender diversity targets and the current representation of women between different companies. Therefore, it seems advisable to

47 For detailed information to the disclosure requirements in accordance to FüPoG I see section 2.2.3.4.

provide a transparent and consistent definition for each management level (*Kajüter* (2020), Rn. 32; *Rotsch/Weninger* (2015), p. 305; DRS 20.K231b).

Subsidiaries

As mentioned, certain subsidiaries are exempt from preparing an autonomous management report if they are included in the group management report of the parent company. This includes subsidiaries covered by the parent company's management report (section 264 (3) HGB) and parent companies included in a higher-level parent company's group management report (sections 291 and 292 HGB). For subsidiaries exempt from the obligation to publish a management report under section 264 (3) HGB, there is **debate in the literature** about whether they must publish an autonomous corporate governance statement on the company's website per section 289f HGB to comply with the disclosure requirements of FüPoG I (*Deutscher BT/BR – DIP* (2020c), BT-Drs. 19/24615, p. 194; *Kajüter* (2020), Rn. 12). The exemption from preparing a management report under section 264 (3) HGB, which includes the application of section 289f HGB and thus also section 289f (4) sent. 2 HGB, argues against the requirement to publish a corporate governance statement (*Hargarten/Seidler* (2016), pp. 2797–2798; *Junker/Schmidt-Pfitzner* (2015), p. 937; *Kajüter* (2020), Rn. 12; *Röhm-Kottmann/Gundel* (2015), pp. 1113–1114).[48] Other interpretations suggest these subsidiaries must publish a corporate governance statement on the company's website per section 289f (4) sent. 2 and 3 HGB (*Fromholzer/Simons* (2015), pp. 464–465; *Herb* (2015), p. 970). If the company does not publish a management report, the disclosure of the corporate governance statement should coincide with the annual financial statement (*Fromholzer/Simons* (2015), p. 465).

Companies included in a higher-level parent company's group management report (sections 291 and 292 HGB) are exempted from preparing a group management report. Hence, section 289f (4) HGB applies accordingly. However, similar to the companies exempted under section 264 (3) HGB, there is **room for interpretation** on whether these companies must separately publish the information required by FüPoG I (*Deutscher BT/BR – DIP* (2020c), BT-Drs. 19/24615, p. 194). As these companies do not prepare financial statements and annual reports per the provisions of HGB, it is reasonable to assume that they are also exempt from the disclosure requirements on gender diversity following FüPoG I.

Audit of the Corporate Governance Statement

Despite the importance of accurate disclosure in a targeted transparency regulation such as FüPoG I, the content of the corporate governance statement is not reviewed in the audit of the management report (section 317 (2) sent. 4 HGB). Thus, the targets for the proportion of women at different hierarchy levels are also not audited. However, auditors are only required to confirm the existence of the corporate governance statement, including information on FüPoG I (*Kajüter* (2020), Rn. 42; *Ruhnke/Schmidt* (2017), p. 2558).

---

[48] For an example on the scope of the application of section 264 (3) HGB in the context of the provisions of FüPoG I, cf. *Hargarten/Seidler* (2016), p. 2797.

Nevertheless, **auditors do not audit the correctness of the content** in accordance with FüPoG I (section 317 (2) sent. 6 HGB).

Additionally, there is controversy in the literature regarding whether the complete absence of the corporate governance statement – neither in the management report nor on the company's website – leads to a **qualification of the auditor's opinion** (*Hargarten/Seidler* (2016), p. 2797; *Ruhnke/Schmidt* (2017), pp. 2558–2559; *Seidler* (2016), pp. 939–942) According to a literal interpretation of the law, the auditor is not obliged to provide information in the auditor's opinion on the absence of information regarding FüPoG I (section 317 (2) sent. 4 HGB; *Seidler* (2016), p. 940). The management report is incomplete if the corporate governance statement or individual details are missing. Therefore, the auditor can restrict or qualify the audit opinion (e.g., *Kajüter* (2020), Rn. 44). In any case, to achieve the statutory provisions' desired transparency, users of companies' reports should be informed about missing information in the context of FüPoG I. Moreover, missing or incorrect disclosures can also result in sanctions beyond the scope of the management report audit.

Sanctions for misconduct

In general, FüPoG I only considers sanctions for non-compliance with the mandatory quota on the supervisory board, not for missing self-set targets for the proportion of women (*BT-Drs.* 18/3784, p. 120; *Kolb/Meyer* (2016), p. 495). In the sense of GDDR, the legislator aims to expose the self-set targets and the achievements in increasing the proportion of women to public pressure (*BT-Drs.* 18/3784, p. 120; *Fromholzer/Simons* (2015), p. 466), that public scrutiny will motivate companies to increase gender diversity (*Fink/Kajüter* (2021b), p. 394). Nevertheless, companies must comply with the disclosure requirements of the corporate governance statement and face sanctions for non-compliance. A deliberate missing, incorrect, or incomplete corporate governance statement constitutes a misdemeanor of the supervisory board or the authorized representative body (section 334 (1) no. 3 HGB, also *Kajüter* (2020), Rn. 43). Such infringements may result in fines up to € 50,000 (section 334 (3) sent. 1 HGB). More severe sanctions may apply if a company **deliberately misstates or conceals its situation** (section 331 no. 1 HGB). For example, this offense can occur by referring to the management report on the website without publishing the corporate governance statement. If a company is not required to prepare a management report, these sanctions do not apply (*Fromholzer/Simons* (2015), p. 465).

Companies and their respective bodies must define self-set targets and target achievement periods by law. Breaching this duty leads to liability for damages according to sections 93 (2) sent. 1, 116 AktG. The same **legal consequences** apply if impermissible targets and target achievement periods are set (*Habersack/Kersten* (2014), p. 2820; *Schulz/Ruf* (2015), p. 1162). Beyond target setting, an inadequate definition of management levels could impose sanctions. However, the legislator grants the executive board "*very great leeway*" (*BT-Drs.* 18/4227, p. 21) in setting targets for the management levels and also expressly points out that no legal consequences arise from the definition of the target "*even if it does not appear* *plausible or obvious to everyone*'[49] (*BT-Drs.* 18/4227, p. 21). A breach of duty can only be considered if the definition of management levels is entirely incomprehensible (*Fromholzer/Simons* (2015), p. 466). In conclusion, it remains doubtful what compensable damage has been caused by any omission or incorrect definition of targets for the proportion of women (*Fromholzer/Simons* (2015), p. 466).

2.2.4 FüPoG II

In 2021, six years after the implementation of FüPoG I, the German legislator revised the gender diversity regulation. On August 12, 2021, the "Act to Supplement and Amend Regulations for the Equal Participation of Women in Leadership Positions in the Private Sector and Public Service" (Zweites Führungspositionengesetz (FüPoG II); (BGBl. 2021 I no. 51, pp. 3311-3335) was enacted. Based on the findings of the evaluation of FüPoG I (*Deutscher BT/BR – DIP* (2020c), BT-Drs. 19/24615), the legislator determined that the **efficacy of the existing regulations was insufficient** (*BT-Drs.* 19/26689, p. 1). Although the mandatory gender quota on supervisory boards was deemed effective, the softer regulation on executive boards had not achieved the intended effects (*BT-Drs.* 19/26689, pp. 1–2). FüPoG II, therefore, builds on the existing regulations and tightens them in certain respects (*Spindler* (2023), Rn. 170).

Firstly, FüPoG II maintains the distinction between companies that are either listed or co-determined and those that are both listed and parity co-determined (e.g., *Seibt* (2021), p. 446; section 2.2.3.2). A central element of the amendments to FüPoG II is the **mandatory minimum representation** of both genders on the executive board (e.g., *Kocher* (2022), p. 104). According to section 76 (3a) AktG, companies that are listed and parity co-determined – i.e., those for which the mandatory gender quota for the supervisory board applies under FüPoG I – must appoint at least one woman or one man to the executive board if it consists of more than three members.[50] From August 1, 2022, the supervisory board must consider the minimum participation when making new appointments or extending an executive board mandate (section 261 (1) EGAktG).[51] Consequently, companies must either replace a member of the executive board or increase the size of the executive board if this is required to meet the legal requirements (*Kocher* (2022), p. 105). Even if it is not a mandatory gender quota in the narrow sense (*BT-Drs.* 19/26689, p. 48), the minimum participation requirement constitutes a stricter regulatory approach. This also underlines the "empty chair" sanction (already introduced under FüPoG I for the supervisory board; section 2.2.3.2) for the executive board (*Spindler* (2023), Rn. 191). If the appointment of an executive board member does not comply with the minimum participation requirement, it is null and void (section 76 (3a) sent. 2 AktG). This can result

---

[49] Note that the quotation is translated from German into English.

[50] Executive boards consisting of ten members have to consist of at least one women or man (resulting in a 10% participation) as well as executive boards consisting of four members (resulting in a 25% participation). Hence, a minimum participation is not equivalent to a mandatory gender quota, cf. *Rimmelspacher/Kliem* (2021), p. 1461; *Spindler* (2023), Rn. 184.

[51] For the particularities of the legal form of a KGaA, cf. *Backhaus* (2021).

in far-reaching consequences for the executive board's ability to operate (*Bürk/Wentz* (2022), pp. 179–180; *Seibt* (2021), p. 443).

Secondly, FüPoG II strengthens the targeted transparency provisions and **reinforces the GDDR**. Companies subject to FüPoG II must state self-set targets for the participation of women and men at each hierarchy level, corresponding to the full number of persons if the targets are percentages (sections 76 (4) sent. 2, 111 (5) sent. 2 AktG). This provision applies to targets set from August 12, 2021, onwards (section 26 (2) EGAktG). This prevents companies from setting a percentage target greater than zero that does not entail hiring a woman (*Bürk/Wentz* (2022), p. 182; *Rimmelspacher/Kliem* (2021), p. 1463).[52] Moreover, companies must provide an explanation if they set a self-set target of zero (sections 96 (4) sent. 3, 111 (5) sent. 3 AktG). This explanation must include a detailed statement of the considerations behind the decision (sections 96 (4) sent. 4, 111 (5) sent. 4 AktG). Since self-set targets of zero should be an exception (*BT-Drs.* 19/26689, p. 85), this provision increases the justification pressure on companies (*Seibt* (2021), pp. 444–445; *Spindler* (2023), Rn. 212). In line with the regulatory mechanisms of GDDR (section 2.1.2), this transparency may contribute to the regulation's efficacy.

In addition to major alterations and amendments of FüPoG I, further provisions are adjusted. This includes regulations for a mandate break for executive board members (section 84 (3) AktG), enabling women to continue their mandate after **maternity leave** (*Kocher* (2022), p. 106).[53] Moreover, FüPoG II **sharpens the sanctions** for violating the disclosure requirements of the corporate governance statement (*Rimmelspacher/Kliem* (2021), p. 1466). It is an administrative offense if companies do not publish the required information correctly or completely within the corporate governance statement (section 334 (1) sent. 1 no. 3 HGB, e.g., also *Spindler* (2023), Rn. 223). Companies are also sanctioned if no targets or target achievement periods have been set or if a target of zero has not been justified (section 334 (1) sent. 2 and 3 HGB). Addressing existing enforcement gaps for reporting obligation breaches in target-setting aims to improve the efficacy of FüPoG II (*BT-Drs.* 19/26689, p. 50).

2.2.5 Supranational gender diversity regulations

In addition to the national efforts by the German Federal Government, supranational regulators also seek to foster gender diversity in the corporate context. Unlike FüPoG I and FüPoG II, which specifically emphasize increasing gender diversity, the regulations implemented by the European Union address a **broader range of corporate diversity** aspects.

In 2014, the **Non-Financial Reporting Directive** (NFRD) (Directive 2014/95/EU) was published. It requires large publicly listed companies within the EU to describe their diversity policy. This directive has been transposed into German law through the CSR-

[52] For example, according to section 76 (4) sent. 2 AktG, it is not permitted to define a target of 10% for a management level comprising six persons, cf. similarly *Bürk/Wentz* (2022), pp. 181–182.

[53] For a further discussion of the mandate break regulations, cf. *Bürk/Wentz* (2022), pp. 182–184; *Kocher* (2022), pp. 106–108.

Richtlinie-Umsetzungsgesetz (CSR-RUG) (*Kajüter* (2020), Rn. 36).[54] In accordance with section 289f (2) no. 6 HGB, affected companies must disclose information regarding the diversity of their executive and supervisory bodies within the corporate governance statement (see section 2.2.3.4). The disclosure requirements encompass information on aspects such as age, gender, educational, and professional backgrounds of the board members, as well as the objectives, implementation methods, and outcomes of the pursued diversity policy (section 289f (2) no 6 HGB; also *Kajüter* (2020), Rn. 39).

Since the directive relies on a **"comply or explain" mechanism** (DRS 20.K231l), the companies are not legally required to pursue a diversity policy (*Velte* (2024), p. 87). Neither the NFRD nor the CSR-RUG specify detailed requirements for the minimum content of diversity policy descriptions (*Fink/Kajüter* (2021b), p. 402), thereby allowing companies substantial flexibility in their reporting (*Velte* (2024), p. 91). Against the backdrop of the national reporting requirements, companies that disclose gender diversity information (e.g., self-set targets) as mandated by FüPoG I and FüPoG II may fulfill the requirement to report on a diversity policy in accordance with section 289f (2) no. 6 HGB (*Fink/Schmidt* (2015), p. 2165). Consequently, these companies are not required to provide explanations for omitting a separate diversity policy (*Fink/Kajüter* (2021b), p. 402).

In 2022, the EU adopted the **Corporate Sustainability Reporting Directive** (CSRD) (Directive (EU) 2022/2464), which will replace the NFRD. In addition to a significantly expanded scope of application[55], the directive has several implications for reporting on the diversity policy. The CSRD mandates publishing a sustainability report, which must be included as a separate section of the management report. Furthermore, the information within this sustainability report is subject to mandatory auditing. Through the European Sustainability Reporting Standards (ESRS), issued by the European Commission via a delegated act (Delegated Regulation (EU) 2023/2772), uniform reporting standards have been established. ESRS 2 and ESRS S1 specifically affect the reporting on diversity policies. ESRS S1 defines "diversity", among other things, as the "*representation of women and/or ethnic groups or minorities in own workforce*" (Delegated Regulation (EU) 2023/2772, p. 198). Consequently, unlike the NFRD, the CSRD mandates explicitly reporting on gender diversity within the diversity policy.

The CSRD has to be implemented in national law until June 6, 2024. However, the German Federal Government failed to meet this deadline (*Lanfermann/Baumüller* (2024), p. 383). Even though the law has not been passed yet, the draft bill for implementing the CSRD largely proposes a direct transposition of the European requirements (*Kajüter* (2024), p. 401). For companies required to prepare a **sustainability report** according to CSRD and to disclose their diversity policy in the corporate governance statement, there is a risk of redundant disclosures (*Velte* (2024), p. 89). To avoid duplication, the draft bill permits relevant information on the diversity policy to be integrated into the sustainability report,

---

[54] In contrast to the requirements of FüPoG I and FüPoG II, the NFRD applies exclusively to publicly listed and large companies, with the latter defined according to section 267(3) HGB. Consequently, the obligation to disclose a diversity concept does not extend to limited liability companies (*Spindler* (2023), Rn. 109).

[55] For detailed information on the scope of application, cf. *Lanfermann/Baumüller* (2024), pp. 384–387.

with the corporate governance statement referencing this information (*BT-Drs.* (20/12787), p. 11).

Apart from the amendments to sustainability reporting, the European Commission intensified its efforts to promote corporate gender diversity with specific regulations. The **European Gender Diversity Directive** (Directive (EU) 2022/2381) mandates listed companies apart from micro, small and medium sized-companies[56] to achieve a mandatory gender quota (*Velte* (2024), pp. 87–88). The directive specifies a target of 40% gender representation for supervisory board members or 33% across both supervisory and executive board members, effective from June 30, 2026 (Directive (EU) 2022/2381, section 5). However, member states can opt to suspend the application of the directive if publicly listed companies must meet a mandatory gender quota of 30% on supervisory boards and 25% on executive boards (Directive (EU) 2022/2381, section 12 (1) lit. b) (i)). Germany's existing provisions under FüPoG II meet these criteria. Accordingly, the German Federal Government has determined that there is no need to transpose the EU directive into national law (*Rothenburg/Moench* (2023), p. 218).

2.3 Summary

This chapter **outlined the regulatory approaches** to promoting gender diversity at a corporate level. It explained the mechanisms of targeted transparency regulations, particularly highlighting the regulatory characteristics of GDDR. The key feature of Germany's gender diversity regulation is its combination of soft and hard laws, targeting hierarchy levels below corporate boards, and serving as a pioneer in implementing GDDR. The targeted transparency regulation introduced by FüPoG I is unique in the context of gender diversity regulation, aiming to shape corporate behavior through increased transparency. While this mechanism was already used in other fields (e.g., animal welfare labeling), Germany was the first country to apply it to gender diversity for ethical goals.

Since GDDR do not legally mandate an increase in the proportion of women in management positions, companies could set targets that did not exceed the current status quo and might choose not to increase gender diversity. The provisions and comprehensive **disclosure requirements** of FüPoG I and FüPoG II, summarized in Figure 2-7, are intended to activate the mechanisms of targeted transparency.

[56] These companies are companies, which employ less than 250 persons and have an annual sales revenues not exceeding €50 million or an annual balance sheet total not exceeding €43 million (section 3 No. 8 Directive (EU) 2022/2381).

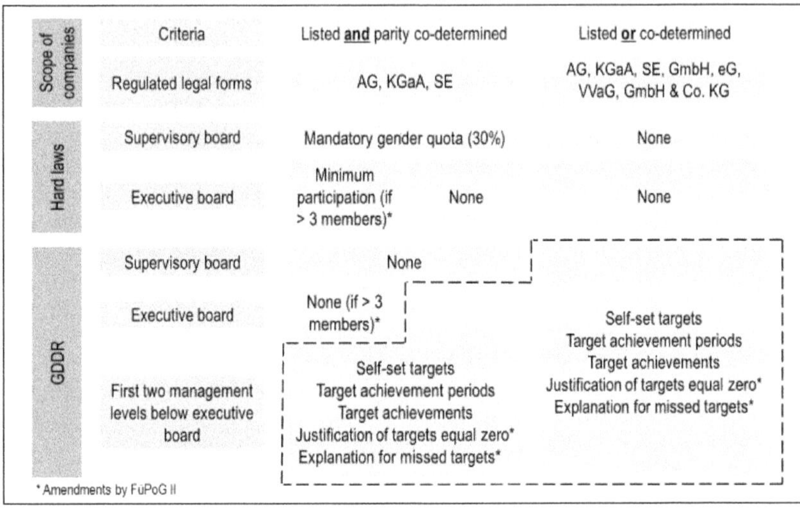

Figure 2-7: Overview of regulatory requirements by FüPoG I and FüPoG II

However, the **efficacy determinants of GDDR are largely unknown**. During the legislative process, its efficacy was controversially debated and contested by some who advocated for stricter regulatory interventions (e.g., a broader application of mandatory gender quotas (*Deutscher BT/BR – DIP* (2015c), pp. 8739–8762)). Nevertheless, the disclosure requirements introduced by FüPoG I are wide-ranging, applying to both publicly listed and private companies. Due to their individual characteristics, companies may differ in their response to the disclosure requirements and potential changes in behavior.

Regardless of the type of regulatory intervention, however, corporate boards are crucial for monitoring and managing the company. Therefore, members of corporate boards and managers at lower hierarchy levels require personal skills. The regulatory intervention by GDDR may **result in changes in appointment decisions** and alterations in the composition of companies' boards and management, potentially leading to altered outcomes.

In summary, the GDDR introduced by FüPoG I leads to several options regarding disclosure practices and responses of regulated companies. The efficacy of GDDR is questionable as **increasing corporate gender diversity remained voluntary**. However, external factors could influence companies' responses to GDDR and, consequently, their appointment behavior on corporate boards. Thus, the study at hand examines companies' disclosure practices in response to FüPoG I and empirically investigates the efficacy of GDDR. Additionally, it explores the determinants of efficacy and the consequences of an increased proportion of women in response to the introduction of GDDR.

3 State of research

Since the introduction of gender diversity regulations in several countries[57], various studies have investigated their regulatory background, efficacy, and consequences. First, section 3.1 reviews descriptive evidence on the presence of women on corporate boards after the introduction of the GDDR in Germany. Due to the scarcity of inferential statistical research on GDDR, section 3.2 examines previous empirical studies on several regulatory approaches, providing important insights into regulatory settings and institutional factors (section 3.2.1). Additionally, it presents research on determinants of regulatory efficacy (section 3.2.2). Section 3.3 provides an overview of studies analyzing the relationship between female board members and financial reporting quality in the absence of gender diversity regulation (section 3.3.1). It also explores studies examining how increased female participation on corporate boards, within the context of gender diversity regulations, is associated with financial reporting quality (section 3.3.2). Given the diverse characteristics of regulatory approaches aimed at promoting gender diversity on corporate boards, the determinants influencing their efficacy and consequences may differ from those of GDDR. Finally, section 3.4 summarizes the current state of research and highlights the research gap.

3.1 Descriptive research on GDDR

Focusing on Germany, the participation of women in management positions is of high public and political interest (section 2.2.3.1). Several groups of researchers and government institutions **continuously monitor** the development of the proportion of women on German corporate boards. Even before the GDDR came into force, the gender composition of supervisory and executive boards was systematically monitored in Germany.[58]

Since 2011, *FidAR e.V.*[59] publishes the "**Women-on-Board-Index**" annually, which offers descriptive data on the gender composition of supervisory and executive boards for 160 German companies that are listed on the DAX, MDAX, SDAX or TecDAX (*FidAR e.V.* (2011); *FidAR e.V.* (2012); *FidAR e.V.* (2013); *FidAR e.V.* (2014b); *FidAR e.V.* (2015); *FidAR e.V.* (2016))). The index provides detailed information on corporate gender diversity, ranking the analyzed companies based on the presence of women on corporate boards. The index strives to attain increased transparency and inform a broad audience in

---

57 For an overview of mandatory gender quotas implemented in European countries, cf. *Kirsch et al.* (2022b). For on overview of regulatory approaches beyond mandatory gender quotas, cf. *Mensi-Klarbach et al.* (2017).

58 Note that the following studies are German sources, which are predominantly only available in German language.

59 *FidAR e.V.* is a registered association recognized as a non-profit organization. It was founded in 2006 by women in leadership positions from business, science and politics with the aim of significantly and sustainably increasing the proportion of women on German supervisory boards. The association works supra-regionally, non-partisan, independently and exclusively on the basis of existing democratic principles in Germany and the EU, cf. *FidAR e.V.* (2018).

a concise form.[60] Before the enactment of FüPoG I, the researchers observe a steady but sluggish increase in the female presence on corporate boards under the voluntary disclosure regime (e.g., *FidAR e.V.* (2015), p. 3). For instance, starting from a proportion of 10.0% in 2011, the presence of female supervisory board members increased in the subsequent years (12.8% in 2012, 15.8% in 2013, 17.2% in 2014) and reached a proportion of 21.4% in 2015 (*FidAR e.V.* (2015), p. 16). The researchers observe a similar increase, though at a lower level, in female participation on executive boards (*FidAR e.V.* (2015), p. 17). For example, the proportion of women on the executive board reached a maximum of 5.2% on average in 2015 (*FidAR e.V.* (2015), p. 22). Despite an overall increase of women on corporate boards, the findings of *FidAR e.V.* indicate **substantial variation in gender diversity** among the analyzed companies (e.g., *FidAR e.V.* (2015), p. 3).

With the enactment of FüPoG I, *FidAR e.V.* expands the sample to include companies on the regulated market subject to the mandatory quota, not previously covered in earlier studies (*FidAR e.V.* (2017); *FidAR e.V.* (2018); *FidAR e.V.* (2019); *FidAR e.V.* (2020); *FidAR e.V.* (2021); *FidAR e.V.* (2022); *FidAR e.V.* (2023)). This extended sample reveals **differences in the efficacy** of the mandatory gender quota compared to the GDDR in influencing gender diversity on supervisory boards (e.g., *FidAR e.V.* (2017), p. 1). The researchers argue for the efficacy of the mandatory gender quota and recommend extending it to a broader range of companies (*FidAR e.V.* (2017), p. 63). The index continuously monitors gender diversity on corporate boards and, thus, contributes to increased transparency. However, the findings of the Women-on-Board-Index concentrate on the composition of supervisory and executive boards. Hence, the researchers focus their evaluation on the upper corporate hierarchy levels. Nevertheless, the series provides some insights into self-set targets, target achievement periods, and actual target achievement for management levels below the executive board. Since the index is based on a sample of the largest listed German companies, it does not include private companies subject to the GDDR. However, private companies make up the majority of companies affected by the GDDR (*Deutscher BT/BR – DIP* (2020a), BT-Drs. 19/20361, p. 17).

The "**Women Executive Barometer**" is another series of descriptive studies conducted by a research collective[61] that monitors the progress in gender diversity on German corporate boards, published annually (*Holst/Kirsch* (2016a); *Holst/Wrohlich* (2017); *Holst/Wrohlich* (2018); *Holst/Wrohlich* (2019); *Kirsch/Wrohlich* (2020b); *Kirsch/Wrohlich* (2021b); *Kirsch et al.* (2022a); *Kirsch et al.* (2023b); *Sondergeld et al.* (2024)). Complementary to the Women-on-Board-Index, these studies analyze a group of large private limited liability corporations alongside large listed companies. The sample encompasses Germany's 200 largest non-financial sector companies measured by total revenues (e.g., *Holst/Kirsch*

[60] For example, a leading German business magazine headlined in the wake of the publication of the first Women-on-Board-Index "The zeros must go"(*Freisinger* (2011)). Note that the quotation is translated from German into English.

[61] The Women Executive Barometer is published by DIW Berlin. DIW Berlin (the German Institute for Economic Research) was founded in 1925 and is one of the leading economic research institutes in Germany. The institute analyzes the economic and social aspects of topical issues, formulating and disseminating policy advice based on its research findings. A member of the Leibniz Association, DIW Berlin is independent and primarily publicly funded, cf. *DIW Berlin* (2024).

(2016a), p. 13).[62] The series of studies offers comprehensive information on the presence of women on supervisory and executive boards. In contrast to the studies of *FidAR e.V.*, the researchers offer further information regarding the women appointed to corporate boards and list them by name. Furthermore, the researchers compare the changes in German corporate boards with the developments in other European Countries (e.g., *Holst/Kirsch* (2016a), pp. 21–23). Besides an aggregated comparison, the observation does not provide a detailed analysis of the other countries' regulatory approaches and their impact on the development of corporate board transparency.

Due to the overlapping samples, despite some minor variations, the findings of the Women Executive Barometer largely align with those of *FidAR e.V.*, showing a **steady increase in the proportion of women on corporate boards** (e.g., *Holst/Wrohlich* (2019), p. 18). Moreover, the researchers observe discrepancies in gender diversity between large listed companies and private companies. However, the study does not provide a structured comparison of listed companies subject to the mandatory quota and those affected by the GDDR. Despite offering valuable insights, the studies face the methodological issue that the 200 largest companies in Germany vary over time, making full comparability between years difficult. Contrary to the surveys of *FidAR e.V.*, these studies do not monitor changes in self-set targets, target achievement periods, and actual target achievement at lower management levels in companies subject to the GDDR. Nevertheless, the Women Executive Barometer enhances transparency by providing publications in English, thus reaching a broader audience of non-German speaking addresses.

In addition to the annual publication of the Women Executive Barometer, the research collective publishes supplementary literature that explores various aspects of gender diversity regulation in Germany. These primary descriptive analyses cover topics such as the trickle-down effect[63] of the mandatory gender quota in Germany (*Kirsch/Wrohlich* (2020a)), the benefits of **gender-diverse supervisory boards in terms of monitoring** (*Kirsch/Wrohlich* (2021a)), the efficacy of different European quota regulations (*Kirsch et al.* (2022b)), and the reporting on women's participation in leadership positions (*Kirsch et al.* (2023a)). The researchers contribute to the literature investigating gender diversity regulation in Germany and provide additional insights beyond the development of the proportion of women.

Furthermore, the German Federal Government commissions the most comprehensive descriptive study analyzing companies' responses to the GDDR. According to section 23 (1) FüPoG I annual information ("**The annual information of the German Federal Government**") is published on the development of the proportion of women and men in management positions and boards in the private and public sectors (*Deutscher BT/BR – DIP* (2017a), BT-Drs. 18/11500; *Deutscher BT/BR – DIP* (2017b), BT-Drs. 18/13333; *Deutscher*

[62] Additionally, the research collective publishes comparable studies investigating the largest German banks and insurance companies. For an example, cf. *Holst/Kirsch* (2016b).

[63] The trickle-down effect describes the phenomenon that female representation on senior management positions (e.g., on the executive board) is positively related with the female representation at the hierarchy level immediately below (e.g., at the first management level below the executive board), cf. *Bilimoria* (2006); *Gould et al.* (2018).

BT/BR – DIP (2020a), BT-Drs. 19/20361; *Deutscher BT/BR – DIP* (2020b), BT-Drs. 19/20362; *Deutscher BT/BR – DIP* (2021), BT-Drs. 19/32704; *Deutscher BT/BR – DIP* (2023a), BT-Drs. 20/5340; *Deutscher BT/BR – DIP* (2023b), BT-Drs. 20/9850). While the first study in 2017 covers solely publicly listed companies (*Deutscher BT/BR – DIP* (2017a), BT-Drs. 18/11500), subsequent studies have included all public and private companies subject to FüPoG I (e.g., *Deutscher BT/BR – DIP* (2017b), BT-Drs. 18/13333). Thus, these studies closely monitor progress in increasing gender diversity at both corporate boards and management levels.

The ongoing studies examine and illustrate data on the level of gender diversity in supervisory boards, executive boards, and lower management levels. For example, the results show an **increase in the presence of women on supervisory boards** (from 17.9% in 2015 to 24.0% in 2020 (*Deutscher BT/BR – DIP* (2023b), BT-Drs. 20/9850, p. 29)) **and executive boards** (from 6.1% in 2015 to 10.3% in 2020 (*Deutscher BT/BR – DIP* (2023b), BT-Drs. 20/9850, p. 30)) on average. These trends align with the findings of the Women-on-Board-Index and Women Executive Barometer. Moreover, the researchers observe the development of the analyzed measures over time and identify trends. The studies additionally analyze data by categorizing companies into subsamples (e.g., whether they are publicly listed or private, parity co-determined or co-determined, or due to their size and industry classification). The studies also provide information on the level of self-set targets and target achievement periods, revealing, for example, that public companies are more likely than private ones to disclose targets across all levels of corporate hierarchy (e.g., *Deutscher BT/BR – DIP* (2023b), BT-Drs. 20/9850, pp. 32-34). However, it is particularly remarkable that the results also indicate that some companies do not comply with the disclosure requirements. For example, less than 75% of the analyzed companies publish self-set targets for the first management level below the executive board (*Deutscher BT/BR – DIP* (2023b), BT-Drs. 20/9850, pp. 124-125). Overall, these studies offer a comprehensive overview of changes in gender diversity among companies subject to FüPoG I.

However, due to the large sample size, these studies **do not cover all relevant information** related to the disclosure requirements of FüPoG I. Firstly, despite the detailed information on self-set targets, the researchers do not examine whether companies ultimately achieve self-set targets within the defined target achievement periods. Furthermore, the studies do not provide any information on narrative explanations from companies that fail to meet their self-set targets. Secondly, the studies do not detail the disclosure practices of regulated companies, such as where they publish the required information. Hence, the studies do not indicate whether companies include the required disclosures in the management report or publish them separately on their company's website. Furthermore, the studies do not specify whether companies integrate gender diversity information into other sections of the management report or allocate a dedicated section for it when they publish information within the management report.

In 2020, an independent study commissioned by the BMFSFJ published an evaluation report to meet the statutory requirement of section 23 (3) FüPoG I (*Deutscher BT/BR – DIP* (2020c), BT-Drs. 19/24615). This evaluation aims to assess the acceptance and efficacy of

FüPoG I, focusing on both the mandatory gender quota and the GDDR. The study expands the understanding of the impact of FüPoG I on internal company processes through a mixed-methods research design. The researchers combine the quantitative data with additional qualitative data from interviews with participating actors.[64] The survey evaluates, inter alia, the familiarity of FüPoG I, its influence on **corporate appointment and recruitment processes**, and the challenges companies face (*Deutscher BT/BR – DIP* (2020c), BT-Drs. 19/24615, pp. 47-49). The researchers conclude that FüPoG I "*has so far not led to the establishment of processes and structures that could systematically anchor the participation of women in leadership within companies (e.g., target quotas for women's participation in succession planning, professionalization of selection processes through diverse selection committees, standardized processes for defining target values)*"[65] (*Deutscher BT/BR – DIP* (2020c), BT-Drs. 19/24615, p. 35).

Overall, the researchers find that the mandatory gender quota considerably impacts the gender diversity on supervisory boards.[66] In contrast, they observe that the **GDDR increased gender diversity** in executive boards and lower management levels **to a more limited extent**. The study reveals a substantially lower increase in the presence of women at corporate levels below the quota-affected supervisory boards. Furthermore, the findings of the qualitative survey suggest that FüPoG I has not yet led to a change in corporate processes and structures necessary for systematically anchoring women's presence in management. This aligns with the finding that the regulation of FüPoG I is less familiar at lower corporate hierarchy levels. Based on their findings, the researchers recommend, inter alia, expanding the mandatory gender quota to a broader range of companies, stricter regulation of executive boards, and requiring companies to explain why they set targets of zero for the proportion of women (*Deutscher BT/BR – DIP* (2020c), BT-Drs. 19/24615, pp. 121-124). However, the evaluation report is limited in terms of quantitative data from 2015 to 2017. The findings cover only the early implementation period of FüPoG I. Additionally, the study does not address the limitations of prior studies regarding the type of publication, whether companies meet their self-set targets, or the reasons for missing them.

In summary, descriptive studies continuously document increasing participation of women on corporate boards after the implementation of FüPoG I, noting a **steady increase in gender diversity across different hierarchy levels**. However, the literature suggests that the mandatory gender quota is more effective than GDDR at improving gender diversity on supervisory boards. Nonetheless, previous studies also observe increased gender diversity on the executive board, which is regulated solely by GDDR. The development of female participation on management levels below the executive board is largely unexplored. Moreover, descriptive research reveals differences in companies' disclosure practices. For instance, most companies publish self-set targets of zero, especially on the executive board. However, no study provides insights into how frequently companies achieve or miss their self-set targets. Yet, prior research on GDDR does not explore company-specific

---

64 These actors include experts (e.g., supervisory and executive board member, member of work councils, and employees) from the political and professional environment (*Deutscher BT/BR – DIP* (2020c), BT-Drs. 19/24615, p. 27).

65 Note that the quotation is translated from German into English.

66 Here and in the following, cf. *Deutscher BT/BR – DIP* (2020c), BT-Drs. 19/24615, pp. 35-36.

determinants of its efficacy or broader consequences beyond increased gender diversity. Therefore, it is crucial to investigate these determinants and potential impacts to fully assess the efficacy of GDDR. Table 3-1 summarizes the descriptive studies on GDDR.

Descriptive research on GDDR		
Series of studies	**Sample**	**Key findings**
Women-on-Board-Index	160 (185 from 2017 onwards) publicly listed companies (DAX, MDAX, SDAX, TecDAX)	The proportion of women on supervisory and executive boards increased after the implementation of FüPoG I. The mandatory gender quota at the supervisory board level lead to a larger increase in gender diversity than the GDDR. Supervisory and executive board chair remain largely male-dominated. Companies frequently disclose self-set targets equal to zero for the executive board. The level of co-determination is associated with the level of self-set targets on each hierarchy level.
Women Executive Barometer	200 largest German non-financial sector companies (both publicly listed and private)	The proportion of women on supervisory and executive boards increased after the implementation of FüPoG I. The dynamic of growth in proportion of women decreases over time and in some cases gender diversity stagnates in certain groups of companies or hierarchical levels. Differences in the development between companies listed on the DAX, MDAX, SDAX, and TecDAX.
Annual information of the German Federal Government	All companies subject to FüPoG I (approx. 2.100)	The proportion of women on supervisory and executive boards increased after the implementation of FüPoG I. The mandatory gender quota at the supervisory board level lead to a larger increase in gender diversity than GDDR. The participation of women on executive boards increases but remains at an overall low level. Companies frequently disclose self-set targets equal to zero for the executive board. The effectiveness of FüPoG I varies between public and private, larger and smaller, and parity co-determined and co-determined companies. Not all companies fully comply to the disclosure requirements of FüPoG I, particularly in terms of disclosing self-set targets for corporate hierarchy levels.

Table 3-1: Descriptive research on GDDR

3.2 Research on gender diversity regulation

3.2.1 Qualitative research

Due to the absence of literature analyzing GDDR beyond descriptive observations, this section broadens the focus by reviewing research on various gender diversity regulations. Prior research explores the **contextual factors** that lead to the enactment of a gender diversity regulation, evaluates their effectiveness, and examines the determinants and consequences of these regulations.

Teigen (2012) analyzes different regulatory approaches to fostering gender diversity on corporate boards using a normative, explorative research method (*Teigen* (2012), p. 115). The study reviews the Norwegian quota legislation process and examines seven other enacted mandatory gender quotas worldwide (*Teigen* (2012), pp. 127–130). Moreover, the author investigates the political debates in other countries considering varying types of gender diversity regulations (*Teigen* (2012), pp. 130–133). *Teigen* (2012) discusses the diffusion of gender diversity regulation on corporate boards against the background of theoretical considerations (*Teigen* (2012), pp. 134–141). Since many Nordic countries discussed a mandatory gender quota following Norway's example, she identifies regional patterns as drivers for considering and legislating gender diversity regulations (*Teigen* (2012), p. 136). Additionally, **national multifactorial circumstances** (e.g., including political traditions and ruling political parties) might influence the type of regulatory approach debated or enacted (*Teigen* (2012), pp. 125–126). Furthermore, the author argues that the existence of other quota regulations beyond gender diversity increases the likelihood of a mandatory gender quota (*Teigen* (2012), p. 142). However, these conclusions are based on qualitative comparisons of several regulations and do not include quantitative empirical results.

Terjesen et al. (2015) investigate the institutional factors that determine the enactment of mandatory gender quotas on corporate boards (*Terjesen et al.* (2015), p. 233). The authors examine a multinational sample of ten countries that enacted mandatory gender quotas and 15 countries that recommend gender-diverse boards voluntarily through corporate governance codes (*Terjesen et al.* (2015), pp. 233–234). In addition to a detailed and structured overview of the different national regulatory approaches (*Terjesen et al.* (2015), pp. 235–237), the authors identify three important institutional factors associated with the legislation of gender diversity regulation on corporate boards. They argue that the likelihood of enacting a gender diversity regulation is higher for countries with greater welfare to support **women's participation in the labor market** (*Terjesen et al.* (2015), pp. 238–242), governed by **left-leaning coalitions** (*Terjesen et al.* (2015), pp. 242–244), and with a **legacy of gender equality initiatives** (*Terjesen et al.* (2015), pp. 244–245). These findings contribute to institutional theory, highlighting the role of government and political institutions in gender diversity regulations (*Terjesen et al.* (2015), p. 246). Furthermore, the study enhances the understanding of why a specific regulatory approach is enacted in a particular country. However, the investigation by *Terjesen et al.* (2015) has limitations in understanding the specific scope, effectiveness, and applicability of these regulations (*Terjesen et al.* (2015), p. 247).

Contributing to qualitative research in the context of gender diversity regulations, *Seierstad et al.* (2017b) survey the processes, actors, and conditions that drive the enactment of a regulatory approach to foster gender diversity on corporate boards (*Seierstad et al.* (2017b), p. 289). Focusing on regulatory approaches in Norway, the UK, Italy, and Germany between 2000 and 2014, the authors explore how various actors and processes influence national gender diversity regulations (*Seierstad et al.* (2017b), pp. 293–294). Through qualitative data, including participant observations, semi-structured interviews, and text analysis of media and political debates, they identify both similarities and considerable differences in the importance of actors across the countries studied (*Seierstad et al.* (2017b), p. 297). Despite the identification of important civil society, corporate, state, and transnational actors, *Seierstad et al.* (2017b) examine actors' motivation and the interaction between individual actors within a country (*Seierstad et al.* (2017b), pp. 297–303). In Germany, for instance, **international norms, women's commitment to gender diversity, and political party negotiations are key factors** supporting the development of national gender diversity policies. (*Seierstad et al.* (2017b), p. 303).[67] The study concludes that institutional factors and environmental conditions in each country lead to *"a picture of many nuances"* (*Seierstad et al.* (2017b), p. 303). While these findings enhance the understanding of how specific contexts shape regulatory approaches, they are limited to West European cultures and cannot be generalized globally. (*Seierstad et al.* (2017b), p. 306). Additionally, the qualitative data does not allow for definitive conclusions on the effectiveness and appropriateness of different regulatory approaches, indicating the need for further empirical research to gain a more precise understanding.

While previous studies mainly distinguish between voluntary targets and mandatory quotas in the context of gender diversity regulation, *Mensi-Klarbach/Seierstad* (2020) enriches the literature with detailed insights into the **specific design of mandatory gender quotas** (*Mensi-Klarbach/Seierstad* (2020), p. 615). They compare and categorize national mandatory gender quotas based on the regulations of all ten European gender quota laws enacted in 2018 (*Mensi-Klarbach/Seierstad* (2020), p. 618). The authors differentiate two dimensions of mandatory quota regulation. First, the regulations vary in enforcement hardness (e.g., the severity of sanctions) and wording precision (e.g., the definition of regulated companies) (*Mensi-Klarbach/Seierstad* (2020), pp. 619–620). Second, the progressiveness (i.e., year of enactment, implementation period, the quota's ambitiousness, and the regulation's scope) differentiates national mandatory gender quota approaches (*Mensi-Klarbach/Seierstad* (2020), pp. 620–621). They argue that an unfavorable institutional setting does not prevent the enactment of quotas but may influence their design and effectiveness (*Mensi-Klarbach/Seierstad* (2020), p. 624). This argument contributes to the findings of *Seierstad et al.* (2017b) by suggesting that the influence of actors and processes beyond the pure institutional setting also determines the regulatory approach. However, despite the valuable overview of quota designs in Europe and the improved understanding of mandatory gender quotas, the study of *Mensi-Klarbach/Seierstad* (2020) does not provide guidance on choosing the most effective regulatory approach to increasing gender diversity on corporate boards.

In summary, prior qualitative research on gender diversity regulations concentrates mainly on mandatory gender quotas. Empirical studies considering the GDDR in Germany are scarce. However, prior research on gender diversity regulations gained valuable insights and explored the factors leading to their adoption, determining their design, and influencing their effectiveness. The enactment of gender diversity regulations is often driven by a combination of **regional patterns, institutional factors, and political dynamics**. For example, countries with strong welfare systems, left-leaning governments, and a history of gender equality initiatives are more likely to enact mandatory gender quotas. The design of these regulations, including the severity of enforcement and the scope of gender quotas, varies substantially and influences the impact on promoting gender diversity. Political negotiations and the involvement of key actors also play a crucial role in shaping the regulatory approach within different national contexts. Despite these insights, research highlights that the effectiveness of gender diversity regulations remains uncertain and context-dependent, with further empirical studies needed to understand how different

[67] For a detailed description of the legislative process in Germany, see section 2.2.3.1.

approaches can be most effectively applied across diverse settings. Table 3-2 summarizes qualitative research on gender diversity regulations.

Qualitative research on gender diversity regulations		
Reference	**Countries/Sample**	**Key findings**
Teigen (2012)	Eight mandatory gender quotas (Belgium, France, Iceland, Italy, Malaysia, Netherlands, Norway, Spain)	National characteristics (e.g., political traditions) and general acceptance of quotas within a country is related to the enactment of mandatory gender quotas.
Terjesen et al. (2015)	Ten mandatory gender quotas (Belgium, Canada, Finland, France, Iceland, Israel, Italy, Kenya, Norway, Spain), and 15 voluntary regimes (Australia, Austria, Denmark, Germany, Ireland, Luxembourg, Malawi, Malaysia, Netherlands, Nigeria, Poland, South Africa, Sweden, United Kingdom, United States)	Institutional factors (i.e., female labor market and gendered welfare state provisions, left-leaning political government coalitions, and path-dependent policy initiatives for gender equality) are related to the enactment of mandatory gender quotas and the design of regulations.
Seierstad et al. (2017)	Mixed regulatory approaches (England, Germany, Italy, Norway)	The legislative process of gender diversity regulation is largely shaped by political maneuvering and influenced by various actors. The advocacy efforts of those pushing for increased gender diversity may play a more critical role than institutional settings.
Mensi-Klarbach/Seierstad (2020)	Ten mandatory gender quotas (Austria, Belgium, France, Germany, Iceland, Italy, Netherlands, Norway, Portugal, Spain)	The design of mandatory gender quotas varies in terms of hardness and progressiveness. Differences in regulatory design, such as the severity of sanctions, influence the effectiveness of mandatory gender quotas.

Table 3-2: Qualitative research on gender diversity regulations

3.2.2 Quantitative research

Due to Norway's pioneering role in the context of mandatory gender quota on corporate boards and due to the *"exogenous policy shock" (Wang/Kelan (2013), p. 463)*,[68] extensive literature examines the contextual conditions of the enactment of the mandatory gender quota in Norway and its effectiveness. *Wang/Kelan* (2013) conducted one of the early studies using the Norwegian setting, analyzing the impact of the mandatory gender quota on the likelihood of women being appointed to executive boards or top management positions. Using a sample of 87 companies listed on the Oslo Stock Exchange subject to the mandatory gender quota between 2001 and 2010, the authors analyze changes in corporate board composition following the introduction of the mandatory gender quota (*Wang/Kelan* (2013), pp. 453–454). Their analysis, consistent with the findings of *Teigen* (2012), revealed a substantial increase in female representation after the mandatory gender quota was enacted (*Wang/Kelan* (2013), p. 458). According to the authors, Norway's mandatory gender quota positively influenced the presence of women in top management positions, with a

[68] For detailed information on the general background, the corporate governance system and legislative process in Norway, cf. *Seierstad/Huse* (2017), pp. 11–45, and *Teigen* (2022), pp. 197–217.

higher proportion of female directors associated with the appointment of female chairpersons (*Wang/Kelan* (2013), pp. 460–461). Their findings, hence, support the concept of the trickle-down effect. Moreover, they identify a positive relationship between a "critical mass"[69] of at least three female directors or female board chairs and the appointment of women as executive board chairs (*Wang/Kelan* (2013), pp. 462–463). The authors conclude that mandatory gender quotas are an **effective regulatory approach to implement top-down changes** to gender diversity in companies (*Wang/Kelan* (2013), p. 463). However, the results are not generalizable due to the small sample size and the unique characteristics of the Norwegian corporate governance system. Furthermore, the study does not address company-specific determinants that could affect the effectiveness and consequences of the mandatory gender quota.

Bøhren/Staubo (2014) provide insights into how Norwegian companies respond to the mandatory gender quota. Analyzing a sample of 2,743 companies in Norway from 2001 to 2010, they find that nearly half of the companies respond to the regulatory intervention by **altering their organizational form to avoid the restrictive regulation** (*Bøhren/Staubo* (2014), 157-160)). The authors argue that the mandatory gender quota imposes costs, leading companies to change their organizational form if these costs outweigh the benefits of maintaining their current structure (*Bøhren/Staubo* (2014), p. 165). Their findings indicate that companies are more likely to change their organizational structure if they are young, small, profitable, and not listed (*Bøhren/Staubo* (2014), pp. 160–161). However, the study of *Bøhren/Staubo* (2014) does not provide detailed information on the specific costs incurred due to the mandatory gender quota, hence limiting conclusions about average cost assumptions. Additionally, the large number of changes in the organizational form of Norwegian companies may be driven by the severe sanctions (liquidation of the company) associated with the mandatory gender quota, making these findings less applicable to regulations with less severe sanctions.

Labelle et al. (2015) extend prior research by investigating the effectiveness of voluntary approaches to increase female representation on corporate boards while considering economic consequences (*Labelle et al.* (2015), p. 339). The authors distinguish between non-regulation and a voluntary (enabling) approach through corporate governance codes (*Labelle et al.* (2015), p. 341). Unlike previous studies that evaluate policy decisions in single-country settings (e.g., *Ahern/Dittmar* (2012)), *Labelle et al.* (2015) utilize a sample of 1,691 companies headquartered in 17 countries from 2009 to 2011 to compare the effect of gender diversity regulations on corporate performance. They find that the proportion of women on corporate boards is roughly four percentage points higher (statistically significant at the 1% level) under an enabling approach compared to no regulatory intervention (*Labelle et al.* (2015), p. 349). Moreover, the results indicate a **negative association between the proportion of women on corporate boards** in the context of an enabling regulatory intervention **and corporate performance**, measured by ROA (*Labelle et al.* (2015), pp. 351–352). Overall, *Labelle et al.* (2015) argue, consistent with

[69] The concept of critical mass is rooted in the work of *Kanter* (1977a), (1977b) and postulates that until a certain threshold or "critical mass" of women in a group is achieved, the group members do not focus on the distinct abilities and skills that women contribute, cf. *Joecks et al.* (2013), p. 64.

Ahern/Dittmar (2012), that gender diversity regulation might not be the optimal approach to achieving the optimal corporate board composition for maximizing financial performance (*Labelle et al.* (2015), p. 355).

Sojo et al. (2016) contribute to the discussion on the effectiveness of regulatory approaches to foster gender diversity on corporate boards. Drawing from various sub-studies, including a US sample of 170 listed companies from 1996 to 2015 and a cross-national dataset covering 91 countries, they examine the impact of legislation through reporting requirements, targets, and quotas to increase female representation on corporate boards (*Sojo et al.* (2016), pp. 521–527). They conclude that implementing regulations incorporating **targets and quotas is more effective in enhancing gender diversity than mere reporting** requirements (*Sojo et al.* (2016), p. 527). Furthermore, the authors find that higher targets and quotas lead to a more pronounced increase in the proportion of women on corporate boards (*Sojo et al.* (2016), p. 527). Based on their findings, *Sojo et al.* (2016) suggest that regulators should consider implementing targets or quotas combined with severe sanctions to foster gender diversity on corporate boards (*Sojo et al.* (2016), pp. 532–534). However, the authors note that their conclusions from cross-national analyses are based on secondary data, and that many quota-regulated countries have not yet met their quota deadlines (*Sojo et al.* (2016), p. 534).

Furthermore, *Klettner et al.* (2016) examine the regulatory environment in Australia[70] to analyze changes in the representation of women at hierarchy levels below corporate boards (*Klettner et al.* (2016), p. 395). By combining qualitative data from interviews and statements from annual reports with quantitative data from the national census of women in leadership positions, the authors find that the underrepresentation of women in leadership is not solely due to a lack of qualified female candidates but further structural issues (*Klettner et al.* (2016), pp. 398–404). Based on the qualitative data, they identify **barriers at the mid-management level** that hinder an increasing number of women in leadership positions (*Klettner et al.* (2016), p. 399). According to the authors, these issues are unlikely to be addressed by mandatory gender quotas on corporate boards (*Klettner et al.* (2016), p. 395). Overall, they conclude that voluntary self-regulation, combined with public disclosure of corporate targets, fosters cultural change within companies and increases women's representation at higher corporate levels (*Klettner et al.* (2016), p. 416).

Gregorič et al. (2017) investigate how institutional pressure determines female representation on corporate boards and provide explanations for resistance to change board appointment processes (*Gregorič et al.* (2017), p. 267). Using a multinational sample of Nordic companies, *Gregorič et al.* (2017) find that **company-specific determinants** like company size, board size, and geographic location affect gender diversity on corporate boards (*Gregorič et al.* (2017), pp. 280–283). Their results partially support the assumption that a company's visibility, exposure to societal pressure, and female representation among its industry peers impact female representation on corporate boards (*Gregorič et al.* (2017), pp. 279–282). Moreover, they find a positive association between institutional investors' ownership levels and female participation on corporate boards, as well as between a high proportion of

---

70 For detailed information on the general background, the corporate governance system and legislative process in Australia, cf. *Terjesen/Trombetta* (2017), pp. 235–260.

female leadership within the industry and female board representation (*Gregorič et al.* (2017), p. 279). *Gregorič et al.* (2017) enhance understanding of both company-specific and industry-specific determinants, highlighting the importance of institutional pressure on board appointment processes. The authors conclude that companies do not expect a positive effect of female board members on financial performance, leading to slow organizational changes in response to societal pressure (*Gregorič et al.* (2017), p. 286). Although the study does not focus on the effectiveness of regulatory interventions, *Gregorič et al.* (2017) call for transparency in the nomination process of corporate boards to ensure the appointment of suitable and qualified candidates (*Gregorič et al.* (2017), p. 286). However, the implications are specific to Nordic boards and cannot be directly applied to the effectiveness of regulatory approaches to foster gender diversity on corporate boards in other countries.

Complementing the study of *Mensi-Klarbach/Seierstad* (2020) on mandatory gender quotas, *Mensi-Klarbach et al.* (2021) investigate the effectiveness of voluntary approaches in improving gender diversity on corporate boards (*Mensi-Klarbach et al.* (2021), p. 577). The authors analyze a sample of 65 listed companies and 61 state-owned companies in Austria from 2006 to 2016 to assess the impact of recommendations aimed at achieving gender-diverse boards under the Austrian corporate governance code (*Mensi-Klarbach et al.* (2021), p. 582). The results indicate that **voluntary approaches**, such as corporate governance codes, **are largely ineffective in fostering gender diversity** on corporate boards (*Mensi-Klarbach et al.* (2021), p. 587). However, *Mensi-Klarbach et al.* (2021) identify certain conditions that may enhance the effectiveness of these regulatory approaches. They note that the prospect of regulators implementing a mandatory gender quota increases compliance with recommendations for gender diversity on corporate boards (*Mensi-Klarbach et al.* (2021), p. 587). The authors acknowledge the limitation that their findings are primarily restricted to Austria. Nevertheless, they suggest that the implications may also apply to countries with similar cultures and corporate governance systems, such as Germany (*Mensi-Klarbach et al.* (2021), p. 589).

Bozhinov et al. (2021) analyze 95 German co-determined companies between 2009 and 2016 to investigate the spillover effects of women on supervisory boards to the presence of women on executive boards (*Bozhinov et al.* (2021), p. 1317). In the context of a voluntary approach based on a corporate governance code and the impending introduction of a mandatory gender quota on corporate boards, the authors use Germany's two-tier board structure (section 2.2.1) to examine the importance of women on nominating committees (*Bozhinov et al.* (2021), p. 1318). The study provides insights into co-determined boards, differentiating between female shareholders and employee representatives due to their varying ownership power (*Bozhinov et al.* (2021), pp. 1318–1319). Their findings suggest that female shareholder representatives on supervisory boards are **positively related to an increased proportion of women on the executive board** (*Bozhinov et al.* (2021), pp. 1323–1324). Additionally, *Bozhinov et al.* (2021) find empirical support for the proposition that female shareholder representatives appointed to a nominating committee positively influence gender diversity on executive boards (*Bozhinov et al.* (2021), p. 1326). Based on their findings, the authors conclude that, due to the observed spillover effects, adding additional quotas on the executive board might not be necessary to increase gender diversity (*Bozhinov et al.* (2021), p. 1326). Nevertheless, the slow increase of female executive board members, even after the legislation of a mandatory quota on the supervisory board, hampers this argumentation. However, the study does not provide evidence of whether the increased proportion of women on the supervisory board in anticipation of the mandatory gender quota in 2015 moderates the spillover effects between the two boards (*Bozhinov et al.* (2021), p. 1326).

Adding to the discussion of determinants and the consequences of institutional conditions, *Peña-Martel et al.* (2022) examine the relationship between media visibility and gender diversity on corporate boards in Spain[71] between 2003 and 2016 (*Peña-Martel et al.* (2022), p. 192). Although Spanish regulations mandate a gender quota, they lack enforcement mechanisms. As a result, many regulated companies treat the quota more as a recommendation than as a mandatory requirement (*Gabaldon/Giménez* (2017), pp. 57–58). *Peña-Martel et al.* (2022) find that **media attention**, as well as the tone of media, has a **positive influence on board gender diversity** (*Peña-Martel et al.* (2022), pp. 198–199). The authors suggest that, within the context of the soft Spanish gender quota, the media acts as a disciplinary tool, affecting the reputation and legitimacy of companies as well as their representatives (*Peña-Martel et al.* (2022), p. 201). The findings indicate that media in comparable countries with similar cultural contexts and the same freedom of the press also influence the presence of women on corporate boards (*Peña-Martel et al.* (2022), p. 203). However, despite their methodological endeavors (*Peña-Martel et al.* (2022), p. 199), the study cannot entirely rule out reverse causality between board gender diversity and media visibility.

Recently, *Poletti-Hughes/Dimungu-Hewage* (2023) investigate the effectiveness of both voluntary approaches and mandatory gender diversity regulations in increasing the proportion of women on corporate boards and their impact on board independence (*Poletti-Hughes/Dimungu-Hewage* (2023), p. 1316). Analyzing a large multi-country sample of 10,313 companies from 41 countries, the authors explore differences between both regulatory approaches and moderating conditions (*Poletti-Hughes/Dimungu-Hewage* (2023), p. 1321). The results indicate that **voluntary gender regulations negatively affect the number of independent women** on corporate boards. Furthermore, *Poletti-Hughes/Dimungu-Hewage* (2023) find that national culture moderates the independence of female board members in the context of voluntary approaches. Conversely, mandatory gender quotas enhance the presence of independent female board members regardless of national culture (*Poletti-Hughes/Dimungu-Hewage* (2023), p. 1334). The authors emphasize the importance of mandatory regulations for appointing independent female board members (*Poletti-Hughes/Dimungu-Hewage* (2023), p. 1335). Despite that, the study does not consider the multifaceted and diverse subtypes of voluntary approaches and mandatory gender regulations across the sample countries. This constitutes an important limitation, as the design of specific regulations can considerably impact the outcomes of gender diversity initiatives (e.g., *Mensi-Klarbach/Seierstad* (2020)). Moreover, due to the scope of analyzed companies, micro-level information cannot be analyzed to identify company-specific determinants and moderators of independent female board members.

---

[71] For detailed information on the general background, the corporate governance system and legislative process in Spain, cf. *Gabaldon/Giménez* (2017), pp. 47–74 and *Lombardo/Verge* (2022), pp. 267–286.

Finally, *Page et al.* (2024) examine the trickle-down effect between women on corporate boards on their presence at senior management levels within a recommendation-based setting (*Page et al.* (2024), p. 1). Using an event study approach, the authors analyze a sample of 219 listed companies in the UK[72] from 2007 to 2018 (*Page et al.* (2024), p. 5). Before the introduction of a recommendation and a voluntary target of 20%, the researchers observe a **positive relationship between women on boards and female participation in upper management levels**. However, the results indicate a significant weakening of this trickle-down effect after the introduction of a voluntary target based on recommendation. *Page et al.* (2024) interpret this finding as an unintended consequence of the regulation (*Page et al.* (2024), p. 11). Furthermore, they suggest that while companies might comply with external regulatory requirements, this does not necessarily translate into intrinsic motivation to promote gender diversity in senior management positions (*Page et al.* (2024), p. 11). The authors conclude that regulatory interventions aimed at fostering gender diversity across corporate hierarchy levels do not inevitably strengthen trickle-down effects and may even mitigate desired outcomes (*Page et al.* (2024), p. 11). However, the study does not provide a causal setting. Nevertheless, it highlights the impact of gender diversity regulation and the risk of unintended negative effects.

Quantitative research on gender diversity regulations for corporate boards highlights key insights into their determinants and regulatory efficacy. Mandatory gender quotas are consistently shown to be effective in increasing female representation on corporate boards, especially when enforcement mechanisms are strong. The presence of a "critical mass" of female directors further amplifies these effects, promoting the trickle-down of women into senior management positions. Voluntary approaches, however, tend to be less effective, often resulting in only superficial compliance. Prior research identifies **institutional factors** (e.g., national culture and company-specific characteristics) as influencing factors of regulatory efficacy. Additionally, national culture moderates the impact of both mandatory regulations and voluntary approaches, underscoring the **need to tailor policies to national contexts**. Moreover, political pressure (e.g., an announcement of mandatory gender quotas) or public pressure (e.g., media coverage and fear of reputational costs) enhance the efficacy of voluntary gender diversity policies. Nevertheless, prior literature reveals that the efficacy of gender diversity regulations is often highly context-specific and influenced by national environments.

Table 3-3 summarizes the findings of quantitative research on voluntary approaches and mandatory gender diversity regulations.

---

72 For detailed information on the general background, the corporate governance system and legislative process in the UK, cf. *Doldor* (2017), pp. 13–44.

Quantitative research on gender diversity regulations		
Reference	**Countries/Sample**	**Key findings**
Wang/Kelan (2013)	Norway 87 listed companies (2001-2010)	Increase in female board representation on corporate boards after implementation of a mandatory gender quota. Female chairs are positively associated with independence status and qualification of female board members (trickle-down effect). The likelihood of female chairs increases with proportion of independent directors and higher qualification of female board members. A critical mass of women enhances female leadership appointments.
Bøhren/Staubo (2014)	Norwegian 2,743 listed and private companies (2001-2010)	Nearly half of the companies altered their organizational form to avoid a mandatory gender quota. Companies are more likely to change if young, small, profitable, and unlisted. The severe sanctions of the gender quota regulation may incentivize these organizational changes.
Labelle et al. (2015)	Multinational (17 countries) 1,691 listed and private companies (2009 and 2011)	The proportion of women on corporate boards is higher (approx. four percentage points) under an enabling approach than under a voluntary approach. Gender-diverse boards are positively associated with corporate performance (measured by ROA) in countries using a voluntary approach but negative in countries using an enabling approach. Gender diversity regulation might result in non-optimal board composition for financial performance.
Sojo et al. (2016)	US and multinational (91 countries) 1,137 listed companies (1996-2015)	Legislation with quotas and quantified targets are more effective in increasing female board representation than reporting requirements. Higher quotas and targets lead to greater increases. Strong enforcement mechanisms (severe sanctions) increase efficacy of gender diversity regulations.
Klettner et al. (2016)	Australia Listed companies	Structural barriers at mid-management levels hinder female participation on corporate boards. Voluntary regulations may be more effective at promoting strategic and cultural change of companies than mandatory gender quotas.
Gregorič et al. (2017)	Denmark, Finland, Sweden, Norway 502 listed companies (2001-2008)	Institutional pressure, public visibility, and industry peer representation positively influence female board representation. Company-specific factors like size and board composition also impact gender diversity on boards. Companies do not anticipate economic benefits from increased gender diversity on corporate boards.
Mensi-Klarbach et al. (2021)	Austria 65 listed and 61 state-owned companies (2006-2016)	Voluntary approaches to foster gender diversity are largely ineffective without being supported by additional forces. Specific quantified targets combined with public monitoring or the credible threat of imposing mandatory gender quotas increase efficacy of voluntary approaches.
Bozhinov et al. (2021)	Germany 95 listed companies (2009-2016)	Female shareholder representatives on supervisory boards positively influence representation of women on executive boards (trickle-down effect). Mere high proportion of female supervisory board members is insufficient for spillover effects on executive boards.
Peña-Martel et al. (2022)	Spain 101 listed companies (2003-2016)	Media visibility positively influences board gender diversity, acting as a disciplinary tool in the absence of strict quota enforcement. Media visibility disciplines companies by inflicting reputational costs.
Poletti-Hughes/Dimungu-Hewage (2023)	Multinational (41 countries) 10,313 companies (2000-2019)	Mandatory gender quotas increase the presence of independent female board members, whereas voluntary approaches decrease them in countries with limited inclusion of women in the labor markets. National culture moderates the effects of gender diversity regulations.
Page et al. (2023)	UK 219 listed companies (2007-2018)	Positive association between proportion of women on corporate boards and women at senior management levels (trickle-down effect). The effect is weakened after the introduction of voluntary, quantified targets.

Table 3-3: Quantitative research on gender diversity regulations

3.3 Research on board gender diversity and financial reporting quality

3.3.1 Female board members in non-regulated contexts

Drawing on the debate about behavioral differences between male and female managers and board members (e.g., *Farrell/Hersch* (2005)), *Krishnan/Parsons* (2008) provide early insights into the relationship between women in senior management positions and earnings quality[73] (*Krishnan/Parsons* (2008), p. 65). The authors analyze a US sample of 353 listed companies (*Krishnan/Parsons* (2008), p. 70). Besides an overall positive association between female senior managers and a company's financial performance, the authors find that these beneficial effects are not driven by lower-quality earnings (*Krishnan/Parsons* (2008), pp. 71–72). In fact, the presence of women in senior management is **positively related to higher earnings quality** (*Krishnan/Parsons* (2008), p. 74). However, although the study struggles with reverse causality issues, it paves the way for further research on the impact of gender diversity on earnings quality.

Adams/Ferreira (2009) investigate the impact of female board members on board characteristics and governance mechanisms (*Adams/Ferreira* (2009), p. 292). Addressing endogeneity problems and reserve causality concerns, they analyze an unbalanced sample of 1,939 listed US companies between 1996 and 2003 (*Adams/Ferreira* (2009), p. 293).[74] Their findings reveal that women are more likely to attend board meetings (*Adams/Ferreira* (2009), pp. 296–297). Additionally, the authors observe that women's presence on corporate boards is positively associated with an increased male attendance rate (*Adams/Ferreira* (2009), pp. 297–298). Moreover, women are more likely to serve on monitoring-related committees (e.g., audit or corporate governance committees) than men, contributing positively to board oversight (*Adams/Ferreira* (2009), pp. 298–299). However, *Adams/Ferreira* (2009) find a **negative association between gender-diverse boards and corporate performance** in companies with strong shareholder rights, and a positive association in companies with weak shareholder rights (*Adams/Ferreira* (2009), pp. 304–306). The authors suggest that over-monitoring due to female presence on boards may decrease shareholder value (*Adams/Ferreira* (2009), p. 306). The study provides valuable insights into the positive relationship between female board members and managerial oversight, though the results are specific to an unregulated setting. The introduction of voluntary approaches or mandatory gender diversity regulations could change appointment patterns, lead to diverging board member characteristics, and potentially result in different outcomes.

Building on previous research, *Srinidhi et al.* (2011) analyze whether gender-diverse boards contribute to higher earnings quality (*Srinidhi et al.* (2011), p. 1610). Using a US sample, the authors find that companies with women on boards exhibit higher-quality earnings and greater reporting discipline, particularly when women serve on audit committees (*Srinidhi et*

---

73 Since the literature sometimes uses the terms "earnings quality" and "financial reporting quality" interchangeable, this study uses them as synonyms. Furthermore, some studies (e.g., *García Lara et al.* (2022); *Schumann et al.* (2024)) use the term "accounting quality" to mention financial reporting quality.

74 For detailed information on the general background, the corporate governance system and legislative process in the US, cf. *Terjesen/Trombetta* (2017), pp. 235–260.

al. (2011), p. 1632). The study uses two different proxies to measure a company's earnings quality. First, the authors use discretionary accruals to estimate the quality of earnings (*Srinidhi et al.* (2011), p. 1615), which reflect managers' accounting choices and are factored into financial markets (*Srinidhi et al.* (2011), p. 1611). Second, the study uses the propensity of companies to manage earnings to meet or slightly exceed benchmarks or analysts' expectations (*Srinidhi et al.* (2011), p. 1616). *Srinidhi et al.* (2011) conclude that **female representation on corporate boards enhances earnings quality** through improved board oversight (*Srinidhi et al.* (2011), p. 1639). However, this study also examines an unregulated setting, leaving open the question of whether these findings would hold under regulatory interventions in board composition.

In a subsequent study, *Lai et al.* (2017) focus on the impact of female board members on auditor choice and audit fees (*Lai et al.* (2017), p. 1681). The authors investigate a sample of 2,990 US companies using a propensity score matching method (*Lai et al.* (2017), p. 1691). They find that the presence of women on corporate boards, particularly on audit committees, is **positively related to higher audit quality**. Gender-diverse boards, on average, pay 6% more for audits and are 6% more likely to hire industry-specialized auditors compared to all-male boards (*Lai et al.* (2017), pp. 1697–1702). Thus, *Lai et al.* (2017) suggest a positive impact of female board members on audit quality, which is related to financial reporting quality (*Lai et al.* (2017), p. 1708). However, the authors caution that these results are specific to the US legal and institutional context (*Lai et al.* (2017), p. 1708).

Abbott et al. (2012) explore whether the presence of at least one woman on corporate boards affects the likelihood of financial restatements (*Abbott et al.* (2012), p. 607). Deviating from previous studies in this field of research, the authors expand the analyzed sample beyond the largest US companies and include remarkably smaller US companies (*Abbott et al.* (2012), p. 609). The results reveal a negative relationship between corporate boards with female board members and the occurrence of financial restatements (*Abbott et al.* (2012), p. 622). *Abbott et al.* (2012) find that the **likelihood of a financial restatement for not all-male boards is 62% lower** compared to a board without female presence (*Abbott et al.* (2012), p. 622). The authors attribute this to the enhanced monitoring effectiveness of gender-diverse boards, reinforcing findings from *Adams/Ferreira* (2009). However, they note that the study does not address whether the observed associations are affected by unmeasured characteristics of female board members (*Abbott et al.* (2012), p. 626).

Hoang et al. (2017) investigate the impact of diversified boards on earnings quality in a sample of 150 listed companies in Vietnam between 2005 and 2011 (*Hoang et al.* (2017), p. 150). Beyond gender diversity, the authors examine other demographic factors, such as age and nationality diversity, which might influence outcomes. In the context of a non-Western culture and in the absence of mandatory gender diversity quotas, the study finds a **positive association between board diversity and earnings quality** (*Hoang et al.* (2017), p. 155). Instead of assessing earnings quality solely through discretionary accruals, the authors employ four different earnings quality proxies (accruals quality, earnings persistence, earnings predictability, and earnings smoothness) to create a highly aggregated weighted score (*Hoang et al.* (2017), pp. 150–151). The findings reveal a non-linear, U-shaped relationship between board diversity and earnings quality (*Hoang et al.* (2017),

p. 156). However, it remains unclear whether this effect is primarily driven by gender diversity or other demographic attributes. Despite limitations in sample size and causality concerns, the study offers valuable insights into the relationship between board diversity and earnings quality in smaller and emerging markets (*Hoang et al.* (2017), p. 159).

Later, *Gull et al.* (2018) expand on previous research by investigating how specific attributes of female board members influence earnings management (*Gull et al.* (2018), p. 255). They examine the role of particular competencies and skills in contributing to higher-quality earnings statements (*Gull et al.* (2018), pp. 259–260). Analyzing a sample of 394 French-listed companies during the pre-law period from 2001 to 2010 (*Gull et al.* (2018), pp. 260–261),[75] they find a **positive relationship between the presence of female board members and earnings quality** (*Gull et al.* (2018), p. 267). However, the results suggest that this association is not initially driven by gender itself but rather by the demographic characteristics of female board members (*Gull et al.* (2018), p. 268). Additionally, *Gull et al.* (2018) find that the presence of women on audit committees reduces earnings management, supporting the findings of *Adams/Ferreira* (2009) regarding the positive association between board gender diversity and monitoring abilities (*Gull et al.* (2018), p. 268). The authors conclude that while women with particular competencies and skills can enhance earnings quality, this does not necessarily justify implementing mandatory gender quotas (*Gull et al.* (2018), p. 272).

In summary, the findings of research on the presence of female board members on financial reporting quality highlight that **gender-diverse boards are positively associated with better corporate governance and higher financial reporting quality**. Across various contexts, the presence of women in senior management and on corporate boards is associated with higher earnings quality, improved oversight, and more rigorous audit processes. These effects are often linked to enhanced monitoring abilities and the unique competencies women bring to corporate boards. However, the positive impact of gender diversity appears to be contingent on the broader organizational and regulatory environment, with some evidence suggesting that these benefits may be more pronounced in settings with weaker governance structures. Overall, while gender diversity enhances corporate accountability, the specific outcomes are shaped by the regulatory and institutional frameworks in place.

Table 3-4 summarizes the research on female board members and financial reporting quality.

[75] For detailed information on the general background, the corporate governance system and legislative process in France, cf. *Zenou et al.* (2017), pp. 108–124.

Research on female board members in non-regulated contexts		
Reference	**Countries/Sample**	**Key findings**
Krishnan/Parsons (2008)	US 353 listed companies (1996-2000)	Female managers are positively associated with financial performance and higher earnings quality. Women in management positions enhance the quality of earnings, indicating better financial discipline and oversight.
Adams/Ferreira (2009)	US 1,939 listed companies (1996-2003)	Female board members contribute to better board oversight by attending more meetings and encouraging higher male attendance. Women are more likely to serve on monitoring-related committees. In companies with strong shareholder rights, the presence of women may lead to over-monitoring, potentially reducing shareholder value.
Shrinidi et al. (2011)	US 2,480 listed company-year observations (2001 and 2007)	Gender-diverse boards are related to higher earnings quality, particularly when women are part of the audit committee. The presence of women on boards leads to greater financial reporting discipline, reducing the likelihood of earnings manipulation and improving overall earnings quality.
Lai et al. (2017)	US 2,990 listed company-year observations (2009-2016)	The presence of women on corporate boards, especially on audit committees, is associated with higher audit quality. Gender-diverse boards tend to pay higher audit fees and are more likely to engage industry-specialized auditors, reflecting greater emphasis on audit quality and financial transparency.
Abbott et al. (2012)	US 278 listed companies (1996-2003)	Boards with at least one female member are less likely to experience financial restatements, indicating more effective oversight. The probability of a financial restatement decreases by 62% for boards with female representation.
Hoang et al. (2017)	Vietnam 150 listed companies (2005-2011)	Board diversity, including gender diversity, is positively related to earnings quality measured by an aggregated proxy. The results reveal a U-shaped relationship between gender-diverse boards and earnings quality.
Gull et al. (2018)	France 394 listed companies (2001-2010)	The presence of female board members is associated with higher earnings quality, primarily due to their specific skills rather than gender alone. Women on audit committees contribute to reducing earnings management, supporting the notion that female directors enhance the monitoring ability of boards.

Table 3-4: Research on female board members in non-regulated contexts

3.3.2 Female board members in the context of gender diversity regulations

While research generally indicates a positive impact of gender-diverse senior management levels and corporate boards on financial reporting quality, there is limited research on how gender diversity regulations influence these outcomes. Prior literature exploring the association between gender diversity regulations and financial reporting quality reports **mixed results**. Some studies utilize the case of Norway to derive insights into mandatory quotas, while others investigate voluntary approaches intended to foster gender diversity.

García Lara et al. (2017) examine whether female representation on corporate boards is positively related to financial reporting quality in the context of voluntary regulation (*García Lara et al.* (2017), p. 651). The authors analyze a sample of 4,785 listed UK companies between 2003 and 2012 (*García Lara et al.* (2017), p. 658), which operate under a voluntary approach based on the comply-or-explain principle. Their findings suggest that **earnings quality**, measured through estimated discretionary accruals (following *Srinidhi et al.* (2011)), is **positively related to the presence of women on corporate boards** (*García Lara et al.* (2017), p. 660). However, this positive relationship holds only for female board members classified as independent directors. No significant positive association is observed for the presence of female board members regardless of their independence (*García Lara et al.*

(2017), p. 666). *García Lara et al.* (2017) emphasize that characteristics beyond gender diversity, such as independence, might be associated with board monitoring ability (*García Lara et al.* (2017), p. 666). However, the study does not address the potential association between the voluntary approaches and the characteristics of appointed female directors.

In a subsequent study, *García Lara et al.* (2022) specifically investigate the association between increased gender diversity on corporate boards in response to a mandatory gender quota and financial reporting quality (*García Lara et al.* (2022), p. 2). The authors use the regulatory setting of Norway, analyzing an unbalanced sample of 81 companies subject to the Norwegian gender quota to assess changes in financial reporting quality (*García Lara et al.* (2022), p. 7). In line with prior research, they employ discretionary accruals as a proxy for financial reporting quality (*García Lara et al.* (2022), pp. 8–9). The authors use the measure provided by *Francis/Wang* (2008), which allows the calculation of discretionary accruals based on a small sample size (*García Lara et al.* (2022), p. 8). Applying various identification strategies, *García Lara et al.* (2022) reveal a **positive effect of companies required to increase gender diversity due to the mandatory quota** on the level of discretionary accruals (*García Lara et al.* (2022), p. 11). The effects are statistically and economically significant, as companies that are forced to increase the proportion of women on their boards by 10% increase their discretionary accruals on average by 0.9% of total assets (*García Lara et al.* (2022), p. 11). This indicates a negative effect of increased gender diversity through mandatory quotas on companies' financial reporting quality (*García Lara et al.* (2022), p. 22). The authors suggest that this negative effect might result from the appointment of less qualified candidates or suboptimal contracting decisions in response to the forced changes in board composition (*García Lara et al.* (2022), p. 22). However, *García Lara et al.* (2022) find that this negative effect appears to be short-lived and that differences in board member characteristics additionally contribute to the decrease in financial reporting quality (*García Lara et al.* (2022), pp. 12–17).

Panzer/Müller (2015) are the first to investigate the impact of gender-diverse boards on financial reporting quality in the context of German companies (*Panzer/Müller* (2015), p. 9). Specifically, they examine the presence of women on the supervisory boards of 64 companies listed on the DAX, MDAX, and SDAX between 2006 and 2011 (*Panzer/Müller* (2015), p. 11). Given the unique characteristics of the German two-tier corporate governance system (section 2.2.1), the authors focus on the supervisory board's distinct monitoring function and its duty to ensure the appropriate audit of financial statements (*Panzer/Müller* (2015), p. 10). Measuring financial reporting quality by discretionary accruals, the results indicate that the **presence of women on supervisory boards improves earnings quality** (*Panzer/Müller* (2015), p. 15). These findings align with prior literature, suggesting a positive effect of female board members on financial reporting quality. However, *Panzer/Müller* (2015) do not thoroughly consider the regulatory environment of the analyzed sample. They do not take into account that a voluntary approach to foster corporate gender diversity was introduced during the period under review (section 2.2.2), which could potentially influence the appointment process for board members and, therefore, alter the financial reporting quality. Additionally, the findings should be interpreted cautiously due to the constrained sample size and their limitation to large publicly listed companies (*Panzer/Müller* (2015), p. 16).

Recently, *Schumann et al.* (2024) contribute to the ongoing debate by investigating the impact of various facets of diversity on earnings quality (*Schumann et al.* (2024), p. 137). The authors analyze a sample of 24 German companies listed on the DAX between 2011 and 2018 (*Schumann et al.* (2024), pp. 146–147). Contrary to prior studies, they focus on diversity of executive boards and its association with financial reporting quality, arguing that executive board members have a higher degree of managerial discretion in financial accounting decisions, making them a relevant group for analysis (*Schumann et al.* (2024), pp. 140–141). *Schumann et al.* (2024) find that, besides the association with other biographical characteristics, **gender-diverse executive boards are related to a decrease in discretionary accruals, thereby indicating higher earnings quality** (*Schumann et al.* (2024), pp. 151–155). However, due to the hand-collected data set, the sample size is relatively small and includes only the largest German companies (*Schumann et al.* (2024), p. 163). Moreover, the study does not account for the regulatory environment in Germany, which may influence board appointment decisions and, by extension, the characteristics of appointed board members. Furthermore, it is debatable whether the composition of the executive board primarily determines discretionary accruals. As discussed in section 2.2.1, in Germany's two-tier corporate governance system, the supervisory board holds the monitoring function and is responsible for ensuring the accuracy of financial reporting.

In summary, studies on the consequences of gender diversity regulations on financial reporting quality report **mixed results depending on the regulatory setting**. In settings with voluntary approaches, prior research finds positive associations between gender-diverse boards and financial reporting quality due to the beneficial attributes of female board members. In the context of mandatory gender quotas, studies find a negative influence of increased female representation on corporate boards and financial reporting quality. Prior literature suggests that the forced increase in gender diversity leads to changes in appointment decisions and results in non-optimal corporate board compositions with poorer monitoring abilities. Table 3-5 summarizes the results of prior research on gender diversity regulations and financial reporting quality.

Research on female board members in the context of gender diversity regulations		
Reference	**Countries/Sample**	**Key findings**
Garcia Lara et al. (2017)	UK 4,785 listed companies (2003-2012)	The presence of independent female board members is positively related to lower earnings management and better financial reporting quality if these women are independent. Results are driven by gender biases, suggesting that financial reporting quality is mostly related to board members' independence.
Garcia Lara et al. (2022)	Norway 81 listed companies (2002-2010)	Increased gender diversity on corporate boards in the context of mandatory gender quotas is negatively associated with financial reporting quality. Companies forced to increase female board representation indicating lower earnings quality, potentially due to suboptimal board composition.
Panzer/Müller (2015)	Germany 64 listed companies (2006-2011)	The presence of women on supervisory boards is positively related to improved earnings quality due to the beneficial role of gender diversity and board's monitoring abilities.
Schumann et al. (2024)	Germany 24 listed companies (2011-2018)	Diversity at the executive board level, including gender diversity, is positively associated with higher earnings quality. Gender diversity alone is not related to higher earnings quality.

Table 3-5: Research on female board members in the context of gender diversity regulations

3.4 Summary and research gap

The research explores different approaches aimed at fostering gender diversity on corporate boards. However, aside from descriptive studies of GDDR, in-depth research on GDDR is scarce. Descriptive literature suggests that GDDR positively affects the presence of women on corporate boards and upper management levels in Germany. These findings primarily focus on changes in the composition of supervisory and executive boards (e.g., *FidAR e.V.* (2017); *Holst/Kirsch* (2016a)), with studies often facing challenges related to data availability on management levels beyond corporate boards (*Deutscher BT/BR – DIP* (2017a), BT-Drs. 18/11500, p. 29). More research on the impact of GDDR on upper management levels could provide valuable insights into its efficacy (e.g., breaking the glass ceiling or strengthening trickle-down effects). Additionally, no prior research has provided detailed information on disclosure practices related to GDDR (e.g., location of corporate governance statement). Since GDDR rely heavily on the power of transparency (section 2.1.2), it is crucial to examine whether and to what extent companies meet disclosure requirements and how they choose their publication options. This study aims to address these gaps by analyzing **changes in the proportion of women across all regulated hierarchy levels** and providing information on **disclosure practices** for publicly listed and private co-determined companies.

Many studies also investigate the contextual factors that **determine** the efficacy of gender diversity regulations. One stream of literature uses multinational samples to examine differences in national gender diversity policies, aiming to identify institutional or company-specific factors that influence the efficacy of regulatory approaches. Due to the multinational samples, these studies often rely on secondary data regarding the proportion of women on corporate boards, limiting the data's level of detail. Additionally, these studies exclusively concentrate on voluntary approaches to foster gender diversity and mandatory gender diversity regulation. Hence, due to the particular mechanisms of GDDR, the findings are not transferable to assess the determinants of efficacy for GDDR. Another closely related stream of literature attempts to identify company-specific determinants based on single-country samples. These studies find that institutional factors, inter alia, company size (e.g., *Page et al.* (2024)), board size (e.g., *Klettner et al.* (2016)), and company age (e.g., *Peña-Martel et al.* (2022)) tend to influence a company's response to gender diversity regulation. However, these studies also focus solely on voluntary approaches or mandatory gender diversity regulations or a combination of both. Additionally, there is little research on the efficacy of gender diversity regulations for private companies, as most prior literature focuses on publicly listed companies.

Specific research on the determinants of GDDR is absent. While some studies analyze German companies, they either choose sample periods that end before the implementation of the GDDR (*Panzer/Müller* (2015)), barely consider the regulatory environment (*Schumann et al.* (2024)) or focus exclusively on listed companies subject to mandatory gender laws on supervisory boards (*Bozhinov et al.* (2021)). Therefore, analyzing **efficacy determinants in the context of GDDR** is an important topic that contributes to calls for further research on targeted transparency regulations. (*Hombach/Sellhorn* (2019), p. 164).

Another stream of literature examines the **effects of gender-diverse boards on the monitoring abilities** of corporate boards in various regulatory settings. In the absence of regulatory interventions, these studies find a positive relationship between the presence of women on corporate boards and financial reporting quality (e.g., *Srinidhi et al.* (2011)), attributing this to the beneficial attributes of female board members (e.g., *Gull et al.* (2018)).

Additionally, a third stream of literature analyzes the **impact of board gender diversity on financial reporting quality** in the context of **regulatory interventions**. In the context of voluntary approaches, researchers support the findings of a positive association between female board members and financial reporting quality (*García Lara et al.* (2017); *Panzer/Müller* (2015)). However, prior literature provides mixed results for this relationship in the context of mandatory gender diversity regulations. *Schumann et al.* (2024) also suggest a positive impact of female board members on financial reporting quality. However, this study analyzes the presence of women on executive boards and, therefore, of women on boards without monitoring functions. Furthermore, the study has methodological weaknesses, including a small sample size, and *Schumann et al.* (2024) barely consider the mandatory gender quota. In contrast, *García Lara et al.* (2022) provide indications for a negative impact of increased board gender diversity on financial reporting quality in the context of mandatory gender quotas. Despite studies like those by *Panzer/Müller* (2015) and *Schumann et al.* (2024) that analyze a sample of German companies, no study investigates the impact of GDDR on financial reporting quality. Given the unique regulatory mechanisms of GDDR compared to voluntary reporting regimes or mandatory gender quotas, there is a gap in research on the consequences of GDDR.

In conclusion, this study first examines the development in the presence of women on corporate boards and upper management positions after implementing a GDDR (RQ1a) as well as companies' disclosure practices in response to GDDR (RQ1b) to address gaps in prior descriptive research. This provides important insights into the reporting behavior of companies subject to GDDR. Second, the study investigates the determinants of GDDR efficacy in increasing gender diversity in top management positions (RQ2). To date, this study is the first to examine the determinants of GDDR. Specifically, determinants of voluntary approaches and mandatory gender diversity regulations provided by prior research are considered and complemented by determinants of public pressure. Third, the study analyzes the relationship between GDDR and financial reporting quality (RQ3). Prior literature presents mixed results on the effects of voluntary approaches and mandatory gender regulations on financial reporting quality. Since regulatory interventions to increase gender diversity on corporate boards may alter optimal board composition, this study sheds light on the unintended consequences of GDDR beyond the regulators' ethical objectives. By doing so, the study enhances the understanding of GDDR and responds to calls for further research on targeted transparency regulations (*Hombach/Sellhorn* (2019), p. 164). The study at hand addresses the research gap, illustrated by Figure 3-1:

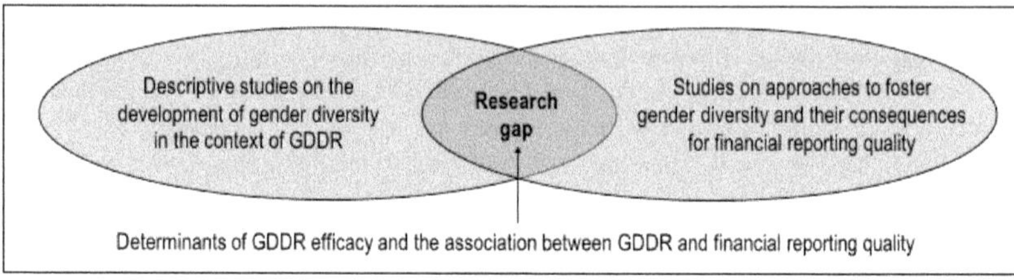

Figure 3-1: Identification of the research gap

4 Theory and hypotheses development

This chapter establishes the theoretical foundation for the analysis. To address the research gap identified in the previous chapter, section 4.1 presents five theories used to explain the efficacy and consequences of GDDR. After introducing principal-agent theory, four system-oriented theories (legitimacy theory, stakeholder theory, institutional theory, and resource dependence theory) are described. In conjunction with the regulatory requirements in Germany (section 2.2) and the findings of prior literature (chapter 3), hypotheses are derived in section 4.2 for the subsequent empirical analysis of this study.

4.1 Theoretical foundation

4.1.1 Principal-agent theory

GDDR aim to shape companies' appointment behavior to increase corporate gender diversity in management positions (section 2.2.3.3). It can be assumed that shareholders, as the owners of the company, strive to appoint a composition of corporate board members that ensures observance in line with their interests (*Ahern/Dittmar* (2012), p. 139). Consequently, the board composition selected by shareholders is considered optimal (*Labelle et al.* (2015), p. 342). GDDR, however, attempt to affect this optimal board composition by fostering gender diversity for political or ethical reasons. Thus, the regulatory intervention can cause changes in appointment behavior and alter the optimal selection of board members. Hence, it is necessary to shed light on the contract design between shareholders and managers in order to understand existing information asymmetries and conflicts of interest between both parties. The principal-agent theory provides a theoretical explanation for the optimal board composition choice of an individual company.

Principal-agent theory, which is part of new institutional economics theory[76], deals with agency relationships that arise out of the **separation of ownership and control** (*Eisenhardt* (1989), p. 58; *Göbel* (2021), p. 103; *Jensen/Meckling* (1976), p. 357). Such relationships appear when one individual – the principal – delegates his or her decision-making authority to another individual – the agent – due to a lack of time or know-how (*Erlei et al.* (2016), p. 71; *Jost* (2001), p. 1). *Jensen/Meckling* (1976) understand an agency relationship

> "[…] *as a contract under which one or more persons (the principal(s)) engage another person (the agent) to perform some service on their behalf which involves delegating some decision-making authority to the agent*". (*Jensen/Meckling* (1976), p. 308).

However, as a result of the separation of ownership and control, information asymmetries and conflicts of objectives may occur, and, therefore, the principals strive to monitor the activities of the agents (*Spremann* (1990), pp. 562–563; *Richter/Furubotn* (2010), p. 173). In a corporate context, there is a contractual relationship between the shareholders of a

---

[76] Cf. *Pfaff D./Zweifel* (1998), p. 184; *Williamson* (2000), p. 595. For an overview of new institutional economics theories, cf. *Richter/Furubotn* (2010).

company (principals) and management (agents).[77] Given the situation where shareholders are not able or willing to personally supervise and manage their company, they appoint managers on corporate boards to run the business (section 2.2.1). Shareholders are interested in aligning managers and their own interests in the best possible way to ensure the optimal functioning of the company (*Fama/Jensen* (1983), pp. 331–333; *Hillman/Dalziel* (2003), p. 385). However, managers may attempt to maximize their personal wealth instead of maximizing shareholder value (*Morris* (1987), p. 54). Thus, to ensure that the management behaves in the interest of the shareholders, the performance of the management needs to be controlled and assessed (*Kieser/Walgenbach* (2010), p. 47; *Richter/Furubotn* (2010), pp. 173–174). The existence of divergence in interests and the information advantage of managers leads to **agency problems** (Table 4-1). Principal-agent theorists differentiate three different types of **information asymmetries** from a principal's perspective (*Breid* (1995), p. 824; *Göbel* (2021), pp. 155–156). These three problems can be classified as problems that occur before and after the conclusion of the contract (*Hart/Holmström* (1987), p. 76).

First, before the contractual agreement, the manager's characteristics and the quality of his or her performance are difficult to assess for shareholders (*Göbel* (2021), p. 157). Before hiring, shareholders do not know if the manager is willing to act in the best interest of the shareholders (*Eisenhardt* (1989), p. 61). In this sense, managers can conceal potential negative characteristics ex-ante (**hidden characteristics**) (*Arrow* (1985), p. 38). Since shareholders are unable to evaluate the quality of managers unequivocally, they assume an average performance and, hence, offer an average compensation for the management position (*Horsch* (2004), p. 532). In turn, high-quality managers offering above-average quality services will refuse an average compensation offer and ultimately are unwilling to offer their services to the market (*Morris* (1987), p. 48). As a result, only average-quality and below-average-quality managers provide their services, reducing the overall quality offered on the market (*Horsch* (2004), p. 532). This phenomenon (**adverse selection problem**) can cause an ongoing reduction in the average quality of managers as well as the offered compensation and, thus, ultimately leads to dysfunctional markets or a market breakdown (*Akerlof* (1970), pp. 488–500).

Second, after the contract's conclusion, two different types of **moral hazards** can arise (*Hart/Holmström* (1987), p. 76; *Meinhövel* (2005), p. 68). Shareholders are not able to thoroughly assess and judge managers' actions (**hidden actions**) (*Arrow* (1985), p. 38). The lack of supervision provides managers with the freedom to minimize their efforts (shrinking) or to misuse corporate resources to achieve personal gains (consumption on the job) (*Eisenhardt* (1989), p. 61). Furthermore, even if the capital provider is able to observe the agent's behavior and actions, it might be challenging for the principals to evaluate the observed performance due to a lack of operational or internal knowledge (**hidden information**) (*Kieser/Walgenbach* (2010), p. 47). Hence, shareholders are confronted with the problem of assessing whether managers' actions are in line with the intended manner

77 Principal-agent relationships also arise, for example, between employer and employee, citizen and state, voters and politicians, patient and doctor (*Hannen* (2017), p. 106; *Nienhaus* (2015), p. 56).

or whether they attempt to maximize managers' personal benefits (fringe benefits) (*Göbel* (2021), p. 159).

Time of origin	Type of problem	Issue	Possible solutions	
			Principal	Agent
Before contract	Hidden characteristics	Adverse selection	Screening	Signaling
After contract	Hidden action	Moral hazard (Shirking, consumption on the job)	Monitoring	Reporting
	Hidden information	Moral hazard (Fringe benefits)		

Table 4-1: Agency problems and possible solutions (based on *Barth* (2009), p. 92; *Göbel* (2021), pp. 156 and 170)

Both principals and agents can engage in several **beneficial activities to mitigate agency problems** before signing the contract. On the one hand, principals can attempt to comprehensively screen the agent's behavior to identify and hire the best available service quality (screening) (*Richter/Furubotn* (2010), p. 303; *Stiglitz* (1975), p. 283). On the other hand, agents can contribute to mitigating the principal's skepticism by providing reliable information about themselves (signaling) and, thus, avoiding a hidden characteristics problem (*Spence* (1973), p. 357; *Spremann* (1990), p. 563). After the conclusion of the contract, principals may put efforts into the supervision of agents' actions (monitoring) to lower information asymmetries between both parties (*Göbel* (2021), p. 173). Agents can also contribute to a reduction of agency problems themselves by reporting about his or her activities (reporting) (*Spence* (1973), p. 355).

However, all of the actions mentioned above are associated with spending resources for at least one of the two parties and are therefore associated with different types of **agency costs** (*Erlei et al.* (2016), p. 71; *Jensen/Meckling* (1976), p. 308). First, monitoring costs arise for shareholders when they supervise management's actions or implement bonus payment systems as a way to incentivize desired behavior (*Hill/Jones* (1992), p. 132; *Göbel* (2021), p. 192). Second, bonding costs occur when managers try to convince shareholders (e.g., through reporting or signaling) of their goal-congruent intentions and activities (*Göbel* (2021), p. 192; *Jensen/Meckling* (1976), p. 308). Despite all efforts, it is still impossible to completely harmonize the interests of both parties (*Hill/Jones* (1992), p. 132; *Jensen/Meckling* (1976), p. 308). As a result, the remaining differing objectives will lead to a residual loss for the principals (*Erlei et al.* (2016), p. 72; *Morris* (1987), pp. 47–48). However, an efficient contract between shareholders and managers can be defined as one that maximizes shareholder value and minimizes agency costs (*Core et al.* (2003), p. 27).

The principal-agency theory contributes to the analysis of GDDR for several reasons. Due to the specific characteristics of the dualistic corporate governance system in Germany (section 2.2.1), a **twofold agency relationship** exists (Figure 4-1).

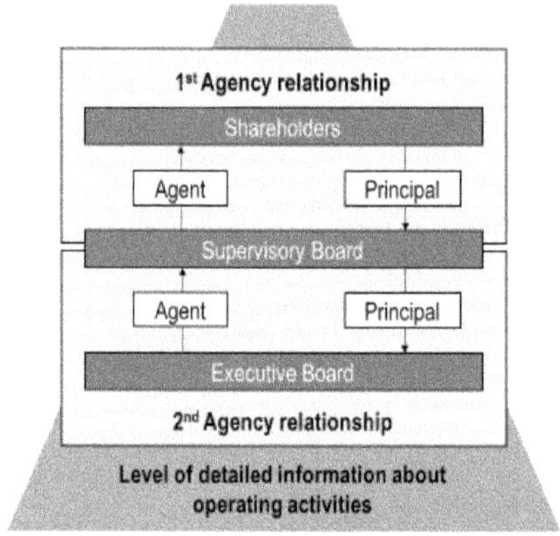

Figure 4-1: Twofold principal-agent relationship in two-tier corporate governance systems

The **first-level agency relationship** prevails between the shareholders and the supervisory board (*Berens/Schmitting* (2004), p. 58). The shareholders (principals) appoint the members of the supervisory board (agents) to control the company's management. In this relationship, the agency problems described above may arise: On the one hand, shareholders are predominantly interested in maximizing their return (*Ahern/Dittmar* (2012), p. 139; *Ramanathan* (1976), p. 516). Therefore, gender diversity in management positions, as intended by GDDR, is not in shareholders' primary interest unless it increases their profits (*Labelle et al.* (2015), p. 342). On the other hand, supervisory board members inherently attempt to maximize their personal power and reputation. This may result in a deviating intention regarding the gender-diverse composition of corporate boards if supervisory board members conclude that increased gender diversity in management positions contributes to achieving their objectives.

The **second-level agency relationship** arises between the supervisory board (principal) and executive board (agent) (*Berens/Schmitting* (2004), p. 58). The supervisory board appoints managers to the executive board to manage the operating business. Due to the regulation of the German GDDR (section 2.2.3.3), this includes the responsibility for gender diversity on lower management levels. Thus, comparable to the first-level agency relationship, discrepancies in the perceptions of appointments to management positions may occur.

However, from the theoretical **optimal contracting** perspective, on both hierarchy levels, principals (shareholders (or supervisory boards)) seek to appoint the best agents (supervisory boards (or executive boards)) to mitigate information asymmetries and agency costs. In the context of GDDR, external authorities (e.g., regulators) may influence corporate governance structures to address the societal issue of gender diversity (section 2.1.2). The forced change in appointment processes and composition of corporate boards, thus, does not result in optimal, shareholder-value maximizing contracts (*Labelle et al.* (2015), p. 343).

In summary, principal-agent theory can explain the decision to appoint specific board members and the resulting **composition of corporate boards**. GDDR aim to increase board gender diversity and, thus, influence the composition of corporate boards. System-oriented theories explain why and how companies may react to GDDR and reshape the composition of corporate boards.

4.1.2 System-oriented theories

The system-oriented theories are part of new institutional sociological theory (*Katz/Kahn* (1966)). In contrast to new institutional economics theory, the system-oriented theories deal with societal and ethical aspects. They describe an **influence of society on corporations** and vice versa (*Deegan* (2002), p. 292). Based on the assumption of such mutual interdependencies (*Deegan/Unermann* (2011), p. 321), these theories examine the motivation of a company to publish certain information and how corporate disclosure may influence the relationship between the company and society (*Gray et al.* (1996), pp. 42–45). System-oriented theories include legitimacy theory, stakeholder theory, institutional theory, and resource dependence theory (Figure 4-2).

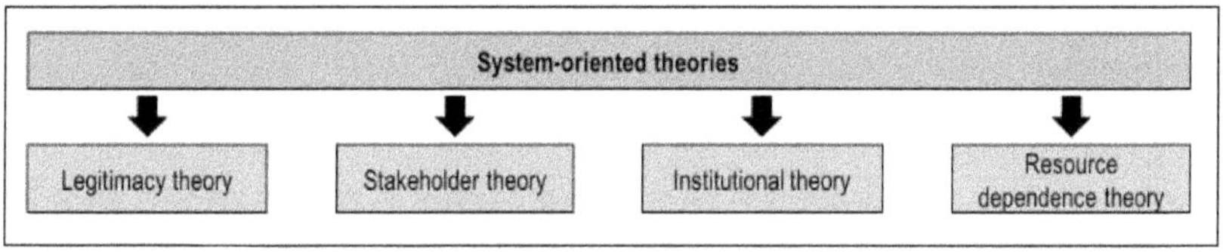

Figure 4-2: Overview of system-oriented theories (based on (*Hannen* (2017), p. 109))

In the context of targeted transparency regulation, it is essential to understand why companies voluntarily disclose information. Thus, system-oriented theories provide a valuable theoretical foundation to investigate why companies exercise specific **disclosure choices** (section 2.2.3.4). Therefore, the system-oriented theories are explained in the following sections.

4.1.2.1 Legitimacy theory

Legitimacy theory examines the congruence between **society's implicit and explicit expectations** of an organization and whether the organization's activities are in line with these expectations (*Lindblom* (2010), pp. 51–53). Following *Shocker/Sethi* (1973)

> "*Any social institution – and business is no exception – operates in a society via a social contract, expressed or implied, whereby its survival and growth are based on:*
>
> *1) the delivery of some socially desirable ends to society in general, and*
> *2) the distribution of economic, social, or political benefits to groups from which it derives its power." (Shocker/Sethi (1973), p. 97)*

Thus, organizations strive to reach and maintain a certain level of legitimacy to ensure its future existence. Organizations can ensure this objective by operating within the social boundaries of **socially acceptable behavior** (*O'Donovan* (2002), p. 344). In detail, the social construct of legitimacy underlies a system of "*norms, values, beliefs, and definitions*"[78] based on the expectations of society (*Suchman* (1995), p. 574). Without being reputed as legitimate, organizations are unable to survive in the social environment in the long term, and thus, legitimacy is of particular importance (*Dowling/Pfeffer* (1975), pp. 123–124).

However, the needs and expectations of society, or which behavior is defined as socially acceptable, are considerably changing over time (*Newson/Deegan* (2002), pp. 184–190; *Patten* (1992), p. 471). The traditional expectation of meeting only the interests of selected stakeholders, in a corporate context, predominantly the profit maximization interest of shareholders (*Ramanathan* (1976), p. 516), is nowadays no longer sufficient to achieve legitimacy (*O'Donovan* (2002), pp. 346–349). During the last decades, companies were increasingly required to consider more and more **environmental and social consequences** of their operating activities (*Heard/Bolce* (1981), p. 247; *O'Donovan* (2002), pp. 344–345). Hence, corporations need to continuously realign their business activities with changing societal expectations. Due to society's effective sanction measures (e.g., the name and shame mechanism), companies have to be concerned about misconduct in the sense of infringing social norms and boundaries (*Newson/Deegan* (2002), p. 185).

To achieve the desired legitimacy, corporations need to **convince society of the congruence** between corporate actions and the expected behavior by society (*Dowling/Pfeffer* (1975), p. 124). However, assessing a company's real actions can be difficult for society (*Suchman* (1995), p. 574). Therefore, it is insufficient for companies to simply align their corporate activities with societal expectations as they additionally need to convince society of their desirable and proper conduct (*Hagemann* (2017), p. 111; *Suchman* (1995), p. 574). In this vein, to obtain the required legitimacy, it can be sufficient to purport desirable and proper conduct in order to manage society's perceptions without truly following through on such claims (*Khor* (2003)).

To maintain or extend legitimacy, companies can apply different **legitimization strategies**.[79] These strategies include:

- the adoption of prevailing constraints and, thus, align corporate activities with societal norms and expectations,
- communicating in a way that aligns with legitimate values, thereby manipulating social perceptions to reinforce the acceptability of corporate behavior,
- altering of existing social definitions in order to justify corporate practices, and
- the modification of external expectations to manage perceptions of corporate conduct.

An established and common way to incorporate one or a **combination** of the described strategies and, thereby, achieve the objective of legitimacy is corporate disclosure (*Khor* (2003), p. 7; *Woodward et al.* (1996), pp. 337–338).

In the context of **GDDR**, companies are required to report on their corporate gender diversity, and thus, companies can utilize the disclosure obligation to ensure or enhance

[78] *Suchman* (1995), p. 574.

[79] Here and in the following, cf. *Dowling/Pfeffer* (1975), p. 127; *Khor* (2003), p. 7; *O'Donovan* (2002), pp. 353–354.

their legitimacy. Companies face pressure to meet society's expectations regarding a certain level of gender diversity on corporate boards. Even if the company does not achieve the expected level of gender diversity, it can demonstrate its willingness to comply with societal expectations (e.g., through an appropriate setting of self-set gender diversity targets). Hence, companies can attempt to convince society about their legitimate conduct and social values through a transparent communication strategy. Even companies that are already facing **public pressure** have the opportunity to maintain their legitimacy through corporate disclosures. For instance, companies confronted with negative media reports use especially environmental disclosure to respond to public pressure (*O'Donovan* (2002), p. 351). However, companies have to fear social sanctions if they do not meet society's expectations. This can weaken legitimacy and, ultimately, jeopardize the existence of the company. Because interests and possible sanctions of different groups are not homogeneous, stakeholder theory examines the relationship between individual groups and the company.

4.1.2.2 Stakeholder theory

Both legitimacy theory as well as stakeholder theory deal with the impact of the environment on organizations and information needs and, therefore, are closely related (*Gray et al.* (1995), p. 52). Whereas legitimacy theory mainly focuses on the congruence between the societal values of an organization and the social system of society as a whole (or rather on the society's expectations), stakeholder theory distinguishes between different stakeholder groups (*Donaldson/Preston* (1995), p. 67; *Chen/Roberts* (2010), p. 653). In contrast to legitimacy theory, stakeholder theory does not examine the unitary expectations of society but takes **individual social contracts between the company and each stakeholder group** into account (*Deegan/Unermann* (2011), p. 348). This is expedient for two reasons: First, the impact and expectations between the various stakeholder groups (e.g., shareholders are interested in profit maximization while NGOs expect ethical behavior) are heterogeneous (*Deegan* (2002), p. 295). Second, stakeholders' interests not only vary but can also be conflicting in some cases (e.g., customers hope for the lowest achievable price for a product, while employees demand appropriate compensation) (*Chen/Roberts* (2010), p. 653). A further crucial contrast between both theories is that they assume different underlying motives for a company's conduct and behavior (*Näsi et al.* (1997), pp. 303–305). Legitimacy theory is restricted to the assumption that companies provide information to obtain the required social legitimacy. In contrast, stakeholder theory assumes that companies have an intrinsic interest in fulfilling the individual stakeholder groups' information needs to ensure the company's survival as a going concern (*Freeman et al.* (2010), pp. 10–12; *Hagemann* (2017), p. 114).

Following *Freeman/Reed* (1983), a stakeholder group of a company is defined as

> "*Any identifiable group or individual who can affect the achievement of an organization's objectives or who is affected by the achievement of an organization's objectives.*"[80] (*Freeman/Reed* (1983), p. 91)

---

[80] For an overview of the chronological development of the shareholder definition, cf. *Mitchell et al.* (1997), p. 858.

Consequently, a company's individual stakeholders or stakeholder groups are diverse and company-specific. Among others, potential stakeholders include investors, employees, political actors, media, trade unions, suppliers, and competitors (*van der Laan Smith et al.* (2005), pp. 126–127). Each stakeholder has **individual expectations** towards a company and, therefore, interacts with the corporate management differently (*Näsi et al.* (1997), p. 303). Depending on the essentiality of resources provided by the stakeholder, stakeholders' power to determine corporate achievement varies (*Ullmann* (1985), p. 552).

Stakeholder theorists incorporate stakeholders' impact on corporate objectives differently, and therefore, stakeholder theory can be distinguished into two branches (*Deegan/Unermann* (2011), p. 348). The **normative branch** posits that managers should include all stakeholders' interests equally, regardless of their ability to affect corporate objectives in terms of financial performance (*Hasnas* (1998), pp. 25–26). Therefore, this approach assumes that the company manages its business activities for the welfare of all stakeholders (*Hasnas* (1998), p. 26; *Stoney/Winstanley* (2001), p. 608). Applying this approach to companies subject to GDDR would require them to consider the interests of investors, political parties, employees, and media similarly. However, as these stakeholders have different expectations regarding gender diversity in management positions, it is hardly feasible for the company to treat the interests equally.

Furthermore, the normative branch postulates that stakeholder power is not directly relevant to influencing corporate achievements (*Deegan/Unermann* (2011), p. 349). This leads to the conclusion that companies should consider the (sometimes far-reaching) demands of some political parties in the same way as the expectations of investors regarding the **optimal composition of corporate boards**. Due to the incompatibility of all interests regarding gender diversity in management positions and the current management practice deviating (*Hagemann* (2017), p. 113), the normative branch cannot serve as an appropriate theoretical basis for this work.

The other branch of stakeholder theory, the **managerial branch**, focuses on prioritizing stakeholder groups regarding their varying interests and power (*Ackermann/Eden* (2011), p. 183). Following *Clarkson* (1995), stakeholders can be differentiated into two groups: **primary and secondary stakeholders**.[81] Primary stakeholders have a direct sphere of influence due to their mutual and direct exchange relationship with the company. Engagement with primary stakeholders is essential for the survival of the company. Hence, the company is highly intertwined with these stakeholders (*Shubham et al.* (2018), p. 912). Therefore, those stakeholders whose economic situation is directly related to the company's performance (e.g., shareholders, creditors, employees, customers, or suppliers) are classified as primary stakeholders (*Vasi/King* (2012), p. 577). In contrast, secondary stakeholders (e.g., NGOs, media, and local communities) do not directly participate in economic transactions with the company and, therefore, lack any formal contractual authority over the company (*Eesley/Lenox* (2006), p. 765). Thus, an asymmetrical relationship arises between companies and their secondary stakeholders. While secondary stakeholders are reliant on the company to realize their objectives, the company is not crucially dependent upon secondary stakeholders (*Shubham et al.* (2018), p. 912; *van der Laan et al.* (2008), p. 302). However, even

[81] Here and in the following, cf. *Clarkson* (1995), pp. 106–107.

secondary stakeholders are able to exert pressure and thus indirectly influence the company (e.g., negative and critical media or other types of protests) (*King/Soule* (2007), pp. 416–417).

Despite the absence of formal contractual bonds, companies cannot completely neglect the interests of secondary stakeholders. *Eesley/Lenox* (2006) argue that these stakeholders can utilize a bundle of actions available at their disposal to exert pressure and urge the company to respect their interests.[82] On the one hand, they can cause **direct operational costs** (e.g., public relations expenses, legal fees, or managerial attention) to increase the awareness of their demands. On the other hand, the initiatives can potentially damage the company's **reputation** and trigger the attention of primary stakeholders. This can result in far-reaching repercussions for the company. The principles of the managerial branch of stakeholder theory can be applied appropriately to GDDR. While primary stakeholders, such as investors and employees, may have disparate interests in considering gender diversity, the targeted transparency approach of GDDR also aims at the interests and power of secondary stakeholders. This regulatory approach relies mainly on information intermediaries. Thus, secondary stakeholders exert pressure on the company to shape its behavior. For instance, companies that are particularly restrictive regarding gender diversity in management positions may risk reputational damage if media coverage is detrimental (name and shame). This may result in negative consequences in the relationship with various primary stakeholders (e.g., certain socially sensitive investors or female employees).

4.1.2.3 Institutional theory

Institutional theory emphasizes how organizations **incorporate societal norms** to ensure their stability (*Chen/Roberts* (2010), pp. 652–653). This theory shares a common foundation with legitimacy theory and stakeholder theory to a certain degree (*Deegan* (2002), pp. 292–299; *Hannen* (2017), p. 110). In essence, the purpose of institutional theory is to explain why organizations in similar environments evolve in a particular way and adopt comparable characteristics (*Hall* (1996), pp. 298–299; *Larrinaga-González* (2007), pp. 151–154). Institutional theorists assume that organizations respond to external pressure from stakeholders by changing their structure and adopting institutionalized norms to maintain their legitimacy (*Meyer/Rowan* (1977), p. 352; *Zucker* (1977), pp. 726–727). Institutional theory provides a beneficial theoretical foundation to investigate organizations' response under external pressure to social or environmental reporting requirements, such as **GDDR** (*Cormier et al.* (2005), pp. 12–13; *Rahaman et al.* (2004), pp. 40–41). Hence, institutional theory can help understand whether companies subject to GDDR disclose information similarly and engage comparably in gender diversity.

DiMaggio/Powell (1983) described the process in which an organization adapts the structures of another organization in a comparable environment as **isomorphism** (*DiMaggio/Powell* (1983), pp. 150–152). They identify three different types: coercive isomorphism, mimetic isomorphism, and normative isomorphism.

---

82 Here and in the following, cf. *Eesley/Lenox* (2006), pp. 765–767.

Coercive isomorphism results from external pressure of regulators, standard setters, or other major stakeholders that seek a change of companies' behavior in a desired manner (*Deegan/Unermann* (2011), p. 363; *DiMaggio/Powell* (1983), p. 150). Regulatory reporting requirements, such as social or environmental reporting, inherently create this type of pressure on companies (*Contrafatto* (2014), p. 418). With regard to GDDR, regulators oblige companies to report about gender diversity on several hierarchy levels to reach increased transparency.

Mimetic isomorphism arises under an organization's uncertainty about institutional practices of comparable organizations. When goals or common practices entail uncertainty, organizations seek orientation and, thus, may imitate other organizations to prevent reputational disadvantages (*DiMaggio/Powell* (1983), p. 151). In the context of GDDR, companies face uncertainty about how other companies respond to the disclosure requirement and their effort to foster gender diversity in management positions. As a result, companies may adapt the disclosure practices of their peer-companies and align their self-set gender diversity targets with those of their competitors to avert legitimacy harm.

The third form is **normative isomorphism** and occurs through pressure from norms and rules most commonly imposed by professional associations (*DiMaggio/Powell* (1983), p. 152). Regarding gender diversity regulations, corporate governance codes are an example of such a norm (section 2.2.2). Even if the standards are not legally binding, companies face external pressure to comply with the corporate governance codes.

Despite their different origins, a clear distinction between the three forms is rather difficult in practice (*DiMaggio/Powell* (1983), p. 150). However, as mentioned above, all three types of isomorphism are theoretically **reasonable regarding GDDR**. Therefore, the study at hand considers the holistic effect and does not make a distinction between the three types of isomorphism.

4.1.2.4 Resource dependence theory

Resource dependence theory, like stakeholder theory and institutional theory, is also linked to legitimacy theory and focuses on the environment's influence on organizations (*Chen/Roberts* (2010), p. 653; *Deegan* (2002), p. 293). However, this theory – grounded on the work of *Pfeffer/Salancik* (1978) – addresses the implications of how environmental constraints affect organizations (*Pfeffer/Salancik* (1978), pp. 1–2). Resource dependence theory posits that organizations operate under environmental constraints, necessitating engagement in exchanges with other organizations and competition for **scant resources** (*Pfeffer/Salancik* (1978), pp. 2–3). Thus, organizations are reliant on their environment and must ensure the ability to acquire and maintain vital resources to secure organizational survival (*Deegan* (2002), p. 293; *Hillman et al.* (2000), p. 236). For instance, *Suchman* (1995) describes "*legitimacy as an operational resource that organizations extract [...] from their cultural environment*" (*Suchman* (1995), p. 576). Accordingly, legitimacy can also be defined as a resource like any other that a company needs to ensure its further survival (*Ashforth/Gibbs* (1990), p. 177; *Deegan* (2002), p. 293; *Dowling/Pfeffer* (1975), p. 125; *Suchman* (1995), p. 576).

Companies can pursue different strategies to manage and mitigate resource constraints. If an external constraint is manageable, organizations can attempt to coordinate their activities by forging **alliances or strategic arrangements** with other organizations (e.g., competitors) facing the same resource constraints (*Chen/Roberts* (2010), p. 657; *Pfeffer* (1972a), pp. 382–383). If organizations are confronted with unmanageable dependencies, they can build strong relationships with powerful organizations (e.g., standard setters or political parties) that control or regulate crucial resources to enhance their position and alter their environmental constraints (*Chen/Roberts* (2010), p. 657).

In a corporate context, companies strive to manage external constraints through an appropriate composition of corporate boards (*Hillman et al.* (2000), pp. 235–239; *Peng* (2004), pp. 453–454; *Pfeffer* (1972b), pp. 218–220; *Pfeffer* (1973), pp. 349–350). Board members are of crucial importance in **mitigating external constraints** because they provide or secure access to essential resources through their individual characteristics (e.g., know-how) or their relationship to the external environment (*Boyd* (1990), p. 419; *Hillman et al.* (2000), p. 236; *Pearce/Zahra* (1992), pp. 411–412). Furthermore, corporate board members provide the ability to incorporate important external organizations (*Hillman et al.* (2007), p. 942; *Pfeffer/Salancik* (1978), p. 176). In this vein, corporate board members can be seen as providers of resources (e.g., legitimacy, expertise, or advice) that accumulate their resources on the corporate board (*Hillman/Dalziel* (2003), p. 383). These accumulated resources, referred to as board capital (*Hillman/Dalziel* (2003), p. 383), determine the provision of resources to the company in return.

Thus, the theoretical assumptions of resource dependence theory are relevant to understanding how **GDDR** shape the compositions of corporate boards. The intended increase in gender diversity on corporate boards results in changed characteristics of board members (*Hillman et al.* (2009), pp. 1408–1409). On the one hand, referring to legitimacy theory, **gender diversity on corporate boards is a resource** for meeting society's expectations and, therefore, gaining legitimacy. Since there is a limited supply of qualified board members (*Ahern/Dittmar* (2012)), a resource dependence exists, and companies may compete for candidates. On the other hand, due to the differences in individual characteristics between male and female board members, boards' ability to manage external dependencies may change in turn (*Hillman et al.* (2000), p. 236).

4.1.2.5 Summary

As outlined above, system-orientated theories are not isolated but overlap, build on and complement each other. The overarching objective of these theories is to examine the relationship between a company and society or separate groups of society. Figure 4-3 illustrates the **relationship among system-oriented theories**.

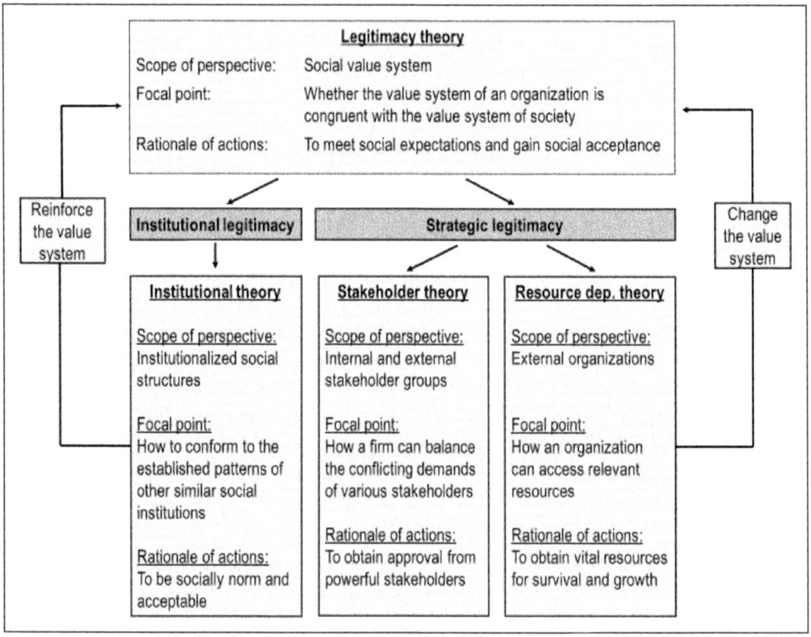

Figure 4-3: The relationship among system-oriented theories (based on *Chen/Roberts* (2010), p. 653)

Although system-oriented theories share the same fundamental objectives, they vary in their **perspectives, specificity, and determination** (*Chen/Roberts* (2010), p. 661). For instance, whereas legitimacy theory assumes one single "social contract" between the company and the society (*Shocker/Sethi* (1973), p. 97), stakeholder theory considers various social contracts between the company and each stakeholder group (*Deegan/Unermann* (2011), p. 348). However, each system-oriented theory supposes companies attempting to reach a certain degree of legitimacy to ensure long-term survival and growth.

While legitimacy theory takes a broad societal view, the other theories adopt a narrower perspective and aim to offer solutions on how companies can achieve legitimacy.[83] Primarily, two types of legitimacy can be differentiated, which depend on the purpose of legitimacy: institutional legitimacy and strategic legitimacy. The former is closely related to institutional theory. In simple terms, companies adapt their behavior and conduct to existing, socially established norms in order to gain institutional legitimacy. However, this behavior pattern also **reinforces the legitimacy** of the current value system, given that companies are aligned with accepted norms of behavior. In contrast, stakeholder theory and resource dependence theory assume an exchange between the company and individual

[83] Here and in the following, cf. *Chen/Roberts* (2010), pp. 660–662.

groups within the society. Due to the different strategies for achieving strategic legitimacy, these theories imply a change in the value system of the society.

In summary, system-oriented theories provide, in combination with principal-agent theory, a suitable theoretical framework to investigate social or environmental disclosure regulations. In particular, system-oriented theories provide reasons to believe that companies are motivated to incorporate gender diversity as intended by GDDR to ensure their long-term survival and growth. Therefore, the next section derives hypotheses based on the theoretical foundation.

4.2 Hypotheses development

This section deduces hypotheses for the following empirical analysis based on the theories presented. Following *Schanz* (1988), hypotheses are assumptions regarding the structural nature of reality (*Schanz* (1988), p. 24). In line with critical rationalism[84], statistical tests consist of two interrelated hypotheses: the **null hypothesis** on the one hand and the **alternative hypothesis** on the other hand (*Döring* (2023), p. 648). The following hypotheses of this study (H_1-H_{12}) are alternative hypotheses and, thus, build the counterpart of the null hypothesis. The null hypotheses are evaluated based on significance tests. The rejection of the null hypotheses leads to an acceptance of the alternative hypotheses. Research hypotheses can be provided in a non-directed (assumption of an association) or directed (assumption of a positive/negative association) form (*Döring* (2023), p. 649). If theory and literature permit a clear prediction of the association, the study uses directed hypotheses. The study uses undirected hypotheses if the theory does not permit a clear prediction or previous studies do not provide consistent findings.

Subsequently, hypotheses are derived addressing the **research questions** regarding the development of the proportion of women in management positions (RQ1a), determinants of GDDR efficacy (RQ2), and the association between GDDR and financial reporting quality (RQ3). Since the findings for disclosure practices in response to GDDR (RQ1b) are of explorative and descriptive nature, no hypotheses are deduced.[85]

4.2.1 GDDR and the development of corporate gender diversity

GDDR do not force companies to increase gender diversity on any corporate hierarchy level. In contrast to mandatory gender quotas, an increasing presence of women in management positions is not stipulated by law. However, due to the regulatory mechanisms of targeted transparency regulations, GDDR aim to shape corporate behavior indirectly through **disclosure requirements** and hence promote increased gender diversity as a result of stakeholder pressure in light of higher transparency.

GDDR require affected companies to disclose specific information regarding corporate gender diversity. Thereby, a broad audience is informed about companies' actual progress and future targets regarding the participation of women on management levels (section 2.1.2). The disclosure required by GDDR enables report users to evaluate and assess

---

84 Critical rationalism goes back to the work of *Popper* (1934), cf. section 1.2.

85 For a comparable approach, cf. *Rave* (2022), p. 79.

companies' conduct in promoting gender diversity. On the one hand, report users can observe companies' real actions by evaluating changes in the actual participation of women. On the other hand, companies subject to GDDR can signal their willingness to foster the presence of women in the company (e.g., by setting ambitious gender diversity targets). Based on the published information, primary report users, as well as society at large, can assess companies' gender diversity on management levels. Thus, according to **legitimacy theory**, the observable behavior can be collated with societal norms and expectations. Report users are empowered to detect companies that fail to meet society's expectations. Accordingly, social sanctions (e.g., name and shame campaigns) may be imposed on these companies, resulting in reduced legitimacy. Ultimately, companies that struggle with reduced legitimacy fear the company's future existence. In order to prevent legitimacy damage, companies can both declare their intention to foster gender diversity and also actually align their behavior with social expectations.

According to **stakeholder theory**, individual stakeholders can also utilize published information to evaluate companies' behavior. Stakeholders can conclude whether companies' actions in respect of gender diversity are in their interest. If the conduct is considered inadequate, stakeholders can utilize their contractual relation to the company and try to shape corporate behavior in an intended manner. Consequently, in line with stakeholder theory, the disclosure requirements lead to an increase in the proportion of women in management positions.

Furthermore, the target-setting provision of GDDR requires companies to set specific targets for the gender composition of management positions (section 2.2.3.3). Prior literature examines the usefulness of target-setting in achieving a goal-relevant outcome (e.g., *Mensi-Klarbach et al.* (2021), p. 580). **Setting goals** leads to increased attention toward the desired outcome (*Locke* (1968); *Latham/Locke* (2013)), thereby increasing the endeavors to reach the respective goal (*Wood et al.* (2013), p. 91). *Sojo et al.* (2016) transmitted the primary individual-centered goal-setting concept to a broader institutional setting and, thus, applied it to a gender diversity regulation context (*Sojo et al.* (2016), p. 520; see further: *Mensi-Klarbach et al.* (2021), p. 580). Hence, self-set targets may increase companies' accountability and enable stakeholders to evaluate companies' progress against the backdrop of stated targets. The target-setting obligation of GDDR, therefore, results in increased gender diversity in management positions.

However, prior literature observes and identifies phenomena that may cause varying increases in the presence of women on different corporate hierarchy levels. On the one hand, the **glass ceiling effect** states that women are hindered from reaching upper management levels due to structural and cultural barriers. Hence, the presence of women at lower management levels may be higher than at upper management levels. On the other hand, the **trickle-down effect** characterizes the fact that women in top-management positions "trickle down" to lower management levels since the company attracts more women and supports gender diversity. Other contextual factors, such as the size of management levels (e.g., executive boards might consist of fewer members than subordinate management levels), may influence the possibility of gradually increasing women's presence.

In summary, a variety of theories suggest an increase in gender diversity in response to the introduction of GDDR. In conjunction with findings of prior literature, this increase may vary across corporate hierarchy levels. Therefore, the following hypothesis postulates:

H_1 The proportion of women in management positions increases after the implementation of GDDR.

4.2.2 Determinants of GDDR efficacy

The second research question (RQ2) focuses on the efficacy of GDDR. Based on principal-agent theory and system-oriented theories, several **determinants** that influence the efficacy of GDDR are identified. On the one hand, some institutional factors affect the whole company and, hence, determine the efficacy of GDDR. On the other hand, hierarchy-level specific contextual factors may also affect the efficacy of GDDR. For example, supervisory boards are larger on average and allow gradual changes in the board composition, while executive boards are smaller on average.[86] Moreover, shareholders or employees appoint members directly to the supervisory boards, while executive board members are appointed by the supervisory board. Therefore, separate hypotheses are derived for different management levels to consider these specific contextual factors. However, due to the restriction in data availability, the hypotheses are limited to supervisory and executive boards. Thus, no hypotheses are derived for management levels below the executive board.

Supervisory board

According to legitimacy theory and stakeholder theory, companies need to consider society's and stakeholders' expectations to reach and maintain a certain level of legitimacy that ensures the future existence of the company.[87] **Stakeholder theory and legitimacy theory** state that companies have to take the needs and expectations of individual stakeholder groups and society at large into account to gain a sufficient legitimacy level (*Deegan* (2002), p. 295). GDDR oblige companies to publish information regarding their gender diversity and sensitize stakeholder demands and their increasing calls for the equal participation of women and men in corporate hierarchy levels. However, the interests of various stakeholder groups may be unaligned when considering gender diversity. While some stakeholders are primarily interested in value-maximization (e.g., shareholders) or financial stability (e.g., debtholders), other stakeholders' primary interests aim for social conduct and therefore demand an appropriate level of gender diversity (e.g., employees). As stakeholder theory suggests, stakeholders can impose different sanctions to penalize companies if they do not meet their expectations. For example, if a company fails to achieve the level of gender diversity desired by its customers, customers may boycott the company's products or services. Thus, customers pressure the company and urge it to realign its behavior in the intended manner. Due to the varying importance of resources provided by different stakeholder groups (resource dependence theory), their abilities to exert pressure

---

[86] For example, in the 200 largest companies in Germany, the size of the supervisory boards is more than twice as large as that of the executive boards on average, cf. *Sondergeld et al.* (2024), p. 19.

[87] An argumentation in a similar vein but based on the assumptions of institutional theory and resource dependence theory, cf. *Gregorič et al.* (2017), p. 269.

differ in efficacy. In total, the pressure of different stakeholders accumulates to public pressure and compounds the interests of various stakeholder groups.

However, particular non-professional stakeholder groups (e.g., employees, customers, or society at large) require publicly available information beyond corporate reporting to notice and assess corporate behavior. Therefore, information intermediaries (e.g., media) prepare information that enables these stakeholders to assess companies' information published according to GDDR. Nevertheless, due to individual characteristics and varying visibility in society, companies subject to GDDR are not equally covered by information intermediaries. Thus, stakeholders do not have equal access to graspable and comprehensible information, resulting in deviating abilities to assess corporate behavior and exert pressure on companies. However, transparency and the resulting **level of public pressure** are assumed to be crucial for the efficacy of targeted transparency regulations (*Hombach/Sellhorn* (2019), p. 164) and, hence, also for GDDR.

Prior studies on the presence of women on corporate boards in other regulatory environments show that companies tend to appoint more women to their boards in the context of voluntary disclosure if they face higher levels of public pressure (*Gregorič et al.* (2017); *Peña-Martel et al.* (2022)). In conjunction with legitimacy theory and stakeholder theory, companies in the **spotlight of public attention** face higher levels of public pressure than companies with average public attention. Thus, these highly visible companies may fear social sanctions from stakeholders or society at large if they do not meet societal expectations. To prevent reputational harm and losses in legitimacy, companies facing high public pressure tend to incorporate stakeholders' expectations regarding gender diversity more frequently. Consequently, companies subject to distinct public pressure appoint more frequently women to their supervisory board than companies that face average public pressure. This leads to the following hypothesis:

H_{2a}	*The efficacy of GDDR on the supervisory board is positively associated with a high level of public pressure.*

Based on the same theoretical assumptions, companies that receive less attention from society are covered sparsely by information intermediaries. Accordingly, stakeholders and interested members of society have limited access to graspable information on corporate gender diversity performance. This leads to stakeholders being less able to observe the behavior of companies with regard to gender diversity and, therefore, not being able to evaluate it accordingly. As a result, these **poorly visible companies have to fear fewer or no societal sanctions** since stakeholders face larger barriers to evaluating corporate conduct.

The low availability of information creates only a low level of public pressure. The lower risk of being sanctioned by stakeholders reduces the pressure on companies to meet social expectations. Thus, the incentives to foster gender diversity and appoint more women to the supervisory board may be **lower than those of average-covered companies**. In response to GDDR, the proportion of women on the supervisory board might be unchanged or increased to a lesser extent.

In consideration of the causal chain underlying a GDDR (section 2.1.2), the regulatory mechanisms driven by increased transparency may fail to achieve the intended objective of enhancing gender diversity on supervisory boards in companies exposed to little or no public pressure. Formulating **two separate hypotheses** – one for companies under high public pressure and one for those under low public pressure – is required for a more precise examination of public pressure as a determinant of GDDR efficacy. This approach is particularly valuable as it accounts for the heterogeneity of GDDR efficacy across different company contexts. In contrast, a single-directed hypothesis positing a positive relationship between public pressure and GDDR efficacy would fail to account for this heterogeneity. By distinguishing between high- and low-pressure contexts, two separate hypotheses offer more nuanced insights into the conditions that drive GDDR efficacy and better reflect the complexity of the phenomenon under investigation. Hence, correspondingly to hypothesis H_{2a}, hypothesis 2b (H_{2b}) postulates:

H_{2b} The efficacy of GDDR on the supervisory board is negatively associated with a low level of public pressure.

Publicly listed companies are often of **major interest and take a central focus** of political and public discussion. Thus, these companies face high external pressure due to their exposed position and visibility. In the context of GDDR, the disclosure practices of listed companies attract the most attention and are analyzed by various professional and non-professional stakeholders. Prior descriptive research that monitors the proportion of women on the supervisory boards of German companies analyzes primarily (e.g., *FidAR e.V.* (2023)) or exclusively (e.g., *Kirsch et al.* (2023b)) large, publicly listed companies. Accordingly, listed companies face a higher level of public visibility compared to private companies. GDDR rely on the mechanisms of targeted transparency (section 2.1), and thus, a higher level of visibility and transparency might be beneficial for the efficacy of the regulation.

Furthermore, from an **institutional theory perspective**, companies tend to adopt structures and strategies from other companies in a comparable environment to maintain their legitimacy. Thus, in line with mimetic isomorphism, companies aim to align their reporting practices in response to GDDR with other companies (e.g., with companies within the same index). If peer companies subject to GDDR increasingly appoint more women to their supervisory board or set ambitious targets for the gender composition (e.g., a proportion of 40% for the underrepresented gender), investors and other stakeholders might expect comparable increases or similar target-setting. Therefore, companies might increase their efforts to appoint female supervisory board members or set more ambitious targets to meet the performance of their benchmark. Besides that, more visible companies are more in the frame of regulators and, therefore, face higher institutional pressure (*Gregorič et al.* (2017), p. 270).

However, FüPoG I introduced different regulatory approaches to the supervisory board of regulated companies. Accordingly, the GDDR only applies to private, co-determined companies and listed companies that are not subject to parity co-determination. By contrast, listed parity co-determined companies are subject to the mandatory gender quota (section 2.2.3.2). As a result, listed companies targeted by the GDDR on the supervisory board tend to be smaller.[88] Hence, although they are publicly listed, companies subject to the GDDR might show lower public visibility than larger companies that have to apply the mandatory gender quota. Due to the **potentially opposing effects**, hypothesis 3 (H_3) supposes an undirected association:

H_3	*The efficacy of GDDR on the supervisory board is associated with companies' capital market orientation.*

Institutional theory states that companies aim to incorporate societal norms to meet the expectations of other organizations or society to ensure their stability. *Greenwood et al.* (2011) argue that a company's age is associated with its status within an institutional environment. Older companies tend to become more integrated into society over time. Due to their position as "*central firms*" (*Greenwood et al.* (2011), p. 340), older companies might be more visible and, thus, are more often the subject of interest, resulting in increased public attention (*Greenwood et al.* (2011), p. 340).

Hence, the theory of **normative isomorphism** suggests that older companies face greater pressure to meet societal expectations due to their exposed position and prominent status within society. Therefore, the age of a company is also a determinant of a company's status within society (e.g., *Gregorič et al.* (2017), p. 277). Professional associations that intend to foster gender diversity on corporate boards often observe the organizational behavior of older companies due to their often larger size. Because of the closer monitoring and greater awareness of corporate conduct, the pressure from normative isomorphism might be higher for older companies.

On the contrary, **principal-agent theory** suggests that shareholders strive to achieve a composition of the supervisory board that mitigates agency problems in order to maximize shareholder value. This gradual optimization process, therefore, leads also to a certain degree of gender diversity on the supervisory board. In this light, *Bøhren/Staubo* (2014) argue that older companies had more time to allocate an optimal gender balance on the supervisory board compared to younger companies (*Bøhren/Staubo* (2014), pp. 156–157). Consequently, older companies might be more restrictive in changing the organizational structure of their supervisory board as the composition is more entrenched and complex. In addition, since men historically dominate corporate boards, supervisory boards of older companies more frequently exhibit the "old boys' club"-phenomenon[89] (*Allemand et al.* (2022)). As a result, it may be more challenging for women to break the glass ceiling and be appointed to corporate boards (*Cotter et al.* (2001)). In this context, the age of a company might negatively affect the efficacy of GDDR.

---

[88] According to section 96 (2) sent. 1 AktG, the requirements for parity co-determination are based on the size of the company (measured by number of employees), cf. section 2.2.3.2.

[89] So-called "old-boys' networks", often referred to as "old boys' clubs", are closed groups of directors mostly dominated by men. According to social network theory, these networks can influence selection processes, favoring male candidates and consequently reducing the number of women among board directors (e.g., *Brass* (1985); *Terjesen et al.* (2009)).

In summary, on the one hand, older companies may be more integrated into society and face higher pressure of normative isomorphism. Thus, a company's age may influence the efficacy of GDDR positively. On the other hand, the institutionalized structures of older, predominantly male-dominated supervisory boards may hinder an increase in gender diversity through GDDR. Hypothesis 4 (H_4) thus postulates an undirected association:

H_4 The efficacy of GDDR on the supervisory board is associated with companies' age.

Companies face uncertainty about strategic goals and reporting practices concerning the corporate gender diversity of peer companies. The theory of **mimetic isomorphism** – as part of institutional theory – assumes that companies may align their reporting practices with the objectives of gender diversity on corporate boards with those of other companies that publish related information. To avoid reputational harm and loss of legitimacy, companies may adapt established practices concerning gender diversity in order to provide comparable information to stakeholders (e.g., investors) and meet their expectations.

Before the GDDR came into force, the GCGC (section 2.2.2) set the framework for reporting practices about corporate governance, including gender diversity, in Germany. However, the GCGC provides only a relatively broad guideline regarding companies' objectives for gender-diverse composition of corporate boards. Thus, **discretion in reporting practices** existed, creating an institutional environment afflicted with uncertainty (mimetic isomorphism).

To emphasize their willingness and sincere efforts to promote gender diversity on the supervisory board, companies can set specific targets for the proportion of women voluntarily. **Setting targets** is beneficial in achieving specific outcomes because targets direct attention and efforts toward the objectives (*Wood et al.* (2013), p. 91). Thus, setting and publishing specific targets on the gender composition of the supervisory board can contribute to increased gender diversity.

Companies that include specific targets on women's presence on supervisory boards in their disclosure may have fostered gender diversity in anticipation of GDDR. In this case, companies that report voluntarily may have addressed concerns of equal participation beforehand. Hence, GDDR and the concomitant requirement to disclose specific targets may **not change the companies' internal information set** (refer to the targeted transparency action cycle, section 2.1.2). From this company-internal perspective, GDDR have no or solely an incremental impact. That could result in GDDR being limited in efficacy.

Nevertheless, changes in the composition of the supervisory board are slow (e.g., due to existing mandates and contractual agreements) and gradual (e.g., due to single changes in board compositions for reasons of continuity). Accordingly, it may take several years before gender diversity is increased sustainably on the supervisory board. In this respect, companies that set gender diversity targets voluntarily may be harvesting the benefits after GDDR came into force. In other words, **companies can benefit from prior engagement** with corporate gender diversity and thus make greater progress after GDDR applies. This may result in increased efficacy of GDDR for companies that voluntarily set targets for corporate gender diversity beforehand. Considering the above arguments, hypothesis 5 (H_5) proposes:

H_5 *The efficacy of GDDR on the supervisory board is associated with companies' reporting practice regarding gender diversity of the supervisory board before the implementation of GDDR.*

Executive board

Within a two-tier corporate governance system, members of the executive board are not appointed directly by the shareholders. The shareholders delegate this task to the supervisory board (section 2.2.1), which determines the size of the executive board and appoints its members (*GCGC* (2022), principle 9). Therefore, the **supervisory board has the authority to determine the composition of the executive board** with regard to gender diversity. Moreover, according to the provisions of GDDR, the supervisory board is also responsible for specifying self-set targets for the proportion of women on the executive board. Overall, the supervisory board has the power to determine the gender diversity on the executive board.

According to **principal-agent theory**, there is a contracting relationship between the supervisory board and shareholders. As the agent of the principal, the supervisory board should act in the interest of the shareholders. In the context of GDDR, shareholders require the appointment of executive board members who primarily serve a value-maximizing interest. Thus, appointing a gender-diverse executive board may be of subordinate importance in the view of shareholders. To ensure adherence to their interests, shareholders can incentivize the supervisory board to make its appointment decisions geared towards value maximization. This might not prioritize fostering gender diversity at the forefront. However, conflicts may arise between shareholders and supervisory boards due to competing interests.

Considering **legitimacy theory and stakeholder theory**, companies strive for an appropriate level of legitimacy and therefore consider society's and stakeholders' expectations. Moreover, the concept of legitimacy and reputation is not limited to companies as a whole but also applies to individuals within a corporate context. Prior research finds that managers notice public attention generated by media and adjust their behavior to avoid personal reputational harm (e.g., *Dyck et al.* (2008); *Fang/Peress* (2009)). Supervisory board members of companies that face a high level of public pressure may foster gender diversity to meet external expectations and avoid negative public attention in conjunction with their names. If supervisory board members consider increased executive board gender diversity as an opportunity to improve their public perceptions, they may appoint more female board members (*Peña-Martel et al.* (2022), p. 195). However, based on the theoretical assumptions, the level of public pressure on supervisory boards has to be high enough for them to yield to it rather than act in the best interests of shareholders. Furthermore, if public pressure is so high that a company's economic performance is affected (e.g., a decrease in sales revenues due to product boycotts), it may be value-maximizing for shareholders to consider societal interests when making executive board appointment decisions. Even if shareholders require enhanced gender diversity on the executive board, additional high public pressure can encourage supervisory boards to appoint more female executive board members.

In summary, the regulatory mechanisms of GDDR may show greater efficacy if companies face a high level of public pressure. In this regard, the hypothesis 6a (H_{6a}), therefore, states:

H_{6a}	*The efficacy of GDDR on the executive board is positively associated with a high level of public pressure.*

In contrast, supervisory boards subject to a low level of public pressure may not intensify their efforts to act in the best interest of the shareholders (**principal-agent theory**). In line with **legitimacy theory and stakeholder theory**, supervisory boards subject to low public pressure may not consider gender diversity as a means to meet external expectations. Therefore, the regulatory mechanisms of GDDR are less effective in contexts with low public pressure, resulting in lower efficacy compared to companies facing average public pressure. Correspondingly, to precisely examine the role of public pressure as a determinant of GDDR efficacy, the hypothesis 6b (H_{6b}) postulates:

H_{6b}	*The efficacy of GDDR on the executive board is negatively associated with a low level of public pressure.*

Similar to the composition of supervisory boards, appointments of executive board members in listed companies are also of high interest and closely observed by society. Due to the intended increase in gender diversity on executive boards mandated by GDDR, the actions of listed companies, particularly large ones, are closely monitored (e.g., *FidAR e.V.* (2023); *Kirsch et al.* (2023b)). Compared to private companies, where changes are less closely observed, progress in **gender diversity of listed companies is more visible and transparent**. In contrast to the supervisory board, all companies are affected by GDDR on the executive board, regardless of whether they are parity co-determined (section 2.2.3.3). Thus, the mechanisms of GDDR may be more effective on the executive board in publicly listed companies than in private companies. Hypothesis 7 (H_7) therefore proposes:

H_7	*The efficacy of GDDR on the executive board is positively associated with companies' capital market orientation.*

A company's status within society is associated with its visibility and related societal expectations (legitimacy theory; institutional theory). Thus, the composition of executive boards of older companies is more often the focus of societal interests than that of younger companies. Since GDDR rely on the power of transparency, this **increased visibility may enhance regulatory efficacy**. However, despite the increased visibility, the appointment process and executive board composition are more institutionalized in older companies than they are in younger companies. Thus, similar to the mechanisms on the supervisory board, executive boards of older companies may more frequently consist of members of the "old boys club" and, hence, be less gender-diverse.

In summary, the direction of the association between companies' age and the efficacy of GDDR is unclear. Therefore, the following hypothesis 8 (H_8) postulates an undirected association:

H_8 *The efficacy of GDDR on the executive board is associated with companies' age.*

Similar to the requirements for supervisory boards, the GCGC also requires companies to consider appropriate gender diversity on the executive board even before GDDR came into force. However, the guidelines for voluntary disclosure of GCGC do not mandate companies to set specific targets for the proportion of women on the executive board. Thus, besides the broad adoption of the GCGC (e.g., *Werder/Turkali* (2015)), the reporting practices regarding gender diversity on the executive board are wide-ranging.

On the one hand, consistent with the **goal-setting concept**, supervisory boards that disclose specific and quantifiable targets for the presence of women on executive boards pay greater attention to gender diversity. Thus, companies providing more precise information may adjust their appointment processes and enhance the presence of female executive board members before they are affected by GDDR. In this case, GDDR might not trigger further increases in gender diversity on the executive board because the regulation does not enhance the company's internal information set. On the other hand, the **availability of appropriate female candidates** for executive board positions may be limited (resource dependence theory). Therefore, companies may face difficulties attracting female candidates with the required knowledge and experience even if supervisory boards are willing to appoint more women to the executive board. If the supply of female candidates is scarce, finding or developing female board members with the necessary skills can require several years. This could impede reaching the intended appointment of women to the executive board. Companies that set specific targets for executive board gender diversity voluntarily may benefit from their previous endeavors and harvest the possibility to appoint women on the executive board time-delayed. Moreover, due to the increased transparency through GDDR, companies may perceive additional incentives to appoint more gender-diverse executive boards and are therefore nudged to appoint more women.

In summary, the direction of an association between the efficacy of GDDR on the executive board and companies' voluntary gender diversity reporting practices is not clear. Therefore, hypothesis 9 (H_9) states the following association:

H_9 *The efficacy of GDDR on the executive board is associated with companies' reporting practice regarding gender diversity of the executive board before the implementation of GDDR.*

Since the supervisory board directly appoints the executive board members, it can determine its gender composition. Prior research shows that supervisory boards in Germany consist **predominantly of male members** and have almost exclusively male chairpersons (e.g., *FidAR e.V.* (2015)). Furthermore, prior research also finds that all-male supervisory boards tend to appoint primarily male executive board members due to their similarities in characteristics ("old boys' club", (*Allemand et al.* (2022))). Therefore, the presence of women on supervisory boards can determine the proportion of women for several reasons.

First, the appointment of gender-diverse supervisory boards by shareholders might indicate their interest in gender-diverse boards. Thus, gender-diverse supervisory boards might also act in the **interest of shareholders in employing gender-diverse executive boards** (principal-agent theory). Second, because women are consistently the underrepresented gender on corporate boards, female supervisory board members may support women's presence on the executive board to foster equal participation (trickle-down effect; *Gould et al.* (2018)). In the context of GDDR, female supervisory board members may promote ambitious target-setting and ensure appropriate attention to gender diversity within the company. Third, according to the concept of critical mass, a higher proportion of women on the supervisory board enhances the power of female board members (*Joecks et al.* (2013)). Hence, more women on the supervisory board may help to enforce an appropriate consideration of gender diversity on the executive board, influence the establishment of self-set targets, and monitor the progress critically. Overall, the presence of women on supervisory boards may lead to a more thorough consideration of gender diversity and ambitious target setting.

The obligation to disclose targets for the executive board is important for the efficacy of GDDR. If companies set minimal targets, they signal that they are unwilling or unable to increase gender diversity. A greater participation of women on the supervisory board may **influence target-setting behavior and appointment decisions** to foster gender diversity on the executive board. Therefore, the following hypothesis 10 (H_{10}) postulates a positive association between the proportion of women on the supervisory board and the efficacy of GDDR:

H_{10} *The efficacy of GDDR on the executive board is positively associated with the proportion of women on companies' supervisory board.*

In the German two-tier corporate governance system, supervisory board members are granted different amounts of rights. Within the supervisory board, the chairperson has, among others, the special right to cast a second vote to avoid stalemates (section 2.2.1). Accordingly, the chairperson has the power to direct corporate decisions, even in the context of gender diversity. Thus, the **chairperson's preferences and perceptions are of major importance**.

Based on the glass-ceiling phenomenon, the so-called **second glass-ceiling problem** describes the situation where women, even if they overcome the first glass-ceiling and reach the supervisory board, face restrictions to access senior positions within the board (*Bozhinov et al.* (2019), p. 387; *Nekhili/Gatfaoui* (2013), p. 228). Minority groups in the boardroom, often female board members, might be seen as tokens[90], thus having limited influence on corporate decisions (concept of critical mass (*Joecks et al.* (2013)). Therefore, in addition to the proportion of women on the supervisory board, their positions might be crucial for their impact on corporate decisions (*Panzer/Müller* (2015), p. 11).

[90] Within the concept of critical mass (*Kanter* (1977b)), a single woman or a small minority of women are referred to as tokens due to their limited influence on decisions of corporate boards (*Torchia, M. et al.* (2011)).

Because the supervisory board appoints members of the executive board, female chairpersons may be more likely to promote gender-diverse executive boards and thus influence supervisory board appointment decisions. The chairperson's position might be particularly important in the context of GDDR. Even if companies cannot actually appoint more women to the executive board (e.g., due to current and ongoing contracts), they can **commit to self-set targets to increase gender diversity in the future**. Thus, GDDR allow companies to affirm their commitment to appointing female executive board members. Consequently, hypothesis 11 (H_{11}) assumes the following relationship between female chairmanship and the efficacy of GDDR on the executive board:

H_{11}	*The efficacy of GDDR on the executive board is positively associated with female chairmanship of companies' supervisory board.*

4.2.3 Consequences of GDDR on financial reporting quality

According to the third research question (RQ3), this section derives the hypothesis to analyze the relationship between GDDR and financial reporting quality. Because GDDR aim to increase corporate gender diversity, a change in the composition of corporate boards is intended. However, against the backdrop of **principal-agent theory**, corporate governance mechanisms should ensure that companies are supervised and controlled in the best interest of their shareholders. Accordingly, shareholders seek to appoint the best possible composition of supervisory board members with the necessary qualifications, expertise, and experience (*Campbell/Mínguez-Vera* (2008), p. 435). Therefore, the composition of the supervisory board is optimized to ensure the efficient operation of the company and to mitigate agency problems.

A central task of the supervisory board is to monitor and control the executive board (*GCGC* (2022), principle 6). In particular, this includes auditing of financial statements and management reports. Regarding the **second agency relationship** in the German two-tier corporate financial system (section 4.1), members of the executive board may try to influence or manipulate corporate earnings statements to maximize their personal benefits (e.g., increasing job security or obtaining bonus payments). Thus, the supervisory board aims to detect and reveal opportunistic earnings management activities by the executive board that are not in line with shareholders' interests. Therefore, the supervisory board must ensure an appropriately high level of **financial reporting quality**.

Prior research has identified **differences in the cognitive and demographic characteristics of board members** that contribute to an increased monitoring ability of the supervisory board. Firstly, some researchers find that the accounting expertise of board members in the audit committee is associated with enhanced financial reporting quality (*Gull et al.* (2018); *Lai et al.* (2017); *Srinidhi et al.* (2011); *Thiruvadi/Huang* (2011); *Zalata et al.* (2019); for no significant association: *Sun et al.* (2011)). Moreover, other studies suggest positive associations between the impact of female board members on board independence (e.g., *Poletti-Hughes/Dimungu-Hewage* (2023)) or further corporate governance outcomes (*Abbott et al.* (2012); *Adams/Ferreira* (2009); *Cumming et al.* (2015); *Zhang* (2012)). For example, *Cumming et al.* (2015) find that more gender-diverse boards reduce the frequency of securities fraud, particularly within male-dominated industries (*Cumming et al.* (2015), pp. 1585–1588). However, various studies investigated the relationship between women on board and financial reporting quality. Depending on the setting and research methodology, most researchers find a positive association, while other studies find no or negative association between the presence of women on board and improved financial reporting quality (*Abbott et al.* (2012); *Gul et al.* (2011); *Hoang et al.* (2017); *Lai et al.* (2017); *Srinidhi et al.* (2011)).

According to **resource dependence theory**, supervisory boards may benefit from female board members. Women are found to be less likely to act unethically in business to gain personal advantage (*Betz et al.* (1989), p. 323). Additionally, under certain conditions, women are also more likely than men to report fraudulent financial reporting (*Kaplan et al.* (2009), p. 25). Furthermore, women often tend to be more risk averse, particularly in terms of financial decision-making (*Powell/Ansic* (1997), pp. 623–624) and accounting conservatism (*Francis et al.* (2015), p. 1314). Therefore, women may provide crucial resources to supervisory boards that contribute to boards monitoring abilities, enhancing detecting earnings management and, hence, increasing financial reporting quality.

However, principal-agent theorists assume that companies' **current nexus of contracts is optimal** (*Labelle et al.* (2015), p. 342). Shareholders are interested in designing contracts that avoid opportunistic behavior of managers (to minimize agency costs; section 4.1.1). Thus, the current composition of the supervisory board results from optimal appointment decisions (*Hermalin/Weisbach* (2006); *Labelle et al.* (2015), p. 342). In light of this assumption, external influences (e.g., regulatory interventions) alter the appointment processes, affecting the optimal composition of contracts.

By implementing gender diversity regulations, regulators **aim to intervene in the institutionalized appointment processes** of supervisory boards. The degree of intervention varies depending on the progressiveness and strictness (section 2.1.1) of the regulatory approach. Under voluntary approaches fostering gender diversity (e.g., through corporate governance codes, section 2.2.2), companies are not forced to change their appointment behavior and increase gender diversity. However, companies may face indirect pressure to increase female participation on the supervisory board. In this regulatory environment, studies find a positive association between increased gender diversity on corporate boards and financial reporting quality (*Abbott et al.* (2012); *Gul et al.* (2011); *Hoang et al.* (2017); *Lai et al.* (2017); *Srinidhi et al.* (2011)). These findings suggest that companies appoint female board members to add valuable resources (resource dependence theory), enhance board competency, and mitigate agency problems (principal-agent theory), leading to increased financial reporting quality.

By contrast, **mandatory gender quotas** directly intervene in appointment decisions. Such gender quotas mandate a certain degree of gender diversity. Thus, shareholders must appoint members of the underrepresented gender to meet legal obligations, potentially disregarding beneficial personal characteristics. Consequently, companies may compete for the resources of well-qualified female candidates, leading to a scarcity of suitable female candidates. Thus, companies may appoint less suitable or less qualified board members to meet legal requirements, which results in a non-optimal board composition (*Rhode/Packel*

(2014), pp. 401–402; *Labelle et al.* (2015), p. 343). Evidence from the Norwegian gender quota law indicates that the regulation results in younger and less experienced board members (*Ahern/Dittmar* (2012)). The appointment of less experienced female board members could reduce the board's monitoring abilities, thereby weakening financial reporting quality. In this context, *García Lara et al.* (2022) provide evidence that enacting a mandatory gender quota in Norway was negatively associated with the affected companies' financial reporting quality.

However, GDDR do not require companies to reach a specific degree of gender diversity and, therefore, do not directly intervene in board appointment decisions. However, compared to voluntary approaches, GDDR require more transparent and comprehensive gender diversity reporting. Due to the mechanisms of targeted transparency regulations, companies may face increased public pressure and be coerced into meeting societal expectations (legitimacy theory). Thus, companies must incorporate external expectations concerning board gender diversity to avoid reputational harm. Similar to mandatory quotas, companies change their appointment behavior in light of increased public pressure and may **nominate less qualified or less experienced board members** due to the lack of suitable female candidates. Consequently, these changed appointment decisions may lead to a non-optimal board composition in terms of qualifications, reducing the board's monitoring ability and resulting in lower financial reporting quality.

In summary, theory suggests that shareholders appoint an optimal composition of supervisory board members in the absence of gender diversity regulations. In this light, the ex-ante proportion of women on the supervisory board is optimal from a shareholder value-maximization perspective. Any external influence that leads to a change in appointment decisions must, therefore, **impair the optimal composition** of the supervisory board, resulting in a poorer financial reporting quality. GDDR do not directly affect the composition of supervisory boards. However, GDDR may indirectly alter corporate appointment decisions in response to public pressure. This leads to a non-optimal nexus of contracts and consequently weakens the supervisory board's ability to monitor and detect earnings management. Therefore, the hypothesis 12 (H_{12}) postulates:

H_{12} *Increased gender diversity on the supervisory board in the context of GDDR is negatively associated with financial reporting quality.*

5 Gender diversity and disclosure practice under GDDR

To address the first research question, this chapter illustrates the change in gender diversity at the regulated management levels in Germany (RQ1a) and presents the descriptive results of the disclosure practice in accordance with GDDR (RQ1b). Section 5.1 describes the research design, including the selection process and general characteristics of the sample companies. Section 5.2 presents the descriptive results. Section 5.3 discusses the results and concludes the findings of the chapter.

5.1 Research design

5.1.1 Content analysis fundamentals

This study utilizes a content analysis to capture the disclosure practices in response to the GDDR. Many studies in accounting research use content analysis to investigate corporate disclosure.[91] Therefore, the content analysis helps researchers to evaluate and describe gender diversity disclosure practices in a structured and standardized way. *Neuendorf* (2017) defines content analysis briefly "*as the systematic, objective, and quantitative analysis of message characteristics*" (*Neuendorf* (2017), p. 2).

This definition, as well as several other definitions of content analysis [92], mention the three characteristics: systemization, objectivity, and quantification. Systemization means the content analysis catalog is theoretically derived and coded according to specific rules to ensure reliability and validity. To achieve objectivity, the content analysis catalog should be defined so precisely that different researchers can obtain the same findings. That ensures that subjectivity concerns are minimized and that the results can be replicated. Lastly, the quantification of the collected data is crucial to allow the application of statistical tests and analysis.

The study at hand ensures that all three characteristics are taken into account. In order to achieve objectivity and avoid inconsistencies, the data collection was carried out exclusively by the author himself. This procedure is intended to prevent possible distortion by different coders and thus ensure the intersubjectivity of the data collection. After the content analysis catalog had been developed, a test coding was carried out using ten randomly selected companies. Based on this, the analysis criteria were reviewed and final adjustments were made to the catalog. The data was collected over a period of five months. After the initial data collection was completed, the first ten companies were resurveyed in order to identify any discrepancies in the assessment. No inconsistencies were found during the review.

With regard to systematization, the author defined the content analysis catalog prior to conducting the study. The items in this catalog were developed closely related with the disclosure requirements of FüPoG I and with consideration of national accounting standards governing the publication of corporate governance statements (section 2.2.3.4).

[91] For instance, the existing descriptive studies investigating disclosure practices of companies subject to the GDDR (section 3.1) utilize content analysis as primary research method.

[92] For an overview of other definitions commonly used in the literature, cf. *Kassarjian* (1977), pp. 8–9. Most of them agree that the distinctive features of a content analysis are systematization, objectivity and quantification.

As a result, most of the items refer directly to the disclosure requirements. Finally, to allow the quantification of every item, almost every item is a binary or category variable.

Structure of the content analysis catalog for GDDR

A) General information

- Company name
- Fiscal year end
- Year
- Parity co-determination
- Legal form
- Index

B) Disclosures

- Location of the corporate governance statement
- Separate section for gender diversity information required the GDDR
- Visualization of information

C) Gender diversity

- Supervisory board
  - Current composition
  - Information required by the GDDR
- Executive board
  - Current composition
  - Information required by the GDDR
- First management level below the executive board
  - Current composition
  - Information required by the GDDR
- Second management level below the executive board
  - Current composition
  - Information required by the GDDR

Figure 5-1: Structure of the content analysis catalog

The content analysis catalog is developed to gather information for two reasons. First, the development of the proportion of women in management positions should be observed (RQ1a). Second, the catalog aims to gather insights into the reporting practice of companies subject to FüPoG I (RQ1b). Therefore, the content analysis catalog consists of **three categories**: general information, disclosures, and gender diversity (Figure 5-1).[93] Firstly, the category **general information** refers to information such as the name of the company, its fiscal year-end, the reporting period, the degree of co-determination legal status, and the index. Secondly, the category **disclosure** considers information about the location of the corporate governance statement, a separate section for information required by FüPoG I, and the visualization of information. Lastly, the category **gender diversity** includes information about the current composition of all corporate hierarchy levels as well as the information about gender diversity required by FüPoG I (e.g., self-set targets). The second and third categories include the most important information on corporate gender diversity, as their items cover all information required by the GDDR. Based on this content analysis

[93] For detailed information on all 57 items of the content analysis catalog, cf. Appendix 1.

catalog, differences in disclosure practices in response to the GDDR can be evaluated. Taken both purposes together, they contribute to assessing the efficacy of GDDR.

5.1.2 Sample selection process

Germany is the subject of this following analysis, as Germany is currently the only country that has implemented a GDDR to promote corporate gender diversity. Thus, the German regulatory setting is required to gain insights into the disclosure practice and developments in corporate gender diversity among companies subject to GDDR.

The sample consists of annual reports and corporate governance statements for the fiscal years from 2014 to 2021. In line with the provisions of FüPoG I, companies were required to comply with these regulations starting June 30, 2015 (section 2.2.3.4). Consequently, corporate reports from the fiscal year 2015 onward contain the required information under FüPoG I. To assess the development of the proportion of women following the implementation of FüPoG I, the study includes data on the composition of supervisory and executive boards in the fiscal year 2014. Since the primary focus of this analysis is on the efficacy of GDDR, the sample period ends in 2021, before the implementation of FüPoG II (section 2.2.4), which introduced regulatory changes (e.g., minimum participation on executive boards).

The sample includes both publicly listed and private companies subject to parity co-determination (i.e., subject to MitbestG) to analyze differences arising from different capital market orientations. Publicly listed companies were selected based on the market capitalization of the regulated market. In Germany, the regular market comprises the DAX, MDAX, and SDAX.[94] The index compositions as of December 31, 2020, totaling 160 companies, served as the basis for this analysis. First, 13 foreign-listed companies were excluded as only companies headquartered in Germany are subject to FüPoG I. Second, annual reports[95] for the fiscal years from 2014 to 2021 were downloaded directly from the companies' websites to gather required information on corporate boards. Third, only companies continuously listed on one of the analyzed indexes throughout the sample period were included to ensure they were subject to the GDDR for the entire period. Fourth, four companies were excluded due to unavailable reports,[96] resulting in a final subsample of 114 publicly listed companies.

Additionally, the sample includes all private companies subject to parity co-determination and affected by FüPoG I. In the fifth step, 373 private companies with parity co-determination as of December 31, 2020 were identified. As many private companies do not

---

[94] The DAX includes the 40 largest listed companies, the MDAX covers the next 50 mid-cap companies, and the SDAX represents the following 70 small-cap companies. Before the index restructuring in September 2021, the DAX consisted of 30 companies. During the sample period, the size of DAX (30 companies until September 2018), MDAX (between 50 (until September 2018) and 60 (until September 2021)), and SDAX (50 until September 2018) changed multiple times.

[95] Some companies publish their corporate governance statements separately on their websites (section 2.2.3.4), rather than in their annual reports. In such cases, the corporate governance statement is downloaded in addition to the annual report.

[96] The issue of unavailable reports is discussed in detail in section 5.2.1.

provide their annual report directly on their website, the reports were downloaded from Germany's official organ of promulgation and publication (Bundesanzeiger). In the sixth step, 176 companies that were not consistently parity co-determined throughout the sample period were excluded. Four more companies are excluded for not providing reports with the required information. In the eighth step, 93 parity co-determined private companies not required to disclose information under FüPoG I (section 2.2.3.4) were removed from the sample. This results in a final subsample of 100 private companies. Combined with the 114 publicly listed companies, the final sample consists of a balanced sample of 214 companies. In total, 1,712 reports were analyzed due to the sample period of eight fiscal years. Table 5-1 summarizes the sample selection process.

Sample selection	Number of companies	Company years
Public companies		
Identification of all listed companies in DAX, MDAX, and SDAX as of December 31, 2020	160	1,280
Less foreign listed companies	-13	-104
Less companies that were not continuously represented in at least one of the stated indexes between January 1, 2015 and December 31, 2021	-29	-232
Less companies with unavailable corporate governance statements	-4	-32
Sample of listed companies	**114**	**912**
Private companies		
Identification of all private companies subject to parity co-determination as of December 31, 2020	373	2,984
Less companies that were not consistently parity co-determined between January 1, 2015 and December 31, 2021	-176	-1,408
Less companies with unavailable corporate governance statements	-4	-32
Less companies that were not required to report according to FüPoG I (e.g., according to section 264 (3) HGB)	-93	-744
Sample of private companies	**100**	**800**
Final sample of companies subject to FüPoG I	**214**	**1,712**

Table 5-1: Sample selection process

Since most publicly listed companies in the sample are subject to parity co-determination, selecting private companies under the same criteria ensures comparability regarding the supervisory board structure.[97] Furthermore, because company size (measured by the number of employees) determines whether a company is parity co-determined, the selected private companies tend to be the largest in Germany. Although structural differences in size between public and private companies cannot be entirely eliminated, this selection mitigates these differences. However, since the scope of companies subject to FüPoG I is difficult to determine (section 2.2.3.2), determining affected private companies is crucial.[98]

97 In the following, the study refers to publicly listed companies as public companies and to private companies subject to parity co-determination as private companies.

98 The annual report on the proportion of women in management, commissioned by the German Federal Government, initially struggled to identify all regulated companies in the years following FüPoG I (e.g., *Deutscher BT/BR – DIP* (2017a), BT-Drs. 18/11500).

To identify these companies, the Hans-Böckler-Stiftung[99] provided a list of all private companies subject to parity co-determination. Moreover, while the number of analyzed reports is smaller than in archival studies due to the manual data collection and evaluation (*Eckerth* (2022), p. 129), focusing on the largest public and private German companies enables a broad coverage of companies targeted by GDDR. Additionally, concentrating on the largest companies ensures comprehensive data availability through electronic databases. All publications were downloaded in German to ensure consistency. [100]

5.1.3 Sample description

Index composition and company size

Table 5-2 presents the distribution of the 100 private companies compared to 114 public companies. The distribution between private (47%) and public companies (53%) is nearly balanced. Public companies are further categorized by their index membership, showing that DAX companies constitute the smallest group (12%), while MDAX and SDAX companies each account for 21% of the sample.

In addition, the average size of the companies, measured by the average number of employees during the sample period, differs markedly between private and public companies. Private companies employ an average of 5,585 employees, whereas public companies are nearly eight times larger, with an average of 41,090 employees. Among public companies, DAX companies are the largest, with an average of 132,834 employees, followed by MDAX (20,812) and SDAX (7,155) companies. Notably, even SDAX companies, on average, exceed the size of private companies.

Sample distribution			
Subsample	**Number of: companies**	**reports**	**Share**
Private companies	100	800	47%
Public companies	114	912	53%
thereof: DAX	*26*	*208*	*12%*
thereof: MDAX	*44*	*352*	*21%*
thereof: SDAX	*44*	*352*	*21%*
Final sample of companies subject to FüPoG I	**214**	**1,712**	**100%**

Table 5-2: Sample distribution by indexes and company size

[99] The Hans-Böckler-Stiftung, part of the German Trade Union Confederation, supports co-determination, research, and academic support. It aids elected representatives in co-determination roles and advocates for extended co-determination rights. The foundation also offers financial and ideal support to students and doctoral candidates in their academic pursuits.

[100] Private companies typically publish their annual reports only in German language.

Industry composition

The industry classification is based on the "Nomenclature statistique des activités économiques dans la Communauté européenne" (NACE).[101] This European classification system is available in the Dafne database and comprises 21 industries. Figure 5-2 presents the industry classification[102] of the sample, which includes 16 different industries. The Manufacturing industry (37%) and the Professional activities industry (14%) account for more than half of the complete sample. Instead, Accommodation and food service (1%), Arts, entertainment, and recreation (1%), Other service activities (1%), Agriculture (<1%), and Public administration, and defence (<1%) account for the smallest share in the sample.

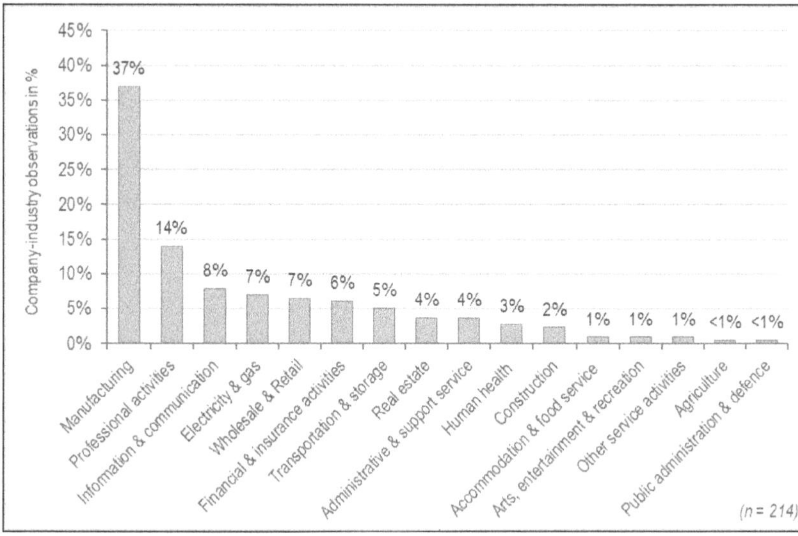

Figure 5-2: Industry composition

Regulatory approaches for the supervisory board

FüPoG I combines the two regulatory approaches of mandatory gender quotas and GDDR for the supervisory board. Because this study aims to investigate the disclosure practice, determinants, and consequences of GDDR, it is important to distinguish between both regulatory approaches. All private companies in the sample are subject to the GDDR because they are parity co-determined. In contrast, public companies are either subject to the mandatory gender quota (in the case of parity co-determination) or subject to the GDDR (in the case of non-parity co-determination). Therefore, Figure 5-3 presents the

[101] NACE is regulated by the EU, mandating the general adoption of the classification in all Member States. NACE was introduced in 1990 by Regulation (EEC) No. 3037/90. The current revision of NACE, which is used in this study, is NACE Rev. 2.

[102] Note that the official designation of the NACE Rev. 2 industry classification is partly shortened to ensure a compact illustration.

proportion of public companies subject to each regulation and shows further the proportion within different indexes.

In 459 out of 798 company-year observations, public companies are subject to the mandatory gender quota.[103] While nearly all companies listed on the DAX (in 161 out of 182 company-year observations) have to appoint 30% women to their supervisory board, companies of the MDAX (in 168 out of 308 company-year observations) and SDAX (in 130 out of 308 company-year observations) are less frequent subject to the mandatory gender quota. The varying size of the companies is the reason for the uneven application of GDDR. Smaller companies – listed on the MDAX and SDAX – are less frequently subject to parity co-determination due to their fewer employees. Therefore, these smaller companies are more often subject to the GDDR on the supervisory board.

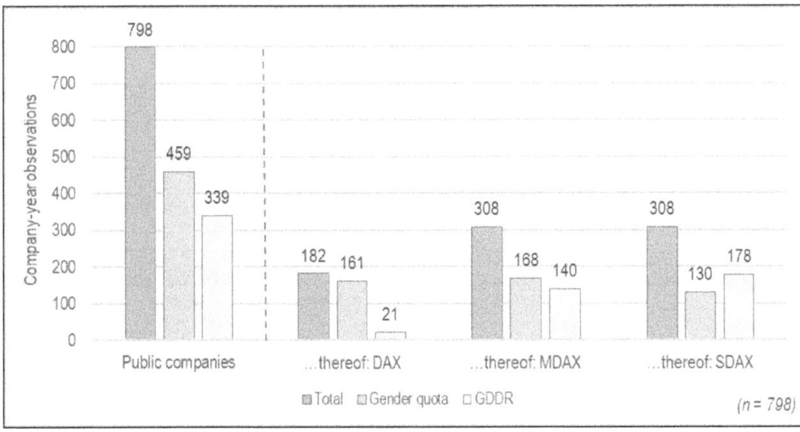

Figure 5-3: Regulatory approaches on the supervisory board

Supervisory board size

When investigating whether the regulation of FüPoG I shapes board gender diversity, it is essential to consider the corporate board size of the sample companies. Focusing on public companies, those listed on the DAX have larger supervisory boards (mean: 16.01; median: 16) compared to those listed on the MDAX (mean: 11.24; median: 12) and SDAX (mean: 9.10; median: 7.5). This suggests that the average supervisory board size decreases with the average company size. This trend is influenced by Germany's co-determination regulations, which require larger companies with more employees to have larger supervisory boards.

---

103 Note, that during the sample period, three companies (CompuGroup Medical SE & Co. KGaA, Indus Holding AG, Ströer SE & Co. KGaA) were subject to changes in the co-determination regulations on the supervisory board. These companies were not initially parity co-determined at the beginning of the period but were subsequently covered by MitbestG due to an increase in employees or court decisions. Accordingly, these companies were not initially affected by the mandatory gender quotas, but were affected to a later point of time.

Table 5-3 provides the supervisory board size of the sample companies. On average, supervisory boards have 12.62 members (mean), with a median of 12 members. The smallest supervisory boards consist of three members while the largest count 21 members. *Bozhinov et al.* (2021) report an average supervisory board size of 13.48 members for German public companies (*Bozhinov et al.* (2021), p. 1322). Additionally, the supervisory boards of companies subject to the GDDR are generally smaller (mean: 11.60; median: 12) than those affected by the mandatory gender quota (mean: 15.43; median: 16). This difference is largely due to the smaller average number of employees in companies regulated by the GDDR.

Furthermore, private companies (mean: 14.21; median: 12) appoint, on average, more members to the supervisory board compared to public companies (mean: 11.50; median; 12). All private companies of the sample are parity co-determined and, therefore, have to appoint at least 12 members to the supervisory board. By contrast, the supervisory boards of public companies can consist of less than 12 members if the company is not parity co-determined.

Among public companies, those listed on the DAX have larger supervisory boards (mean: 16.01; median: 16) compared to companies listed on the MDAX (mean: 11.24; median: 12) and SDAX (mean: 9.10; median: 7.5). This suggests that the average supervisory board size decreases with the average company size. This trend is influenced by Germany's co-determination regulations, which require larger companies with more employees to have larger supervisory boards.

	Supervisory board size							
Sample	**n**	**Mean**	**Std. dev.**	**Min.**	**Q25**	**Median**	**Q75**	**Max.**
Full sample	1,712	12.62	4.80	3	12	12.00	16	21
Type of regulatory interventions								
Quota companies	523	15.43	3.42	11	12	16.00	20	21
GDDR companies	1,189	11.60	4.83	3	6	12.00	12	20
Capital market orientation								
Private companies	800	14.21	3.26	6	12	12.00	16	20
Public comapnies	912	11.50	4.80	3	12	12.00	16	21
thereof: DAX	*208*	*16.01*	*4.41*	*5*	*12*	*16.00*	*20*	*20*
thereof: MDAX	*352*	*11.24*	*5.20*	*3*	*6*	*12.00*	*16*	*20*
thereof: SDAX	*352*	*9.10*	*4.70*	*3*	*6*	*7.50*	*16*	*21*

Table 5-3: Supervisory board size

Additionally, Figure 5-4 provides further information on the most frequent supervisory board size. Most companies constitute a supervisory board of 12, 20, 16, six, three, or nine members. With respect to the legal requirements for the size of a parity co-determined supervisory board (section 2.2.1), 20, 16, and 12 members are the proposed number of members. Supervisory boards consisting of nine, six, or three members usually arise from the co-determination provisions of DrittelbG. The other supervisory board sizes result from temporary vacancies (e.g., due to unplanned retirements) or company-specific characteristics (e.g., honorary chairmanship).

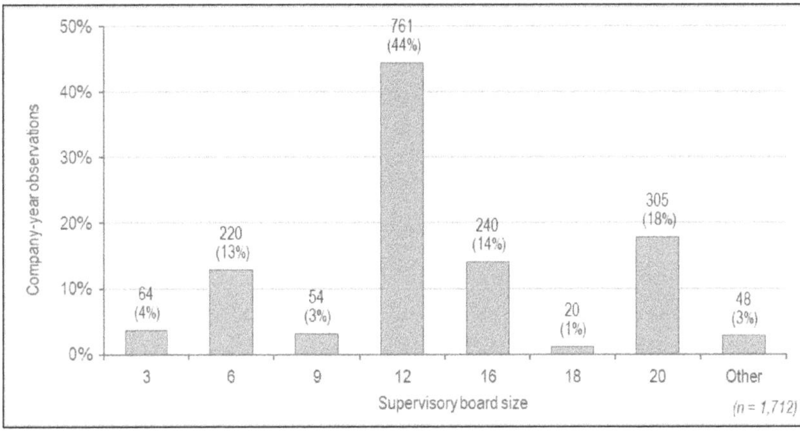

Figure 5-4: Frequency of supervisory board size

Executive board size

Due to FüPoG I, all sample companies are subject to the GDDR on the executive board. For the full sample,[104] findings indicate that companies appoint an average of 3.94 members (mean) with a median of 4 members to the executive board. The analysis of the size of executive boards indicates a difference between private and public companies. The executive boards of public companies (mean: 4.39) are slightly larger than those of private companies (mean: 3.48). However, the range of private companies' executive board size is broader (min: 1; max: 13) compared to public companies (min: 2; max: 10). On average, the executive boards of DAX companies consist of 6.72 members (mean) and are therefore larger than those of MDAX (mean: 3.93) and SDAX companies (mean: 3.56). Hence, the size of the executive boards is positively associated with company size.

	Executive board size							
Sample	**n**	**Mean**	**Std. dev.**	**Min.**	**Q25**	**Median**	**Q75**	**Max.**
Full sample	1,608	3.94	1.87	1	3	4.00	5	13
Private companies	800	3.48	1.70	1	2	3.00	4	13
Public companies	808	4.39	1.85	2	3	3.00	5	10
thereof: DAX	*176*	*6.72*	*2.05*	*2*	*5*	*7.00*	*5*	*10*
thereof: MDAX	*320*	*3.93*	*1.30*	*2*	*3*	*4.00*	*5*	*8*
thereof: SDAX	*312*	*3.56*	*1.23*	*2*	*3*	*3.00*	*4*	*7*

Table 5-4: Executive board size

Figure 5-5 illustrates that, in contrast to supervisory boards, the frequency of executive board sizes is more dispersed. Over 70% of the executive boards consist of three (28%),

[104] Note the smaller sample size of 1,608 company-year observations. The reduced sample size results from the exclusion of companies that are organized as KGaA, because this legal form does not provide for an executive board.

four (23%) or two (21%) members. Thus, a gradual increase in gender diversity on the executive board is not possible for the majority of the companies in the sample. In particular, for companies with a board of two members, only a quota of 50% is conceivable unless they aim for a gender-uniform executive board (section 2.2.3.4). In rare cases, executive boards consist of more than eight members (other: 4%).

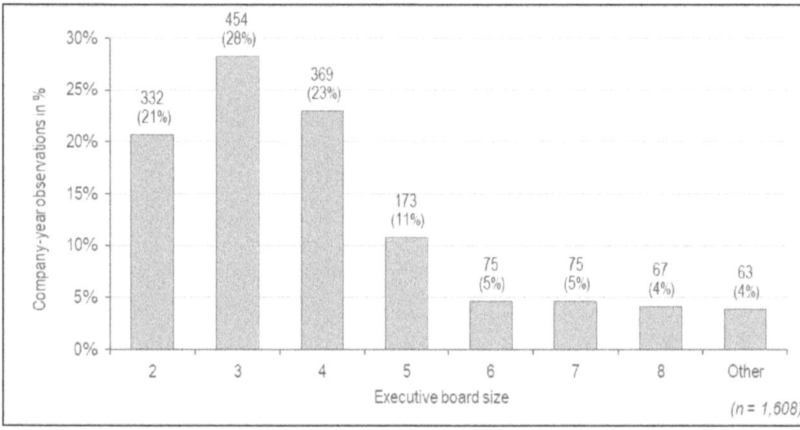

Figure 5-5: Frequency of executive board size

5.2 Results

This section presents the results of the descriptive analyses. Before evaluating whether GDDR shape the proportion of women in management positions (RQ1a), the compliance of companies with the disclosure requirements and the publication options they choose are examined. Subsequently, the disclosure practices are presented in detail (RQ1b).

5.2.1 Compliance with disclosure requirements

Availability of corporate governance statements

GDDR rely on transparency and the power of information. Therefore, compliance with the disclosure requirements is crucial to ensure the regulatory mechanisms of GDDR. First and foremost, users of gender diversity information must be able to access the disclosures (section 2.1.2). Therefore, it is remarkable that eight companies are excluded from the sample (see Table 5-1) because **no or not all corporate governance statements are available**. Disclosures are missing for both public companies (four companies) and private companies (four companies). Furthermore, five companies made the required reports available only upon request by the author.

To disclose the required information, FüPoG I provides two options: the integration within the management report or a separate publication on company's website (section 2.2.3.4). In line with these legal requirements, a considerable proportion of companies **opt to publish the corporate governance statement separately** on their website (Figure 5-10).

However, separately published corporate governance statements of 13 companies could not be retrieved during the data collection process. In order to rule out technical problems or human failure, written inquiries were sent to all affected companies.

In five out of these 13 cases, the companies provided the corporate governance statements on request. However, in the remaining eight out of 13 missing corporate governance statements, the companies were **unable or unwilling to provide the corporate governance statement** for the relevant fiscal years. Of these eight companies, four are listed, and four are private companies. Two of these private companies, both subsidiaries of a parent company that is also subject to the legal requirements of FüPoG I, stated that their gender diversity disclosures were included in the parent company's corporate governance statement. Lastly, two private companies did not provide any information on the availability of the corporate governance statement and did not respond to the researcher's multiple requests for information. On the contrary, all four public companies with unavailable reports respond to the researcher's request. However, all four companies stated that they either do not provide the requested information or, while they provide current information, can no longer make reports from past periods available. In total, 214 companies made their corporate governance statements available for the entire sample period.

Completeness of disclosed information

An assessment of the available reports published to meet the **disclosure requirements of FüPoG I** is necessary to determine whether the disclosed information is complete and in line with regulatory requirements. The information required by FüPoG I aims to inform a broad audience and, thereby, ensure the proper functioning of GDDR. Thus, companies need to disclose all the information regarding their gender diversity targets required by FüPoG I to make it accessible to report users. The information published by *Brenntag AG* provides an example[105] of a disclosure that complies with the requirements of FüPoG I:

> "*In accordance with Section 76, para. 4 and Section 111, para. 5 of the German Stock Corporation Act, Brenntag AG is required to set targets for the percentage of women on the Supervisory Board, Board of Management and on the first two management levels below the Board of Management. By resolution passed in September 2015, the Supervisory Board set the target for the percentage of women on the Supervisory Board at 33.3% and the target for the percentage of women on the Board of Management at 0% in the period up to June 30, 2017. By resolution passed in September 2015, the Board of Management set a target of 30% for the percentage of women on the only management level in the company below the Board of Management in the period up to June 30, 2017.*"
>
> (*Brenntag AG* (2016), p. 34)

This statement **meets all disclosure requirements**. *Brenntag AG* discloses self-set targets for the proportion of women and a target achievement period for each hierarchy level

[105] Note that *Brenntag AG* is a publicly listed company that is not parity co-determined. Therefore, the GDDR also applies on supervisory board (section 2.2.3.2). Moreover, *Brenntag AG* states that its organization consists of only one management level below the executive board. Accordingly, the company only discloses information for the first management level below the executive board.

targeted by the requirements of FüPoG I. However, not all analyzed reports contain information sufficient to meet the disclosure requirements.

Figure 5-6 presents the completeness of the disclosed information. Overall, nearly four-fifths (78%) of the reports are in line with the disclosure requirements. However, **more than one-fifth** (22%) of the reports **does not contain all information** required by the GDDR. Therefore, these reports are not in line with the legal disclosure regulation stipulated by FüPoG I.

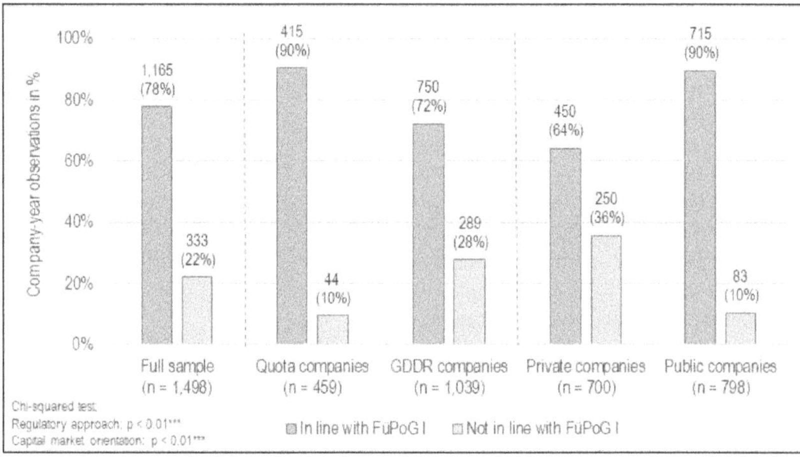

Figure 5-6: Compliance with GDDR disclosure requirements

Going into more detail, the results reveal **differences in compliance** due to the regulatory approach applied to the supervisory board and companies' capital market orientation. Companies forced by law to constitute a supervisory board comprising at least 30% women or men meet the disclosure requirements in 90% of the reports. By contrast, only 72% of the reports published by companies subject to the GDDR on all hierarchy levels comply with the disclosure requirements. Thus, companies regulated by the mandatory gender quota less frequently infringe the reporting requirements of FüPoG I.

Moreover, public companies listed on the stock exchange also disclose the required information in 90% of their reports. In comparison, the results show that **private companies meet the disclosure requirements** solely in **less than two-thirds** (64%) of the reports. Reversely, the results reveal that private companies do not comply with the legally binding disclosure requirements in more than one out of three (36%) reports. The results from a Chi-squared test[106] are statistically significant at the 1% level, thus confirming the differences observed between the groups within the subsamples.

The sample of public companies is divided into the three indexes to evaluate differences in compliance with disclosure requirements depending on company size (Figure 5-7). The large companies listed on the DAX only account for 1% of the 83 reports of public companies that are not in line with FüPoG I. By contrast, 41% of the reports with missing information are attributed to the MDAX companies. Further, the small companies of the SDAX publish most of the non-compliant reports (58%). Accordingly, the results indicate that **compliance** with reporting requirements among public companies **tends to decrease with decreasing company size**. Additionally, the results of a Chi-squared test indicate that the differences between indexes are statistically significant at the 1% level.

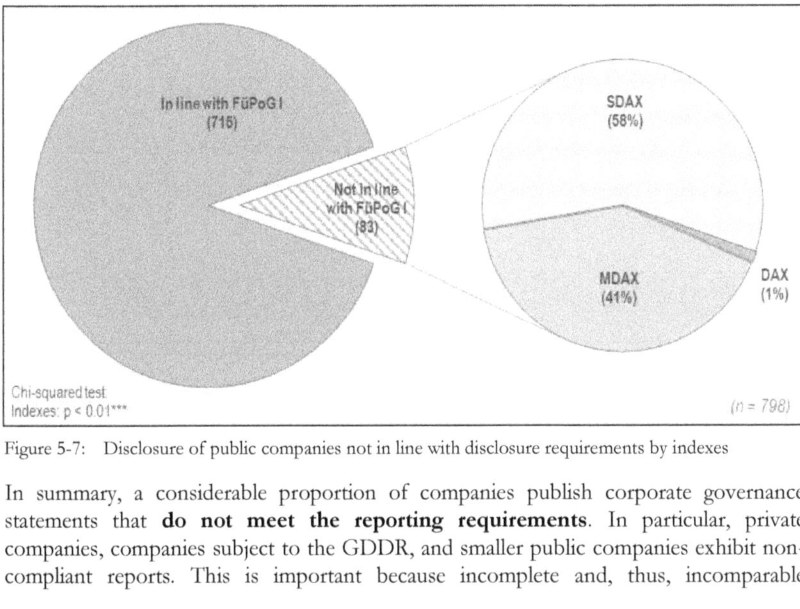

Figure 5-7: Disclosure of public companies not in line with disclosure requirements by indexes

In summary, a considerable proportion of companies publish corporate governance statements that **do not meet the reporting requirements**. In particular, private companies, companies subject to the GDDR, and smaller public companies exhibit non-compliant reports. This is important because incomplete and, thus, incomparable

106 The Chi-squared test is a statistical test used to determine whether there is a significant association between categorical variables (*Pearson* (1900)). The Chi-squared test is non-parametric that, unlike parametric tests, does not require assumptions about the normal distribution of variables (*McHugh* (2013), p. 143). It is applicable to data measured on a nominal scale and can be used to test for independence in contingency tables (*Agresti* (2013), p. 70). In the context of this study, the test evaluates whether the observed frequencies of categories deviate significantly from the expected frequencies under the null hypothesis, which posits no association between the variables (*Auer/Rottmann* (2020), pp. 104–105). If the p-value is below a chosen significance level, the null hypothesis is rejected, indicating a statistically significant relationship between the variables (*Büning/Trenkler* (1994), pp. 75–76). However, the Chi-squared test does not provide information on the strength or direction of the association. Moreover, if the expected frequencies are less than 10, the test yields inaccurate results. (*Bortz/Schuster* (2016), p. 159; *Büning/Trenkler* (1994), p. 227). In these cases, the study applies the Fisher Exact test.

information undermines transparency. Since GDDR primarily rely on the power of information (section 2.1.2), incomplete disclosure may affect the efficacy of the regulation and, thereby, impede the fostering of gender diversity.

Since FüPoG I requests a bunch of information due to corporate gender diversity targets, there can be **many causes for incomplete reports**. Firstly, companies may publish a corporate governance statement in accordance with section 289f HGB but do not include information on gender diversity required by FüPoG I. Figure 5-8 provides information about these 59 corporate governance statements, divided into multiple subsamples.

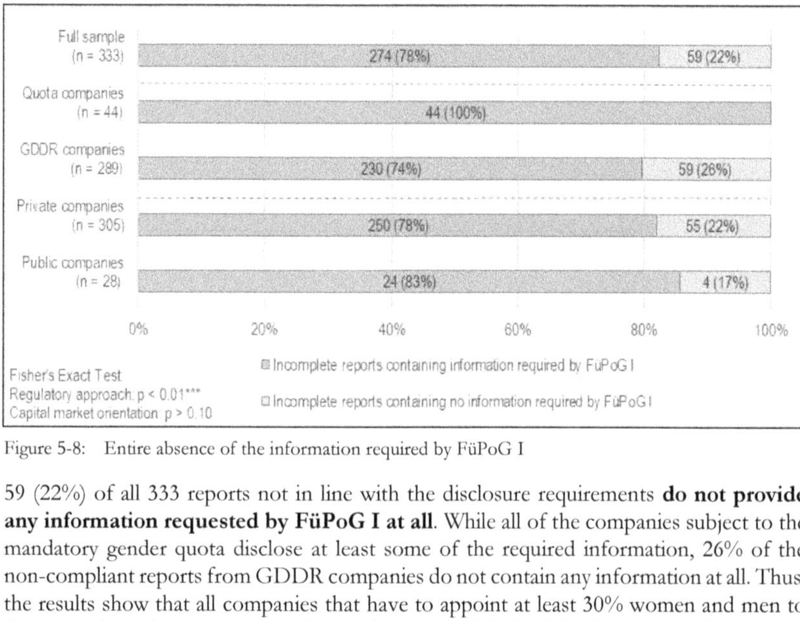

Figure 5-8: Entire absence of the information required by FüPoG I

59 (22%) of all 333 reports not in line with the disclosure requirements **do not provide any information requested by FüPoG I at all**. While all of the companies subject to the mandatory gender quota disclose at least some of the required information, 26% of the non-compliant reports from GDDR companies do not contain any information at all. Thus, the results show that all companies that have to appoint at least 30% women and men to the supervisory board mention the requirements of FüPoG I. The results of a Fisher's Exact Test[107] report a statistically significant difference at the 1% level and hence support the observations. Considering the capital market orientation of the companies, slight differences in compliance occur. While only four reports (17%) of public companies do not contain any information in the context of FüPoG I, private companies publish 55 reports (22%) that do not provide any required information. Despite the absolutely higher proportion of reports not being in line with FüPoG I, private companies more frequently

[107] Due to the low expected frequencies (<10), the Chi-squared test is not reliable (*Bortz/Schuster* (2016), p. 159), so Fisher's Exact Test is applied instead *Büning/Trenkler* (1994), p. 228. Fisher's Exact Test is a non-parametric test used to determine the significance of the association between two categorical variables in contingency tables, especially when sample sizes are small (*Fisher* (1935)). Unlike the Chi-squared test, it provides an exact p-value without relying on large-sample approximations, making it more accurate for small or unbalanced datasets (*Agresti* (2013), pp. 108–109).

ignore the disclosure requirements completely. However, a Fisher's Exact Test does not indicate statistically significant differences between private and public companies. Due to only four reports of public companies that do not contain any content, a further investigation considering the company size is not performed.

Furthermore, Figure 5-9 presents the **explanations provided for non-compliance** in the corporate governance statements (274 reports) that do not fully comply with the requirements of FüPoG I but still include some of the required information. In many cases, companies fail to provide information at the first management level (61%), target achievement periods (60%), or information at the second management level (54%). The missing information on the management level can include details on self-set targets, the target achievement periods, or the actual target achievement. Moreover, missing target achievement periods can arise on all targeted hierarchy levels. On the executive board (52%) and supervisory board (48%), the information provided by the companies is incomplete in fewer cases. Lastly, in some reports, companies do not separate the two management levels or do not state separate targets for each management level. However, a separate definition of self-set targets and target achievement periods is required by FüPoG I.

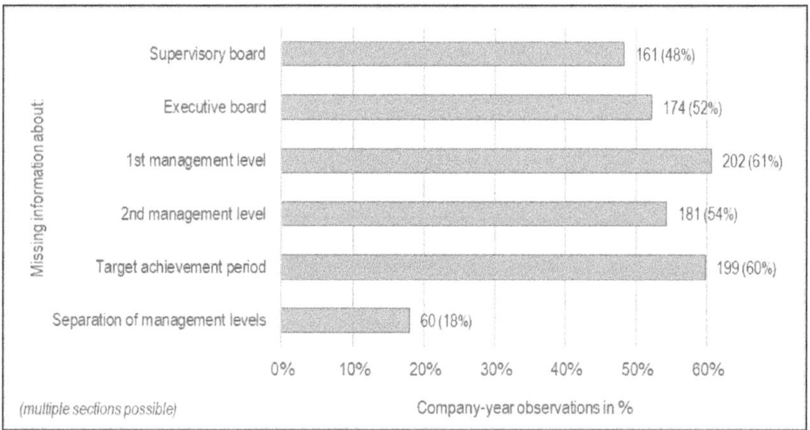

Figure 5-9: Explanations for non-compliance with disclosure requirements

5.2.2 Disclosure practices

The GDDR provides companies with certain options and **leeway in fulfilling the disclosure requirements**. Firstly, public companies subject to section 289f HGB have the option to choose between publishing the corporate governance statement within the management report or disclosing the report separately on the company's website.[108] Figure 5-10 illustrates which publication option the sample companies choose. Overall, the

[108] Note that private companies are not subject to section 289f HGB and therefore do not have a publication option. Private companies need to include the information required by FüPoG I in their management report (section 2.2.3.4).

majority of companies (87%) integrate the corporate governance statements, and therefore the information required by the GDDR, into their management reports.

Additionally, some **differences** appear between the groups of companies based on the **regulatory approach** on the supervisory board. Most companies (90%) subject to the mandatory gender quota include the corporate governance statement in the management report, whereas companies entirely subject to the GDDR do so only in roughly four out of five reports (79%). The results of a Chi-squared test report that the difference is statistically significant at the 1% level.

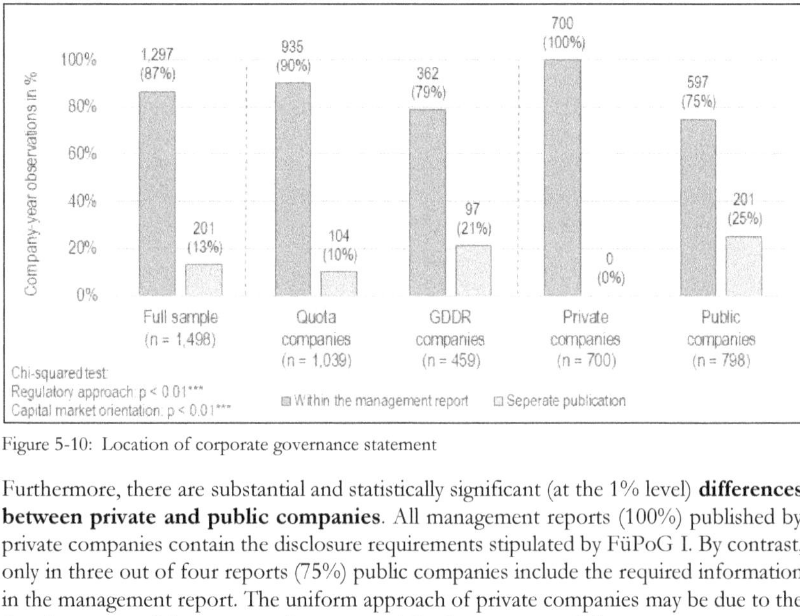

Figure 5-10: Location of corporate governance statement

Furthermore, there are substantial and statistically significant (at the 1% level) **differences between private and public companies**. All management reports (100%) published by private companies contain the disclosure requirements stipulated by FüPoG I. By contrast, only in three out of four reports (75%) public companies include the required information in the management report. The uniform approach of private companies may be due to the fact that many of these companies are not obliged to prepare a full corporate governance statement. In these cases, they only have to supplement the management report with the information required by FüPoG I. In addition, unlike public companies, private companies often do not offer financial reports for download on their websites. Integration into the management report is therefore obvious.

The **choice of publication location** may **influence the report's visibility** for users.[109] If integrated into the management report, the information on gender diversity could also be perceived by users who read the management report for other reasons. If the corporate

[109] The placement of information in reports can influence the perception of the report users. For instance, non-professional users of financial reports typically follow a sequential reading strategy, evaluating the information in the order in which it is presented (*Meinhövel/Schaumann* (2021), p. 38). For insights into the differences in the decision-making processes between experienced and non-experienced report users, cf. *Bouwman* (1984), p. 326.

governance statement is published separately, the report must be searched for and downloaded accordingly. It can be assumed that this will not be done by private stakeholders but primarily by professional investors or professionally organized stakeholder groups.

Moreover, embedding gender diversity information required by the GDDR may vary among sample companies. There is **no legal obligation** that determines how companies have to integrate the information into their corporate report. Basically, companies can dedicate information required by the GDDR to a separate section or integrate it into other sections. A report is classified as a separate section if the information is separated from other text passages and includes a corresponding heading. Figure 5-11 shows how many reports integrate gender diversity information without a separate heading and how often a distinct section is provided. Overall, **in more than three of four reports (77%), the information** required by the GDDR is published in a **separate section**. Even considering the subsamples, the option of a separate section predominates within both subsamples. Considering the regulatory approach, 80% of companies affected by the mandatory gender quota and 76% of the GDDR companies publish the information in a separate section. A Chi-squared test reports a statistically insignificant result.

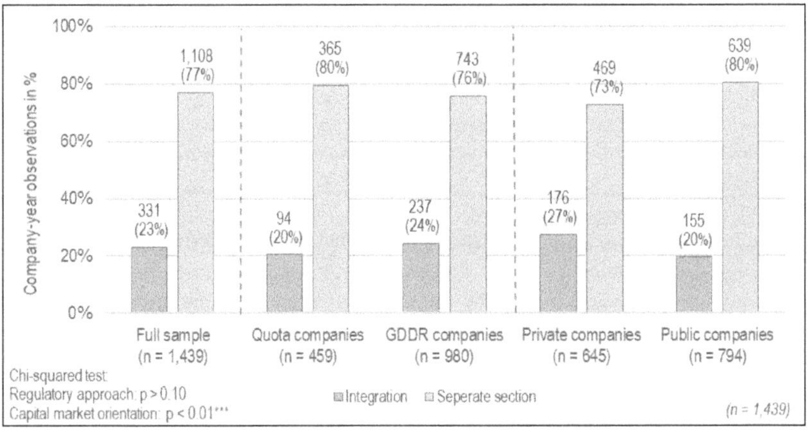

Figure 5-11: Integration of gender diversity information into corporate reports

By contrast, the subsample referring to companies' capital market orientation reveals slightly larger differences. While 73% of private companies publish the information required by the GDDR in a separate section, 80% of the public companies use this disclosure option. The results of a Chi-squared test reveal that the differences between private and public companies are statistically significant at the 1% level. However, embedding the diversity-specific information in a separate section may lead to better accessibility and higher visibility due to the concentrated format.

5.2.3 Development of the proportion of women in management positions

This section provides the results for the analysis of the **proportion of women on corporate hierarchy levels** targeted by the obligations of FüPoG I, thereby addressing RQ1a. Since mandatory gender quotas and GDDR aim to foster gender diversity, the change in the proportion of women on each hierarchy level is a crucial indicator of the impact of the regulatory approach. The results are presented separately for each corporate hierarchy level.

5.2.3.1 Supervisory board

Participation of women on supervisory board

For the full sample, the **presence of women on supervisory boards increases constantly** between 2014 and 2021 (Figure 5-12).[110] In 2014, before the introduction of a gender diversity regulation[111], women accounted for roughly every fifth (20%) seat on a supervisory board. The proportion of women has increased continuously since the implementation of FüPoG I. In 2021, almost one-third (32%) of supervisory board members were female. However, shareholder and employee representatives do not evenly contribute to the overall increase. In 2014, the presence of women among shareholder representatives (17%) was notably lower than employee representatives (23%). Every year of the sample period, the proportion of women increases among both groups of representatives. In 2021, the proportion of women among representatives elected by shareholders (31%) has caught up but is still below the proportion of employee representatives (32%). Thus, despite the converging development, employee representatives contribute more to gender-diverse supervisory boards than shareholder representatives.

In addition, the **different regulatory approaches** on the supervisory board indicate different developments in the presence of women (Figure 5-12). In 2014, companies subject to the mandatory gender quota (22%) appointed more women to their supervisory boards compared to companies affected by the GDDR (19%). With the implementation of FüPoG I in 2015, the presence of women among quota companies increased at a comparatively rapid rate. In 2017, the proportion of women on supervisory boards reached 31%, meeting the legally defined quota of 30% on average. In the subsequent years, the average proportion of women continuously increased and substantially exceeded the required minimum of 30%. Although the companies are not forced to increase gender diversity beyond the threshold of 30% by law, the proportion of women reached over 36% in 2021.

---

[110] For a tabular overview of the development of the proportion of women on the supervisory board during the sample period, cf. Appendix 2. The table contains percentages with two decimal places. Decimal places are omitted in the figures (Figure 5-12 and Figure 5-13) for reasons of clarity. In addition, Appendix 2 contains a breakdown of each subsample by shareholder and employee representatives.

[111] Note that gender diversity regulation includes mandatory gender quota and GDDR.

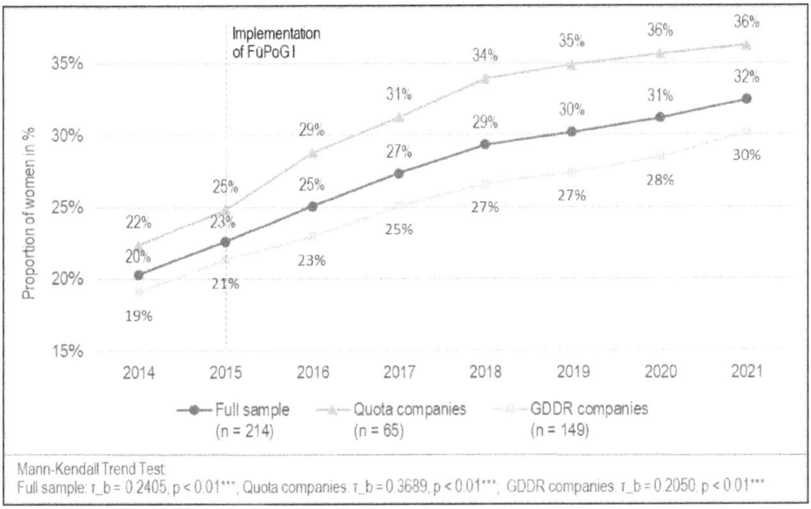

Figure 5-12: Development of the proportion of women on supervisory boards by regulatory approaches

GDDR companies also constantly increased the proportion of women on supervisory boards between 2014 (19%) and 2021 (30%), but at a lower level than the quota companies. Moreover, compared to companies affected by the mandatory gender quota, the increase is more gradual with the implementation of FüPoG I in 2015. However, the companies affected by the GDDR elect steadily more female board members in the following years, reaching 30% in 2021. Therefore, on average, GDDR companies would also comply with the mandatory gender quota of 30% since 2021, even if they are not legally required to enhance gender diversity of their supervisory boards. Results of a Mann-Kendall Trend Test[112] indicate a positive and strong statistically significant trend for both regulatory approaches in the presence of female supervisory board members. Consequently, **both regulatory approaches result in the level of female participation intended by the regulator**. Nevertheless, the increase caused by the mandatory gender quota is faster and results, on average, in an overfulfillment.

Furthermore, depending on the regulatory approach, shareholder and employee representatives contribute to a considerably different extent to the increased gender

[112] The Mann-Kendall Trend Test is a non-parametric test used to detect trends in time series data (*Mann* (1945); *Kendall* (1975)). This test does not require the data to be normally distributed, making it ideal for analyzing trends in continuous data (*Hirsch et al.* (1982), p. 110). The Mann-Kendall Trend Test is particularly useful when assessing whether there is a significant upward or downward trend over time (*Hirsch et al.* (1982), p. 111). Instead of focusing on the magnitude of changes, it determines the consistency of the trend direction across the time series. The trend is quantified using Kendall's Tau-b (τ_b), which adjusts for tied ranks in the data, providing a more accurate measure of association for continuous variables (*Kendall* (1975), pp. 53–55). Tau-b values range from -1 to 1, where values near -1 indicate a strong negative trend, values near 1 indicate a strong positive trend, and values around 0 suggest no trend (*Agresti* (2010), pp. 188–189).

diversity. Whereas **shareholder representatives account for fewer female board members** within the companies affected by the mandatory gender quota, they roughly comprise the same proportion of women as employee representatives within GDDR companies. Thus, in GDDR companies, both representative groups tend to contribute equally to more gender-diverse supervisory boards.

Private and public companies also exhibit differences in the development of the proportion of women on supervisory boards (Figure 5-13). Starting from an identical proportion in 2014 (20% for private companies; 20% for public companies), the presence of female supervisory board members has developed slightly differently. While private companies reached a participation of women of 31% in 2021, **public companies exceeded the level of private companies** and staffed more than every third seat (34%) with a woman. Even if gender diversity of private companies lags behind that of public companies, both values are above the quota of 30% intended by the regulator.

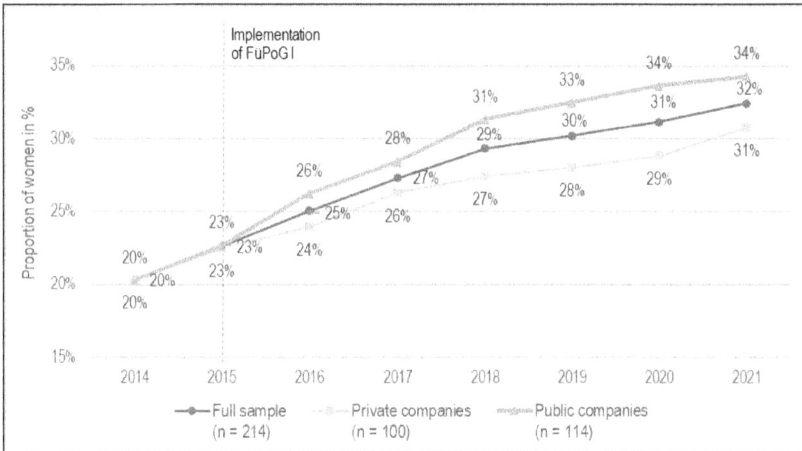

Mann-Kendall Trend Test
Full sample: $\tau_b = 0.2405$, $p < 0.01$***; Private companies: $\tau_b = 0.1947$, $p < 0.01$***; Public companies: $\tau_b = 0.2867$, $p < 0.01$***

Figure 5-13: Development of the proportion of women on supervisory boards by capital market orientation

Concerning the distribution of women between shareholder and employee representatives, there are considerable differences between private and public companies. Although employee representatives (27%; 29% for shareholder representatives in 2021) contribute slightly less to the presence of women in private companies, the overall level is comparable. In public companies, however, employee representatives (38% in 2021) account for a noticeably larger share of female supervisory board members compared to shareholder representatives (32% in 2021). Consequently, the results indicate that in public companies, **employee representatives contribute more to the increase in the proportion of**

women.[113] In contrast, the participation of both groups of representatives in private companies is more balanced.

Participation of women in supervisory board chairs

The chairperson of the supervisory board holds a **particularly important position** within the supervisory board - not least because of the right to a second vote in stalemate situations (section 2.2.1). Therefore, the chairperson of the supervisory board has a crucial role in promoting gender diversity within the company.

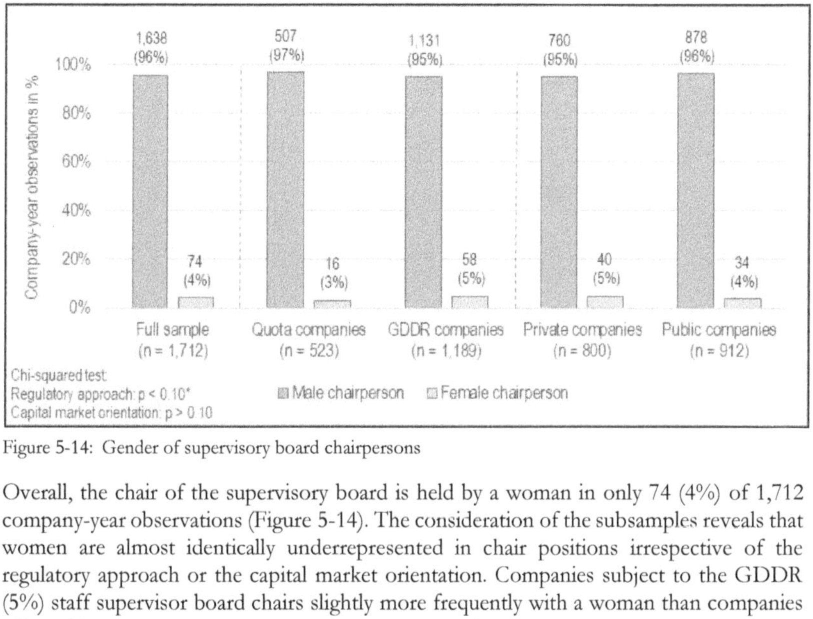

Figure 5-14: Gender of supervisory board chairpersons

Overall, the chair of the supervisory board is held by a woman in only 74 (4%) of 1,712 company-year observations (Figure 5-14). The consideration of the subsamples reveals that women are almost identically underrepresented in chair positions irrespective of the regulatory approach or the capital market orientation. Companies subject to the GDDR (5%) staff supervisor board chairs slightly more frequently with a woman than companies affected by the quota regulation (3%). No substantial differences are observable between private (5%) and public companies (4%). Although the proportion differs slightly between the groups of companies, it remains at a low level for all of them. Thus, the chairs of supervisory boards are strongly male-dominated. Consequently, **women are seen to be elected** as chairperson of the supervisory board **only in rare cases**. The results of a Chi-squared test support the observation of solely slight differences within the subsamples. The difference within the regulatory approach subsample is marginally statistically significant at the 10% level, whereas the difference within the capital market orientation subsample is statistically insignificant.

113 An additional analysis of public companies by company size (i.e., by indexes) is not performed, as public companies are affected by different regulatory approaches. The consideration of regulatory approaches leads to very small groups of companies (e.g., only three companies listed on the DAX are affected by the GDDR on the supervisory board) that skew the analysis results.

Figure 5-15 visualizes the percentage of female supervisory board chairpersonship throughout the sample period to shed light on the development in female participation at supervisory board chairs. There are no noticeable differences between the subsamples, so the analysis is based on the full sample. In the first two years after the implementation of FüPoG I, the number of female supervisory board chairs declined from eight (3.74%) in 2014 to six (2.80%) in 2015 and 2016. In subsequent years, the share of female chairpersons grew yearly between 2017 (eight chairs (3.74%)) and 2020 (14 chairs (6.54%)). However, in 2021 (11 chairs (5.14%)), the share dropped by 1.40 percentage points (three female chairs). The low absolute number of female supervisory board chairs demonstrates that individual observations can impact the average. However, the **linear trendline indicates a moderate increase in the chairs held by women** over time. On average, the share of supervisory board chairs that are held by women increases yearly by about 0.45 percentage points (Figure 5-15).

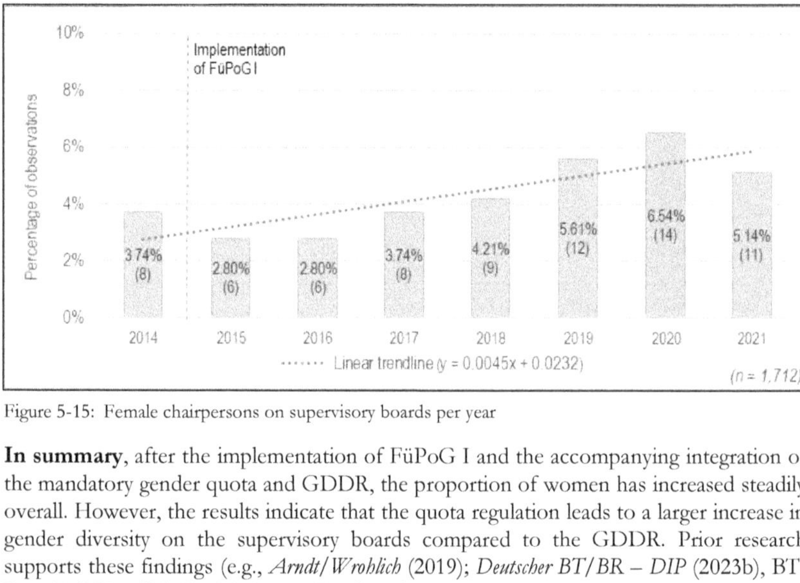

Figure 5-15: Female chairpersons on supervisory boards per year

In summary, after the implementation of FüPoG I and the accompanying integration of the mandatory gender quota and GDDR, the proportion of women has increased steadily overall. However, the results indicate that the quota regulation leads to a larger increase in gender diversity on the supervisory boards compared to the GDDR. Prior research supports these findings (e.g., *Arndt/Wrohlich* (2019); *Deutscher BT/BR – DIP* (2023b), BT-Drs. 20/9850; *FidAR e.V.* (2022); *Kirsch et al.* (2022b)). Besides the overall larger increase, the findings reveal that companies subject to the mandatory gender quota increase the proportion of women on supervisory boards more rapidly compared to companies subject to the GDDR. Furthermore, public companies tend to staff more gender-diverse supervisory boards than private companies (similar findings: e.g., *Deutscher BT/BR – DIP* (2023b), BT-Drs. 20/9850). However, overall, employee representatives account for a higher proportion of women than shareholder representatives. This is particularly true for public companies and companies subject to the mandatory gender quota (similar findings: e.g., *FidAR e.V.* (2022)). Despite the increasing proportion of women on supervisory boards in general, the results portend that supervisory board chairs are still heavily male-dominated (similar findings for public companies: e.g., *FidAR e.V.* (2022)). The presence of women in these positions increases over time but still remains in a low single-digit percentage range.

5.2.3.2 Executive board

Participation of women on executive boards

This section analyzes the development of the **proportion of women on executive boards**. Due to the legal requirements of FüPoG I, all companies are affected by the GDDR on this corporate hierarchy level. However, to observe a potential trickle-down effect from the supervisory board to the executive board, the sample is also analyzed regarding the type of regulatory approach on the supervisory board. Since the mandatory gender quota results in a sharper increase in the proportion of women, this effect may trickle down to the executive board. Furthermore, it has to be considered that 13 companies are organized in a legal form (e.g., KGaA) that does not foresee an executive board. Therefore, the sample is reduced to 201 companies (1,608 company-year observations). Correspondingly to the analysis of the supervisory board, the development of the proportion of women on executive boards during the sample period is presented in Figure 5-16 and Figure 5-17.[114]

Overall, in 2014 – in the run-up of FüPoG I – 9% of all executive board members were female. In the following years, **the presence of women on executive boards steadily increased** year after year, reaching an all-time high in 2021 (16%). It is conspicuous that, between 2020 (13%) and 2021 (16%), the increase was particularly sharp. This may result from anticipatory effects in advance of the extended requirements of FüPoG II (section 2.2.4; similar findings and interpretation, cf. *FidAR e.V.* (2022)).

Considering the type of regulatory approach on the supervisory board, the results indicate differences in the increase of female executive board members. While the companies affected by the mandatory gender quota employed, on average, 7% female executive board members in 2014, GDDR companies appointed every tenth seat (10%) with a woman. After the implementation of FüPoG I, the **quota companies have caught up** and appointed women to their executive board more frequently. Thus, in 2021, there is only a small gap observable between the participation of women on the executive boards of quota companies (15%) and GDDR companies (16%). Nevertheless, the results of the Mann-Kendall Trend Test indicate positive and statistically highly significant trends for both groups.

---

114 Cf. Appendix 2 for a tabular overview of the development of the proportion of women on the executive board during the sample period. The table contains percentages with two decimal places. Decimal places are omitted in the figures (Figure 5-16 and Figure 5-17) for reasons of clarity.

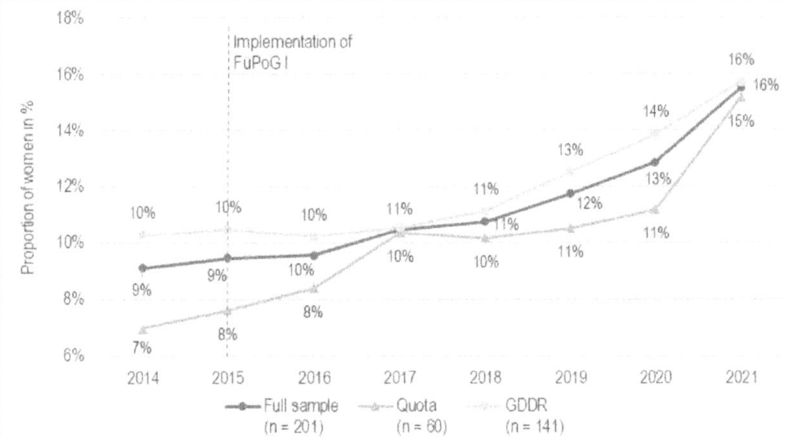

Mann-Kendall Trend Test
Full sample: τ_b = 0.0939, p < 0.01***; Quota companies: τ_b = 0.1451, p < 0.01***; GDDR companies: τ_b = 0.0776, p < 0.01***

Figure 5-16: Development of the proportion of women on executive boards by regulatory approaches

Furthermore, an even more pronounced difference in the starting point (in 2014) emerges between private (13%) and public companies (6%) (Figure 5-17). Thus, the presence of women on executive boards was more than twice as high in private companies as in public companies. In the subsequent year in which the GDDR was applied, both groups of companies increased the representation of women on the executive board. However, the **public companies show a larger increase** and reached an all-time high in 2021 (14%), which is beyond the proportion of private companies (18%) but to a smaller extent. This observation corresponds to the findings considering the type of regulatory approach because all quota companies are public companies by nature. However, the same does not apply vice versa. Irrespective of the capital market orientation, the results of the Mann-Kendall Trend Test report for both private and public companies a positive and statistically significant trend in the female participation on executive boards.

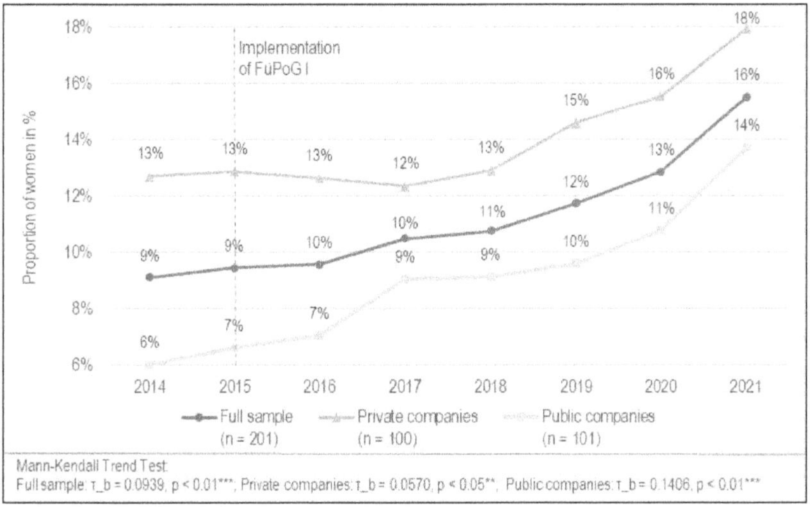

Figure 5-17: Development of the proportion of women on executive boards by capital market orientation

Due to the pronounced increase in the participation of female executive board members of public companies, Figure 5-18 illustrates the development split into indexes to identify differences in company size. Overall, **the participation of women increased in all indexes**. In 2014, the DAX companies (8%) employed more female executive board members than companies listed on the MDAX (5%) or SDAX (4%). Among indexes, the proportion of women developed unevenly in the initial phase – from 2015 to 2017. While the companies listed on the DAX increased the level of gender diversity from 8% (2014) to 14% (2017), the increase of MDAX companies (5% in 2014 to 7% in 2017) and SDAX companies (4% in 2014 to 6% in 2017) was less pronounced. However, it should be noted that due to the small sample sizes within the indexes, even single companies can influence the average. The initially tentative increase in the proportion of women on executive boards may be caused by ongoing mandates that did not permit a swifter change. In the second phase of the GDDR – from 2017 to 2021 – the DAX companies pursue to appoint more female executive board members (14% in 2017 to 19% in 2021). However, the development in the participation of women in DAX companies staggered until 2020 (13%) and only rose sharply in 2021 (19%). The pronounced increase of DAX companies in 2021 may be driven by anticipatory effects in the run-up of FüPoG II (section 2.2.4).[115] By contrast, there was a steady increase in MDAX (7% in 2017 to 13% in 2021) and a marginal increase in SDAX companies (6% in 2017 to 8% in 2021). In line with the observed increases in gender

[115] For example, out of 62 companies that will have to appoint at least one female executive board member under FüPoG II, 16 companies have an all-male executive board by the end of 2021 (*FidAR e.V.* (2022)). By the end of 2020, however, 24 of these companies had a gender-uniform executive board (*FidAR e.V.* (2022)). This suggests that these companies were already appointing women to their boards in anticipation of future regulations.

diversity, the results of a Mann-Kendall Trend Test substantiate a positive and statistically significant trend for all indexes. However, while the increase of DAX and MDAX companies is statistically significant at the 1% level, the positive trend of SDAX companies is slightly less statistically significant (at the 5% level).

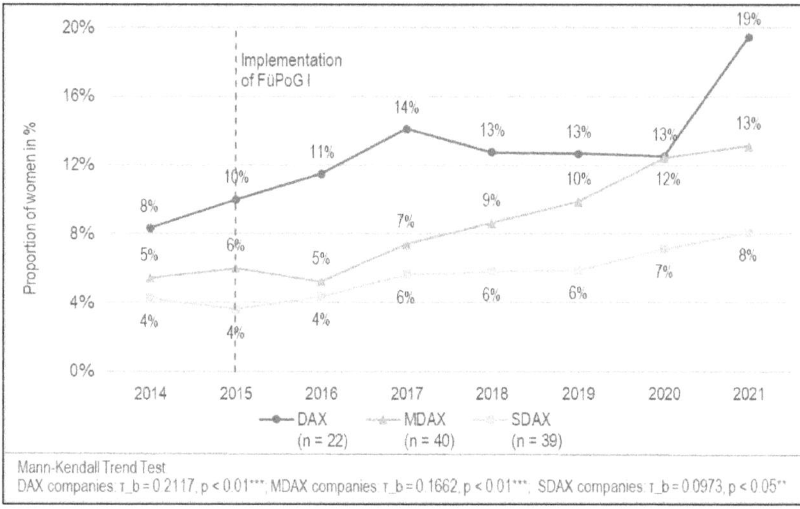

Figure 5-18: Development of the proportion of women on executive boards by indexes

Participation of women in executive board chairs

The chairperson of the executive board, frequently referred to as Chief Executive Officer (CEO), is granted additional administrative competencies. These competencies, which can vary depending on the company's articles of association, may extend those of the regular members of the executive board (*Gerum et al.* (2007), pp. 120–121).

Figure 5-19 illustrates the gender of executive board chairpersons. Overall, in only 42 out of 1,608 company-year observations (3%) the chair of the executive board was held by a woman. However, irrespective of the regulatory approach companies face on the supervisory board and their capital market orientation, **all subsamples indicate a small proportion of female chairmanships**. The results of a Chi-squared test confirm that there are no statistically significant differences within the subsamples. The underrepresentation of women on executive board chairs is comparable to the underrepresentation on supervisory board chairs (Figure 5-14). Additionally, the proportion of female executive board chairpersonships lags even further behind those of supervisory boards (4% female chairs for the full sample).

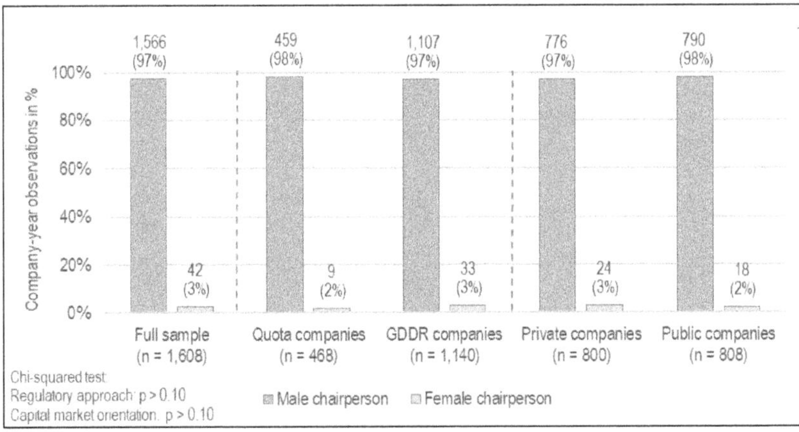

Figure 5-19: Gender of executive board chairpersons

Figure 5-20 shows the development of female chairpersons on the executive boards over the sample period. Before the introduction of the GDDR in 2014, women accounted for five chairs (2.49%) of all executive board chairs. After the introduction of the GDDR, the female presence on executive board chairs declined to four chairs (1.99%) in 2015 and 2016. Even though the participation of women slightly increased in subsequent years, reaching seven chairs (3.48%) in 2019, **female chairs remain exceptional cases**. In 2021, still only six (2.99%) of the executive board chairpersons were female. Therefore, the increase between 2014 (five chairs (2.49%)) and 2021 (six chairs (2.99%)) is due to certain individual new appointments. Similar to the supervisory board, single changes in the appointment of chairpersons can considerably impact the level of gender diversity.

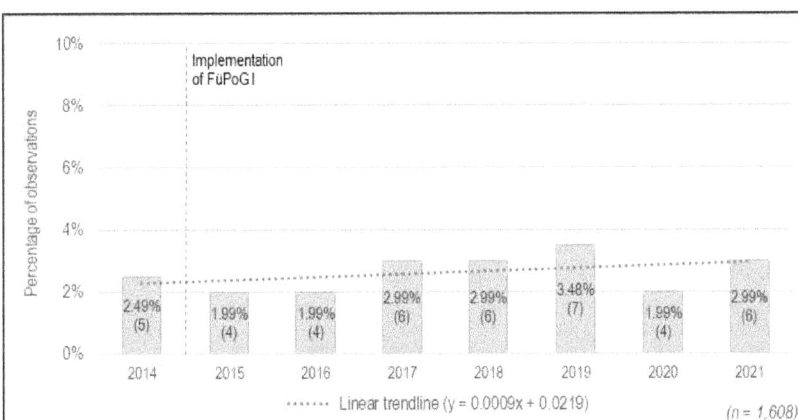

Figure 5-20: Female chairpersons on executive boards per year

5.2.3.3 Management levels

Since the GDDR also targets the first two management levels below the executive board, this section presents the results for these management levels. In light of the glass ceiling phenomenon, **fostering gender diversity at lower corporate hierarchy levels aims to reduce barriers for women** to staff positions on executive or supervisory boards. However, because FüPoG I does not define the scope of management levels, the disclosed information may vary across companies. In contrast to executive and supervisory boards, companies do not present the members of management levels in detail in their corporate reports. Therefore, information needs to be gathered solely from disclosure required by the GDDR. As presented in section 5.2.1, corporate disclosure frequently lacks comprehensive information on gender diversity at management levels because companies are incompliant with disclosure requirements. Furthermore, companies are not obliged to report annually about the current proportion of women at the respective management level (section 2.2.3.4). These restrictions in observing the development of the proportion of women in management positions result in considerably reduced sample sizes and automatically lead to distortions in relation to the full sample.

First management level below the executive board

Table 5-5 presents the development of gender diversity at the first management level below the executive board. The reduced sample consists only of companies that disclose the actual composition of the first management level at least every second year after the introduction of the GDDR (2015, 2017, 2019, and 2021). This ensures a consistent and comparable data base, since companies do not disclose information continuously. Due to this restriction, the analysis consists of a sample of 56 companies (392 company-year observations). **The adjusted sample accounts for 26% of the full sample** (56 out of 214 companies). Because of the reduced sample size, the results are only presented by type of regulatory approach and capital market orientation. Dividing the public companies by indexes would result in less than ten observations for some indexes and is therefore not performed.

Porportion of women at the 1st management level below the executive board					
Sample	**n**	**2015**	**2017**	**2019**	**2021**
Full sample	56	14.70%	17.04%	18.82%	20.62%
Type of regulatory approach					
Quota companies	20	12.80%	13.05%	16.04%	17.33%
GDDR companies	36	15.76%	19.25%	20.36%	22.45%
Capital market orientation					
Private companies	20	16.19%	19.91%	19.16%	19.48%
Public companies	36	13.88%	15.44%	18.63%	21.26%

Mann-Kendall Trend Test:
*Full sample: $\tau_b = 0.1330$, $p < 0.01$****
*Quota companies: $\tau_b = 0.1300$, $p > 0.10$; GDDR companies: $\tau_b = 0.1347$, $p < 0.05$***
*Private companies: $\tau_b = 0.0950$, $p < 0.05$**; Public companies: $\tau_b = 0.1542$, $p > 0.10$*

Table 5-5: Proportion of women at the first management level below the executive board per year

The results indicate a **growing proportion of women at the first management level** below the executive board over time. Overall, in 2015, 14.70% of all managers at the first management level were female. This proportion increased steadily in subsequent years, resulting in more than one-fifth (20.62%) of female managers in 2021. Moreover, the results of a Mann-Kendall Trend Test suggest a positive and strongly statistically significant increase in the proportion of women during the sample period.

The consideration of the regulatory approach reveals differences in the proportion of women. While quota companies increased the presence of women at the first management level from 12.80% in 2015 to 17.33% in 2021, the increase among GDDR is even more pronounced. These companies increased the presence of female managers from 15.76% in 2015 to 22.45% in 2021. These differences between both groups are confirmed by the results of a Mann-Kendall Trend Test. While the increase among quota companies is positive but statistically insignificant, the increase among GDDR companies is positive and statistically significant at the 5% level. Thus, **GDDR companies tend to increase the proportion of female managers** on the highest management level below the executive board to a greater extent than quota companies.

However, slightly varying developments are observable when considering companies divided into their type of market orientation. While in 2015, public companies (13.88%) employed fewer female managers than private companies (16.19%), the proportion developed differently during the sample period. In 2021, the proportion of women at the first management level of public companies (21.26%) exceeded that of private companies (19.48%). The results of a Mann-Kendall Trend Test reveal that the increase among public companies is positive but statistically insignificant, whereas the trend among private companies is positive and moderately statistically significant. Since all private companies are subject to the GDDR on the supervisory board, the results are not surprising and reinforce the results of the regulatory approach subsample. Nonetheless, the results show a **larger increase among public companies compared to private companies** under the GDDR.

Second management level below the executive board

Corresponding to the first management level, the same restrictions apply to the second management level below the executive board. Moreover, in particular, smaller companies frequently lack a second management level. Thus, these companies are technically unable and, therefore, not legally required to publish information on their second management level. Compared to the sample of the first management level, the number of observations is even more reduced. The restrictions result in an adjusted sample of 33 companies (231 company-year observations). **The subsample accounts for 15% (33 out of 214 companies) of the full sample.** Despite the small subsample size and its sensitivity to outliers, Table 5-6 provides the results for the second management level below the executive board. Therefore, consistency with the analysis of the first management level should be ensured. Nevertheless, the results must be considered with caution since single observations may substantially influence the overall average.

Proportion of women at the 2nd management level below the executive board					
Sample	**n**	**2015**	**2017**	**2019**	**2021**
Full sample	33	20.84%	23.87%	23.98%	23.09%
Type of regulatory approach					
Quota companies	16	16.87%	20.10%	20.26%	21.29%
GDDR companies	17	24.58%	27.42%	27.49%	24.78%
Capital market orientation					
Private companies	11	25.47%	27.27%	29.15%	23.07%
Public companies	22	18.53%	22.17%	21.40%	23.09%
Mann-Kendall Trend Test:					
*Full sample: $\tau\_b = 0.1218$, $p < 0.10$**					
Quota companies: $\tau\_b = 0.1651$, $p < 0.10$; GDDR companies: $\tau\_b = 0.1011$, $p > 0.10$*					
*Private companies: $\tau\_b = 0.0621$, $p > 0.10$; Public companies: $\tau\_b = 0.1552$, $p < 0.10$**					

Table 5-6: Proportion of women at the second management level below the executive board per year

Overall, the results indicate an **increase in the proportion of women at the second management level** below the executive board during the sample period. However, the overall increase results from the period between 2015 (20.84%) and 2017 (23.87%). Between 2017 and 2021 (23.09%), the participation of women stagnated. The results show that, when considering companies based on the type of regulatory approach they are subject to, only quota companies demonstrate an increase in gender diversity (16.87% in 2015 to 21.29% in 2021). By contrast, GDDR companies do not reveal a higher proportion of female managers at the second management level (24.58% in 2015 to 24.78% in 2021). The results of a Mann-Kendall Trend Test indicate only for the quota companies a positive and marginally statistically significant trend. Considering companies' capital market orientation, the level of gender diversity varied at the time the GDDR was introduced. Whereas less than every fifth position (18.53%) was staffed by a woman among public companies in 2015, it was more than every fourth (25.47%) among private companies. During the sample period, the proportion of women among public companies (23.09% in 2021) and private companies (23.07% in 2021) converged. Accordingly, only public companies exhibit a statistically significant increase at the 10% level, indicated by a Mann-Kendall Trend Test. However, as stated at the beginning of this section, the results should be interpreted with caution. The subsample sizes are especially small and susceptible to outliers.

5.2.4 Development of self-set targets for women in management positions

A key aspect of the GDDR is the requirement for companies to set and disclose their targets for the proportion of women at each hierarchical level. The following section examines how companies report these self-set targets and analyzes their development over time. Examples and excerpts from the reports of the sampled companies illustrate the reporting practices and support the findings.

5.2.4.1 Supervisory board

Level of self-set targets

According to the provisions of FüPoG I, public companies subject to co-determination are affected by the **mandatory gender quota**. These companies are **not required to disclose additional self-set targets** for the supervisory board. Therefore, this group of companies (68 companies, see section 5.1.3) is not subject to the following evaluation. Moreover, as described in section 5.2.1, the information provided by companies regulated by the GDDR is not always in line with the disclosure requirements of FüPoG I. Hence, companies that publish incomplete information (e.g., missing self-set targets or target achievement periods) are excluded from the sample (56 companies). Consequently, the sample to analyze the self-set targets for the supervisory board consists of 90 companies (630 company-year observations).

Table 5-7 presents the development of the self-set targets for the supervisory board. Overall, the **self-set targets for the proportion of women on supervisory boards increased** during the sample period. In the year FüPoG I came into force, in 2015, the companies targeted, on average, a presence of 20.76% female board members. This target increases to an intended participation of 23.62% in 2021. The results of a Mann-Kendall Trend Test reveal a statistically significant increase for the full sample. Considering the capital market orientation subsamples, a comparable trend is observable. Both private and public companies exhibit increasing targets during the sample period. However, each year, private companies aimed for more gender-diverse supervisory boards than public companies. While public companies targeted a presence of female board members of 21.57% in 2021, private companies aimed to staff more than every fourth position (25.21%) with a woman. However, the results of a Mann-Kendall Trend Test indicate for private companies a marginally statistically significant increase and for public companies an insignificant positive trend.

Self-set targets for the proportion of women on supervisory boards								
Sample	**n**	**2015**	**2016**	**2017**	**2018**	**2019**	**2020**	**2021**
Full sample	90	20.76%	20.67%	20.72%	22.47%	22.49%	22.85%	23.62%
Capital markt orientation								
Private companies	50	22.88%	22.71%	22.81%	25.30%	24.96%	24.96%	25.21%
Public companies	40	18.03%	18.03%	18.03%	18.83%	19.30%	20.13%	21.57%

Mann-Kendall Trend Test:
*Full sample: τ_b = 0.0649, p < 0.05***
Private companies: τ_b = 0.0790, p < 0.10; Public companies: τ_b = 0.0564, p > 0.10*

Table 5-7: Self-set targets for the proportion of women on supervisory boards per year

For both the full sample and the subsample of private companies, the sharpest increase can be observed between 2017 and 2018 (1.75 percentage points for the full sample, 2.49 percentage points for private companies). The comparably large increase may be associated with the regulatory requirements of the GDDR. The first target achievement period was not allowed to exceed June 30, 2017 (section 2.2.3.4, cf. Appendix 2). Therefore, all companies were required to disclose new self-set targets for the fiscal year 2018 at the latest.

An increase in the proportion of women on the supervisory board for GDDR companies is already observable in the early implementation period (section 5.2.3.1), which could be associated with the increase in self-set targets (e.g., prohibition of deterioration (section 2.2.3.4)).

In more detail, Figure 5-21 illustrates the development of self-set targets on supervisory boards for public companies categorized according to their index. Since most DAX companies are subject to the mandatory gender quota, only three companies disclose self-set targets. However, DAX companies are also included in the figure to ensure consistency, but they are not discussed in detail due to the small sample size. **MDAX companies aimed to appoint more women** to the supervisory board **than SDAX companies** during the sample period. While companies listed on the MDAX aimed to reach 24% female members, SDAX companies targeted to appoint solely every fifth position (20%) with a woman in 2021. The results of a Mann-Kendall Trend Test reveal no statistically significant trend for any of the analyzed indexes.

Summarizing, on average, the self-set targets of the sample companies increase during the sample period. However, the target setting lags behind the female participation targeted by the mandatory gender quota of 30%.

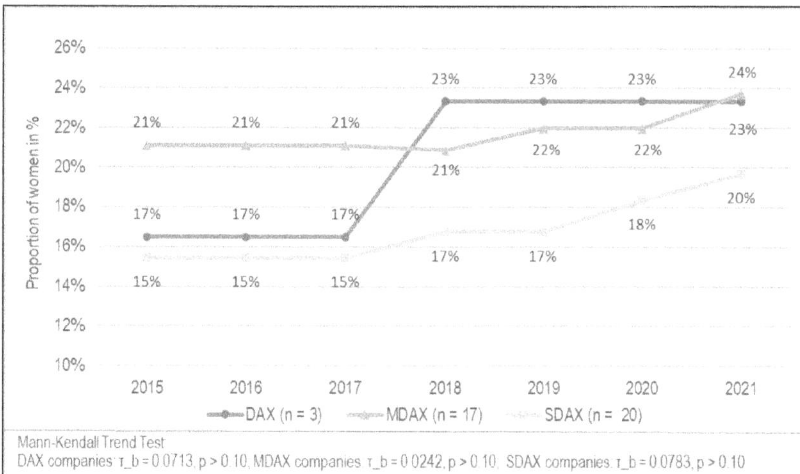

Figure 5-21: Development of self-set targets for the proportion of women on supervisory boards per year

The GDDR allows companies to independently determine the level of their targets as long as they comply with the prohibition of deterioration. Thus, a **self-set target of 0%** is permissible for gender-uniform supervisory boards. Figure 5-22 presents the proportion of companies that do not aim to increase board gender diversity and, therefore, disclose a target of 0%. Overall, the majority of the sample companies (90%) set targets that are larger than zero. This includes companies that are forced to set targets unequal to zero due to their actual board composition as well as companies that aim to increase their gender diversity on their gender-uniform supervisory board. Overall, however, in 10% of the reports, companies publish a self-set target of zero.

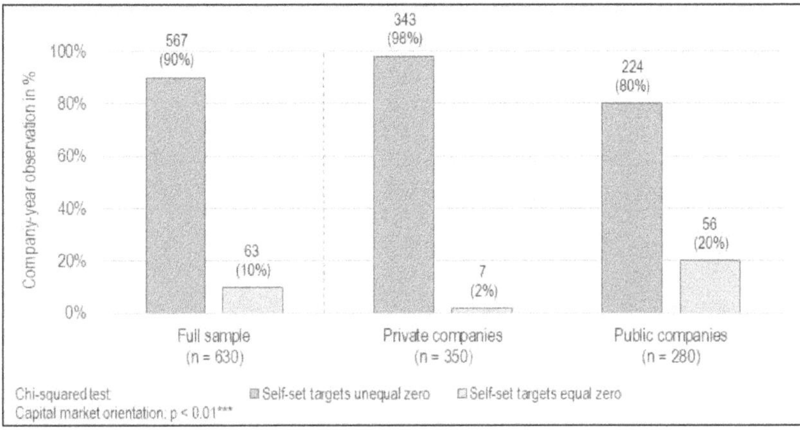

Figure 5-22: Self-set targets of zero for supervisory boards

The subsamples of **private and public companies reveal substantial differences** in the frequency of zero targets. Whereas private companies (2%) make use of the option to declare a target of zero in only rare cases, public companies disclose such targets more frequently (20%). Correspondingly, public companies define a target that does not intend to increase gender diversity on the supervisory board in 56 reports. The result of a Chi-squared test confirms that the difference between private and public companies is highly statistically significant at the 1% level.

Furthermore, the subsamples of public companies indicate a **negative association between company's index and the definition of self-set targets of zero** (Figure 5-23). In only 5% of the reports comprising such a target, DAX companies published the report. However, this figure should be assessed against the background that only three DAX companies are required to set targets. By contrast, companies listed on the MDAX (36%) and SDAX (59%) account for most of the reports that contain a target of zero for the participation of women on the supervisory board. The result of a Fisher's Exact Test reveals that the differences between the indexes are statistically insignificant. However, even if the differences are not statistically significant and in consideration of the small number of large companies, smaller public companies account for a larger proportion of reports with targets of zero.

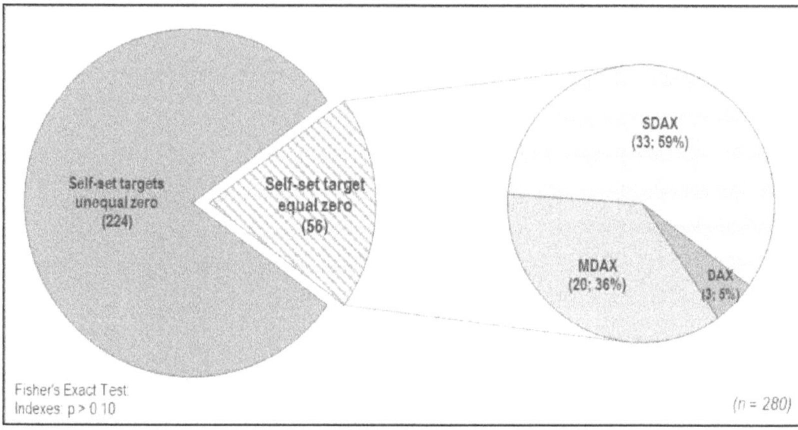

Figure 5-23: Self-set targets of zero for supervisory boards reported by public companies by indexes

Target achievement

According to the provisions of the GDDR, companies set the targets for the participation of women on supervisory boards independently. These **self-set targets are not legally binding**. Thus, companies subject to the GDDR are not forced to meet the aimed level of gender diversity. Figure 5-24 provides an overview of how many companies achieve their self-set targets on the supervisory board and how often these targets are missed. Furthermore, the figure illustrates which indexes account for missed targets within the group of public companies.

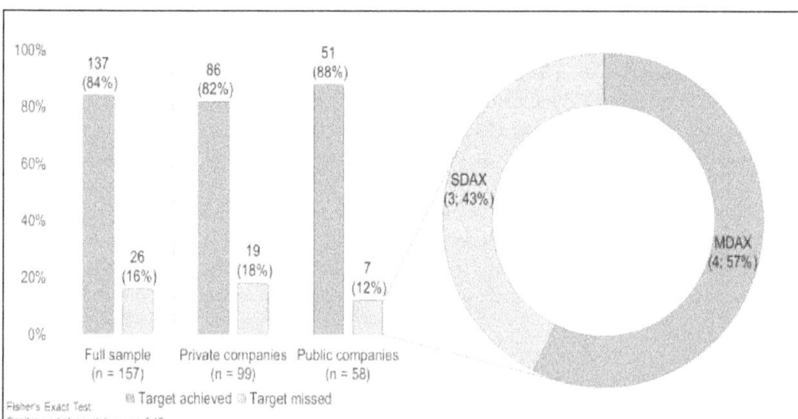

Figure 5-24: Achievement of self-set targets for supervisory boards

The achievement of self-set targets on supervisory boards is analyzed based on the **company-year observations in which a self-set target achievement period has expired**. Accordingly, only reports from companies whose target period has ended are considered. In such periods, companies are required by law to state whether the self-set target is ultimately achieved or missed. In total, a target achievement period ends in 157 reports.

Overall, companies meet the self-set targets in 84% of all analyzed reports. Thus, the results indicate that **in the majority of cases, companies achieve the aimed participation of women** on supervisory boards. The results reveal that private companies (18%) tend to miss their targets more frequently than public companies (12%). However, the targets were achieved in more than four out of five reports for both groups. The result of a Fisher's Exact Test shows that the difference between these companies is statistically insignificant. Investigating which companies caused the missed targets for public companies shows that all three DAX companies have achieved their targets. However, companies listed on the MDAX missed their target four times (57% of seven reports) and SDAX companies three times (43% of seven reports).

Explanations for missed self-set targets

The GDDR requires companies to state reasons for missing their self-set targets for the participation of women on the supervisory board. Hence, 26 reports have to include an explanation of why the companies do not achieve their gender diversity target within the self-set target achievement period. However, a **noticeable proportion of companies do not comply with the requirements** of the GDDR (section 5.2.1) in general. Accordingly, not all companies state reasons for missing their self-set targets for the supervisory board.

In eight of 26 reports (31%) companies explain why they have not reached the striven level of proportion of women on their supervisory board. Accordingly, only in less than one-third of the observations involving failed self-set targets, companies comply with the disclosure requirements of the GDDR. This implies that, in the majority of the observations, **users of the reports cannot assess and understand the reasons** for missing the intended level of gender diversity. However, in roughly one-third of the reports, companies justify the circumstances that result in underperforming the self-set targets for the presence of women at the top of the company's hierarchy.

To gain a further understanding of why companies do not manage to achieve their targets regarding the proportion of women on the supervisory board, Table 5-8 shows the **explanations provided by the companies**. These eight narrative explanations for missed targets are clustered into five categories to provide a coherent structure.

In two reports each, companies state that they lack a **vacant position** on the supervisory board during the sample period, make an **unexpected change**, or the **qualification of the female candidates** does not fulfill the appointment criteria. In one report, a company justifies the missed target with a change in the supervisory board size. Another company explains the underrepresentation of women with the appointment decision of employee representatives.

Explanations for missed targets on supervisory boards	
Explanation	**Frequency**
No vacant position	2
Unexpected changes	2
Qualification of female candidates	2
Change in supervisory board size	1
Appointment of employee representatives	1

Table 5-8: Narrative explanations for missing self-set targets for supervisory boards

Wabco Holding GmbH, for example, states that "*the target could not be achieved at this time, as the new Supervisory Board members are to be appointed in coordination with the new elections in 2018*"[116] (*Wabco Holding GmbH* (2018), p. 13). This statement points to the fact that the target could not be achieved because new regular appointments to the supervisory board will be made after the target achievement period has expired. However, the company does not explain why they defined a target that could not be achieved under regular circumstances.

Two companies explain the missed self-set targets with the **qualification of female candidates**. *Capgemini Deutschland GmbH*, for example, states that "*the reasons for this lie on the one hand in the limited availability of suitable female managers within the industry*"[117] (*Capgemini Deutschland GmbH* (2019), p. 3). Moreover, *DIC Asset AG* provides a comparable explanation and declares that "*the Supervisory Board was primarily guided by the company's interest in keeping the positions constantly staffed by individuals with proven professional expertise and a thorough understanding of the company*" (*DIC Asset AG* (2018), p. 168). The explanations provided by the companies reveal that the self-set targets were not achieved for a variety of reasons. While some justifications rely on technical reasons (e.g., change in the size of the supervisory board), other companies point to reasons that result from the company's appointment preferences (e.g., lack of suitable female candidates).

In summary, the reporting practice on self-set targets for the supervisory board shows significant differences between the company's capital market orientation and company size. It is remarkable that despite the legal foundation of the GDDR, a considerable proportion of companies does not comply with the disclosure requirements. This includes the lack of self-set targets, self-set target achievement periods, and explanations for missed targets. Nevertheless, on average, the participation of women on the supervisory board increased during the sample period. However, female chairpersons remain exceptions. Further, despite the overall increase in the proportion of women, the results indicate that the lack of enforcement induces companies to violate their reporting obligations.

[116] Because the publication is only available in German language, the quotation is translated from German into English.

[117] Because the publication is only available in German language, the quotation is translated from German into English.

5.2.4.2 Executive board

Level of self-set targets

Companies subject to the GDDR have to disclose **self-set targets for the composition of the executive board** in terms of gender diversity. Therefore, Table 5-9 provides the development of self-set targets on executive boards between 2015 and 2021. Due to the varying regulatory approaches introduced by FüPoG I, the sample has to be adjusted. It has to be considered that some companies are organized in a legal form (e.g., KGaA) that does not foresee an executive board. These companies (three companies) are removed from the sample (section 5.2.2). Moreover, 63 companies that do not consistently disclose information in line with the requirements of the GDDR are excluded from the sample. In summary, the subsample for this analysis consists of 138 companies.

Self-set targets for the proportion of women on executive boards								
Sample	**n**	**2015**	**2016**	**2017**	**2018**	**2019**	**2020**	**2021**
Full sample	138	8.35%	8.59%	8.93%	13.69%	14.10%	14.44%	16.85%
Type of regulatory approach								
Quota companies	52	8.65%	8.97%	8.92%	14.64%	15.03%	15.07%	17.37%
GDDR companies	86	8.17%	8.35%	8.94%	13.09%	13.52%	14.04%	16.53%
Capital market orientation								
Private companies	50	10.99%	11.29%	11.90%	16.88%	16.88%	16.88%	18.71%
Public companies	88	6.87%	7.06%	7.26%	11.91%	12.56%	13.07%	15.82%
Mann-Kendall Trend Test:								
*Full sample: $\tau_b = 0.1673$, $p < 0.01$****								
*Quota companies: $\tau_b = 0.2459$, $p < 0.01$***; GDDR companies: $\tau_b = 0.2016$, $p < 0.01$****								
*Private companies: $\tau_b = 0.1250$, $p < 0.01$***; Public companies: $\tau_b = 0.2755$, $p < 0.01$****								

Table 5-9: Self-set targets for the proportion of women on executive boards per year

Overall, the companies set a self-set target for the proportion of women on executive boards of 8.35% in 2015. The targets increased consistently during the sample period, doubling to 16.85% in 2021. The largest increases in the self-set targets can be observed between 2017 (8.93%) and 2018 (13.69%) and between 2020 (14.44%) and 2021 (16.85%). The same applies to the requirements for the target achievement periods for executive boards as for supervisory boards (section 2.2.3.4). Thus, in particular, the large increase between 2017 and 2018 could be caused by the disclosure of new self-set targets due to expired target achievement periods (cf. Appendix 2). Additionally, the results suggest that **the type of regulatory approach** applied to the company's supervisory boards **does not affect the target-setting behavior** for executive boards. Both quota and GDDR companies targeted a comparable presence of female executive board members during the sample period. This observation is confirmed by the results of a Mann-Kendall Trend Test that report for both groups positive and strongly statistically significant trends.

Nevertheless, **differences in the target-setting of private and public companies** are observable. While private companies initially targeted a proportion of women of 10.99% in 2015, public companies aimed for a lower representation (6.87% in 2015). Even though both groups of companies steadily increased their targets in the subsequent years, the gap in the targets has not narrowed noticeably. Additionally, the results reveal that the most significant increase occurred between 2017 and 2018. Both private and public companies increased their targeted participation of women on executive boards by around five percentage points on average between these two reporting periods. Conclusively, the results indicate that private companies tend to set more ambitious targets for the presence of women on executive boards than public companies.

Furthermore, dividing the subsample of public companies according to indexes reveals noticeable differences regarding companies' size (Figure 5-25). During the complete sample period, DAX companies set the highest targets. In 2015, for example, DAX companies aim for a proportion of female executive board members of 11%, whereas companies listed on the MDAX (5%) and SDAX (6%) disclose targets that are roughly half of the targets set by DAX companies. However, the level of self-set targets for the participation of women on executive boards develops differentially. Even though the companies on all indexes increased their targets during the sample period, the extent of the increase varies. The companies listed on the MDAX more than tripled their self-set targets during the sample period (5% in 2015 to 16% in 2021). SDAX companies also increase their targets considerably and double them between 2015 (6%) and 2021 (13%). By contrast, DAX companies increase their targets less than twofold (11% in 2015 to 20% in 2021). The results of a Mann-Kendall Trend Test indicate a statistically significant increase in the self-set targets. Nevertheless, the results suggest an **association between companies' size and the level of gender diversity targets** on executive boards.

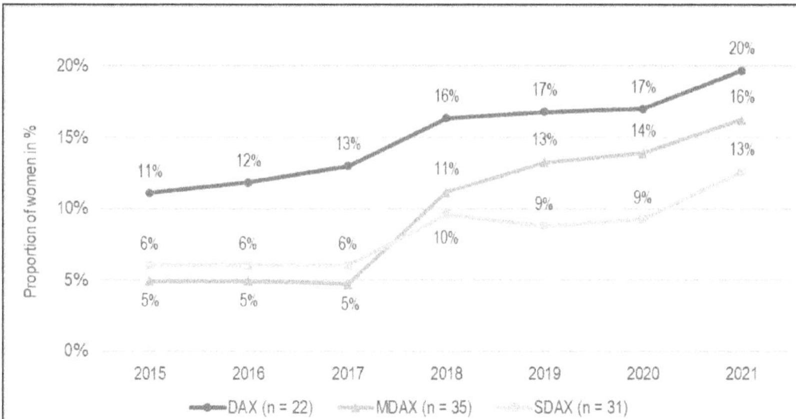

Mann-Kendall Trend Test
DAX companies: τ_b = 0.2459, p < 0.01***, MDAX companies: τ_b = 0.2755, p < 0.01***, SDAX companies: τ_b = 0.1363, p < 0.05**

Figure 5-25: Development of self-set targets for the proportion of women on executive boards per year

Similar to the provisions for the supervisory board, the GDDR also allows companies to set targets of zero for the participation of women on the executive board, as long as the executive board is gender-uniform. To analyze how often companies use this option, Figure 5-26 illustrates the number of reports consisting of targets of zero. Overall, **in**

exactly half of the reports (50%), companies set a target of zero for the participation of women on the executive board. Compared to the target-setting behavior for the supervisory board, companies set a target equal to zero more frequently.

The results reveal differences when considering the subsamples based on regulatory approach and capital market orientation. Whereas companies affected by the mandatory gender quota set more frequently (60%) a target unequal to zero than the average, GDDR companies define targets aimed at an increase in only 44% of the reports. The result of a Chi-squared test indicates that the difference is highly statistically significant at the 1% level. Thus, **companies subject to the mandatory gender quota** on the supervisory board **tend to set more ambitious targets** than GDDR companies.

Moreover, the results do not indicate substantial differences between private and public companies. Although private companies disclosed more often targets that aim to increase gender diversity on the executive board (53%) than public companies (48%), both values do not differ significantly from the overall average (50%). Accordingly, a Chi-squared test confirms that the difference between private and public companies is statistically insignificant. In summary, companies set in half of the reports targets that do not aim at female representation on the executive board. While **no considerable differences** appear **between private and public companies**, companies subject to the GDDR tend to define targets that equal zero more frequently than quota companies.

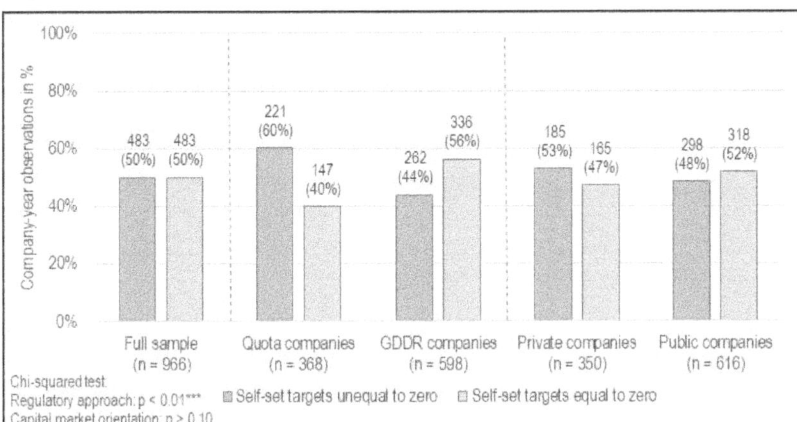

Figure 5-26: Self-set targets of zero for executive boards

Target achievement

Similar to the supervisory board, self-set targets for the participation of women are also non-binding for the executive board (section 2.2.3.4). Thus, Figure 5-27 presents **how often companies achieve** their **self-set targets**. Corresponding to the procedure for the supervisory board, the analysis solely includes company-year observation with an expiring target achievement period for the executive board. Overall, in 240 reports, companies have to evaluate an expiring target achievement period.

In 35 out of 240 observations (15%), the aimed proportion of women on executive boards could not be met. Therefore, this **target achievement ratio is comparable to that observed for the supervisory board** (16%; Figure 5-24).

The **type of regulatory approach** for the supervisory board as well as the **capital market orientation do not seem to determine the company's target achievement** on the executive board. Although companies subject to the mandatory gender quota (17%) missed their self-set targets slightly more often, GDDR companies (13%) also missed their targets in a frequency comparable to the full sample. The same applies when considering the company's capital market orientation. While private companies (17%) missed their self-set targets slightly more frequently than public companies (13%), both do not differ substantially from the overall average. The results of a Chi-squared test support this conclusion and report that the differences within the subsamples are statistically insignificant.

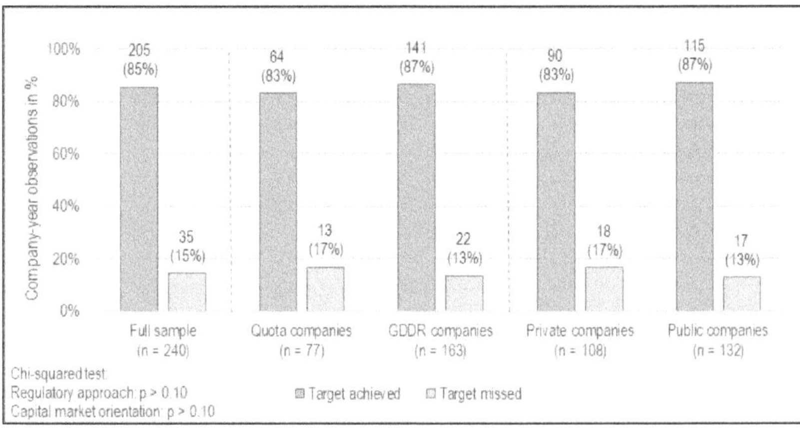

Figure 5-27: Achievement of self-set targets for the executive board

Explanations for missed self-set targets

Similar to the supervisory board, companies have to state a reason for missing a self-set target for the executive board (section 2.2.3.4). In 35 out of 240 reports, companies are legally required to **provide an explanation** for missing the target. Consistent with the analysis of the supervisory board, the investigation evaluates if and how companies justify their conduct in case of missed targets (Figure 5-28).

In 22 out of 35 (63%) reports, companies state the reasons for not meeting the targeted proportion of women on the executive board. However, the remaining 13 (37%) lack the legally required justification. Thus, more than one out of three observations reveal an **infringement of the disclosure obligation** required by the GDDR.

Considering the type of regulatory approach companies face for the supervisory board, the results indicate **differences in the reporting practice of companies**. Companies affected by the mandatory gender quota explained in ten out of 13 reports (77%) why the targets are missed. By contrast, companies exclusively subject to the GDDR disclosed only in slightly more than half of the reports (55%) why they could not meet the intended proportion of women on the executive board. Thus, quota companies justify their missed targets more often than GDDR companies.

Comparable differences are observable between private and public companies. While private companies explain why they did not achieve the self-set target in 50% of the reports, public companies provide an explanation for the missed targets in 13 out of 17 reports (76%). Thus, **private companies infringe the justification obligation more frequently** than public companies. However, the results of a Fisher's Exact Test do not indicate statistically significant differences within the regulatory approach subsample, whereas the test reveals a marginally statistical difference between private and public companies. However, irrespective of the capital market orientation or type of regulatory approach, it is remarkable that a considerable proportion of companies do not comply with the disclosure requirements.

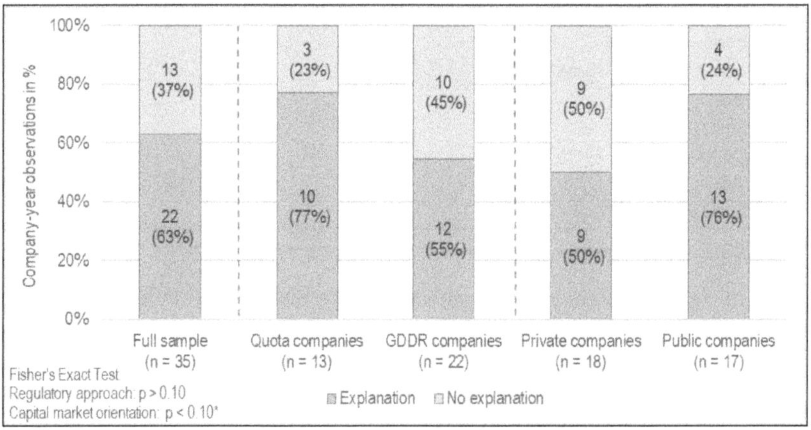

Figure 5-28: Existence of explanations for missed self-set targets on the executive board

In 22 of the 35 reports that contain an **explanation for missed targets** on the executive board, Table 5-10 provides an overview of the explanations stated. Some of the most frequently mentioned explanations are comparable to those already frequently stated for missed targets on the supervisory board (e.g., qualification of female candidates (Table 5-8)). Identical to the procedure for the supervisory board, the explanations are clustered into categories. Nevertheless, each explanation is a company-specific, individual statement.

In seven of the 22 reports, companies stated that they failed to appoint more women to the executive board because the **female candidates did not offer the desired qualifications** or because the male candidates were better qualified than the female candidates. For example, during the sample period, *HUGO BOSS AG* was unable to reach its self-set target on the executive board twice. Firstly, in 2017, *HUGO BOSS AG* explained that the new male executive board member "*was ultimately selected on account of his professional qualifications*" (*HUGO BOSS AG* (2018), p. 17). Secondly, in 2021, *HUGO BOSS AG* explained in more detail that the "*Supervisory Board strives to ensure an appropriate representation of women on the Managing Board. However, personnel decisions are always made with a view to the qualifications of all candidates*" (*HUGO BOSS AG* (2022), p. 151). This statement demonstrates that the company generally wants to increase the proportion of women and achieve the self-set target but has decided to favor a male candidate due to the candidate's qualifications. *Vaillant GmbH* argues in the same vein for missing the self-set target expiring in 2017, that the target "*has not yet been achieved, as there were no suitably qualified female candidates available*"[118] (*Vaillant GmbH* (2019), p. 9). These examples illustrate that various companies criticize the supply of qualified female candidates for board positions and claim this as a reason for missing gender diversity targets on their executive board.

Explanations for missed targets on executive boards	
Explanation	**Frequency**
Qualification of female candidates	7
Change in executive board size	5
Departure of a female executive board member	4
Low fluctuation	2
Vacant executive board seat	1
Internal succession planning	1
Reorganisation	1
More comprehensive diversity concept	1

Table 5-10: Narrative explanations for missing self-set targets for the executive board

In five of the 22 reports, companies justify their failure to meet the striven presence of women on the executive board with **changes in the board size**. *Siemens AG*, for example, argues in the context of the missed self-set target and the appointment of a male board member in 2017 that because the executive board "*now has eight members, the target for the Managing Board of 2/7 until June 30, 2017 has been missed since April, 1 2017*" (*Siemens AG* (2018), p. 146). Similarly, *Deutsche Börse AG* also argues that "*this quota, however, declined due to the increase of the Executive Board to six members as of 1 July 2018, despite the fact that the actual number of women on the Executive Board did not change*" (*Deutsche Börse AG (2022)*, p. 132). Accordingly, the self-set target is missed not due to the retirement of a female board member but because of the appointment of a man. Thus, the absolute number of women on the executive board is constant. However, the mathematically calculated proportion of women declines under the targeted participation.

In contrast to the examples with an increased executive board size, the target achievement can also be affected by a reduced size of the executive board. *GEA Group AG*, for example, states that "*one reason for the decline in the share of women on the Executive Board to 0 percent is the*

118 Because the publication is only available in German language, the quotation is translated from German into English.

reduction in the size of the Executive Board to its current size of only three members: After the only female member of the Executive Board left the Group" (*GEA Group AG* (2022), pp. 76-77). However, due to a decline in the size of the executive board, the proportion of women is not inevitably declining. In contrast, if a male executive board member leaves the board, the proportion of women increases ceteris paribus. Consequently, in the example of *GEA Group AG*, the reduction in executive board size is related to the departure of a woman.

In four of the 22 reports, companies explain the underperforming of the targeted gender diversity level due to the **unexpected departure of a female executive board member**. *Morphosys AG*, for example, declares that „*the reason this target has not been met is the unplanned departure*" (*Morphosys AG* (2018), p. 81) of a female board member and the replacement with a man. In the same sense, *Philips GmbH* states regarding the target achievement period expired in 2017, that "*due to the departure of the managing director in the meantime, the target regarding the management is currently no longer achieved*"[119] (*Philips GmbH* (2018), p. 13). Both examples indicate that companies fail to reach the targeted level of gender diversity on executive boards due to a reduction in female board members. However, even though companies do not attribute the missed targets to the unavailability of qualified female candidates, the explanations raise the question of why women leaving the executive board are not replaced by other female executive board members.

In summary, the examples extracted from reports illustrate a broad range of reasons that led to a failure to meet the desired level of gender diversity. Some companies base their justification on shortcomings on the supply side (e.g., insufficient pool of well-qualified female candidates). In contrast, other companies refer to more organizational or technical reasons (e.g., changes in the executive board size). However, the multitude of different explanations provided by the companies suggests that the causes for not achieving the desired gender diversity on executive boards can be multifactorial and, therefore, complex.

5.2.4.3 Management levels

Contrary to other European gender diversity regulations that target solely corporate boards, the GDDR also aims to foster gender diversity at management levels below corporate board positions. Therefore, the GDDR requires companies to disclose **self-set targets** for the proportion of women **on the first and second management level** below the executive board. As explained in section 5.2.3.3, these lower management levels are analyzed on a reduced sample size due to restrictions in data availability.

5.2.4.3.1 First management level below the executive board

Level of self-set targets

Table 5-11 outlines the development of self-set targets for the proportion of women at the first management level below the executive board. The analysis includes 56 companies that disclose at least every second year a targeted gender diversity level.

[119] Because the publication is only available in German language, the quotation is translated from German into English.

Self-set targets for the proportion of women at the 1st managmement level					
Sample	**n**	**2015**	**2017**	**2019**	**2021**
Full sample	56	15.35%	15.78%	18.30%	19.12%
Capital market orientation					
Private companies	20	16.43%	17.08%	19.91%	20.48%
Public companies	36	14.73%	15.04%	17.47%	18.42%

Mann-Kendall Trend Test:
*Full sample: $\tau_b = 0.0964$, $p < 0.10$**
*Private companies: $\tau_b = 0.0654$, $p > 0.10$; Public companies: $\tau_b = 0.1147$, $p < 0.10$**

Table 5-11: Self-set targets for the proportion of women at the first management level below the executive board per year

In 2015, when companies initially set targets for the presence of women at the lower management levels, the companies aimed overall for a proportion of women of 15.35% on average. In the subsequent years, the **self-set targets constantly increased** to 15.78% in 2017, 18.30% in 2019, and reached the highest level of 19.12% in 2021. Accordingly, companies target, on average, to staff roughly every fifth position at the first management level with a female manager at the end of the sample period. Similar to the findings on the supervisory (section 5.2.4.1) and executive board (section 5.2.4.2), the sharpest increase is observable after 2017. Since companies must disclose new self-set targets after June 30, 2017, at the latest, the impact of the new targets is observable for the fiscal year 2019 (cf. Appendix 2). The results of a Mann-Kendall Trend Test suggest that the increase in self-set targets is positive and statistically significant at the 10% level.

When analyzing the subsamples based on the **capital market orientation** of the companies, an increase in desired gender diversity is observable in both groups. Private companies steadily increased the targeted proportion of women at the first management level. While these companies defined an average target of 16.43% in 2015, this target increased to 20.48% in 2021. Thus, private companies aim to staff roughly every fifth position with a female manager. In 2015, public companies strived to reach a female participation of 14.73%. Hence, their self-set targets were below the overall average. However, during the sample period, the public companies increased the level of self-set targets and aiming in 2021 for a proportion of women of 18.42%. The results of a Mann-Kendall Trend Test indicate a positive and marginally statistically significant increase at the 10% level for public companies. In contrast, the increase among private companies is statistically insignificant.

Moreover, similar to the higher hierarchy levels of the supervisory and executive board, companies can set a target of zero for the participation of women at management levels. However, the prerequisite for such a target is that no woman was employed at the relevant management level at the time the target was set **(prohibition of deterioration)**. Figure 5-29 illustrates the frequency of targets for the participation of women at the first management level below the executive board, which are equal to zero.

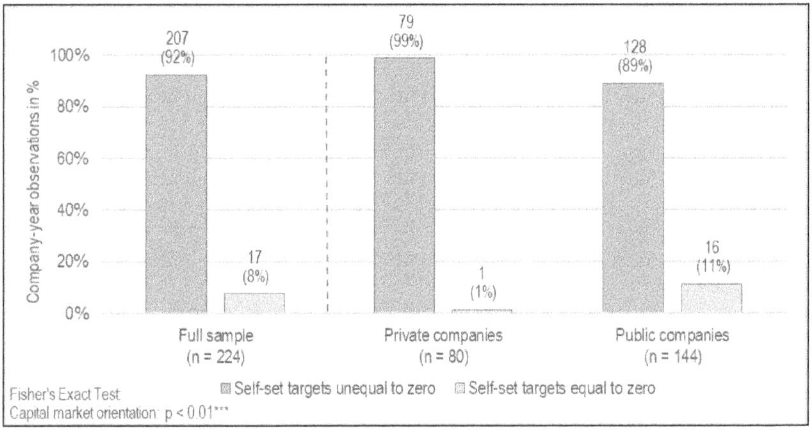

Figure 5-29: Self-set targets of zero at the first management level below the executive board

In 17 out of 224 (8%) reports, companies target a gender-homogeneous first management level below the executive board. Solely one of these 17 targets (1%) was set and disclosed by private companies. However, although public companies account for the remaining 16 targets of zero, the vast majority (89%) of public companies still target a presence of female managers unequal to zero. The results from a Fisher's Exact Test show that the difference between private and public companies is statistically significant at the 1% level. Nevertheless, with few exceptions, **private and public companies set targets that aim to employ female managers** at the first management level. Compared to the frequency of targets of zero for executive boards (50% (Figure 5-26)), companies set such targets less often for the first management level. This deviation seems reasonable, as companies have to respect the prohibition of deterioration. The findings of the annual information of the German Federal Government suggest that the first management level consists, on average, of a larger number of positions (roughly 15 persons, *Deutscher BT/BR – DIP* (2023b), BT-Drs. 20/9850, p. 57).[120] In contrast, the average executive board of the analyzed sample consists of roughly four members (mean 3.94 (Table 5-4)). Due to the larger size of the first management level, companies are more likely to have staffed at least one position with a woman, prohibiting a self-set target equal to zero.

Target achievement

Due to the provisions of the GDDR, companies can define the target achievement period for each hierarchy level separately. Overall, 63 of 224 reports include an ultimately expiring target achievement period at the first management level. Therefore, Figure 5-30 presents

[120] The study faces restrictions in data availability on management levels below the executive board. Thus, the evaluation of the average size of first management levels is performed on a subsample consisting of 1.4% (29 companies) of the full sample (*Deutscher BT/BR – DIP* (2023b), BT-Drs. 20/9850, p. 57). Therefore, the average number of positions at first management levels must be considered with caution.

how frequently companies met their self-set targets for the proportion of women and how often they missed these targets.

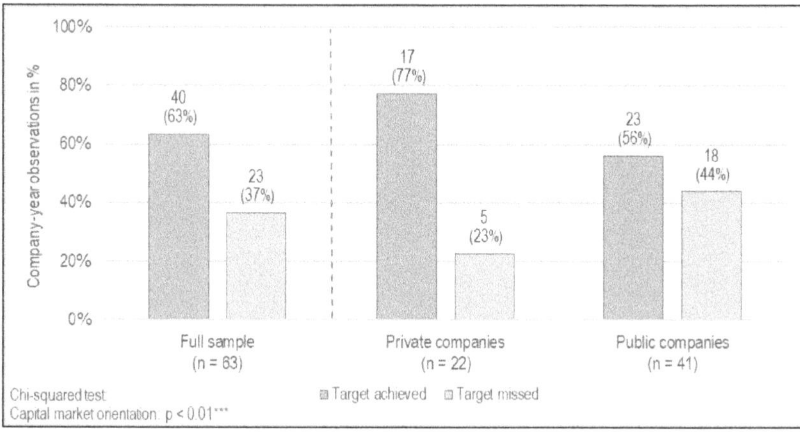

Figure 5-30: Achievement of self-set targets at the first management level below the executive board

In 40 of 63 (63%) reports, companies disclose that the striven level of gender diversity is met and, therefore, the target is achieved. For the group of public companies, the results show that companies achieve just slightly more than every second self-set target (56%). The observations of **private companies show a differing performance**. In 17 out of 22 (77%) expired target achievement periods, companies report that the aimed proportion of female managers is achieved. The results of the Chi-squared test report that the differences between private and public companies are statistically significant at the 1% level. Thus, the findings indicate that public companies miss their self-set targets more frequently than private companies.

Explanations for missed self-set targets

The GDDR requires companies to justify the reasons if they fail to meet their self-set target at the expiration date. Overall, **14 out of 23 reports (61%) contain an explanation** for missing the target. Considering private companies, these companies justify one of five (20%) missed targets. In contrast, public companies more frequently provide reasons for failing to achieve the target proportion of women. In 13 out of 18 reports (72%), including a missed self-set target, public companies state the reasons for missing the target. Accordingly, in five out of 18 (28%) reports, public companies do not justify a missed self-set target. The results of an untabulated Fisher's Exact Test indicate a statistically significant difference between private and public companies at the 10% level.

To gain further insights into why the self-set targets at the first management level could not be achieved, Table 5-12 shows the **frequency of stated explanations**. Because several companies mention multiple reasons, multiple selections are possible.

Explanations for missed targets at the 1st management level	
Explanation	**Frequency**
Qualification of female candidates	6
Reorganisation	4
Low fluctuation	4
Parental or maternity leave	1
Short target achievement period	1
(multiple category selection possible)	

Table 5-12: Narrative explanations for missed targets at the first management level below the executive board

The most frequently cited justification (in six out of 14 reports) for failing to achieve the envisaged proportion of women at the first management level is the lack of **availability of qualified female** or better-qualified male **candidates.** For example, *Wacker Neuson SE* explained: "*It has not been possible, however, to identify or hire sufficient ideal women candidates from inside or outside the company to achieve the targets for line one below the Executive Board*" (*Wacker Neuson SE* (2021), p. 18). First, this statement suggests that although the company endeavored to achieve its target by considering internal and external candidates. Second, the statement indicates that the company is unsure if they are able to identify female candidates with the required qualifications.

In addition, in four of the 14 reports, companies indicated that the target was not met due to **reorganization measures**. These activities can include, for example, changes in the size of the first management level or redefined organizational structures. For example, *Bilfinger SE* explained: "*The target as of June 30, 2017 in management level 1 was not fully met. As a result of restructuring at headquarters, particularly in the upper levels of management, in level 1 an increase from four percent to six percent was achieved and the target of eight percent was nearly achieved*" (*Bilfinger SE* (2018), p. 125). However, this statement does not reveal whether the absolute number of women at the first management level was affected by the reorganization of the headquarters. Thus, users of the report cannot evaluate if the missed target is caused by a reduction of absolute female managers or an increase in the size of the first management level.

Other companies justify the missed targets with **low fluctuation** (4 out of 14 reports). Some companies state multiple reasons to explain missing the intended level of gender diversity. For instance, *Aurubis AG* stated that "*in the first and second management levels under the Executive Board, there were limited open positions in the reporting period. For these, men and women were considered equally. The vacant positions were ultimately filled by the most suitable applicants.*" (*Aurubis AG* (2018), p. 20). On the one hand, this statement indicates that the fluctuation at the first management level was low and hindered substantial changes in the composition. On the other hand, the explanation implicitly suggests that male candidates have offered better qualifications than female candidates, impeding a larger increase in gender diversity. However, the statement reveals that the reasons for the under-representation of female managers at the first management level can be multifactorial.

5.2.4.3.2 Second management level below the executive board

Level of self-set targets

In line with the provisions for the first management level, the GDDR also requires companies to set targets for the second management level below the executive board. Since management levels are not defined by law, some companies **lack a second management level due to their definition or organizational structure**. Therefore, the sample for the analysis of the second management level must be further reduced to 33 companies. Table 5-13 presents the development of the level of self-set targets for the second management level.

Self-set targets for the proportion of women at the 2nd managmement level					
Sample	**n**	**2015**	**2017**	**2019**	**2021**
Full sample	33	19.44%	20.29%	22.07%	22.36%
Capital market orientation					
Private companies	11	20.53%	21.73%	23.03%	23.63%
Public companies	22	18.88%	19.54%	21.61%	21.76%

Mann-Kendall Trend Test:
Full sample: $\tau_b = 0.0776$, $p > 0.10$
Private companies: $\tau_b = 0.0161$, $p > 0.10$; Public companies: $\tau_b = 0.1097$, $p > 0.10$

Table 5-13: Self-set targets for the proportion of women at the second management level below the executive board per year

Overall, the **targeted presence of women** at the second management level **slightly increases** during the sample period. In 2015, the companies strived to reach a proportion of women of 19.44% on average, whereas in 2021, they targeted a participation of 22.36%. A comparable development can be observed considering the groups of public and private companies. Private companies increased the targeted proportion of women from 20.53% in 2015 to 23.63% in 2021. On a slightly lower level, public companies increased the targeted level of gender diversity from 18.88% at the initial target-setting year to 21.76% at the end of the sample period. Similar to the first management level (Table 5-11), the increase in self-set targets is sharpest between 2017 and 2019. Again, the comparably large increase may be caused by the definition of new self-set targets, as most target achievement periods expired in 2017 (cf. Appendix 3).

Contrary to the findings for the first management level, where public companies slightly exceeded the targeted participation of women, the opposite trend is observed at the second management level. Private companies show a similar pattern on both levels. However, the results of a Mann-Kendall Trend Test indicate that neither the increase for the full sample nor the increase of private or public companies is statistically significant. Given the small sample sizes, these results should be interpreted with caution.

Moreover, to evaluate the detailed target-setting practice for the second management level, the analysis **procedure is identical to that of the first management level**. In accordance with the provisions at the first management level, companies are allowed to set targets equal to zero and, therefore, not strive to employ at least one woman at the second management level. Untabulated results reveal that none of the 132 reports aims for a target equal to zero. There are two possible explanations for this homogeneous result. Firstly, companies do not have the option to set a target equal to zero (prohibition of deterioration), as they already employ at least one woman at the second management level. This assumption is supported by the findings of the annual information of the German Federal Government, which provide data on the absolute number of positions at the second management level (roughly 70 positions (*Deutscher BT/BR – DIP* (2023b), BT-Drs. 20/9850, p. 60)) is even larger than at the first management level (roughly 15 positions (*Deutscher BT/BR – DIP* (2023b), BT-Drs. 20/9850, p. 58)).[121] The larger absolute number of management positions may increase the probability of at least one female manager at the second management level. Secondly, companies could willingly set targets unequal to zero as they strive to increase the proportion of women at the second management level. However, since the GDDR does not require companies to provide more detailed information regarding the composition of their management levels (e.g., absolute number of female managers), no further conclusion can be drawn on the company's intentions.

Target achievement

Figure 5-31 presents **how frequently companies meet the targets** for the proportion of women at the second management level. In total, 38 target achievement periods expired during the sample period. In 25 out of these 38 reports (66%), companies manage to employ a sufficient number of female managers to achieve targeted participation of women. Thus, on average, one-third of the targets (33%) are missed.

Considering the capital market orientation of the analyzed companies, the target achievement rates are comparable. Private companies meet their self-set targets in nine out of 13 reports (69%) at the second management level. Public companies achieve their targets in 16 out of 25 reports (64%) with an expiring target achievement period. Furthermore, the results of a Fisher's Exact Test do not indicate statistically significant differences between private and public companies. However, the results indicate differences in comparison to the first management level. While private companies meet their self-set targets more frequently than public companies at the first management level (Figure 5-30), the results of the second management level do not support these findings. Nevertheless, as mentioned above, the results on both management levels face the restrictions of small sample sizes. Thus, single observations may influence the results and lead to biased findings.

[121] The study faces restrictions in data availability on management levels below the executive board. Thus, the evaluation of the average size of second management levels is performed on a subsample consisting of 1.2% (25 companies) of the full sample (*Deutscher BT/BR – DIP* (2023b), BT-Drs. 20/9850, p. 60). Therefore, the average number of positions at the second management level must be considered with caution.

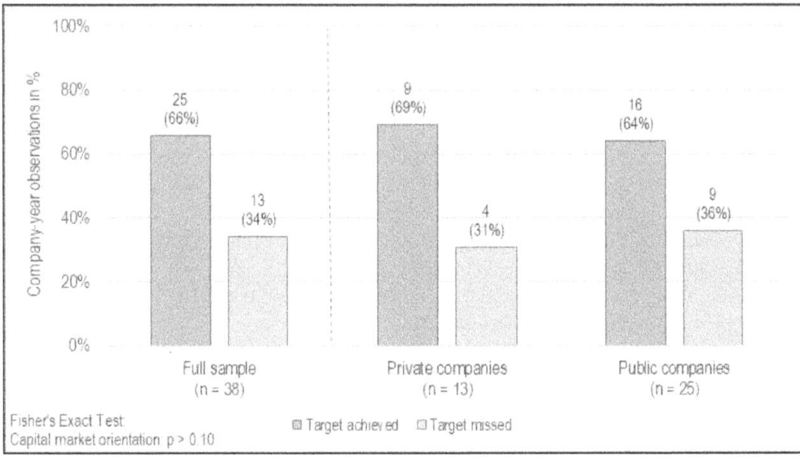

Figure 5-31: Achievement of self-set targets at the second management level below the executive board

Explanations for missed self-set targets

Since a considerable proportion of companies fail to reach the targeted gender composition at the second management level, companies have to state the **reasons for missing the self-set target**. Untabulated results show that in eight out of 13 missed targets (62%) the failure of the target is justified by the company. Accordingly, in more than every third report (38%), companies do not comply with the disclosure requirements of the GDDR and do not state the reason for missing the self-set target. Thus, the ratio for the second management level is comparable to that of the first management level (61% of missed targets are justified). Furthermore, the results suggest that private companies (one out of four reports (25%)) provide explanations less frequently than the group of public companies (seven out of nine reports (78%)). However, the results are not further statistically tested or interpreted due to the very small number of observations, particularly in the subsample of private companies.

Table 5-14 provides information on the **frequency of explanations** provided in reports that justify missed self-set targets at the second management level. The results are organized into the same categories as those for the first management level (Table 5-12). Furthermore, identically to the justifications for failed targets at the first management level, companies most frequently point to reorganization measures (in three out of eight reports) and the lack of qualified female candidates (in two out of eight reports). Since the character of the explanations at the second management level is comparable to that of the first management level (e.g., reorganization measures), solely differing or particularly interesting explanations are examined in detail.

Explanations for missed targets at the 2nd management level	
Explanation	**Frequency**
Reorganisation	3
Qualification of female candidates	2
Low fluctuation	2
Parental or maternity leave	1
Short target achievement period	1

Table 5-14: Narrative explanations for missed targets at the second management level below the executive board

The **overlap in the explanations** is due to the fact that some companies that fail to meet their targets at both management levels justify this with a joint justification. For example, *Sartorius AG* states for both management levels: "*although the percentage of women at these levels increased, both targets were not quite reached. [...] The reasons these targets were not met were the low fluctuation in the management team and, therefore, a lower number of positions to be filled [...]*" (*Sartorius AG* (2018), p 74). However, such statements do not enable users of the reports to assess differences in gender diversity achievement among management levels below the executive board.

However, some explanations for failed targets at the second management level differ in nature from the explanations at the first management level. For example, *Software AG* draws attention to problems in the development of young female managers. They highlight that "*the percentage of women trained in technical professions is less than 30 percent worldwide. For that reason, the advancement of young female managers is not leading to an increase in the percentage of women in management positions as quickly as hoped*" (*Software AG* (2018), p. 22). This indicates that some **companies struggle to externally employ female managers** due to general or industry-specific circumstances. Presuming such problems are an industry-specific phenomenon, a large number of companies tend to be affected.

In summary, a majority of the explanations at the first and second management level are comparable. In some cases, companies provide joint justifications for both management levels, which impedes users of the reports from assessing detailed reasons for missing the self-set targets. Moreover, justifications may vary due to industry- or hierarchy-specific circumstances. Nevertheless, the analyzed reports represent a small proportion of the full sample. Since only explanations of companies that provide at least every second year the actual proportion of women at management levels are analyzed, the findings are not transferable to the full sample.

5.3 Discussion

This section critically discusses the results presented in previous sections against the background of the research questions RQ1a and RQ1b. First, the section examines the development of the proportion of women on all targeted hierarchy levels (RQ1a) compared to the findings of prior descriptive research. Secondly, the disclosure practices are critically reviewed (RQ1b). These results are additionally evaluated in light of exceptions from normative research.

5.3.1 GDDR and corporate gender diversity

Targeted transparency regulations (such as GDDR) rely on the power of transparency. Theories suggest that companies change their behavior in an intended manner to align their actions with societal expectations. Therefore, hypothesis H_1 postulates that the proportion of women in management positions increases after the implementation of the GDDR. Results from Mann-Kendall Trend Tests support this hypothesis for supervisory boards (Figure 5-12) and executive boards (Figure 5-16). Companies affected by GDDR significantly increase the proportion of female board members following its implementation. This aligns with stakeholder theory, suggesting that companies intensify their efforts to meet stakeholders' demand for greater gender diversity after the GDDR is implemented. The finding is further supported by the theoretical framework of targeted transparency regulations. However, data availability on management levels below executive boards is an issue, making statistical tests difficult due to the small sample size at the first management level (n = 56 (Table 5-5)) and the second management level (n = 33 (Table 5-6)).[122] Therefore, hypothesis H_1 is evaluated based on the findings on supervisory and executive boards. Nevertheless, since this study is the first to evaluate the development of gender diversity on lower hierarchy levels after implementing the GDDR and to address the first research question (RQ1a) more broadly, the descriptive results on management levels are included in the discussion. Figure 5-32 summarizes the observed proportion of women on each hierarchy level subject to the GDDR.

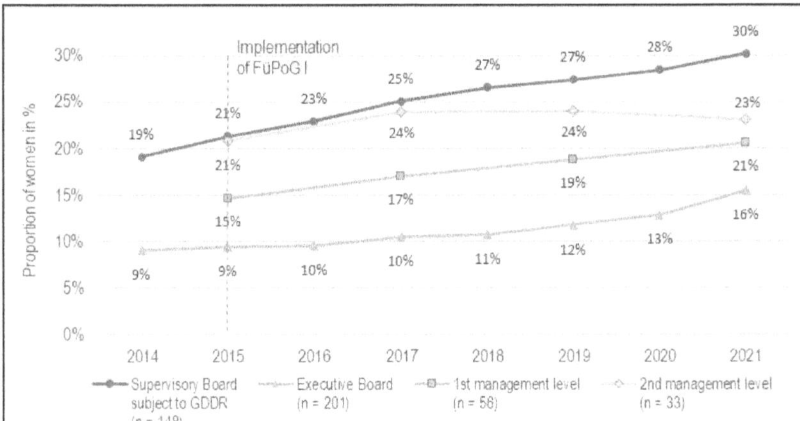

Mann-Kendall Trend Test
Supervisory Boards: $\tau\_b = 0.2050, p < 0.01^{***}$, Executive Boards: $\tau\_b = 0.1673, p < 0.01^{***}$,
First management levels: $\tau\_b = 0.0964, p < 0.010^{*}$, Second management levels: $\tau\_b = 0.0776, p > 0.010$

Figure 5-32: Development of the proportion of women on hierarchy levels targeted by the GDDR

[122] The annual information of the German Federal Government encounters similar issues regarding data availability at the management levels below executive boards and does not provide detailed insights at these corporate hierarchy levels (*Deutscher BT/BR – DIP* (2023b), BT-Drs. 20/9850).

Overall, an increased presence of women is observable on all hierarchy levels. Apart from a stagnating development at the second management level, gender diversity exhibits increasing trends. These findings indicate that the **intended objective of the GDDR is achieved** and that the GDDR paved the way for a higher participation of women at various corporate hierarchy levels. It is necessary to examine the trends on a hierarchy-level basis to consider the nuances in the developments and compare the findings with prior research.

On the **supervisory board**, the findings show a statistically significant increase in the proportion of seats held by women from roughly 19% in 2014 to over 30% in 2021. *Deutscher BT/BR – DIP* (2023b) and *FidAR e.V.* (2022) report similar results. The observed increases of prior research differ slightly due to the varying samples but suggest comparable levels of gender diversity for each year. Notably, companies subject to the GDDR – and therefore not legally required to appoint more female board members – seem to be guided by the target of the mandatory gender quota. In conclusion, the statistically significant increase indicates that the GDDR is effective and associated with increased gender diversity.

Furthermore, apart from the GDDR, the provisions of FüPoG I also include a mandatory gender quota for the supervisory board. The results of this study show that companies affected by the mandatory gender quota statistically significantly increase the presence of women on supervisory boards to a large extent and reach or even exceed the legally binding gender quota (Figure 5-12). Thus, **the mandatory gender quota is an effective regulatory tool**. However, the efficacy of mandatory gender quotas is not the focus of the study at hand. A bunch of prior research confirms the efficacy of gender quotas and, hence, discussed elsewhere (e.g., *Arndt/Wrohlich* (2019); *Hughes et al.* (2017); *Mensi-Klarbach/Seierstad* (2020); *Sojo et al.* (2016); *Wang/Kelan* (2013)).

On the **executive board**, starting from less than 10%, the share of women constantly increased and reached over 16% at the end of the sample period. The increase is statistically significant. Prior research observes a similar trend (*Deutscher BT/BR – DIP* (2023b), BT-Drs. 20/9850; *FidAR e.V.* (2022); *Kirsch et al.* (2022a)). However, the overall level of female representation differs among prior research findings due to the varying sample sizes and sample characteristics (e.g., *Kirsch et al.* (2022a) report 8% female executive board members based on the 200 largest companies in Germany in 2021, whereas *FidAR e.V.* (2022) find nearly 15% among the public and co-determined companies in Germany in 2021). Additionally, as observed on the supervisory board, a similar association between company size and participation of women among public companies is apparent on the executive board.

Since no mandatory gender quota applies to executive boards, all companies affected by FüPoG I are subject to the GDDR. However, the largest increase (more than three percentage points) in the proportion of women is observable between 2020 and 2021. This relatively large increase can be explained by **anticipation effects of FüPoG II** (section 2.2.4). The mandatory minimum representation introduced by FüPoG II affects approximately more than 60 public companies (*FidAR e.V.* (2021); *FidAR e.V.* (2022)). At the time the law was passed, 24 of these companies still had an all-male executive board (*FidAR e.V.* (2021)). Therefore, the affected companies anticipated the upcoming mandatory minimum representation and appointed at least one woman to the executive board to ensure future compliance with the requirements of FüPoG II (*FidAR e.V.* (2022); *Kirsch et al.* (2023b), p. 28; *Sondergeld/Wroblich* (2021)).

Compared to the findings on supervisory boards, the trend is statistically stronger but remains at a lower absolute level. The larger increase may be explained by the difference in average board size (i.e., total number of board members) between both corporate boards. While the average supervisory board consists of 12.62 members (Table 5-3), the average executive board has only 3.94 members (Table 5-4). Therefore, an **incremental increase in female board members is less achievable on executive boards** (*Terjesen et al.* (2009), p. 332). The appointment of one woman to the executive board corresponds, on average, to an increase in female representation of over 25%. Nevertheless, despite the lower level compared to supervisory boards, the presence of women on executive boards significantly increased after the implementation of the GDDR. Thus, the results indicate that the GDDR shapes the proportion of female executive board members.

In addition to assessing the general development of the proportion of women on corporate boards, the results show that women are rarely appointed to supervisory or executive board chairs. However, increasing gender diversity among corporate board chairs is not part of the stated mission of the GDDR. Despite the overall slightly increasing time trend, the participation of women in supervisory and executive board chairs is at a low level. The findings of *FidAR e.V.* (2022) and *Kirsch et al.* (2022a) support these observations. This indicates a "**second glass ceiling**" within corporate boards (*Bozhinov et al.* (2019)). Despite an overall increase in the presence of women on corporate boards, it does not seem to accompany a considerably higher share of female chairpersonship. Moreover, the results are supported by the finding that employee representatives account for a larger share of the overall increase on supervisory boards (similar results: *FidAR e.V.* (2022)). Since chairpersons of the supervisory board are appointed from shareholder representatives (section 2.2.1), increased gender diversity among employee representatives does not directly affect the selection of the chairperson.

On **management levels below the executive board**, the results show on both levels an increase in the presence of female managers for companies that report the actual composition of at least a two-year rhythm. The study at hand is the first to evaluate the development of the proportion of women at the lower management levels since the introduction of the GDDR.[123] The increase at the first management level is marginally statistically significant[124] and indicates a steady increase. Since the members of executive boards are primarily appointed from this management level (*Deutscher BT/BR – DIP*

[123] The annual information published by the German Federal Government contains comparable information on the composition of management levels below the executive board since 2020 (e.g., *Deutscher BT/BR – DIP* (2020a), BT-Drs. 19/20361). However, these studies only examine reports that provide information on the absolute number of management positions, which results in a small subsample compared to the overall large sample size. Moreover, the examinations solely cover a current year of investigation and do not provide information on time trends on the management levels below the executive board.

[124] As mentioned above, statistical tests need to be interpreted with caution due to the small sample size.

(2023b), BT-Drs. 20/9850, p. 54), an increase in the presence of female managers may contribute to a higher proportion of women on the executive board in the future. The same applies to the second management level below executive boards. Although the increase in the proportion of female managers is statistically insignificant,[125] the proportion of female managers has slightly increased in terms of relative numbers. Consequently, more female managers from the second management level may move up to the first management level and ultimately to the executive board in the future.

In summary, this section discusses whether the implementation of GDDR influence the proportion of women on corporate hierarchy levels. The detailed results on the development of the proportion of women enhance the overall understanding of the effectiveness of GDDR. Besides a statistically significant increase in the proportion of female supervisory and executive board members, gender diversity increases on all corporate hierarchy levels during the sample period. However, differences in the extent of the increases exist and can be explained, for example, by the size of the respective hierarchy level. Overall, the results indicate that GDDR shape the proportion of women in management positions. Therefore, hypothesis H_1 is supported. Figure 5-33 summarizes the result for hypothesis H_1.

H_1:	The proportion of women in management positions increases after the implementation of GDDR.	**Supported**

Figure 5-33: Test result for the GDDR and development of corporate gender diversity hypothesis

5.3.2 Disclosure practice

Compliance with disclosure requirements

Since disclosure of information is an essential element of GDDR, the first research question (RQ1b) investigates the disclosure practice of companies affected by the regulation. The results show that some companies – knowingly or inadvertently – do not comply with the legally binding reporting obligations or do not meet them comprehensively and, thereby, **circumvent the mechanisms of the GDDR**. A substantial share (22%) of the analyzed companies do not respect the GDDR at all or do not fully comply with the disclosure requirements stipulated by the GDDR. For instance, for eight companies, reports providing information on gender diversity at corporate hierarchy levels were not available at all or for every year of the sample period. Since the mechanisms of a GDDR rely on transparency and the power of information, comprehensive publication by regulated companies is crucial for the efficacy of such a regulation.

The finding of unavailable corporate governance statements raises questions regarding **auditors' practices** in dealing with the disclosures required of FüPoG I and the oversight mechanisms of enforcement institutions. In accordance with section 317 (2) sent. 4 HGB auditors are required to verify the availability of information required by FüPoG I (*Kajüter* (2020), Rn. 42). Assuming auditors regularly meet their auditing obligations, reporting

[125] As mentioned above, statistical tests need to be interpreted with caution due to the small sample size.

companies may still fail to comply with regulations. In particular, older reports were unavailable or only made available at the researcher's request. Companies may neglect the ten-year retention period stipulated by section 257 (4) HGB in such cases. However, irrespective of the reason for the unavailability of disclosure required by FüPoG I, this should have been identified by enforcement institutions and led to a fine according to section 334 (1) no. 3 HGB[126]. However, there is no such information on hand that a company received a fine for disregarding the disclosure requirements.

Thus, the results suggest that the considerable proportion of missing or incomplete disclosure weakens the mechanisms intended by the GDDR. Therefore, a **tighter audit of disclosure requirements and stricter enforcement** could contribute to the efficacy of the GDDR as intended by the regulator. In consideration of the theoretical assumptions, complete and comparable disclosure contributes to increased stakeholder pressure and strengthens the regulatory mechanisms of targeted transparency regulations. The regulator has recognized existing weaknesses in the sanction mechanisms and addressed some weaknesses with the introduction of FüPoG II. For example, FüPoG II codified that a self-set target equal to zero must be justified. Otherwise, it is an administrative offense (section 334 (1) no. 3a HGB).

Furthermore, the findings from the available reports reveal differences based on the type of regulatory approach companies are subject to, as well as between public and private companies. Companies that are affected by the mandatory gender quota statistically significantly infringe the disclosure requirements of FüPoG I less frequently than companies that are solely subject to the GDDR (Figure 5-6). Furthermore, quota companies statistically significantly integrate the information required by FüPoG I more frequently into the management report and dedicate them to a separate section within the management report than GDDR companies (Figure 5-10). Thus, the findings indicate that **quota companies' disclosure practice ensures more visible reporting** for report users. By contrast, stakeholders of GDDR companies have to search for a separate publication more often and find less prominently placed information within the report.

Irrespective of the regulatory approach, public companies statistically significantly infringe the requirements of the GDDR less frequently than private companies (Figure 5-6). Moreover, among public companies, meeting the disclosure requirements is positively and statistically significantly associated with index classification of the company (Figure 5-7). Therefore, smaller companies listed on the SDAX publish more frequently reports that are not in line with the GDDR. Drawing a more holistic view, the results indicate that the level of companies' public visibility may determine compliance with the disclosure requirements. In line with theory, public companies are more at the center of interest and exhibit higher societal visibility (section 4.1.2.3). Therefore, **more visible companies tend to comply with disclosure requirements**. Consequently, that may lead to a higher efficacy of the GDDR due to regulatory mechanisms that rely on transparency.

However, the results reveal that reports that are not in line with the disclosure requirements lack different legally required information. Most non-compliant reports fail to meet the

[126] Note that this information refers to the version of the law prior to the amendment on August 7, 2021.

required information regarding gender diversity targets on the first and second management level below the executive board (Figure 5-9). Since positions at higher hierarchical levels are often recruited internally (e.g., *Deutscher BT/BR – DIP* (2023b), BT-Drs. 20/9850, p. 54), **it is essential to increase the representation of women at management levels** below the executive board. Due to the non-compliant and incomplete reports, report users cannot identify companies with low female representation at management levels or non-ambitious targets. Against the background of the GDDR causal chain (Figure 2-3), incomplete information interferes with the ability of report users or information intermediaries to evaluate a company's performance regarding the participation of women.

Development of self-set targets for women in management positions

A **pivotal tool of GDDR** is the requirement to publish self-set targets for the proportion of women of each targeted hierarchy level. The results reveal that the level of self-set targets statistically significantly increase during the sample period for the supervisory and executive boards. Corresponding to the evaluation of the development of the proportion of women on lower management levels, statistical tests of the development of self-set targets are an issue due to small sample sizes. Nevertheless, the self-set targets for the proportion of female managers at the first and second management level below executive boards suggest a slight increase during the sample period.

Additionally, the results do not point to substantial differences in the target-setting behavior for executive boards due to the type of regulatory approach applied on the supervisory board. While quota companies do not have to set targets for the supervisory board, both the absolute targets and the development of targets for the executive board align with those of GDDR companies (Figure 5-25). The annual information of the German Federal Government observes comparable trends (*Deutscher BT/BR – DIP* (2023b), BT-Drs. 20/9850, p. 52). However, since the findings of prior research do not explicitly distinguish between quota and GDDR companies, the results are only comparable to a restricted extent.

Furthermore, the findings indicate that private companies tend to set targets that are higher on average compared to public companies. This observation holds for the supervisory board (Figure 5-21), the executive board (Figure 5-25), as well as the first (Figure 5-11) and second management level below the executive board (Table 5-13). **Different reasons can cause this differing target-setting behavior**. Firstly, due to the prohibition of deterioration, companies are not allowed to set targets that aim at a proportion of women that fall below the actual value. Since private companies exhibit, on average, a higher presence of women on supervisory and executive boards during the sample period, and at least partially on the first and second management level, they are legally required to set a higher minimum target on average. Besides this technical reason, another cause may be the characteristics of private and public companies. As supervisory boards of private companies consist, on average, of more members than public companies subject to the GDDR, private companies can set targets that imply a more gradual increase. On the contrary, the size of public companies' executive boards slightly exceeds that of private companies. However, on average, the proportion of female executive board members is higher in private companies during the sample period. This may cause higher self-set targets despite the smaller average board size.

Comparable trends are observable for the management levels below the executive board. While private companies employ, on average, more female managers on both management levels than public companies, they also disclose higher self-set targets most of the time. Another factor that may contribute to the higher targets of private companies may be reasoned by companies' organizational structures. Public companies listed on the major indexes tend to be larger on average than private companies. Therefore, the **hierarchal structures of private companies may be flatter**, resulting in a higher presence of female managers and more ambitious target-setting behavior. However, due to the lack of legally binding definitions of management levels, varying corporate-specific definitions may cause fuzzy and limited comparable targets on management levels.

In addition, besides differences in the level of target-setting, the results find discrepancies in the frequency of self-set targets equal to zero. By disclosing targets that do not aim for the participation of women, companies meet the disclosure requirements without showing an intention to increase gender diversity. The results reveal that companies regularly make use of this option, particularly on the executive board (Figure 5-26). While companies use targets equal to zero on the supervisory board only in 10% of the reports, **every second self-set target for the executive board is equal to zero**. These findings are supported by prior research. Although the annual information of the German Federal Government does not report accumulated results since the introduction of the GDDR, it finds targets equal to zero in 60% to 70% of the analyzed reports, depending on the year. Thus, the researchers observe a more frequent target-setting of zero for the executive board, which may be explained by the larger sample size, which includes many small private companies. *FidAR e.V.* (2022) also do not provide accumulated results but report comparable ratios ranging between 65% (for 2015) and 30% (for 2021). The high number of non-positive targets for the composition of the executive board could be particularly related to the small average size of the executive board. While supervisory boards consist of double-digit numbers of members, executive boards typically consist of a low to mid single-digit number of members. Consequently, incremental increases in gender diversity are not possible.

Whereas private companies set targets that do not envisage the appointment of a woman to the supervisory board in only rare exceptions, public companies statistically significantly set more frequently self-set targets of zero (Figure 5-22). The annual information of the German Federal Government find more frequent targets greater than zero among private companies than public companies subject to the GDDR. The apparent differences can be explained by the provisions of FüPoG I. Public companies that are required to set targets for the supervisory board are not subject to parity co-determination. Accordingly, they are not affected by the mandatory gender quota. By contrast, the private companies of the sample are all parity co-determined. Due to the greater participation of employee representatives on parity co-determined supervisory boards, these boards may set positive targets more frequently. This assumption is supported by the finding that, on average, the proportion of women is higher among employee representatives than shareholder representatives.[127] Even if the results indicate that public companies set more frequent targets equal to zero, this should always be considered against the background of the different levels of co-determination. However, on the executive board, the frequency of negative targets does not differ significantly between private and public companies (Figure 5-26).

Target achievement of self-set targets

Setting a target of zero has the inherent characteristic that companies cannot fail to achieve it. Suppose a company is considering increasing gender diversity on the executive board (or at another management level) but is unsure whether it can achieve it. In this case, it can define such a target as a precaution. In this respect, the regulations of the **GDDR provide communicative leeway** for companies subject to reporting requirements. On the one hand, by setting ambitious targets, companies can signal the intention to increase gender diversity. Hence, in line with stakeholder and legitimacy theory, companies affirm that they intend to foster gender diversity within their company and, hence, pretend to align corporate behavior with societal expectations. However, if a company does not achieve the targeted gender diversity contrary to its communicated targets, it must publish this following the requirements of the GDDR. In this case, the company may have to fear sanctions from stakeholders because it has failed to achieve its targets and has not demonstrated the behavior society desires. On the other hand, companies may fail to signal their efforts to encourage an increase in gender diversity. If they increase the level of gender diversity contrary to the previously stated targets, they can exploit it in their reports and highlight their socially desirable behavior. Which strategy is the most promising may depend on the characteristics of powerful stakeholder groups due to their individual expectations or the behavior of industry peer-companies. Companies have to evaluate an appropriate target-setting behavior against the backdrop of company-specific influencing factors. With the introduction of FüPoG II, the regulator is taking countermeasures by stipulating the obligation to justify setting a zero target, thus making it more difficult for companies to set such a target for strategic reasons.

An indicator of which strategy may be performed by the companies is the frequency of how often they achieve their self-set targets on various hierarchy levels. Irrespective of the hierarchy level, the companies tend to achieve their self-set targets overall. However, while targets for supervisory (16% (Figure 5-24)) and executive boards (15% (Figure 5-27)) are missed roughly in every seventh report, the failure rates on the first (37% (Figure 5-30)) and second management level (34% (Figure 5-31)) are remarkably higher. Besides the frequency of target achievement at the first management level, the results indicate no significant differences between companies due to the capital market orientation. In conclusion, **companies tend to set achievable targets**, especially on the supervisory and executive boards. This finding indicates that companies avoid defining and disclosing targets that may result in failure and, thus, need to be justified. The larger hierarchy size may explain the higher missing rates on the first and second management level. While appointments to supervisory boards and executive boards are usually planned for the long

[127] For an overview on the development in the proportion of women on supervisory boards by representatives, cf. Appendix 2.

term and contractually regulated, lower hierarchical levels can be affected by unforeseen changes (e.g., the resignation of an employee). This makes predictability more difficult and results in a higher failure rate. Since achieving self-set targets is not required by the GDDR, it is up to the users of the reports to judge missed targets.

Explanations of the reasons that lead to missed self-set targets provide valuable insights. However, the results show that a considerable proportion of companies does not consistently comply with the reporting obligation of the GDDR and does not disclose the reasons for not achieving the target. This observation holds for all hierarchical levels. Moreover, there are slight differences in terms of capital market orientation. At all hierarchical levels, public companies more frequently explain why they were unable to achieve the target. However, solely on the first management level, the difference between private and public companies is statistically significant. In line with legitimacy and institutional theory, public companies are more in the focus of public attention. Accordingly, **higher public perception could mean that companies are exposed to greater pressure to justify their actions** and provide explanations more frequently. However, as the justification of missed targets is a mandatory reporting requirement, it is, in any case, remarkable that it is not applied more broadly.

Companies state a bunch of reasons why the intended gender diversity is not met during the target achievement period. Companies frequently justify the underrepresentation of women on the supervisory and executive board with technical reasons. For example, companies state that the target was not achieved due to changes in the corporate board size or the departure of female board members. However, the most stated explanation for the executive board is the unavailability of qualified female candidates (Table 5-10). This explanation is also mentioned second most frequently at the first and second management level. Accordingly, companies do not attribute the reason for missing the target to their own organization but rather to **inadequacies on the supply side**. The justifications of the companies indicate that more well-qualified female managers are needed to increase gender diversity at higher management levels. Accordingly, the GDDR regulations already target the second management level below the executive board to promote young female talents. However, it could be long before young female talent is trained to break through the glass ceiling.

However, at the first and second management level, companies most frequently state that the self-set target is not achieved due to reorganizational measures. As the hierarchy levels were not legally defined by FüPoG I and companies are not obliged to publish their own definition (2.2.3.4), this is a **difficult reason for report users to verify**. It also gives companies the discretion to adjust the definition of management levels at short notice if it is foreseeable that the objectives cannot be achieved. Furthermore, a short-term redefinition is not noticeable, as the content of the disclosures is not reviewed by an auditor. The regulator is also taking countermeasures in this regard with FüPoG II and obliging companies to disclose the absolute number of positions in addition to the percentage target. Based on this information, report users can track and review changes in composition.

In summary, the study at hand describes the disclosure practice in accordance with FüPoG I in detail. Firstly, most companies comply with the mandatory disclosure requirements. Nevertheless, a non-negligible proportion of companies infringe the reporting obligations. Secondly, companies that are subject to the mandatory gender quota for the supervisory board set more ambitious targets for gender diversity on the executive board and tend to report more transparently on target achievement than companies exclusively subject to the GDDR. Moreover, the capital market orientation seems to influence the level of self-set targets and the degree of transparent reporting. Private companies tend to aim for a higher degree of gender diversity at all hierarchy levels than public companies. By contrast, public companies integrate the information more transparently within their management report and justify the reasons for missed targets more often. Within public companies, the size of the companies also seems to determine the reporting practice. Small companies often set lower targets and reports and are less compliant with the reporting standards. Overall, on the one hand, the study at hand indicates that the levels of self-set targets (frequently statistically significant) increase during the sample period. In combination with the actual increase in the proportion of women in management positions (RQ1a), the findings show that the GDDR promote gender diversity in management positions. On the other hand, the results reveal weaknesses and inadequacies in the regulatory design of FüPoG I. For instance, many companies do not meet the regulatory requirements of the GDDR, indicating insufficient regulation enforcement. However, with the amendments to FüPoG II, the legislator appears to have addressed critical points of criticism of the existing reporting obligations.

6 Determinants of GDDR efficacy

This chapter addresses the second research question (RQ2) and analyzes the determinants of GDDR efficacy. Section 6.1 describes the research model, the variables included in the regression models, and the sample selection process. Section 6.2 presents the empirical results for both the supervisory board and the executive board subsample, comprising descriptive statistics, bivariate analyses, and multivariate regressions for each sub-study. Moreover, the section is complemented by sensitivity analyses and a critical evaluation of each sub-study. Finally, section 6.3 concludes with a comparative discussion of the empirical results of both sub-studies.

6.1 Research design

6.1.1 Multivariate panel regression model

The analysis of determinants of GDDR efficacy is performed on a balanced panel data set. A **balanced panel data set** considers repeated observations of an outcome variable (e.g., the proportion of women) and other variables for each cross-sectional unit (e.g., a company) over a certain period (*Zeger/Liang* (1986), p. 121).

The dependent variable of the multivariate panel regression model is continuous. To analyze a continuous dependent variable of a panel data set, an ordinary least squares (OLS) regression can be used (*Das* (2023), pp. 476–477). Estimating regression parameters based on an **OLS regression** requires different prerequisites to provide valid results.[128] First, it is assumed that the variables are normally distributed to allow valid results. A minimum of 30 observations is required to assume a normal distribution (central limit theorem (*Auer/Rottmann* (2020), pp. 285–286)). Second, the relationship between the independent and dependent variables has to be linear (*Backhaus et al.* (2023), p. 104). The study uses the natural logarithm of certain variables (e.g., company size) to avoid non-linear variables. This procedure is in line with prior literature (e.g., *Gregorič et al.* (2017); *Peña-Martel et al.* (2022)). The third assumption requires that all variables included in the model are relevant and that no relevant exogenous variables are missing (*Backhaus et al.* (2023), p. 107). The study at hand derives variables from theory and literature. In addition, all variables are well-established in prior literature. Therefore, the study addresses the prerequisite and is likely to include all relevant variables. Additionally, the application of regression specification error tests (RESET) shows that the models are correctly specified and that no significant non-linear terms or interaction effects have been omitted (*Ramsey* (1969), p. 361).

Fourth, the explanatory variables must be independent from each other to avoid **multicollinearity** (*Backhaus et al.* (2023), pp. 118–119). A model including multicollinear variables can lead to biased regression results (*Das* (2023), p. 144). A perfect correlation between two variables exists if changes in one variable always result in proportional and consistent changes in the other variable (*Auer/Rottmann* (2020), p. 511). This implies that the second variable does not provide any additional explanatory value. The study addresses multicollinearity issues in two ways. Firstly, correlation coefficients are determined to identify collinear variables. If multicollinear variables are identified, a regression model

[128] Cf. *Backhaus et al.* (2023), pp. 101–135.

without these variables is performed to mitigate multicollinearity issues. Secondly, variance inflation factors (VIFs) are calculated for every regression. A VIF that exceeds the value of 10 indicates multicollinearity (*Auer/Rottmann* (2020), p. 514).

Finally, OLS regressions presuppose some assumptions regarding the **error terms**. OLS regressions rely on the assumption that the expected value of the error terms is zero for all observations (*Backhaus et al.* (2023), p. 113). Systematic errors in the measurement (heteroscedasticity) can violate the assumption of the expected value of zero (*Auer/Rottmann* (2020), pp. 446–447). The regression models consider robust standard errors to overcome these issues (*Wooldridge* (2010), pp. 56–57; for panel data sets with fixed effects structures: *Das* (2023), p. 491). Moreover, another issue for OLS regression assumptions is the correlation between independent variables and the error term (autocorrelation *Auer/Rottmann* (2020), p. 539). In panel data sets, correlations of residuals across companies or across time are an issue and result in biased coefficients (*Das* (2023), pp. 552–553). Time-invariant or industry-invariant characteristics may bias the analysis of determinants of GDDR efficacy. For example, the proportion of female employees within a certain industry may be higher than in other industries, resulting in greater participation of women in management positions in more-female industries. Such time-invariant characteristics can influence the validity of the analysis. Considering year and industry fixed effects addresses this issue (*Wooldridge* (2020), p. 463).

Furthermore, the regression tables report statistics to show the goodness of fit of the performed regression, which indicate how well the OLS regression fits the data (*Wooldridge* (2020), p. 35). First, F-statistics (F-stat) are provided for every model, indicating the overall significance of the regression.[129] Secondly, the tables report the **adjusted R^2** statistic.[130] The adjusted R^2 indicates how much of the total variance of the dependent variable is explained by the independent variables (*Backhaus et al.* (2023), p. 88). A higher adjusted R^2 means the independent variables explain a larger portion of the total variance of the dependent variable. If the independent variables explain the complete variance, the adjusted R^2 reports a value of 100% (*Auer/Rottmann* (2020), p. 430).

6.1.2 Variables

The study at hand analyzes the determinants of GDDR efficacy based on multivariate regression models described in the previous section. The models employ **two proxies as dependent variables** to measure the efficacy of GDDR. Furthermore, the independent variables are two proxies for the determinants of GDDR efficacy. These independent variables are derived based on theoretical considerations and findings of prior literature (section 4.2.2) and consist of determinants that consider public visibility and corporate board gender diversity in advance of GDDR.

This analysis performs **two sub-studies** to evaluate the efficacy of GDDR: a supervisory board sub-study and an executive board sub-study. Although most independent variables are the same for both sub-studies, some determinants are specific to the executive board

---

[129] For a discussion of the F-stat results, cf. *Auer/Rottmann* (2020), pp. 468–469.

[130] For an explanation of the differences between R^2 and adjusted R^2 statistics, cf. *Backhaus et al.* (2023), pp. 93–96.

sub-study. It is explicitly stated if certain variables are conducted only in the executive board sub-study. The descriptive analysis in chapter 5 revealed that data availability for gender diversity at the first and second management levels below the executive board is limited. The data base is insufficient for inferential statistical analysis, and therefore, a sub-study on these management levels is not conducted.

GDDR efficacy measures

The efficacy of GDDR cannot be evaluated based on legal definitions. However, the regulator argues that the increase in corporate gender diversity is the main objective of GDDR (*BT-Drs.* 18/4227, p. 2). Following *Mensi-Klarbach et al.* (2021), the efficacy of gender diversity regulation can be measured by what is demanded, i.e., an increase in gender diversity on the targeted corporate hierarchy level (*Mensi-Klarbach et al.* (2021), p. 582).[131] Hence, the **increase in the proportion of women** is measured to assess the efficacy of GDDR. Depending on the sub-study under investigation, the composition of supervisory boards or executive boards is examined. The proportion of female supervisory board members is calculated in a given company and year to measure gender diversity of supervisory boards by dividing the number of female supervisory board members by the total number of supervisory board members (also: *Mensi-Klarbach et al.* (2021); *Peña-Martel et al.* (2022); *Perrault* (2015)). The calculation method is applied analogously to the executive board. The calculated gender diversity in 2014 – the year before GDDR was introduced – is used as the base year. Accordingly, gender diversity in a given year determines the change in the proportion of women in relation to the base year. Equations 6.1 and 6.2 illustrate the delta calculation in the proportion of women for the supervisory and executive board. These proxies are continuous variables. Therefore, they can be analyzed using the OLS panel regression model.

$$(6.1) \quad \Delta PoWoSB_{i,t} = \frac{PoWoSB_{i,t}}{PoWoSB_{i,2014}}$$

where,

$\Delta PoWoSB_{i,t}$	is the dependent variable measuring the delta of the proportion of women on the supervisory board between year *t* and the base year,
$PoWoSB_{i,t}$	is the proportion of women on the supervisory board in year *t*,
$PoWoSB_{i,2014}$	is the proportion of women on the supervisory board in the base year 2014,
i	is an item in the company index, and
t	is an item in the period index (years).

131 For a similar measurement of the efficacy of gender diversity regulation, cf. *Gregorič et al.* (2017) which follow *Ingram/Simons* (1995).

$$(6.2) \quad \Delta PoWoEB_{i,t} = \frac{PoWoEB_{i,t}}{PoWoEB_{i,2014}}$$

where,

$\Delta PoWoEB_{i,t}$	is the dependent variable measuring the delta of the proportion of women on the executive board between the current year and the base year,
$PoWoEB_{i,t}$	is the current proportion of women on the executive board, and
$PoWoEB_{i,2014}$	is the proportion of women on the executive board in the base year 2014.

An alternative proxy to assess the efficacy of GDDR is the development of **self-set gender diversity targets** on the respective hierarchy levels. Achieving a de facto increase in gender diversity can take several years due to existing mandates and contractual relationships. Accordingly, companies can disclose self-set targets to signal their intention to increase the proportion of women in the future. Although these targets entail no legal commitment to actual implementation, companies are incentivized to set realistic targets in order to avoid reputational damage (section 4.1). Therefore, the self-set targets can be used as a proxy for GDDR efficacy. The variables $\Delta TarWoSB$ (for the supervisory board sub-study) and $\Delta TarWoEB$ (for the executive board sub-study) are measured as the percentage value retrieved from corporate disclosure of a given company and year.[132]

Determinant variables

To assess the **determinants of GDDR efficacy** identified in section 4.2.2, several proxies are used. First, determinant variables that consider public visibility and corporate board gender diversity in advance of GDDR are explained. Second, additional determinant variables for GDDR efficacy on the executive board are introduced.

Prior literature indicates that the **level of public pressure** determines the efficacy of gender diversity regulations in voluntary regulatory contexts. Media attention[133] is a frequently used proxy for public pressure in prior literature in multiple research disciplines (*Chang et al.* (2023); *Dyck et al.* (2008); *Liu/McConnell* (2013); *Fang/Peress* (2009); *Fiss/Zajac* (2006); for a gender diversity context: *Anca/Gabaldon* (2013); *Peña-Martel et al.* (2022); for an overview: *Graf-Vlachy et al.* (2020)). Media attention exerts pressure on companies to consider the interests of their stakeholders or society at large due to the increased public visibility of the company. The more media attention a company attracts, the more pressure stakeholders can exert (*Fiss/Zajac* (2006), p. 1177). In order to maintain their reputation and ensure the long-term survival of the company, companies must strive to meet the expectations of their

[132] In certain reports, companies disclose the self-set target as absolute number of women on the respective hierarchy level instead of providing a self-set target as percentage figure. To determine the percentage figure, the aimed absolute number of women is divided by the total number of board members.

[133] Media attention is also referred to as media coverage or media visibility. For the purpose of this study, the terms are used interchangeable.

stakeholders (*Peña-Martel et al.* (2022), p. 194). Consequently, a high level of media attention can positively influence the efficacy of GDDR.

The FACTIVA database provides the number of newspaper articles containing information about a given company in a given year. The number of newspaper articles is retrieved for each company and each year between 2014 and 2021 and serves as a **proxy for media attention**. The data include newspaper articles in the German and English press. Alerts, announcements of dividend payments, or quotes are excluded from the data to retrieve solely newspaper articles that provide informative content (*Peña-Martel et al.* (2022), p. 194). Accordingly, the data consists of two separate datasets. The first one comprises the number of German newspaper articles for each company and each year. The second one comprises the number of English newspaper articles for each company and each year.

Theory proposes that a **high level of public pressure** (H_{2a}/H_{6a}) or a **low level of public pressure** (H_{2b}/H_{6b}) is associated with the efficacy of GDDR. In accordance with the hypotheses derived in section 4.2.2, it is assumed that high public pressure is positively associated with GDDR efficacy. In contrast, low public pressure is assumed to be negatively associated with GDDR efficacy. A dummy variable (*high pressure*) serves as a proxy for high public pressure. It takes the value of one, if a company belongs to the top 20%-percentile of German and English news counts in the current year, and zero otherwise. Equivalently, another dummy variable (*low pressure*) serves as a proxy for low public pressure. The variable takes the value of one, if a company belongs to the low 20%-percentile of German and English news counts in the current year, and zero otherwise.

Theory also suggests an association between **capital market orientation** and the efficacy of GDDR (H_3/H_7). Hypotheses H_3 assumes an undirected and H_7 positive association between companies' capital market orientation and GDDR efficacy. The company's listing status serves as a proxy (*listed*) in this regard. The dummy variable takes the value of one, if a company is listed on a regulated market, and zero otherwise. Data regarding the legal forms of the companies is downloaded from the BvD Dafne database.

Furthermore, theory proposes that a **company's age** is a determinant of the efficacy of GDDR (H_4/H_8). On the one hand, due to the more central position of older companies within society, they are subject to more public attention and higher visibility. Therefore, these companies tend to face more pressure to meet societal expectations. On the other hand, institutionalized structures of older, often predominantly male-dominated boards may inhibit an increase in gender diversity. Consequently, in line with hypotheses H_4 and H_8, an undirected association is assumed between companies' age and GDDR efficacy. *Firm age* is measured as the natural logarithm of the current year subtracted by the company's year of incorporation (*Gregorič et al.* (2017), p. 277; *Peña-Martel et al.* (2022), p. 195).

Moreover, theory and literature suggest that the **reporting practice** of companies before GDDR was implemented determines the efficacy of GDDR (H_5/H_9). Companies that voluntarily set quantified targets for the proportion of women on the supervisory or executive board indicate that they considered gender diversity issues before the introduction of GDDR. An undirected association is assumed between the voluntary reporting practice on the respective board level and GDDR efficacy (section 4.2.2). The study uses *pre-law TarWoSB* and *pre-law TarWoEB* as proxies for voluntary quantifiable gender diversity targets in advance of GDDR. Both variables are binary. *Pre-law TarWoSB* takes the value of one, if a company has disclosed quantified targets about the proportion of women on the supervisory board before the implementation of GDDR, and zero otherwise. Similarly, *Pre-law TarWoEB* takes the value of one, if a company has disclosed quantified targets for the proportion of women on the executive board before the implementation of GDDR, and zero otherwise. The data is hand-collected from annual reports of the fiscal year 2014.

Due to the mechanisms of the German two-tier corporate governance system, the supervisory board appoints the members of the executive board. In this regard, theory proposes that **gender diversity on the supervisory board** is associated with the efficacy of GDDR on the executive board (H_{10}). To consider the extent of gender diversity of the supervisory board, the variable *PoWoSB* is calculated as the number of female supervisory board members divided by the total number of supervisory board members in a specific year (*Mensi-Klarbach et al.* (2021); *Peña-Martel et al.* (2022); *Perrault* (2015)). This proxy is solely used to determine GDDR efficacy on the executive board. The data is hand-collected from annual reports.

The chairperson of the supervisory board is vested with special rights. He or she has a particular influence on appointment decisions and, thus, on gender diversity of the executive board. Theory suggests a positive association between the **gender of the supervisory board chairperson** and GDDR efficacy on the executive board (H_{11}). *SB chair* is measured by the gender of the supervisory board chairperson. The dummy variable takes the of one, if the supervisory board chairperson of a company is female in the current year, and zero otherwise. This proxy is solely used to determine GDDR efficacy on the executive board. The data is hand-collected from annual reports.

Control variables

Besides the determinant variables, literature finds further variables associated with the presence of women on corporate boards. Since research has not yet examined the efficacy of GDDR (by means of inferential statistics), this study uses variables identified by research investigating the effectiveness of voluntary and mandatory regulations. **Prior literature** suggests that board size, the presence of a woman on the board before a gender diversity regulation was implemented, company size, leverage ratio and growth are associated with the efficacy of different regulatory interventions (*Arena et al.* (2015); *Bozhinov et al.* (2021); *Gregorič et al.* (2017); *Mensi-Klarbach et al.* (2021); *Page et al.* (2024); *Peña-Martel et al.* (2022); *Poletti-Hughes/Dimungu-Hewage* (2023); *Sojo et al.* (2016); *Terjesen et al.* (2009)). These variables are included in the regression models.

Board size is proposed to be positively associated with increased proportion of women on corporate boards under regulatory intervention (*Arena et al.* (2015); *Bozhinov et al.* (2021); *Gregorič et al.* (2017); *Mensi-Klarbach et al.* (2021); *Page et al.* (2024); *Peña-Martel et al.* (2022); *Poletti-Hughes/Dimungu-Hewage* (2023); *Sojo et al.* (2016); *Terjesen et al.* (2009)). As explained in the hypotheses development (section 4.2.2), a higher number of board members allows more incremental changes in the board composition in terms of gender diversity (*Terjesen et al.* (2009), p. 332). The proxy for the supervisory board size (*SB size*) is measured as the number of supervisory board members of a company in the current year. Identically, the executive board size (*EB size*) is measured as the number of executive board members of a company at fiscal year-end.

Larger companies are found to have a more prominent perceived status and thus to be more visible in society (*Gregorič et al.* (2017), p. 277). Therefore, larger companies tend to employ more female board members (*Bozhinov et al.* (2021); *Hillman et al.* (2007); *Grosvold et al.* (2007); *Mensi-Klarbach et al.* (2021); *Page et al.* (2024); *Peña-Martel et al.* (2022); *Poletti-Hughes/Dimungu-Hewage* (2023)). Consequently, a positive association between company size and GDDR efficacy is assumed. **Company size** (*firm size*) is the natural logarithm of a company's total assets at fiscal year-end (e.g., *Bozhinov et al.* (2021), p. 1322).

Besides company size, the **presence of a female board member before a gender diversity regulation was implemented** is associated with the impact of the regulation. Companies with at least one woman on their boards have less potential to increase gender diversity, indicating that the objective of gender diversity regulation is partially or fully met in these cases. Accordingly, a negative association is assumed between pre-existing female board membership and the increase in board gender diversity. However, due to the prohibition of deterioration (section 2.2.3.4), a positive relationship is anticipated between pre-existing female board members and the level of self-set targets. The proxy for the pre-law proportion of women on supervisory boards (*pre-law WoSB*) is binary. It takes the value of one if the supervisory board consists of at least one female member in 2014, and zero otherwise. Similarly, the proxy for the executive board (*pre-law WoEB*) takes the value of one if the executive board consists of at least one female member in 2014, and zero otherwise.

Furthermore, an association is assumed between the **leverage** of a company and the proportion of female board members (*Gregorič et al.* (2017); *Peña-Martel et al.* (2022); *Poletti-Hughes/Dimungu-Hewage* (2023)). Companies with a higher leverage ratio face higher pressure to ensure their liquidity and to avoid covenant violation. In cases where companies are highly indebted, they prioritize maintaining financial stability over addressing issues such as gender diversity. Therefore, leverage is assumed to be negatively associated with the proportion of women on corporate boards. *Leverage* is defined as total debt divided by total assets (e.g., *Peña-Martel et al.* (2022), p. 195).

Companies that exhibit **growth rates** are suggested to attract more female candidates and can focus on gender diversity (*Gregorič et al.* (2017), p. 277). Thus, growth rates are found to be positively associated with the proportion of women on corporate boards (*Gregorič et al.* (2017); *Peña-Martel et al.* (2022); *Poletti-Hughes/Dimungu-Hewage* (2023)). The proxy *growth* is measured as the difference between total assets at the fiscal year-end and the fiscal year-end of the base year, divided by total assets at the fiscal year-end of the base year.

Data for the control variables *SB size*, *EB size*, *Pre-law WoSB*, and *Pre-law WoEB* is hand-collected from the annual reports. The financial data for the control variables, *company size*, *leverage*, and *growth* are collected from BvD Dafne. Missing values are added manually. To control for similarities that are unobservable for all companies within a given year or industry, year and industry fixed effects are included in the regression models (*Hillman et al.* (2007); *Mensi-Klarbach et al.* (2021); *Peña-Martel et al.* (2022)).

The determinants of GDDR efficacy are tested based on the **regression models** summarized in equations (6.3) and (6.4). Equation 6.3 presents the empirical model for the efficacy of GDDR determinants on the supervisory board. As a proxy for GDDR efficacy, *ΔPoWoSB* and *TarWoSB* are used to measure the efficacy of GDDR on the supervisory board. Moreover, equation 6.4 illustrates the OLS panel regression model for the analyses of determinants of GDDR efficacy on the executive board. Likewise, the proxies *ΔPoWoEB* and *TarWoEB* are used to measure the efficacy of GDDR on the executive board.

$$(6.3) \quad GDDR_{i,t} = \beta_0 + \beta_1 * high\ pressure_{i.t} + \beta_2 * low\ pressure_{i.t} + \beta_3 * listed_{i.t} + \beta_4 * firm\ age_{i.t} + \beta_5 * pre - law\ TarWoSB_{i.2014} + \sum\gamma_n * Controls_{i,t} + \sum\delta_n * FE + \varepsilon_{i,t}$$

where,

$GDDR_{i,t}$	is any dependent variable measuring GDDR efficacy,
$high\ pressure_{i,t}$	is a dummy variable that takes the value of one, if company *i* belongs to the top 20%-percentile of German and English news counts in year *t*, and zero otherwise,
$low\ pressure_{i,t}$	is a dummy variable that takes the value of one, if company *i* belongs to the low 20%-percentile of German and English news counts in year *t*, and zero otherwise,
$listed_{i,t}$	is a dummy variable that takes the value of one, if company *i* is listed on a regulated market in year *t*, and zero otherwise,
$\text{firm age}_{i,t}$	is the natural logarithm of year *t* subtracted by the year of incorporation of company *i*,
$Pre - law\ TarWoSB_{i,2014}$	is a dummy variable that takes the value of one, if a company *i* has disclosed a quantified target about the proportion of women on the supervisory board before the implementation of GDDR, and zero otherwise,
$\sum Controls_{i,t}$	are the control variables as previously defined,[134]
$\sum FE$	are industry and year fixed effects,
$\varepsilon_{i,t}$	is the error term for company *i* in year *t*, and

all other variables as defined above.

[134] For an overview of the control variables and their calculation, cf. Appendix 4.

$$(6.4)\quad GDDR_{i,t} = \beta_0 + \beta_1 * high\,pressure_{i.t} + \beta_2 * low\,pressure_{i.t} + \beta_3 * listed_{i.t} + \beta_4 * firm\,age_{i.t} + \beta_5 * Pre - law\,TarWoEB_{i.2014} + \beta_6 * PoWoSB_{i.t-1} + \beta_7 * SB\,chair_{i.t-1} + \sum\gamma_n * Controls_{i,t} + \sum\delta_n * FE + \varepsilon_{i,t}$$

where,

$EB\_pre - law\,reporting_{i,2014}$ is a dummy variable that takes the value of one, if company *i* has disclosed quantified targets about the proportion of women on the executive board before the implementation of GDDR, and zero otherwise,

$\text{PoWoSB}_{i,t-1}$ is the ratio of female supervisory board members over the total number of supervisory board members of company *i* in year *t-1*,

$SB\,chair_{i,t-1}$ is a dummy variable that takes the value of one, if the supervisory board chairperson of company *i* is female in year *t-1*, and zero otherwise,

$\sum Controls_{i,t}$ are the control variables as previously defined,[135]

$\sum FE$ are industry and year fixed effects,

$\varepsilon_{i,t}$ is the error term for company *i* in year *t*, and

all other variables as defined above.

The next section presents the sample adjustments made to investigate the GDDR efficacy of each subsample.

6.1.3 Sample adjustments

Sample adjustments are required to assess GDDR efficacy on the supervisory and executive board. Both sub-studies are based on the **final sample for the analysis selected for descriptive analyses in chapter 5** (Table 5-1). Due to their different business model and to ensure consistency with prior research, eight companies that provide financial services (banks and insurance companies) are excluded from the sample (*Farrell/Hersch* (2005); *Gregorič et al.* (2017)). Furthermore, the initial sample comprises subsidiary companies that are required to publish information regarding GDDR in accordance with FüPoG I (section 2.2.3.4). However, these subsidiaries are included in the consolidated financial statements of their parent companies and, therefore, do not provide separate financial statements. Since some control variables[136] rely on financial information from the financial statements, 63 companies are excluded from the sample.

[135] For an overview of the control variables and their calculation, cf. Appendix 5.

[136] The calculation of the control variables *firm size*, *leverage*, and *growth* requires financial information.

To analyze the determinants of GDDR efficacy on the supervisory board, 63 companies that are subject to the **mandatory gender quota** on the supervisory board have to be removed from the sample. The GDDR does not regulate these companies on the supervisory board. Therefore, these companies are not in the scope of the investigation.

For the analysis of the executive board, 13 companies that are organized in a legal form that does not foresee an executive board are excluded (e.g., KGaA). Figure 6-1 presents the final sample **composition for both sub-studies**.

Sample adjustments		
	Number of companies	Company years
Final sample used in descriptive analyses (chapter 5)	**214**	**1,498**
Less financial institutions (banks, insurance companies)	-8	-56
Less subsidiaries	-63	-441
Base sample for GDDR efficacy determinants analysis	**143**	**1,001**
Sub-study of supervisory boards:		
Less companies subject to the mandatory gender quota	-63	-441
Final sample (6.2.1)	**80**	**560**
Sub-study of executive boards:		
Less companies that have an organizational structure that has no formal executive board (e.g., KGaA)	-13	-91
Final sample (6.2.2)	**130**	**910**

Table 6-1: Sample adjustments for the analysis of determinants of GDDR efficacy

6.2 Results

This section presents the results of the determinants analysis of GDDR efficacy to address the second research question (RQ2). The results are structured into the two sub-studies. First, section 6.2.1 examines the determinants of GDDR efficacy on the supervisory board. Second, section 6.2.2 presents the results on the executive board. Both sub-studies are structured similarly. Initially, the determinants and control variables are described. Next, the bivariate correlations of variables used in the regression model are analyzed. Subsequently, the results of the multivariate regression models, sensitivity analyses, and robustness tests are presented. Finally, the determinants of GDDR efficacy on each hierarchy level are critically evaluated against the backdrop of the hypotheses.

6.2.1 Supervisory board

6.2.1.1 Descriptive statistics

The descriptive statistics for all variables used in the multivariate panel regression model (equation 6.1) are presented in Table 6-2 and Table 6-3. First, the **determinant variables** of GDDR efficacy on the supervisory board are tabulated in Table 6-2. Second, Table 6-3 presents the descriptive statistics for the control variables. For the continuous determinant and control variables, the table reports the sample size (n), mean, standard deviation (Std. dev.), 25% percentile (Q25), median, and 75% percentile (Q75). Some of the used variables are dummy variables. Consequently, the statistics for these binary variables report solely the proportion of company-year observations that exhibit certain characteristics. Because prior research does not examine the determinants of GDDR efficacy, comparable studies on voluntary disclosure or, if applicable, studies on mandatory gender quotas are considered to compare the results of this study with prior research.

Descriptive statistics for the (continuous) determinant variables of the supervisory board							
Variables[a]	Sample	n	Mean	Std. dev.	Q25	Median	Q75
Firm age	Full sample	1,001	53.08	48.14	19.00	27.00	88.00
	SB sample	560	39.83	38.54	17.00	23.00	43.00

Descriptive statistics for the (binary) determinant variables of the supervisory board			
Variables[a]	Sample	n	# of company-years (% of company-years)
High pressure	Full sample	1,001	156 (16%)
	SB sample	560	74 (13%)
Low pressure	Full sample	1,001	185 (18%)
	SB sample	560	72 (13%)
Listed	Full sample	1,001	742 (74%)
	SB sample	560	301 (54%)
Pre-law TarWoSB	Full sample	1,001	644 (64%)
	SB sample	560	238 (43%)

[a]Firm age is the difference between the current year and the year of incorporation of a firm. High pressure is a dummy variable that takes the value of one, if a company belongs to the top 20%-quantile of German and English news counts, and zero otherwise. Low pressure is a dummy variable that takes the value of one, if a company belongs to the low 20%-quantile of German and English news counts, and zero otherwise. Listed is a dummy variable that takes the value of one, if the firm is listed on a regulated market, and zero otherwise. Pre-law TarWoSB is a dummy variable that takes the value of one, if a quantified target about the proportion of women on the supervisory board was disclosed before the enactment of the GDDR, and zero otherwise.

Table 6-2: Descriptive statistics for the determinant variables of the supervisory board

High pressure is a proxy for companies being subject to high public pressure. For the full sample, 16% of the company-year observations are subject to high public pressure. This value is slightly below the 20%-percentile since companies must be covered in both German and English news counts in the top 20%-percentile. For the supervisory board subsample (SB sample), 13% of the company-year observation companies face high public pressure. Additionally, Table 6-2 shows that 18% of the company-year observations in the full sample and 13% of the supervisory board subsample are subject to **low pressure**. Hence, both high pressure and low pressure are slightly less frequently represented in the supervisory board subsample.

74% of the companies in the full sample are **listed** on a regulated market. This type of capital market orientation is 20 percentage points less frequently represented in the supervisory board subsample (54%). Companies are excluded from the supervisory board subsample if they are subject to the mandatory gender quota on the supervisory board. Since this regulatory approach solely affects listed and parity co-determined companies, the mandatory gender quota is not applied to private companies. Thus, the fact that all excluded companies are listed explains the lower share of listed companies in the supervisory board subsample.

For the full sample, the mean **firm age**[137] is 53.08 years. The companies considered in the supervisory board subsample are younger on average, with a mean of 39.83 years. The median age differs considerably, with 27.00 years for the full sample and 23.00 years for the supervisory board subsample. The distinctive differences in the magnitude of mean and median indicate that the samples consist of companies considerably older than the average of companies, resulting in a right-skewed distribution of the firm age variable. With regard to the Q75, the supervisory board subsample (43.00 years) consists of fewer large companies than the full sample (88.00 years). The observable differences can be attributed to the regulatory design of FüPoG I. For the analysis of GDDR efficacy, companies not regulated by GDDR on the supervisory board are excluded. Many companies listed on the DAX and MDAX are not affected by GDDR (section5.1.3). These companies are generally larger and, therefore, tend to be older than the rest of the analyzed companies.

Pre-law TarWoSB is a proxy for voluntary target-setting for the proportion of women on the supervisory board before GDDR came into force. For the full sample, 64% of the companies set a quantified target for the presence of women on the supervisory board in 2014. For the supervisory board subsample, less than half of the companies (43%) set such a target, indicating that companies subject to the mandatory gender quota are more likely to set voluntary targets for the supervisory board gender diversity. The results are in line with theory proposing that listed, larger, and older companies are more in the focus of public attention and, therefore, signal their willingness to consider societal demands. Thus, theory supports the result.

Table 6-3 presents the descriptive statistics for the control variables included in the multivariate regression models. The variables **pre-law WoSB** and **SB size** have already been discussed in section 5.1.3 and section 5.2.3.1 and thus are not re-examined in this chapter.

Firm size is a proxy for the size of a company.[138] For the full sample, companies' total assets average €17.20 billion (mean) with a median of €2.74 billion. The standard deviation is €44.70 billion. By contrast, the companies of the supervisory board subsample are remarkably smaller on average. They exhibit a mean of €2.92 billion, a median of €1.63 billion, and a standard deviation of €4.30 billion. The Q75 (€8.30 billion) of the full sample is substantially lower than its mean (€17.20 billion), suggesting that the full sample consists of companies that are considerably larger than the average and increase the mean. By contrast, the Q75 of the supervisory board subsample exhibits a smaller magnitude (€3.09 billion). This indicates that the supervisory board subsample consists of fewer large companies that substantially influence the mean. The sample composition explains the considerable difference in both samples. Companies subject to the mandatory gender quota (large listed companies) are excluded from the supervisory board subsample, resulting in smaller companies on average for this subsample. Based on the same measurement, *Bozhinov et al.* (2021) report a mean company size of €22.61 billion (*Bozhinov et al.* (2021),

137 *Firm age* is reported as an absolute value for descriptive purpose only. The following regression analyses use the natural logarithm of *firm age*.

138 The proxy for *firm size* is measured by total assets. Total assets are reported as an absolute value for descriptive purpose only. The following regression analyses use the natural logarithm of total assets.

p. 1322). Moreover, *Panzer/Müller* (2015) find a comparable mean company size of €22.52 billion (*Panzer/Müller* (2015), p. 13). The mean company size in these studies is slightly larger because both studies examine a sample of companies listed on the German prime standard, which tend to be larger than private companies.

Descriptive statistics for the (continuous) control variables on the supervisory board							
Variables[a]	**Sample**	**n**	**Mean**	**Std. dev.**	**Q25**	**Median**	**Q75**
SB size	Full sample	1,001	12.45	5.37	6.00	12.00	16.00
	SB sample	560	10.37	5.61	6.00	9.00	16.00
Firm size	Full sample	1,001	17.20	44.70	1.21	2.74	8.30
	SB sample	560	2.92	4.30	0.66	1.63	3.09
Leverage	Full sample	1,001	0.60	0.18	0.49	0.60	0.71
	SB sample	560	0.57	0.21	0.45	0.57	0.70
Growth	Full sample	1,001	0.54	1.23	0.05	0.23	0.57
	SB sample	560	0.60	1.29	0.04	0.22	0.63
Descriptive statistics for the (binary) control variables on the supervisory board							
Variables[a]	**Sample**	**n**	**# of company-years (% of company-years)**				
Pre-law WoSB	Full sample	1,001	826 (83%)				
	SB sample	560	399 (71%)				

[a]SB size is the total number of supervisory board members at fiscal year-end. Firm size is the total assets of the company in € billion. Leverage is the ratio of total liabilities over total assets. Growth is the change in total assets compared to the base year. Pre-law WoSB is a dummy that takes the value of one if the company had at least one female supervisory board member before the enactment of the GDDR, and zero otherwise. The control variables Firm size, Leverage, and Growth are winsorized at the 1st and 99th percentiles.

Table 6-3: Descriptive statistics for the control variables on the supervisory board

Leverage measures the ratio of total liabilities over total assets. The greater the ratio of liabilities over total assets, the more the company is indebted. For the full sample, a mean and median of 0.60 suggest that, on average, liabilities account for 60% of the total assets of a company. With a mean and median of 0.57, the companies in the supervisory board subsample exhibit slightly lower values. However, the mean and median only differ slightly between the two samples. Thus, no considerable differences in the leverage are observable. *Panzer/Müller* (2015) report a comparable mean leverage of 0.65 for companies listed on the German prime standard (*Panzer/Müller* (2015), p. 13). By contrast, *Schumann et al.* (2024) report a considerably higher leverage of 2.23 (mean) (*Schumann et al.* (2024), p. 152). However, this finding must be treated cautiously because *Schumann et al.* (2024) analyze a small sample of companies listed on the DAX.

Growth is a proxy for the growth rates of a company. The proxy is measured by the change in total assets compared to the base year. The mean growth rates of 0.54 (full sample) and 0.60 (supervisory board sample) indicate that, on average, the companies in the samples grew by approximately 54% and 60%, respectively, during the sample period. The median growth (full sample (0.23); supervisory board sample (0.22)) is also comparable and indicates growth for companies in both samples. *Panzer/Müller* (2015) use sales revenues instead of total assets to measure growth rates. Moreover, they calculate the growth rates on a yearly basis. They report a yearly growth of 6.7% for companies listed on the German prime standard (*Panzer/Müller* (2015), p. 14). Using the calculation of the study at hand, this would result in a mean growth of 0.57. Thus, the magnitude of the average growth rate is comparable with the average growth rate found by the study at hand.

6.2.1.2 Correlation analysis

For the study of determinants of GDDR efficacy, first, a bivariate correlation analysis is performed to examine the isolated relationship between the variables (*Döring* (2023), p. 667). This study uses **Spearman's rank correlation**, which enables the investigation of the statistical correlation between two variables.[139] Two variables are compared, and the rank correlation coefficient (Spearman Rho) shows the strength of the monotonic correlation between the two ranks. The rank correlation analysis, according to Spearman, requires that the variables are at least ordinally scaled. Moreover, this test is nonparametric and does not require normal distributed variables. Thus, in contrast to the Bravais-Pearson correlation, which requires continuous variables and assumes a linear association, the Spearman rank correlation is more robust.

In general, **correlation coefficients** are the results of correlation analyses (*Auer/Rottmann* (2020), p. 90). The correlation coefficient can range between -1 and +1.[140] The closer the value is to +1, the more likely a perfectly positive monotonic correlation is assumed. Values close to -1 indicate a perfectly negative monotonic correlation. In contrast, a value of zero or close to zero indicates that there is no correlation. In this study, a correlation coefficient between 0.0 and 0.5 indicates a weak correlation, a medium correlation between 0.5 and 0.7, a strong correlation between 0.7 and 1, and a perfect correlation exists at a value of 1.0. The threshold values apply similarly to positive and negative correlation coefficients (*Kobelt/Steinhausen* (2006), p. 122).[141]

Table 6-4 presents the **correlation analysis for both GDDR efficacy** measures on the supervisory board and the independent variables. The correlation matrix shows the correlation coefficients and the significance levels (p-values in parentheses) for each pairwise correlation. When a pairwise correlation between dependent and independent variables is significant, the correlation coefficient and p-values are printed in bold.

---

[139] Here and in the following, cf. *Auer/Rottmann* (2020), pp. 98–100.

[140] Here and in the following, cf. *Schulze* (2007), p. 130.

[141] Note, that different classification threshold exists in literature, For instance, *Auer/Rottmann* (2020), p. 93, the threshold values for a weak correlation is between 0.0 to 0.5, for a moderate correlation between 0.5 and 0.8 and for a strong correlation between 0.8 to 1.0. By contrast, *Eid et al.* (2017) classify weak correlations between 0.0 and 0.1, moderate correlations between 0.1 and 0.3 and strong correlations between 0.3 and 1.0 (*Eid et al.* (2017), p. 540).

Correlation matrix for the supervisory board sub-study							
Variables[a]	ΔPoWoSB	TarWoSB	High pressure	Low pressure	Listed	Firm age	Pre-law TarWoSB
ΔPoWoSB	-						
TarWoSB	-	-					
High pressure	**0.2375 ***** **(0.0000)**	**0.1819 ***** **(0.0000)**	-				
Low pressure	**-0.0732 *** **(0.0824)**	-0.0180 (0.6722)	-0.1499 *** (0.0000)	-			
Listed	**0.0762 *** **(0.0715)**	-0.0366 (0.3867)	0.3302 *** (0.0000)	-0.3927 *** (0.0000)	-		
Firm age	-0.0021 (0.9613)	-0.0647 (0.1263)	-0.1047 ** (0.0131)	-0.1464 *** (0.0005)	0.1462 *** (0.0005)	-	
Pre-law TarWoSB	**0.0958 **** **(0.0235)**	**-0.0898 **** **(0.0337)**	0.3579 *** (0.0000)	-0.3086 *** (0.0000)	0.7975 *** (0.0000)	0.0851 ** (0.0440)	-

[a]The table reports Spearman correlation coefficients for a pairwise correlation of the GDDR efficacy measures on the supervisory board and determinant variables. Respective p-values are presented below the coefficients in parentheses.
*, **, and *** indicate statistical significance at the 10%, 5%, and 1% levels, respectively.

Table 6-4: Correlation matrix for the supervisory board sub-study

First, *high pressure* (0.2375), *listed* (0.0762), and *pre-law TarWoSB* (0.0958) show a **statistically significant positive correlation** with the delta in the proportion of women on the supervisory board (*ΔPoWoSB*) as the dependent variable. The coefficients are smaller than 0.5, indicating a weak correlation. The coefficient for *high pressure* is highly significant at the 1% level. The coefficients for *pre-law TarWoSB* (5% level) and listed (10% level) exhibit a weaker significance. The results suggest that companies that are subject to *high pressure,* or are listed on a regulated market (*listed*), or set targets for the proportion of women on the supervisory board before GDDR was implemented (*pre-law TarWoSB*) are more likely to increase the presence of women on the board. Furthermore, *low pressure* (-0.0732) reports a **statistically significant negative correlation** with the dependent variable at the 5% level. Accordingly, companies that face low public pressure are less likely to increase the presence of women on the supervisory board. However, *firm age* is negatively correlated with the dependent variable but not on a statistically significant level.

Second, *high pressure* (0.1819) is **highly statistically significant and positively correlated** with target-setting for the proportion of women on the supervisory board (*TarWoSB*). Hence, companies that face higher pressure are more likely to set higher targets for the presence of female supervisory board members. However, the correlation is classified as weak. Moreover, the coefficient of *pre-law TarWoSB* (-0.0898) indicates a **weak statistically significant negative correlation** with *TarWoSB*. Thus, companies that set voluntary targets before GDDR came into force are less likely to disclose higher self-set targets for the proportion of women on the supervisory board. However, the correlation coefficients of low pressure (*low pressure*), listed (*listed*), and company age (*firm age*) are close to zero. These determinant variables are not statistically significantly correlated.

High correlation coefficients between independent variables can suggest **multicollinearity issues**. The independent variables *listed* and *pre-law TarWoSB* exhibit a strong positive and statistically highly significant correlation (0.7975). The correlation indicates that companies listed on a regulated market are more likely to set voluntary targets for the presence of women on the supervisory board before GDDR was implemented. Nevertheless, from a theoretical perspective, the collinearity between these independent variables is reasonable. Listed companies are more frequently the focus of public attention and political debates (section 4.1.2). Moreover, certain large listed companies initiated a voluntary commitment to foster gender diversity before GDDR came into force (section 2.2.3.1), which could further contribute to the high correlation. Finally, to mitigate multicollinearity concerns, the collinear variables are included in separate regression models. Nevertheless, a full regression with all variables included is also performed.[142]

The results of the bivariate correlation analysis indicate that the efficacy of GDDR is associated with several factors. For the first proxy of GDDR efficacy (*ΔPoWoSB), high pressure*, *low pressure*, *listed*, and *pre-law TarWoSB* show an association. By contrast, for the second proxy of GDDR efficacy (*TarWoSB*), only *high pressure* and *pre-law TarWoSB* exhibit an association. However, the bivariate analysis can solely provide a **first indication of the correlations** since only relationships between two variables are investigated. A multivariate regression is performed to take different variables simultaneously into account.

6.2.1.3 Multivariate analyses

This section examines the determinants of the efficacy of GDDR on the supervisory board to address the second research question (RQ2). To this end, hypotheses H_{2a} – H_5 are tested. GDDR efficacy is measured with **two alternative proxies**: *ΔPoWoSB* (Panel A) and *TarWoSB* (Panel B).

Table 6-5 presents the results of the **multivariate panel regression of Panel A**. To mitigate potential multicollinearity issues identified in the correlation analysis, six different regression models are used. Model 1 is the general model without any control variables and fixed effects. Model 2 includes control variables but does not consider fixed effects. Model 3 is the full model that takes into account industry and year fixed effects. Model 4 to Model 6 address the multicollinearity issues for each pairwise correlation identified in the correlation analysis.

[142] The pairwise correlation between independent variables and control variables as well as among control variables indicate some multicollinearity issues: *SB size* and *pre-law WoSB* exhibit a strongly positive and statistically highly significant correlation. Moreover, *SB size* is strongly negative and statistically highly significantly correlated with *listed* and *pre-law TarWoSB*. To avoid multicollinearity issues, the same procedure is used as for the determinant variables. For the full correlation matrix of *ΔPoWoSB*, cf. Appendix 6. For the full correlation matrix of *TarWoSB*, cf. Appendix 7.

Multivariate panel regression models for determinants of GDDR efficacy on the supervisory board								
Panel A: Proportion of women on the supervisory board ΔPoWoSB as dependent variable								
Variables	**Hypothesis**	**Expected sign**	**Model 1**	**Model 2**	**Model 3**	**Model 4**	**Model 5**	**Model 6**
High pressure	H_{2a}	(+)	0.101*** (6.61)	0.091*** (5.90)	0.063*** (3.29)	0.058*** (3.34)	0.062*** (3.21)	0.057*** (3.18)
Low pressure	H_{2b}	(-)	-0.004 (-0.24)	0.005 (0.31)	-0.018 (-1.42)	-0.019 (-1.43)	-0.014 (-1.04)	-0.018 (-1.34)
Listed	H_3	(+/-)	0.005 (0.30)	-0.010 (-0.42)	-0.004 (-0.13)	-0.032 (-1.57)		
Firm age	H_4	(+/-)	0.010 (1.51)	0.002 (0.35)	-0.010 (-1.30)	-0.009 (-1.25)	-0.010 (-1.27)	-0.013* (-1.67)
Pre-law TarWoSB	H_5	(+/-)	-0.002 (-0.15)	-0.022 (-1.42)	-0.021 (-1.00)		-0.029 (-1.63)	
SB size		(+)		0.001 (0.76)	0.002 (0.81)			0.001 (0.53)
Pre-law WoSB		(-)		-0.052*** (-4.45)	-0.053*** (-3.48)	-0.048*** (-3.36)	-0.048*** (-3.46)	
Firm size		(+)		0.017*** (3.90)	0.028*** (5.84)	0.030*** (6.24)	0.029*** (5.78)	0.032*** (6.72)
Leverage		(-)		-0.131*** (-5.14)	-0.062** (-2.57)	-0.058** (-2.46)	-0.059** (-2.45)	-0.065*** (-2.69)
Growth		(+)		0.005 (1.43)	-0.003 (-0.87)	-0.004 (-0.96)	-0.004 (-1.05)	-0.005 (-1.35)
Constant			0.016 (0.72)	-0.085 (-1.35)	-0.244*** (-2.94)	-0.246*** (-3.11)	-0.234*** (-2.97)	-0.319*** (-4.49)
Control variables			NO	YES	YES	YES	YES	YES
Fixed effects: Year, Industry			NO	NO	YES	YES	YES	YES
N			560	560	560	560	560	560
Adj. R^2			8.20%	15.90%	39.60%	39.60%	39.60%	38.00%
F-stat			10.93***	11.54***	11.84***	14.54***	14.55***	14.12***
Max. VIF			3.01	6.72	6.72	3.08	1.75	1.40

The table reports the results (OLS coefficients, t-statistics in parentheses) of the multivariate panel regression for Model 1 (model without control variables and fixed effects), Model 2 (full model without fixed effects), Model 3 (full model with fixed effects), Model 4 (listed and pre-law WoSB), Model 5 (pre-law TarWoSB and pre-law WoSB), and Model 6 (SB size). The expected directions are presented next to the variables.

*, **, and *** indicate significance at the 10%, 5%, and 1% level, respectively.

Table 6-5: Multivariate panel regression models for GDDR efficacy on supervisory boards (Panel A)

All regression models (Model 1 to Model 6) are statistically significant (F-stat). Moreover, the **adjusted R^2** indicates that the different models explain the total variance to varying extents. The Model 1 shows the lowest adjusted R^2 with a value of 8.20%. Model 3, Model 4, and Model 5 exhibit the largest explanatory power with an adjusted R^2 of 39.60%. Prior literature that investigates the effects of voluntary regulatory approaches or mandatory gender quotas report comparable adjusted R^2 values (e.g., *Page et al.* (2024), p. 9; *Poletti-Hughes/Dimungu-Hewage* (2023), p. 1328). The considerable differences in the degree of explanation between Model 1 and Model 3 to Model 5 are due to the inclusion of fixed effects. Moreover, because some control variables are statistically significantly correlated with GDDR efficacy, these variables explain a substantial portion of the total variance (see also Model 2, which improves over Model 1 by including control variables). Finally, none of the models show multicollinearity issues based on the maximum VIF values.

Model 1 does not include control variables and fixed effects. The results indicate a positive and statistically significant relationship between *high pressure* and GDDR efficacy at the 1% level. The coefficients of the other determinant variables report associations in the expected directions but are statistically insignificant. However, due to the low goodness of fit and the low explanatory power, the results of Model 1 are not further discussed.

Model 2 includes the control variables. Compared to Model 1, the adjusted R^2 increases considerably from 8.20% (Model 1) to 15.90% (Model 2). Considering the control variables derived from theory and literature thus increases the explanatory power of the model. *High pressure* is still positive and statistically significantly associated with the efficacy of GDDR at the 1% level. Additionally, the signs of the coefficients of all control variables exhibit the expected direction. *Pre-law WoSB*, *firm size*, and *leverage* are statistically significantly related to GDDR efficacy on the supervisory board at the 1% level.

Model 3 considers control variables and industry and year fixed effects. First, industry fixed effects should be considered because time-invariant industry-specific factors may drive the efficacy of GDDR. In some industries, the proportion of the female workforce is larger than in others. Thus, GDDR may be more effective in industries with more female employees (*Mensi-Klarbach et al.* (2021), p. 583). Second, year fixed effects should be considered because the general trends in the employment behavior of companies may change over time. To measure the efficacy of GDDR and not an overall time trend, year fixed effects enhance the empirical model.[143] Considering industry and year fixed effects increases the goodness of fit and the adjusted R^2 to 39.60%. Thus, Model 3 better explains the determinants of GDDR efficacy on the supervisory board and should be preferred. Similar to Model 1 and Model 2, Model 3 reports a positive statistically significant association between *high pressure* and the delta in the proportion of female supervisory board members (*ΔPoWoSB*) at the 1% level. However, the magnitude of the coefficient is lower (0.063) than in Model 1 (0.101) and Model 2 (0.091). The coefficient suggests that, compared to the base year, companies subject to high public pressure (*high pressure*) increase the proportion of women on the supervisory board, on average, 6.3 percentage points more than companies not facing high public pressure. Moreover, similarly to Model 2, the other determinant variables do not exhibit a statistically significant relationship with GDDR efficacy. The coefficients of the control variables show a similar direction, similar statistical significances (apart from *leverage*, which statistical significance decreases from the 1% level

[143] Note that the observed effects cannot be controlled against a group of companies not being subject to the GDDR, because unaffected domestic companies do not publish comparable gender diversity information and often differ significantly in size from regulated companies. Additionally, creating a control group from companies in other countries is not feasible, because such countries have either implemented similar gender diversity regulations or exhibit cultural differences so that gender diversity cannot be meaningfully compared. Nevertheless, the different regression models and robustness tests address this limitation as effectively as possible.

to the 5 % level), and comparable magnitudes. However, the coefficient of *growth* changes direction, but it remains close to zero and statistically insignificant. In summary, in addition to *high pressure*, *firm size* (0.028) is positively associated with GDDR efficacy, whereas *pre-law WoSB* and *leverage* exhibit a negative association with GDDR efficacy. Apart from *leverage* (5% level), all variables are statistically significant at the 1% level.

Model 4 to Model 6 address multicollinearity issues and therefore include only one of the correlated variables (*listed* or *pre-law TarWoSB*, *listed* or *SB size*, *pre-law TarWoSB* or *SB size*, and *SB size* or *pre-law WoSB*). Compared to Model 3, the adjusted R^2 values are nearly constant (at least 38.00% (Model 6)). Thus, excluding correlated independent variables does not affect the explanatory power of the full model. Furthermore, the coefficients in Model 4 to Model 6 (Table 6-5) do not change their direction or substantially in their magnitude. However, addressing multicollinearity issues influences the statistical significance of some variables. In Model 6 (without *listed*, *pre-law TarWoSB*, and *pre-law WoSB*) the coefficient of *firm age* (-0.013) is marginally significant at the 10% level, and the coefficient of *leverage* (-0.065) slightly increases in statistical significance from the 5% level to the 1% level. The coefficients reported from Model 4 and Model 5 remain identical in statistical significance.

To further investigate the determinants of the efficacy of GDDR, Table 6-6 aggregates the results for an **alternative GDDR efficacy proxy** (*TarWoSB* (Panel B)) as introduced in equation 6.4 (section 6.1.2). Model 1 to Model 6 of Panel B are structured identically to the models presented in Table 6-5 for Panel A. Therefore, solely the differences between Panel A and Panel B are discussed in detail. However, Model 1 to Model 6 of Panel B are also statistically significant (F-stat), and each model exhibits a comparable adjusted R^2 compared to Panel A ($\Delta PoWoSB$ as dependent variable).

The results of **Panel B reveal a comparable association** for the determinant variable of *high pressure* that exhibits a statistically significant relationship to GDDR efficacy in Panel A. However, other determinant variables as well as some control variables are statistically significantly associated with GDDR efficacy when considering the target-setting behavior (*TarWoSB* (Panel B)) as dependent variable. In contrast to Panel A, Model 1 (Panel B) reports a negative and highly statistically significant relationship between *pre-law TarWoSB* (-0.058) and GDDR efficacy. Contrary to the first GDDR efficacy proxy (Panel A), Model 2 (Panel B) shows statistically significant associations of some independent variables with GDDR efficacy. *Listed* is negatively and statistically significantly (at the 1% level) associated with GDDR efficacy. Furthermore, *firm age* shows a negative and statistically significant association at the 5% level. Additionally, *SB size* is significantly positively related to the target-setting for the proportion of women on the supervisory board (*TarWoSB*). In contrast to Panel A, *firm size* is not positively and statistically significantly associated with GDDR efficacy. In line with expectations, the coefficient of *pre-law WoSB* (-0.083) changes the direction from negative (Panel A) to positive (Panel B) and suggests a statistically significant association with the dependent variable (*TarWoSB*). The implications of the changed coefficient direction are discussed when considering the full model of Panel B (Model 3).

Multivariate panel regression models for determinants of GDDR efficacy on the supervisory board								
Panel B: Target-setting for the proportion of women on the supervisory board TarWoSB as dependent variable								
Variables	**Hypothesis**	**Expected sign**	**Model 1**	**Model 2**	**Model 3**	**Model 4**	**Model 5**	**Model 6**
High pressure	H_{2a}	(+)	0.081*** (4.58)	0.074*** (4.16)	0.032** (2.17)	0.030** (2.01)	0.027* (1.70)	0.039*** (2.59)
Low pressure	H_{2b}	(-)	-0.022 (-1.26)	-0.013 (-0.76)	-0.049** (-2.58)	-0.040** (-2.11)	-0.037** (-2.01)	-0.052*** (-2.68)
Listed	H_3	(+/-)	0.008 (0.42)	0.081*** (2.97)	0.092*** (2.89)	-0.023 (-1.27)		
Firm age	H_4	(+/-)	-0.012 (-1.63)	-0.015** (-2.12)	-0.012 (-1.64)	-0.006 (-0.88)	-0.007 (-0.99)	-0.005 (-0.71)
Pre-law TarWoSB	H_5	(+/-)	-0.058*** (-3.14)	-0.046** (-2.53)	0.005 (0.28)		-0.003 (-0.14)	
SB size		(+)		0.005*** (2.69)	0.011*** (4.84)			0.008*** (5.86)
Pre-law WoSB		(+)		0.083*** (6.08)	0.072*** (5.36)	0.083*** (6.87)	0.089*** (6.64)	
Firm size		(+)		-0.000 (-0.06)	0.004 (0.72)	0.007 (1.13)	0.007 (1.13)	0.001 (0.22)
Leverage		(-)		-0.084*** (-2.88)	0.010 (0.28)	-0.001 (-0.02)	0.008 (0.22)	0.004 (0.12)
Growth		(+)		-0.004 (-0.90)	-0.002 (-0.57)	-0.001 (-0.47)	-0.002 (-0.77)	0.002 (0.62)
Constant			0.237*** (9.21)	0.143* (1.96)	-0.060 (-0.62)	0.063 (0.71)	0.046 (0.51)	0.093 (1.06)
Control variables			NO	YES	YES	YES	YES	YES
Fixed effects: Year, Industry			NO	NO	YES	YES	YES	YES
N			560	560	560	560	560	560
Adj. R^2			5.40%	14.10%	39.40%	36.40%	36.20%	36.10%
F-stat			7.42***	10.15***	8.33***	6.61***	6.42***	6.99***
Max. VIF			3.01	6.72	6.72	3.08	1.75	1.40

The table reports the results (OLS coefficients, t-statistics in parentheses) of the multivariate panel regression for Model 1 (model without control variables and fixed effects), Model 2 (full model without fixed effects), Model 3 (full model with fixed effects), Model 4 (listed and pre-law WoSB), Model 5 (pre-law TarWoSB and pre-law WoSB), and Model 6 (SB size). The expected directions are presented next to the variables.

*, **, and *** indicate significance at the 10%, 5%, and 1% level, respectively.

Table 6-6: Multivariate panel regression models for GDDR efficacy on supervisory boards (Panel B)

Model 3 (Panel B) also includes industry and year fixed effects. The results indicate differences to Model 3 of Panel A. First, *high pressure* is still positively and significantly associated with GDDR efficacy. However, the variable is only moderately statistically significant at the 5% level (at the 1% level in Panel A) and has a smaller magnitude of 0.032 (0.063 in Panel A). Second, in contrast to Panel A, *low pressure* (-0.049) is negatively and statistically significant (at the 5% level) associated with GDDR efficacy. The results suggest that companies facing low public pressure (*low pressure*) set targets for the proportion of women on the supervisory board that are, on average, 4.9 percentage points lower than those of companies not subject to low public pressure. Third, the results of Panel B indicate a positive and highly significant relationship at the 1% level between *listed* (0.092) and GDDR efficacy. This result suggests that listed companies tend to set higher targets for the proportion of women on supervisory boards (*TarWoSB*). Fourth, the control variables *SB size* and *pre-law WoSB* show a positive and statistically significant association with the dependent variable (*TarWoSB*). In contrast to Panel A, *pre-law WoSB* in Panel B changes the direction and exhibits a positive instead of a negative relationship. As explained in section 4.2.2, this is reasonable as companies must consider the prohibition of deterioration (section 2.2.3.4). Thus, companies that had appointed a female supervisory board member before GDDR came into force (*pre-law WoSB*) must set higher targets (*TarWoSB*). The coefficients of the remaining control variables (*firm size* and *leverage*) are not statistically significant.

Model 4 to Model 6 of Panel B address multicollinearity issues. The statistically significant associations between *high pressure* and GDDR efficacy, as well as between *low pressure* and GDDR efficacy, hold in all models. Model 5 (without *listed* and *SB size*) reports a slightly weaker statistical significance (at the 10% level) and a slightly lower magnitude (0.027) for *high pressure*. In contrast, Model 6 (without *listed, pre-law TarWoSB*, and *SB size*) suggests a slightly stronger statistical significance (at the 1% level) and a slightly greater magnitude (-0.052) for *low pressure*. When considering multicollinearity issues, *listed* does not indicate a statistically significant association with GDDR efficacy of Panel B. Thus, *listed* is sensitive to collinear variables in the multivariate regression model. Overall, since all other variables remain statistically significant and show only slight changes in magnitude, multicollinearity is not an issue for most results of Panel B.

6.2.1.4 Robustness tests and sensitivity analyses

Robustness tests are employed to assess whether the results remain stable under different conditions and assumptions. The effect of the classification of public pressure is analyzed to test the robustness of the main regression results (Model 3 in Panel A and Panel B). The binary variables *high pressure* and *low pressure* are alternatively **measured solely on the basis of German or English news counts**, instead of a combined measurement. Model 7 (modified Model 3, c. p.) presents the results for the main regression when considering only German news counts. Similarly, Model 8 (modified Model 3, c. p.) presents the results for English news counts. Table 6-7 presents the results for Model 7 and Model 8 for Panel A and Panel B.

The findings of Panel A are robust against an alternative definition of *high pressure* and *low pressure*. The results remain unchanged when considering German news counts (Model 7; Panel A) or English news counts (Model 8; Panel A). Additionally, the findings of Panel B are robust and do not alter when using German news counts (Model 7; Panel B). Moreover, *firm age* is associated marginally statistically significantly at the 10% level with the GDDR efficacy measure (*TarWoSB*). However, the results of Panel B do not hold when using **English news counts** as a proxy for *high pressure* and *low pressure* (Model 8; Panel B). The coefficients of *high pressure* and *low pressure* indicate no statistically significant association with GDDR efficacy. Furthermore, the goodness of fit (adjusted R^2) for Model 8 of Panel B

(38.16%) is lower than that of the unmodified model (Model 3; adjusted R^2 = 39.40%). Thus, the robustness test suggests that the level of public pressure based on English news counts does not determine GDDR efficacy in terms of target-setting behavior for the supervisory board. Overall, the robustness test indicates that the public pressure variables generated by German newspapers shape the target-setting more than the public pressure resulting from English newspaper coverage.

Robustness tests for GDDR efficacy determinants on supervisory boards

Variables	Hypothesis	Expected sign	Model 7 (Panel A)	Model 7 (Panel B)	Model 8 (Panel A)	Model 8 (Panel B)
High pressure	H_{2a}	(+)	0.053***	0.031**	0.044***	0.003
			(2.98)	(2.26)	(2.91)	(0.20)
Low pressure	H_{2b}	(-)	-0.020	-0.062***	-0.017	-0.001
			(-1.49)	(-3.06)	(-1.56)	(-0.04)
Listed	H_3	(+/-)	-0.003	0.098***	-0.005	0.095***
			(-0.09)	(3.11)	(-0.15)	(3.06)
Firm age	H_4	(+/-)	-0.011	-0.015*	-0.010	-0.013*
			(-1.42)	(-1.94)	(-1.36)	(-1.65)
Pre-law TarWoSB	H_5	(+/-)	-0.017	0.009	-0.011	0.009
			(-0.83)	(0.50)	(-0.58)	(0.52)
SB size		(+)	0.002	0.013***	0.002	0.011***
			(1.18)	(5.26)	(1.01)	(4.46)
Pre-law WoSB		(+/-)	-0.054***	0.072***	-0.056***	0.074***
			(-3.50)	(5.59)	(-3.59)	(5.21)
Firm size		(+)	0.028***	0.004	0.030***	0.009
			(5.51)	(0.64)	(6.14)	(1.55)
Leverage		(-)	-0.064**	0.006	-0.065**	-0.004
			(-2.70)	(0.18)	(-2.71)	(-0.12)
Growth		(+)	-0.003	-0.001	-0.003	-0.001
			(-0.66)	(-0.29)	(-0.73)	(-0.34)
Constant			-0.243***	-0.061	-0.262***	-0.123
			(-2.91)	(-0.63)	(-3.18)	(-1.31)
Control variables			YES	YES	YES	YES
Fixed effects: Year, Industry			YES	YES	YES	YES
N			560	560	560	560
Adj. R^2			39.46%	40.23%	39.12%	38.16%
F-stat			11.68***	9.10***	11.33***	7.09***
Max. VIF			6.72	6.72	6.72	6.72

The table reports the results (OLS coefficients, t-statistics in parentheses) of the multivariate panel regression for Model 7 (modified model with German news counts) for Panel A and Panel B and Model 8 (modified model with English news counts) for Panel A and Panel B. The expected directions are presented next to the variables.
*, **, and *** indicate significance at the 10%, 5%, and 1% level, respectively.

Table 6-7: Robustness tests for determinants of GDDR efficacy on supervisory boards

Additionally, various sensitivity analyses are conducted for the multivariate regression model to examine the susceptibility of the full regression model (Model 3 in Panel A and Panel B) against minor changes in the measurement of determinant variables and alternative proxies for control variables. First, the **thresholds for the categorization** of the binary variables *high pressure* and *low pressure* may drive the results. A lower value (15%-percentile) and a higher value (25%-percentile) are used as alternative thresholds to determine the quartiles categorizing the companies into high and low public pressure. These alternative thresholds do not change the results of Panel A and the implications drawn. Moreover, *low pressure* suggests a negative and statistically significant association at the 5% level to GDDR efficacy. Panel B is also robust to changes in the categorization thresholds. However, *low pressure* loses statistical significance when using the 15% threshold and exhibits a greater statistical significance (at the 1% level) when using the 25% threshold. The change in the significance can be explained by the reduced number of observations when applying the 15%-percentile threshold. Due to the tighter categorization, fewer company-year observations drive the results. Thus, extreme observations may influence the coefficient, resulting in insignificant results.

Second, it is examined how **alternative proxies** of *firm size* affect the results of the multivariate regression model. Instead of the natural logarithm of total assets, the natural logarithm of sales revenues or number of employees is used. The alternative *firm size* measure based on sales revenues does not affect the results of Panel A. However, using the number of employees as the measure for *firm size* increases the magnitude of *high pressure* (0.085; p = 4.23) at a highly statistically significant level. Additionally, when considering the number of employees, *low pressure* indicates a statistically significant negative relationship at the 5% level (-0.031; p = -2.50) and *pre-law TarWoSB* a statistically significant negative relationship at the 5% level (-0.044; p = -2.11). Thus, the sensitivity analyses suggest that measuring *firm size* by the number of employees further affects the results and exhibits more statistically significant variables. However, using the number of employees as a proxy for *firm size* may involve unobserved characteristics that drive the results (e.g., companies in employee-intensive business models are referred to as large companies). Since the statistical significance increases when considering the number of employees from *firm size*, the findings support the implications drawn from the full model (Model 3 (Panel A)). For Panel B, the alternative proxies for *firm size* do not alter the results. However, both alternative measures strengthen the associations of *high pressure* and *low pressure* to GDDR efficacy in terms of magnitude and statistical significance compared to the measurement by total assets. Accordingly, the alternative proxies for *firm size* do not affect the implications drawn for the full model (Model 3) of Panel B.

Third, companies' **growth rates** (*growth*) can be alternatively measured based on the changes in sales revenues (*Panzer/Müller* (2015); *Poletti-Hughes/Dimungu-Hewage* (2023)) or changes in the number of employees. Identically to the calculation based on total assets, the alternative measures are defined as the difference between sales revenues (number of employees) at the fiscal year-end and the base year divided by sales revenues (number of employees) of the base year. These sensitivity analyses do not affect the results in magnitude or statistical significance, thus supporting the findings of the main model (Model 3) and the implications drawn.

Finally, an **alternative clustering for industry fixed effects** is used. Instead of clustering the companies based on the two-digit NACE codes, Standard Industrial Classification (SIC) codes can be used. Although SIC codes were developed to categorize US companies, they should produce identical results. Besides a slight decrease in the statistical significance of *low pressure* (from the 5% to the 10% level) and *listed* (from the 1% level to the 10% level), the statistical significance of the other variables remains unchanged. Thus, the alternative industry classification does not alter the results of both Panel A and Panel B.

6.2.1.5 Critical evaluation of the results

The previous section analyzed the determinants of GDDR efficacy on the supervisory board. To address the objective of the second research question (RQ 2), the results are **discussed with respect to the hypotheses** derived from theory and literature in section 4.2.2. The results are compared with prior literature investigating the determinants of gender diversity regulations in a corporate context. However, prior research does not examine the efficacy of GDDR. Instead, prior research evaluating the determinants of voluntary regulatory approaches or mandatory gender quotas is considered. However, the results may diverge since other regulatory approaches are based on different regulatory mechanisms. Moreover, most prior research is restricted to one-tier corporate governance systems and, therefore, is not directly comparable.

GDDR rely on the regulatory mechanisms of targeted transparency regulation. The causal chain developed by *Hombach/Sellhorn* (2019) suggests that the level of public pressure determines the efficacy of GDDR. Stakeholder theory and dependence theory support this association. Findings of prior literature complement the theoretical considerations. Consequently, hypothesis H_{2a} postulates a positive association between **high public pressure** and GDDR efficacy on the supervisory board. The empirical results support this hypothesis. Companies subject to high public pressure increase the proportion of women on the supervisory board to a greater extent than companies not exposed to high public pressure (Panel A). Furthermore, high public pressure tends to positively influence the level of gender diversity target-setting on the supervisory board (Panel B). However, the association is marginal and, therefore, should be interpreted cautiously. The results indicate that companies that face high public pressure incorporate stakeholders' demand for a more gender-diverse supervisory board more frequently. These findings are in line with prior literature, as *Peña-Martel et al.* (2022) also report a positive association between a high level of public pressure and the efficacy of mandatory gender quotas (*Peña-Martel et al.* (2022), p. 199).[144]

In the same vein, the study at hand presumes a negative association between a **low public pressure** and GDDR efficacy. Theory assumes that companies less visible in society experience less pressure to consider societal expectations in their corporate decision-making. Consequently, hypothesis H_{2b} suggests a negative association between low public pressure and GDDR efficacy on the supervisory board. The empirical results partially support this hypothesis. While low public pressure is not negatively associated with the

[144] *Peña-Martel et al.* (2022) investigate the efficacy of the mandatory gender quota in the Spanish regulatory setting. The Spanish mandatory gender quota does not stipulate any sanctions in the case of non-compliance and, therefore, companies often do not comply to the mandatory gender quota. For further details on the Spanish mandatory gender quota, cf. *Gabaldon/Giménez* (2017), pp. 47–74.

increase in the proportion of women on the supervisory board (Panel A), it is negatively associated with the level of self-set targets for the presence of women on the supervisory board (Panel B). The diverging results indicate that companies that receive less public attention less frequently signal a willingness to appoint more female supervisory board members. However, this does not result in an actual significantly lower increase in the proportion of women on the supervisory board. Consequently, companies subject to low public pressure do not appoint women less frequently to the supervisory board but do not feel compelled to disclose targets for increased gender diversity.

Moreover, institutional theory suggests that GDDR result in a larger efficacy for listed companies due to increased public interest and their central role in society. However, due to the specific characteristics of the analyzed sample, this association may not hold. The sample of listed companies analyzed in the supervisory board sub-study comprises companies that are not parity co-determined and may therefore incorporate stakeholders' social demands less intensively. Hypothesis H_3 postulates an undirected association between listed companies and the efficacy of GDDR on the supervisory board. Results of the multivariate analyses partially support the hypothesis. On the one hand, the **capital market orientation** is not associated with actual larger increases in supervisory board gender diversity (Panel A). On the other hand, listed companies disclose more ambitious self-set targets for the proportion of women on the supervisory board (Panel B). These findings can be interpreted twofold. First, listed companies may intend to foster gender diversity on the supervisory board in the future but cannot put the intended proportion of women into action. As shown by anecdotal evidence in section 5.2.4.1, companies face various challenges in appointing female supervisory board members. However, if the disclosed targets indicate a company's actual intention, GDDR efficacy may unfold in a long-term perspective. Second, companies may use the disclosure of gender diversity targets to signal the consideration of gender diversity issues without truly aiming for an increased presence of female supervisory board members. In that case, companies may frequently miss their self-set targets, and according to legitimacy and stakeholder theory, they risk their legitimacy. However, the empirical analyses of the study at hand investigate the disclosure practices of companies subject to GDDR (chapter 5), but do not examine the underlying disclosure strategies that drive these practices. Prior literature does not provide insights into the influence of a company's capital market orientation on gender diversity regulation, as prior research mainly focuses solely on listed companies.

Furthermore, principal-agent theory suggests that the **age of a company** negatively determines the efficacy of GDDR. In contrast, institutional theory suggests a positive association between a company's age and GDDR efficacy. According to these theories, hypothesis H_4 postulates an undirected association between a company's age and GDDR efficacy on the supervisory board. The empirical results do not support this hypothesis. The age of a company does neither determine the actual extent of the increase in the presence of female supervisory board members (Panel A) nor the level of gender diversity target-setting on the supervisory board (Panel B). The findings of prior literature are inconsistent. *Gregorič et al.* (2017) report an insignificant association between companies' age and gender diversity regulation efficacy (*Gregorič et al.* (2017), p. 281), whereas *Peña-Martel et al.* (2022) report a negative association (*Peña-Martel et al.* (2022), p. 199). However, *Gregorič* *et al.* (2017) investigate a voluntary regulatory setting, while *Peña-Martel et al.* (2022) examine a mandatory gender quota. Thus, the inconsistent results may be reasoned by the different regulatory settings.

The variables discussed so far mostly consider companies' public visibility and structural characteristics. Additionally, there could also be a link between companies' **voluntary gender diversity targets** and GDDR efficacy. As explained in section 4.2.2, the voluntary target-setting for the proportion of female supervisory board members can be positively or negatively associated with GDDR efficacy (H_5). On the one hand, voluntary targets indicate companies' intention to foster gender diversity and, therefore, may positively influence the efficacy of GDDR. On the other hand, companies that addressed gender diversity issues before GDDR was implemented may have already increased the proportion of women on the supervisory board, resulting in a less effective GDDR. The empirical results do not support the hypothesis. The findings may be explained by the described counteractive effects, which result in an insignificant association. However, prior research does not provide results for the effect of voluntary target-setting before a gender diversity regulation came into force.

In summary, empirical results of the multivariate regression analyses for the supervisory board indicate that high public pressure, low public pressure, and capital market orientation are determinants associated with GDDR efficacy (RQ2). However, the findings do not provide evidence that voluntary target-setting behavior and companies' age determine the efficacy of GDDR on the supervisory board. Moreover, high public pressure has the largest influence on the increase in the proportion of women on supervisory boards (H_{2a}), whereas the level of self-set targets is mostly influenced by companies' capital market orientation (H_3). Nevertheless, the results for different GDDR efficacy proxies suggest **discrepancies in the identified determinants**. Figure 6-1 summarizes the results of the determinants analysis of GDDR efficacy on the supervisory board with respect to the hypotheses.

H_{2a}:	The efficacy of GDDR on the supervisory board is positively associated with a high level of public pressure.	**Supported**
H_{2b}:	The efficacy of GDDR on the supervisory board is negatively associated with a low level of public pressure.	**Partially supported**
H_3:	The efficacy of GDDR on the supervisory board is associated with companies' capital market orientation.	**Partially supported**
H_4:	The efficacy of GDDR on the supervisory board is associated with companies' age.	**Not supported**
H_5:	The efficacy of GDDR on the supervisory board is associated with companies' reporting practice regarding gender diversity of the supervisory board before the implementation of GDDR.	**Not supported**

Figure 6-1: Results for the determinants hypotheses on the supervisory board

6.2.2 Executive board

This section analyzes determinants of **GDDR efficacy on the executive board**. Due to the varying appointment processes of supervisory and executive board members within a two-tier corporate governance system (section 2.2.1), it is questionable whether the identified determinants of GDDR efficacy on the supervisory board (high public pressure, low public pressure, and capital market orientation) also determine the regulatory efficacy on the executive board. Examining another corporate hierarchy level helps uncovering similarities and differences between different corporate hierarchy levels targeted by GDDR.

6.2.2.1 Descriptive statistics

The procedure for the analysis of determinants of GDDR efficacy is identical to the analysis of the supervisory board. Therefore, the structure of the tables and the variables used in both subsamples are not explained in detail.

Table 6-8 presents the descriptive results for the variables of the GDDR determinant regression analyses for the executive board. In the executive board subsample (EB sample), 15% of the company-year observations are subject to high public pressure (**high pressure**), whereas 18% of the company-year observations face low public pressure (**low pressure**). Similar to the supervisory board, these values are slightly below the 20%-percentile since companies must belong to the top or low 20%-percentiles of German and English news counts.

72% of the executive board subsample are companies listed on a regulated market (**listed**). Compared to the full sample, listed companies are slightly less frequently represented. This is due to the necessary sample adjustments made for the executive board subsample (Table 6-1). The companies excluded from the executive board subsample are all listed because only listed companies can exhibit an organizational form that lacks an executive board (e.g., KGaA, section 2.2.3.4). In contrast to the supervisory board subsample (Table 6-2), the proportion of listed companies in the executive board is 18 percentage points larger. The difference is reasonable because companies that are affected by the mandatory gender quota on the supervisory board are removed from the supervisory board subsample. This regulatory approach applies solely to listed companies (section 2.2.3.3).

Compared to the average **firm age** of 53.08 years (mean) of the full sample, companies of the executive board subsample are, on average, 50.02 years (mean) old and thus slightly younger. The same holds true for the median (27.00 years for the full sample; 25.00 years for the EB sample). The results indicate that the companies removed from the sample due to their organizational form are slightly older than those remaining in the executive board subsample. However, since the differences are marginal, no considerable deviations in the characteristics of the companies are assumed. Furthermore, companies in the executive board subsample are considerably older than those in the supervisory board subsample (Table 6-2). The difference in the average age of companies has to be considered when interpreting and comparing the results of both sub-studies.

Descriptive statistics for the (continuous) determinant variables on the executive board							
Variables[a]	Sample	n	Mean	Std. dev.	Q25	Median	Q75
Firm age	Full sample	1,001	53.08	48.14	19.00	27.00	88.00
	EB sample	910	50.02	47.05	18.00	25.00	72.00
PoWoSB	Full sample	1,001	0.26	0.13	0.17	0.30	0.33
	EB sample	910	0.26	0.13	0.17	0.30	0.33

Descriptive statistics for the (binary) determinant variables on the executive board			
Variables[a]	Sample	n	# of company-years (% of company-years)
High pressure	Full sample	1,001	156 (16%)
	EB sample	910	141 (15%)
Low pressure	Full sample	1,001	185 (18%)
	EB sample	910	161 (18%)
Listed	Full sample	1,001	742 (74%)
	EB sample	910	651 (72%)
Pre-law TarWoEB	Full sample	1,001	196 (20%)
	EB sample	910	196 (22%)
SB chair	Full sample	1,001	34 (3%)
	EB sample	910	27 (3%)

[a]Firm age is the difference between the current year and the year of incorporation of a firm. PoWoSB is number of female supervisory board members divided by the total number of supervisory board members. High pressure is a dummy variable that takes the value of one, if a company belongs to the top 20%-percentile of German and English news counts, and zero otherwise. Low pressure is a dummy variable that takes the value of one, if a company belongs to the low 20%-percentile of German and English news counts, and zero otherwise. Listed is a dummy variable that takes the value of one, if the firm is listed on a regulated market, and zero otherwise. Pre-law TarWoEB is a dummy variable that takes the value of one, if a quantified target about the proportion of women on the Executive Board was disclosed before the enactment of the GDDR, and zero otherwise. SB chair is a dummy variable that takes the of one if the supervisory board chairperson is female, and zero otherwise.

Table 6-8: Descriptive statistics for the determinant variables on the executive board

The number of companies that voluntarily set targets for the proportion of women on the executive board before GDDR came into force (**pre-law TarWoSB**) is identical for the full sample and the executive board sample. This is reasonable because companies that lack an executive board are removed from the full sample. Consequently, those companies cannot define gender diversity targets for the executive board. However, the proportion of companies that set voluntary targets for the executive board (20%) is considerably lower than the voluntary target-setting for the supervisory board (64% (Table 6-2)) for the full sample. This result indicates that companies tend to consider gender diversity issues on supervisory boards more frequently than on executive boards. Overall, the diverging pre-law target-setting behavior on both hierarchy levels may influence GDDR efficacy.

In contrast to the multivariate regression for the supervisory board, the analysis for the executive board includes the variables **PoWoSB** and **SB chair**. The gender composition of the supervisory board may impact the efficacy of GDDR on the executive boards because the supervisory board appoints the executive board members (section 4.2.2). Since these variables are already discussed in section 5.2.3.1, they are not discussed in this section again.

Descriptive statistics for the (continuous) control variables on the executive board							
Variables[a]	**Sample**	**n**	**Mean**	**Std. dev.**	**Q25**	**Median**	**Q75**
EB size	Full sample	1,001	3.93	1.73	3.00	4.00	5.00
	EB sample	910	3.93	1.73	3.00	4.00	5.00
Firm size	Full sample	1,001	17.20	44.70	1.21	2.74	8.30
	EB sample	910	17.60	46.50	1.20	2.75	8.20
Leverage	Full sample	1,001	0.60	0.18	0.49	0.60	0.71
	EB sample	910	0.60	0.19	0.49	0.60	0.72
Growth	Full sample	1,001	0.54	1.23	0.05	0.23	0.57
	EB sample	910	0.55	1.30	0.04	0.21	0.55

Descriptive statistics for the (binary) control variables on the executive board			
Variables[a]	**Sample**	**n**	**# of company-years (% of company-years)**
Pre-law WoEB	Full sample	1,001	224 (22%)
	EB sample	910	224 (25%)

[a]SB size is the total number of supervisory board members at fiscal year-end. Firm size is the total assets of the company in € billion. Leverage is the ratio of total liabilities over total assets. Growth is the change in total assets compared to the base year. Pre-law WoSB is a dummy that takes the value of one if the company had at least one female executive board member before the enactment of the GDDR, and zero otherwise. The control variables Firm size, Leverage, and Growth are winsorized at the 1st and 99th percentiles.

Table 6-9: Descriptive statistics for the control variables on the executive board

Table 6-9 shows the descriptive results for the control variables used in the multivariate regression analyses for the determinants of GDDR efficacy on the executive board. The size of the executive boards (**EB size**) and the proportion of companies that set voluntary targets for the executive board before GDDR was implemented (**pre-law WoEB**) are identical in the full sample and the executive board subsample. This is reasonable because, in companies without an executive board, neither board size nor target-setting behavior at that level can be determined. As EB size and pre-law WoEB are already covered in section 5.1.3, they are not revisited in this section.

Companies of the executive board subsample exhibit a marginally larger **firm size** ((mean: €17.60 billion) and (median: €2.75 billion)) than the companies of the full sample ((mean: €17.20 billion) and (median: €2.74 billion)). Since the differences between the executive board subsample and the full sample are negligible, no considerable deviations in the characteristics of the companies are assumed. However, the companies in the executive board subsample are substantially larger than those in the supervisory board subsample (mean: €2.92 billion (Table 6-3)). This is reasonable because large listed companies are excluded from the supervisory board subsample due to the different regulatory approaches for the supervisory board. The different company sizes in both subsamples may affect the regression results. Accordingly, these differences should be taken into account when comparing the results of both sub-studies to assess the determinants of GDDR efficacy.

Comparable to the firm size, **leverage** ((full sample (0.60: mean); EB sample (0.60: mean)) and **growth** (full sample (0.54: mean); EB sample (0.55: mean)) indicate no considerable differences between the full sample and the executive board subsample. Since the results for the full sample are already discussed in section 6.2.1.1, the discussion is not repeated in this section. Moreover, the differences in both control variables between the supervisory board subsample (Table 6-3) and the executive board subsample are marginal.

6.2.2.2 Correlation analysis

Similar to the bivariate analysis performed for the supervisory board (section 6.2.1.2), Table 6-10 presents **Spearman's rank correlation** coefficients for the executive board subsample. It reports the correlation coefficients and the significance level (p-values in parentheses) for the dependent variables and independent determinant variables. The correlation coefficients and p-values of statistically significant pairwise correlations are printed in bold.

First, *high pressure* (0.1866), *listed* (0.0853), and *pre-law TarWoEB* (0.1522) **are positively and statistically significantly correlated** with the GDDR efficacy proxy *ΔPoWoEB* at the 1% level. By contrast, *firm age* (0.0616) is only marginally significantly correlated (at the 10% level) with *ΔPoWoEB*. The positive correlations of these variables are plausible, as they are in line with the theoretical considerations presented in section 4.2.2. Moreover, *low pressure* shows a **negative and statistically significant correlation** with the delta in the proportion of women on the executive board (*ΔPoWoEB*). This is reasonable as companies that face low public attention (*low pressure*) are less pressured to consider stakeholders' demand for increased gender diversity. Moreover, *PoWoSB* and *SB chair* are positively correlated with the dependent variable but not on a statistically significant level.

Correlation matrix for the executive board sub-study

Variables[a]	ΔPoWoEB	TarWoEB	High pressure	Low pressure	Listed	Firm age	Pre-law TarWoEB	PoWoSB	SB chair
ΔPoWoEB	-								
TarWoEB	-	-							
High pressure	**0.1866 ***** **(0.0000)**	**0.2281 ***** **(0.0000)**	-						
Low pressure	**-0.0650 **** **(0.0493)**	**0.1059 ***** **(0.0016)**	-0.1985 *** (0.0000)	-					
Listed	**0.0853 ***** **(0.0098)**	**-0.0963 ***** **(0.0039)**	0.2701 *** (0.0000)	-0.6676 *** (0.0000)	-				
Firm age	**0.0616 *** **(0.0634)**	**0.0805 **** **(0.0152)**	0.2141 *** (0.0000)	-0.2103 *** (0.0000)	0.2173 *** (0.0000)	-			
Pre-law TarWoEB	**0.1522 ***** **(0.0000)**	**0.1020 ***** **(0.0023)**	0.2558 *** (0.0000)	-0.1799 *** (0.0000)	0.3305 *** (0.0000)	0.1201 *** (0.0003)	-		
PoWoSB	0.0025 (0.9406)	**0.2615 ***** **(0.0000)**	0.2150 *** (0.0000)	0.0299 (0.3675)	-0.0315 (0.3417)	-0.0458 (0.1673)	0.0481 (0.1468)	-	
SB chair	0.0412 (0.2141)	0.0553 (0.1013)	-0.0391 (0.2293)	0.0038 (0.8686)	-0.0476 (0.1611)	0.0002 (0.9961)	-0.0286 (0.3988)	0.1296 *** (0.0001)	-

[a]The table reports Spearman correlation coefficients for a pairwise correlation of the GDDR efficacy measures on the executive board and determinant variables. Respective p-values are presented below the coefficients in parentheses.
*, **, and *** indicate statistical significance at the 10%, 5%, and 1% levels, respectively.

Table 6-10: Correlation matrix for the executive board sub-study

Second, *high pressure* (0.2281), *firm age* (0.0805), and *pre-law TarWoEB* (0.1020) are **positively and statistically significantly correlated** with the alternative GDDR efficacy proxy (*TarWoSB*). Similar to the first GDDR efficacy proxy, *firm age* exhibits a weaker significance (at the 5% level) than the other variables. Furthermore, the correlation between *PoWoSB* (0.2615) and *TarWoEB* is also positive and statistically significant at the 1% level. Thus, the bivariate analysis indicates that the proportion of women on the supervisory board (*PoWoSB*) significantly positively influences gender diversity target-setting for the executive board (*TarWoEB*). *SB chair* is also positively correlated with *TarWoEB* but not on a statistically significant level. Contrary to the correlation with the first GDDR efficacy measure (*ΔPoWoEB*), *listed* (-0.0963) exhibits **a weakly negative and strongly statistically significant correlation** with *TarWoEB*. The correlation suggests that a listing on a regulated market (*listed*) positively influences *ΔPoWoEB*, whereas the influence on *TarWoEB* is negative, suggesting that the influence of capital market orientation differs between both GDDR efficacy proxies. However, as explained in section 4.2.2, the theoretical considerations do not point to a positive or negative direction of the correlation.

Furthermore, against expectations, *low pressure* (0.1059) is weakly positively correlated with *TarWoEB*. The correlation is strongly statistically significant at the 1% level. This finding is counterintuitive as it suggests that companies facing a low level of public pressure (*low pressure*) tend to set higher targets for the proportion of women on the executive board (*TarWoEB*). However, the bivariate analysis only provides a **first indication**. The unexpected correlation may be caused by other variables not considered in a bivariate analysis. For instance, companies subject to low public pressure may have voluntarily appointed more women to their executive board before GDDR came into force. Due to the prohibition of deterioration (section 2.2.3.4), these companies may have to set higher targets for the proportion of women on the executive board (*TarWoEB*).

The independent variable *listed* (-0.6676) correlates **strongly and statistically highly significantly** with the independent variable *low pressure*. This correlation coefficient suggests that listed companies face less frequently low public pressure than non-listed companies. The correlation can be attributed to the fact that listed companies are more in the focus of public attention and thus are more frequently covered by the media, resulting less frequently in low public pressure. Nevertheless, the strong correlation indicates a multicollinearity issue that should be addressed in the multivariate regression analyses.

In summary, *high pressure*, *low pressure*, *listed*, *firm age*, and *pre-law TarWoEB* exhibit a **statistically significant correlation** with the first proxy for GDDR efficacy on the executive board (*ΔPoWoEB*). Moreover, *high pressure*, *low pressure*, *listed*, *firm age*, *pre-law TarWoEB*, and *PoWoSB* correlate statistically significantly with the alternative GDDR efficacy proxy (*TarWoEB*). A multicollinearity issue arises from the strong negative and statistically significant correlation between the independent variables *listed* and *low pressure*.

6.2.2.3 Multivariate analyses

This section investigates the determinants of GDDR efficacy on the executive board to gain further insights regarding the second research question (RQ2) and to test **hypotheses H_{6a} – H_{11}**. To this end, the results of the multivariate regression models are presented, which assess the correlation while considering the independent variables simultaneously. Similar to the procedure on the supervisory board, collinear variables are included in separate regression models to address multicollinearity issues.[145] Nonetheless, a complete regression, including all variables, is conducted to consider all independent variables simultaneously.

Similar to the determinants analysis of GDDR efficacy on the supervisory board (section 6.2.1.3), two alternative proxies are used to measure GDDR efficacy: *ΔPoWoEB* (Panel A) and *TarWoEB* (Panel B). Table 6-11 reports the results of the multivariate regression of **Panel A**. The multicollinearity issues identified in the previous section are considered in different regression models. The general model without control variables and fixed effects is conducted in Model 9. Model 10 takes all variables into account but does not include fixed effects. Model 11 is the full regression model and comprises control variables, industry, and year fixed effects. To address multicollinearity issues, Model 12 to Model 15 exclude collinear variables for each pairwise correlation identified in the correlation analysis.

Model 9 to Model 15 are statistically significant (F-stat). Moreover, Table 6-11 reports the **adjusted R^2** to indicate the total variance that each model explains. According to the multivariate regression in section 6.2.1.3, Model 9 exhibits the lowest adjusted R^2 (1.94%) and has nearly no explanatory power. Considering control variables (Model 10) increases the adjusted R^2 (18.66%) and, therefore, enhances the methodological goodness of fit. Furthermore, including industry and year fixed effects (Model 11; full model) increases the adjusted R^2 to 32.07%. When taking multicollinearity issues into account, the adjusted R^2 remains nearly unchanged. Model 14 has the lowest adjusted R^2 with 29.35%, while Model 13 exhibits a marginally increased adjusted R^2 of 32.18% compared to the full model (Model 11). Since prior literature does not examine the efficacy of voluntary regulatory approaches or mandatory gender quotas in a two-tier corporate governance system, the adjusted R^2 values cannot be compared. However, the values for Model 9 to Model 16 can be compared to the analysis on the supervisory board (Model 1 to Model 6; Table 6-5). The full model (Model 11), which explains 32.07% of the total variance (adjusted R^2), is less powerful than the full model (Model 3) of the analysis on the supervisory board (39.40%). Thus, the comparison of the adjusted R^2 values indicates that the full model (Model 3) for the GDDR efficacy analysis on the supervisory board explains more of the total variance than the full model for the executive board (Model 11). However, the differences between both regression models are not substantial. Therefore, Model 11 can also contribute to examining the determinants of GDDR efficacy. Finally, none of the models suggest multicollinearity issues based on the maximum VIF values.

---

145 The pairwise correlation between independent variables and control variables as well as among control variables indicate some multicollinearity issues: *EB size* and *firm size* exhibit a strongly positive and statistically highly significant correlation. Moreover, *firm size* is strongly positive and statistically highly significantly correlated with *high pressure*. To avoid multicollinearity issues, the same procedure is used as for the determinant variables. For the full correlation matrix of *ΔPoWoEB*, cf. Appendix 8. For the full correlation matrix of *TarWoEB*, cf. Appendix 9.

Multivariate panel regression models for determinants of GDDR efficacy on the executive board									
Panel A: Proportion of women on the executive board ΔPoWoEB as dependent variable									
Variables	**Hypothesis**	**Expected sign**	**Model 9**	**Model 10**	**Model 11**	**Model 12**	**Model 13**	**Model 14**	**Model 15**
High pressure	H_{6a}	(+)	0.026** (2.24)	0.041*** (2.87)	0.070*** (4.27)	0.063*** (4.69)	0.067*** (4.91)		
Low pressure	H_{6b}	(-)	-0.003 (-0.20)	0.010 (0.82)	-0.009 (-0.56)	0.003 (0.24)		0.003 (0.24)	
Listed	H_7	(+/-)	0.000 (0.01)	-0.027** (-2.27)	-0.024 (-1.54)		-0.021 (-1.51)		-0.019 (-1.34)
Firm age	H_8	(+/-)	-0.001 (-0.12)	0.001 (0.17)	0.000 (0.03)	-0.001 (-0.11)	0.000 (0.02)	0.003 (0.60)	0.003 (0.67)
Pre-law TarWoEB	H_9	(+/-)	0.025** (2.49)	0.038*** (4.13)	0.040*** (3.86)	0.036*** (3.67)	0.039*** (3.84)	0.040*** (3.79)	0.042*** (3.96)
PoWoSB	H_{10}	(+)	-0.017 (-0.56)	0.025 (0.86)	-0.048 (-1.49)	-0.042 (-1.32)	-0.049 (-1.51)	-0.027 (-0.85)	-0.034 (-1.04)
SB chair	H_{11}	(+)	0.071*** (3.09)	0.071*** (3.38)	0.072** (2.24)	0.073** (2.29)	0.072** (2.25)	0.066** (2.10)	0.065*** (2.05)
EB size		(+)		0.008*** (3.07)	0.011*** (3.70)	0.011*** (3.56)	0.011*** (3.66)		
Pre-law WoEB		(-)		-0.125*** (-13.52)	-0.120*** (-10.06)	-0.119*** (-10.04)	-0.120*** (-10.11)	-0.104*** (-9.09)	-0.105*** (-9.14)
Firm size		(+)		0.004 (1.31)	-0.002 (-0.43)			0.012*** (3.48)	0.013*** (3.77)
Leverage		(-)		-0.018 (-0.89)	-0.008 (-0.37)	-0.006 (-0.29)	-0.010 (-0.49)	0.001 (0.06)	-0.003 (-0.13)
Growth		(+)		-0.000 (-0.11)	-0.003 (-1.36)	-0.003* (-1.77)	-0.003 (-1.43)	-0.004** (-2.18)	-0.004** (-1.97)
Constant			0.015 (0.72)	-0.045 (-0.99)	0.047 (0.81)	0.004 (0.20)	0.019 (0.78)	-0.148*** (-3.23)	-0.152*** (-3.45)
Control variables			NO	YES	YES	YES	YES	YES	YES
Fixed effects: Year, Industry			NO	NO	YES	YES	YES	YES	YES
N			910	910	910	910	910	910	910
Adj. R^2			1.94%	18.66%	32.07%	31.97%	32.18%	29.35%	29.51%
F-stat			3.57***	18.38***	15.49***	18.24***	18.56***	15.89***	16.14***
Max. VIF			2.09	2.74	2.74	1.57	1.61	1.48	1.55

The table reports the results (OLS coefficients, t-statistics in parentheses) of the multivariate panel regression for Model 7 (model without control variables and fixed effects), Model 8 (full model without fixed effects), Model 9 (full model with fixed effects), Model 10 (high pressure, low pressure, and EB size), Model 11 (high pressure, listed and EB size), Model 12 (low pressure, listed, and firm size), and Model 13 (listed and firm size). The expected directions are presented next to the variables.

*, **, and *** indicate significance at the 10%, 5%, and 1% level, respectively.

Table 6-11: Multivariate panel regression models for GDDR efficacy on executive boards (Panel A)

Model 9 is the general model without control variables and fixed effects. The results indicate a positive and statistically significant relationship at the 5% level between *high pressure* and GDDR efficacy. Furthermore, the associations of *pre-law TarWoEB* (at the 5% level) and *SB chair* (at the 1% level) are positive and statistically significant. The other potential determinants (*low pressure*, *listed*, *firm age*, and *PoWoSB*) are not significantly related to GDDR efficacy. The association direction of these variables is mostly in line with the expectations. However, against the assumption of hypothesis H_{10}, *PoWoSB* is negatively but statistically insignificantly associated with the dependent variable. Nevertheless, because the adjusted R^2 is low, the results of Model 9 are not further discussed.

Model 10 presents the multivariate regression results when considering the control variables. The explanatory power of Model 10 (18.66%) is substantially larger compared to Model 9 (1.94%). Thus, taking the control variables into account increases the goodness of fit. The results of Model 10 report a positive and strong statistically significant association between *high pressure* and GDDR efficacy at the 1% level. Moreover, the relationship between *listed* and GDDR efficacy becomes statistically significant at the 5% level and shows a negative direction. Additionally, the magnitude and statistical significance of the association between *pre-law TarWoEB* and GDDR efficacy increases in Model 10. *SB chair* remains unchanged in significance and magnitude. *Low pressure* and *growth* relate in the opposite direction compared to the expectations. However, both variables are statistically insignificant. The coefficients of the remaining independent variable exhibit the predicted signs but are statistically insignificant.

Model 11 is the full model and considers control variables and industry and year fixed effects. Including industry and year fixed effects in the model is appropriate for the same reasons as in the analyses of the supervisory board (section 6.2.1.3).[146] Including these fixed effects in the regression model increases the adjusted R^2 to 32.07% and therefore improves the explanatory power of the model. Hence, based on the goodness of fit, Model 11 is most suitable for explaining determinants of GDDR efficacy on the executive board and should be preferred. The association between *high pressure* and GDDR efficacy is positive and statistically significant at the 1% level. Compared to Model 10, the coefficient's magnitude increases from 0.041 to 0.070. The coefficient suggests that companies subject to high public pressure (*high pressure*) increase the proportion of women on the executive board, on average, 7.0 percentage points more than companies not subject to the same level of public attention. Consequently, the results of Model 11 (Table 6-11) indicate that *high pressure* positively determines the efficacy of GDDR. Furthermore, *pre-law TarWoEB* (0.040) and *SB chair* (0.072) also relate positively and statistically significantly at the 1% level (*pre-law TarWoEB*) and 5% level (*SB chair*) with GDDR efficacy. The interpretation of the coefficients is consistent with that of *high pressure*. However, due to the few company-year observations with a female chairperson on the supervisory board (*SB chair*), the coefficient of *SB chair* should be interpreted carefully.

---

[146] Note that the observed effects cannot be controlled against a group of companies that is not subject to the GDDR, which is similar to the analyses of the supervisory board. Therefore, it cannot be completely ruled out that a general trend of employing more female managers is observed. However, the different regression models and several robustness tests address this problem as good as possible.

Finally, the remaining potential determinants (*low pressure*, *listed*, *firm age*, and *PoWoSB*) show **no significant association with GDDR efficacy**. In contrast to the assumption of hypothesis H_{10}, *PoWoSB* (-0.048) is negatively associated with the delta in the proportion of women on the executive board. Thus, the presence of women on the supervisory board does not seem to positively affect gender diversity on the executive board. However, the association is statistically insignificant.

Model 12 to Model 15 consider multicollinearity issues. Thus, only one correlated variable (*high pressure* or *firm size*, *low pressure* or *listed*, and *firm size* or *EB size*) is included in each model. Compared to the full model (Model 11), the goodness of fit slightly changes (at least an adjusted R^2 of 29.35% (Model 14)). Hence, excluding correlated variables does not enhance the explanatory power of the full model (Model 11). Furthermore, the coefficients in Model 12 and Model 13 do not alter the direction of the statistically significant determinant variables. However, Model 14 (excluding *high pressure*, *listed*, and *EB size*) and Model 15 (excluding *high pressure*, *low pressure*, and *EB size*) report a positive and strong statistically significant association of *firm size* and GDDR efficacy, which contradicts the results from the full model (Model 11). This finding is reasonable as excluding three potential determinants reduces the regression's influencing factors. The lower adjusted R^2 (29.35% (Model 14); 29.51% (Model 15)) supports this explanation. Moreover, the statistical significance of all other variables remains mostly constant between Model 12 and Model 15 and only shows small changes in the magnitudes of the coefficients.

Similar to the procedure on the supervisory board (section 6.2.1.3), the efficacy of GDDR on the executive board is further investigated based on an **alternative proxy**. Table 6-12 aggregates the results for *TarWoEB* as the dependent variable (**Panel B**) to examine the target-setting behavior instead of the delta in the proportion of women on the executive board (Panel A). The structure of Model 9 to Model 15 of Panel B is identical to the results presented in Table 6-11 for Panel A. Since both proxies intend to measure GDDR efficacy, only the differences between the results of both panels are discussed in detail. Similar to Panel A, Model 9 to Model 15 of Panel B are all statistically significant (F-stat). Moreover, the adjusted R^2 values of Panel B are higher than the models investigated in Panel A. The higher adjusted R^2 values suggest a higher goodness of fit of the results of Panel B compared to Panel A. Thus, based on the empirical model presented in section 6.1.1, the results of Panel B (*TarWoEB* as dependent variable) have a higher explanatory power and explain more of the total variance.

The results of **Model 9** reveal some differences between Panel A and Panel B. *High pressure* (0.058) reports a stronger statistical significance (1% level) and a greater magnitude of the positive relationship compared to Panel A (*high pressure* (0.026)). In contrast to Model 9 of Panel A (low pressure (-0.003)), the same model in Panel B indicates a positive and marginally statistically significant association between *low pressure* (0.028) and GDDR efficacy. Furthermore, Model 9 of Panel B indicates a negative and statistically significant association at the 1% level of *listed* (-0.045) and the dependent variable. In contrast to Model 9 of Panel A (*PoWoSB* (-0.017)), the coefficient of *PoWoSB* (0.246) is positive and statistically significant at the 1% level in Panel B. However, the results for *SB chair* (0.030) in Panel B exhibit a positive but insignificant association with *TarWoEB*.

Multivariate panel regression models for determinants of GDDR efficacy on the executive board

Panel B: Target-setting for the proportion of women on the executive board
TarWoEB as dependent variable

Variables	Hypothesis	Expected sign	Model 9	Model 10	Model 11	Model 12	Model 13	Model 14	Model 15
High pressure	H_{6a}	(+)	0.058***	0.024	0.030*	0.020	0.016		
			(4.37)	(1.43)	(1.70)	(1.36)	(1.08)		
Low pressure	H_{6b}	(-)	0.028*	0.018	-0.007	-0.016		-0.019	
			(1.82)	(1.20)	(-0.39)	(-0.99)		(-1.18)	
Listed	H_7	(+/-)	-0.045***	-0.032**	0.030		0.028*		0.035**
			(-3.25)	(-2.32)	(1.63)		(1.70)		(2.15)
Firm age	H_8	(+/-)	0.011**	0.009*	0.016***	0.015***	0.015***	0.016***	0.016***
			(1.97)	(1.68)	(3.04)	(2.88)	(2.84)	(3.17)	(3.16)
Pre-law TarWoEB	H_9	(+/-)	0.027**	0.012	0.048***	0.050***	0.046***	0.052***	0.048***
			(2.33)	(1.15)	(4.13)	(4.37)	(4.09)	(4.46)	(4.17)
PoWoSB	H_{10}	(+)	0.246***	0.200***	0.212***	0.200***	0.208***	0.207***	0.217***
			(6.99)	(5.98)	(5.60)	(5.23)	(5.50)	(5.40)	(5.75)
SB chair	H_{11}	(+)	0.030	0.028	0.030	0.026	0.028	0.026	0.029
			(1.13)	(1.17)	(1.09)	(0.95)	(1.04)	(0.93)	(1.06)
EB size		(+)		-0.007**	-0.001	-0.003	-0.003		
				(-2.22)	(-0.42)	(-0.97)	(-1.03)		
Pre-law WoEB		(+)		0.126***	0.125***	0.125***	0.126***	0.125***	0.126***
				(11.78)	(9.70)	(9.57)	(9.87)	(10.07)	(10.36)
Firm size		(+)		0.004	-0.008			-0.002	-0.004
				(1.02)	(-1.48)			(-0.61)	(-1.05)
Leverage		(-)		-0.024	-0.040	-0.051**	-0.048**	-0.043*	-0.038
				(-0.99)	(-1.58)	(-2.10)	(-1.97)	(-1.67)	(-1.48)
Growth		(+)		0.010***	0.008**	0.008**	0.008**	0.008**	0.008**
				(3.11)	(2.41)	(2.48)	(2.31)	(2.55)	(2.36)
Constant			0.026	-0.011	0.075	0.005	-0.019	0.020	0.011
			(1.09)	(-0.20)	(1.08)	(0.19)	(-0.65)	(0.38)	(0.23)
Control variables			NO	YES	YES	YES	YES	YES	YES
Fixed effects: Year, Industry			NO	NO	YES	YES	YES	YES	YES
N			910	910	910	910	910	910	910
Adj. R^2			12.38%	24.20%	37.20%	36.99%	37.16%	36.95%	37.20%
F-stat			19.35***	25.18***	19.70***	23.08***	23.37***	25.46***	25.94***
Max. VIF			2.09	2.74	2.74	1.57	1.61	1.48	1.55

The table reports the results (OLS coefficients, t-statistics in parentheses) of the multivariate panel regression for Model 7 (model without control variables and fixed effects), Model 8 (full model without fixed effects), Model 9 (full model with fixed effects), Model 10 (high pressure, low pressure, and EB size), Model 11 (high pressure, listed and EB size), Model 12 (low pressure, listed, and firm size), and Model 13 (listed and firm size). The expected directions are presented next to the variables.
*, **, and *** indicate significance at the 10%, 5%, and 1% level, respectively.

Table 6-12: Multivariate panel regression models for GDDR efficacy on executive boards (Panel B)

Model 10 (Panel B) considers industry and year fixed effects. In contrast to Panel A (*high pressure* (0.041)), *high pressure* (0.024) in Panel B exhibits no statistically significant relationship to the dependent variable. Moreover, the coefficient of *firm age* (0.009) is still positive but shows a marginal statistical significance at the 10% level. Contrary to Model 10 of Panel A (*pre-law TarWoEB* (0.038)), the same model does not indicate a statistically significant association between *pre-law TarWoEB* (0.012) and GDDR efficacy. However, the coefficient of *PoWoSB* (0.200) is positive and suggests a strongly statistically significant relationship with the dependent variable (*TarWoEB*). Panel A (*PoWoEB* (0.025)) does not report a statistically significant coefficient for this association.

For the full model (**Model 11**), the multivariate regression of Panel A and Panel B shows some differences in the directions of coefficients, the statistical significances, and the magnitudes of the determinant variables. *High pressure* (0.030) is still positively associated with GDDR efficacy but at a marginally statistically significant level (1% level (Panel A); 10% level (Panel B)). Panel A reports a negative and statistically insignificant relationship between *listed* (-0.024) and the dependent variable, whereas Panel B indicates a positive and statistically insignificant association (0.030). Furthermore, the results of Panel B presented in Table 6-12 show a strong statistically significant and positive relationship between *firm age* (0.016; 1% level) and GDDR efficacy. In Panel A, the same coefficient does not exhibit any statistical significance (*firm age* (0.000)). Besides, contrary to Panel A (*PoWoSB* (-0.048)), the results of Model 11 (Panel B) indicate a positive and statistically significant association between *PoWoSB* (0.212) and GDDR efficacy at the 1% level. The positive direction of the coefficient is in line with the expectation assuming that the proportion of women on the supervisory board positively affects GDDR efficacy on the executive board. Moreover, Panel B indicates a positive but statistically insignificant association between *SB chair* (0.030) and GDDR efficacy, whereas Panel A reports a positive and strong statistically significant relationship between both variables. Lastly, the control variables *pre-law WoEB* (0.125) and *growth* (0.008) exhibit a positive and statistically significant association with GDDR efficacy. The change in the coefficient direction of *pre-law WoEB* is reasonable and in line with expectations. The results suggest that the presence of at least one woman on the executive board positively influences the target-setting behavior (*TarWoEB*) due to the prohibition of deterioration (section 2.2.3.4). In contrast to Panel A, Model 11 of Panel B does not report a statistically significant relationship between *EB size* and GDDR efficacy. This insignificant coefficient indicates that the number of executive board members is not statistically significantly associated with the target-setting for the executive board.

Model 12 to Model 15 of Panel B again consider multicollinearity issues. The marginally statistically significant relationship of *high pressure* (Model 11) to GDDR efficacy does not hold when considering multicollinearity issues (Model 12 and Model 13). Thus, the coefficient must be interpreted cautiously because the statistical significance may result from collinear variables. The statistical significance of the other determinant variables is mostly robust when addressing multicollinearity issues. In contrast to Model 11, *listed* (0.028) exhibits a marginally statistically significant association at the 10% level with GDDR efficacy in Model 13 (without *low pressure* and *firm size*). Moreover, when excluding the collinear variables *high pressure*, *low pressure*, and *EB size* (Model 15), the statistical significance of *listed* (0.035) increases to a 5% level. Thus, Model 13 and Model 15 indicate a marginal or moderate statistically significant association between companies' capital market orientation and the target-setting for the executive board (*TarWoEB*). Similar to the procedure performed in section 6.2.1, the following section presents sensitive analyses and robustness tests for the results of the full regression (Model 11) of Panel A (($\Delta PoWoEB$ as the dependent variable) and Panel B (*TarWoEB* as the dependent variable).

6.2.2.4 Robustness tests and sensitivity analyses

Due to the **identical structure** of the regression models analyzing GDDR efficacy on the supervisory board, identical sensitivity analyses and robustness[147] tests are carried out for the regression model on the executive board.

Similar to the analysis of determinants of GDDR efficacy on the supervisory board, identical robustness tests are performed for Model 11. Accordingly, *high pressure* and *low pressure* are measured **solely based on German news counts or English news counts** instead of a combined consideration. Model 16 (modified Model 11, c. p.) presented in Table 6-13 reports the results when considering only German news counts. Model 17 (modified Model 11, c. p.) shows the regression results for English news counts. The results of Panel A remain the same and do not affect the implications drawn when using German (Model 7 (Panel A)) or English news counts (Model 8 (Panel A)). Thus, Model 11 of Panel A is robust against an alternative definition of *high pressure* and *low pressure*. By contrast, the findings of Panel B are more diverging. The results indicate some changes when considering only German news counts (Model 16 (Panel B)). *High pressure* (0.034) becomes statistically significant at the 5% level and hence supports the findings of Model 11 (Panel B) that high pressure is positively associated with GDDR efficacy. Moreover, Model 16 reports a positive but statistically insignificant coefficient of *low pressure* (0.028). This finding contradicts hypothesis H_{12}, which postulates a negative association between low public pressure and GDDR efficacy. However, the association is statistically insignificant. Furthermore, Model 17 (consideration of English news counts) also reveals some changes in the significance of GDDR determinant variables. *High pressure* (0.002) is statistically insignificant. Moreover, both Model 16 (0.049) and Model 17 (0.045) indicate a statistically significant relationship between *listed* and GDDR efficacy. These findings suggest that combined consideration of German and English news counts affects the association of *listed* and *TarWoEB,* leading to an insignificant result for the full model (Model 11). However, all other determinant variables remain unchanged apart from marginal changes in the magnitude of the coefficients. For both panels and both measures of *high pressure* and *low pressure*, the goodness of fit (adjusted R^2) varies only slightly. Overall, besides the changes of some variables with low statistical significance, the results are **mostly robust against changed databases** for the measurement of the proxies for high public pressure and low public pressure.

---

[147] For the reasoning of the sensitivity analyses and robustness tests, see section 6.2.1.2.

Robustness tests for GDDR efficacy determinants on executive boards						
Variables	Hypothesis	Expected sign	Model 16 (Panel A)	Model 16 (Panel B)	Model 17 (Panel A)	Model 17 (Panel B)
High pressure	H_{6a}	(+)	0.030** (2.24)	0.034** (2.17)	0.051*** (3.43)	0.002 (0.11)
Low pressure	H_{6b}	(-)	0.000 (0.02)	0.028 (1.53)	-0.008 (-0.47)	0.016 (0.90)
Listed	H_7	(+/-)	-0.020 (-1.22)	0.049*** (2.52)	-0.023 (-1.29)	0.045** (2.36)
Firm age	H_8	(+/-)	0.001 (0.19)	0.017*** (3.18)	0.001 (0.22)	0.017*** (3.20)
Pre-law TarWoEB	H_9	(+/-)	0.042*** (3.92)	0.046*** (3.96)	0.041*** (3.96)	0.046*** (3.99)
PoWoSB	H_{10}	(+)	-0.037 (-1.14)	0.216*** (5.75)	-0.044 (-1.38)	0.216*** (5.72)
SB chair	H_{11}	(+)	0.068** (2.09)	0.030 (1.08)	0.071** (2.22)	0.030 (1.10)
EB size		(+)	0.012*** (3.89)	-0.001 (-0.33)	0.012*** (3.92)	-0.001 (-0.28)
Pre-law WoEB		(+)	-0.117*** (-9.72)	0.125*** (9.77)	-0.119*** (-9.88)	0.127*** (9.83)
Firm size		(+)	0.003 (0.61)	-0.008 (-1.58)	-0.000 (-0.00)	-0.003 (-0.63)
Leverage		(-)	-0.002 (-0.07)	-0.040 (-1.58)	-0.008 (-0.37)	-0.038 (-1.49)
Growth		(+)	-0.004** (-2.03)	0.007** (2.27)	-0.003 (-1.58)	0.008** (2.35)
Constant			-0.035 (-0.60)	0.061 (0.86)	0.012 (0.20)	-0.010 (-0.15)
Control variables			YES	YES	YES	YES
Fixed effects: Year, Industry			YES	YES	YES	YES
N			910	910	910	910
Adj. R^2			30.87%	37.58%	31.67%	37.07%
F-stat			16.50***	20.26***	14.99***	19.51***
Max. VIF			2.74	2.74	2.74	2.74

The table reports the results (OLS coefficients, t-statistics in parentheses) of the multivariate panel regression for Model 16 (modified model with German news counts) for Panel A and Panel B and Model 17 (modified model with English news counts) for Panel A and Panel B. The expected directions are presented next to the variables.

*, **, and *** indicate significance at the 10%, 5%, and 1% level, respectively.

Table 6-13: Robustness tests for determinants of GDDR efficacy on executive boards

The same sensitivity analyses are conducted as those applied in the analysis of determinants of GDDR efficacy on the supervisory board. First, **alternative thresholds for categorizing** the binary variables *high pressure* and *low pressure* are used to examine the sensitivity of the full regression model (Model 11 in Panel A and Panel B). The alternative thresholds (15%-percentile and 25%-percentile) do not alter the results of Panel A (Model 11) apart from minor changes in the magnitude of the coefficients. By contrast, the results of Model 11 in Panel B are sensitive to changes in the thresholds for *high pressure* and *low pressure*. As indicated by the multivariate regression analyses (Table 6-12), the statistical significance of *high pressure* (at the 10% level) is sensitive to changes in the regression model. Thus, *high pressure* becomes statistically insignificant when using the 15%-percentile. However, when considering the 25%-percentile, the coefficient of *high pressure* (0.049; p = 3.08) is statistically significant at the 1% level. The other variables are mostly unaffected. Thus, a larger threshold for the categorization of *high pressure* tends to strengthen the association with the GDDR efficacy proxy (*TarWoEB*).

Second, the natural logarithm of sales revenues or number of employees is used instead of the natural logarithm of total assets as a proxy for **company size**. For Panel A and Panel B, the models mostly remain robust using the alternative *firm size* measures. For Panel A, *listed* (-0.026; p = -1.71) and *PoWoSB* (-0.055; p = -1.65) become marginally statistically significant at the 10% level when using the number of employees. However, none of the alternative firm size measures indicate a statistically significant relationship to the dependent variable. For Panel B, both alternative firm size measures affect the marginal statistical significance of *high pressure*, resulting in an insignificant coefficient. This supports the findings of the analyses of multicollinearity issues (Model 12 to Model 15) and the first sensitivity analysis, which shows that *high pressure* is sensitive to changes in the regression model. Furthermore, the association of *firm size* (-0.007; p = -1.68) and GDDR efficacy is statistically significant at the 10% level in Panel B when using the number of employees as an alternative proxy. Overall, apart from marginal changes in the statistical significance of some variables, Model 11 is mainly robust to alternative proxies for company size.

Third, **growth rates** (*growth*) are alternatively measured as the changes in sales revenues or the number of employees, respectively. For Panel A, the sensitivity analyses of growth rates do not alter the implications drawn regarding Model 11. However, *growth* (-0.004; p = -1.89) indicates a marginally statistically significant association with GDDR efficacy when using the change in the number of employees as a proxy for companies' growth rates. All other variables remain unchanged in statistical significance for alternative growth rate proxies. For Panel B, *high pressure* (0.027; p = 1.49) is statistically insignificant when *growth* is measured based on the change in sales revenues. Furthermore, the coefficient of *growth* (-0.011; p = -1.61) is negatively and statistically insignificantly associated with GDDR efficacy when measured based on the change in sales revenues. Despite these marginal changes in the statistical significance of *high pressure* and *growth* in one of the alternative growth rates proxies, the results of Model 11 (Panel B) are mostly robust.

Finally, **industry fixed effects** are alternatively clustered based on SIC codes. For both Panel A (adjusted R^2 = 26.93%) and Panel B (adjusted R^2 = 29.58%), the goodness of fit and, therefore, the explanatory power of Model 11 decreases substantially. The varying classification of SIC codes may cause changes in results, as they were developed for categorizing US companies. However, for Panel A, the alternative industry fixed effects strengthen the results of Model 11 and increase the statistical significance of *listed* (-0.060; p = -3.87) to the 1% level and *PoWoSB* (-0.063; p = -2.18) to the 5% level. However, for Panel B, the alternative industry fixed effects lead to a statistically insignificant coefficient of *high pressure* (0.009; p = 0.48) and a weaker statistical significance for *pre-law TarWoEB*

(0.023; p = 1.97). However, using industry fixed effects based on SIC codes results in a lower goodness of fit of the models. Therefore, the initial Model 11 (with industry fixed effects based on NACE codes) should be preferred.

6.2.2.5 Critical evaluation of the results

This section discusses the empirical results for the determinants of GDDR efficacy on the executive board **against the backdrop of the hypotheses** developed in section 4.2.2 (hypotheses H_{6a} - H_{11}). Wherever possible, the results are discussed in the context of previous research. However, the study at hand is the first to examine the determinants of GDDR efficacy on the executive board. Thus, previous findings are scarce. Nevertheless, to gain valuable insights into the findings of prior research, studies examining the determinants of voluntary regulatory approaches or mandatory gender quotas are considered. These varying types of regulations and diverging corporate governance systems in other countries can cause differences in the results of this study and the findings of prior literature.

Theory and prior research suggest that companies subject to **high public pressure** incorporate stakeholders' expectations more frequently and, hence, appoint more female executive board members. Consequently, hypothesis H_{6a} postulates a positive association between high public pressure and GDDR efficacy on the executive board. The results of both panels of the multivariate regression model provide evidence that supports this hypothesis. However, high public pressure has a stronger influence (both in magnitude and statistical significance) on the actual increase in the proportion of women (Panel A) than on the level of target-setting for the presence of women on the executive board (Panel B). Thus, high public pressure seems to push corporate behavior to an increased consideration of gender diversity on the executive board. This finding supports the theoretical assumption of *Hombach/Sellhorn* (2019) that the efficacy of targeted transparency regulations (such as GDDR; section 2.1.2) is driven by the mechanisms of public pressure. Moreover, since the study at hand measures the level of public pressure based on the number of newspaper articles about a company, it uncovers the potential importance of information intermediaries (e.g., the media) for the efficacy of GDDR. Furthermore, the findings regarding the impact of media coverage on board gender diversity are in line with prior literature. *Peña-Martel et al.* (2022) find a positive relationship between the efficacy of the Spanish mandatory gender quota and the level of media attention to a comparable extent (*Peña-Martel et al.* (2022), p. 199).

Based on the same theoretical idea as for high public pressure, the study at hand expected a negative association between **low public pressure** (H_{6b}) and GDDR efficacy on the executive board. Results from the multivariate regression models of both panels cannot support this hypothesis. Companies subject to a low level of public pressure do not seem to appoint women less frequently to their executive board (Panel A) or to set statistically significantly lower targets for the proportion of women on the executive board (Panel B). The result may be explained by the fact that companies subject to low public pressure do not act considerably differently than companies that perceive average public pressure. Accordingly, both groups of companies could make their appointment decision among female and male candidates without attributing decisive importance to the social demands of society. However, prior research has not yet investigated the influence of low public pressure in the context of gender diversity regulation.

Moreover, as explained in the hypotheses development (section 4.2.2), the **capital market orientation** of a company may also determine the efficacy of GDDR (H_7). Theory suggests that companies listed on a regulated market receive more attention from stakeholders and regulators due to their prominent position within society. However, since the gender diversity of these companies was closely covered before GDDR came into force, these companies may already have exploited some of the gender diversity potential. Therefore, hypothesis H_7 postulates an positive association between listed companies and the efficacy of GDDR on the executive board. The empirical results cannot support this hypothesis. The capital market orientation of the companies is not associated with the efficacy of GDDR on executive boards. The results suggest that listed companies do not appoint more/fewer women to their executive board (Panel A) or set higher/lower targets for the presence of women on the executive board (Panel B). Since most gender diversity regulations are solely applied to listed companies[148], prior research does not provide evidence about the potential impact of capital market orientation on the efficacy of gender diversity regulations.

While institutional theory proposes a positive association between **company age** and the efficacy of GDDR, principal-agent theory suggests a negative association due to institutionalized and male-dominated appointment processes. Accordingly, hypothesis H_8 postulates an undirected association between company age and GDDR efficacy. Empirical results of the multivariate regression analyses partially support the hypothesis and indicate a positive association. Although company age does not influence the increase in the presence of female executive board members (Panel A), it positively impacts the level of self-set targets for the proportion of women on the executive board (Panel B). Thus, in line with institutional theory, older companies tend to set higher targets and consider gender diversity issues for the executive board. However, the disclosure of ambitious gender diversity targets does not necessitate an actual increase in the presence of women. Furthermore, the result cannot explain the differences in the influence of GDDR efficacy measures. A possible cause for the discrepancies in the appointment behavior and target-setting behavior may be provided by the anecdotal evidence presented in section 5.2.4.2. Many companies that fail to meet their self-set targets for the executive board justify the missed target by the lack of suitable qualified female candidates. Thus, older companies may be willing to enhance gender diversity on their executive board and set ambitious targets. Due to the lack of suitable qualified female candidates, they cannot achieve the targeted proportion of women and do not appoint significantly more female board members. On the contrary, companies can use the disclosure of self-set targets to signal their willingness to enhance board gender diversity without intending to achieve an actual increase in the presence of women on the executive board. However, such opportunistic behavior could be debunked by stakeholders since companies have to disclose the target achievement at the end of the target achievement period. The result is contrary to the

[148] For detailed information on the designs of mandatory gender quotas implemented in Europe and their regulatory background, cf. *Gabaldon et al.* (2017), pp. 240–253.

findings of prior research that find no (*Gregorič et al.* (2017), p. 281) or a negative relationship (*Peña-Martel et al.* (2022), p. 199) between a company's age and the efficacy of gender diversity regulation.

While the variables discussed so far relate to public visibility due to company-specific characteristics, the following three variables (existence of **quantified targets for the proportion of women on the executive board** before GDDR was implemented, proportion of women on the supervisory board, and female supervisory board chairpersons) consider corporate gender diversity before GDDR came into force or gender diversity on the higher hierarchy level. Theory suggests that voluntarily setting quantified targets for the proportion of women before GDDR was implemented is associated with GDDR efficacy on the executive board (H_9). Results from the empirical analysis support this hypothesis. Companies that voluntarily disclose targets for gender diversity on the executive board before the introduction of GDDR increase the proportion of women more than companies that do not (Panel A). Moreover, these companies set higher targets for the proportion of women on the executive board (Panel B). These findings suggest that GDDR are more effective for companies that address gender diversity issues beforehand. Since altering appointment processes and increasing gender diversity can be a protracted process, these companies can more efficiently respond to GDDR and appoint more female executive board members. Finally, the mandatory reporting requirements may have an additional impact that nudges companies to increase executive board gender diversity. However, prior research does not examine the impact of voluntary target-setting behavior.

For two-tier corporate governance systems, prior research indicates that the composition of the supervisory board influences the appointment behavior of the executive board. In this light, hypothesis H_{10} postulates that the **proportion of women on the supervisory board** positively influences GDDR efficacy on the executive board. Empirical results partially support this hypothesis. On the one hand, a larger proportion of women on the supervisory board does not result in a greater increase in the presence of female executive board members (Panel A). On the other hand, supervisory boards consisting of a larger proportion of women set higher targets for the proportion on the executive board (Panel B). Thus, the empirical results suggest that a more gender-diverse supervisory board is not associated with the actual appointment of more female executive board members but instead with the proposition and disclosure of higher gender diversity targets. This suggests that female supervisory board members have the power to influence the target-setting for the executive board. Nevertheless, further barriers seem to prevent appointing female executive board members. As presented in section 5.2.4.2, companies justify missed self-set targets for the executive board with the lack of suitable female candidates. In general, supervisory board members need to ensure the optimal composition of the executive board to mitigate agency problems and avoid opportunistic behavior (principal-agent theory). This theoretical concept holds irrespective of the gender of the supervisory board members. Hence, gender-diverse supervisory boards may prefer male executive board members if they provide better qualifications. In that sense, a larger proportion of women on the supervisory board positively impacts the disclosure of ambitious targets, whereas the actual appointment is based on characteristics beyond gender. This finding is supported by the study of *Bozhinov et al.* (2021), which investigates a sample of German listed and co-determined companies. They find that women on the supervisory board influence the probability of having at least one female executive board member under certain circumstances (e.g., position on the nominating committee (*Bozhinov et al.* (2021), p. 1324)).

Finally, similar to the previous hypothesis and due to the importance of supervisory board chairpersons, chairs held by women are supposed to be positively associated with the efficacy of GDDR on the executive board (H_{11}). Results of the multivariate regression partially support this association. However, as stated in section 6.2.2.1, the results must be interpreted cautiously due to the small number of **female chairpersonships** (section 5.2.3.1). Women hold the supervisory board chair in only 27 out of 910 company-year observations (Table 6-8). While female chairpersons are positively associated with GDDR efficacy in terms of the actual increase in the proportion of women on the executive board (Panel A), they do not positively impact the target-setting behavior (Panel B). Thus, female chairpersons seem to use their power within the board to support appointing female executive board members. However, companies whose supervisory board is chaired by a woman may address gender diversity issues more frequently in general. Hence, the association measured by female chairpersons may be an overall indicator of companies' conduct in terms of gender diversity. Moreover, the fact that female supervisory board chairpersons are not positively associated with more ambitious target-setting is against the expectation. This indicates that the small number of observations may limit the explanatory power of this variable.

In summary, the results from the multivariate regression analysis suggest that high public pressure, the age of a company, the voluntary target-setting behavior, the proportion of women on the supervisory board, and the gender of the supervisory board chairperson are determinants associated with GDDR efficacy on the executive board (RQ2). By contrast, low public pressure and a company's capital market orientation do not seem to determine the efficacy of GDDR on the executive board for the analyzed sample. However, the results **indicate that GDDR efficacy varies depending on its specific measurement**. High public pressure, the voluntary target-setting before GDDR was implemented, and female supervisory board chairmanship influence the actual appointment behavior of gender-diverse boards. By contrast, the age of a company, the voluntary target-setting behavior, and, especially the proportion of women on the supervisory board seem to influence GDDR efficacy regarding the level of disclosed gender diversity targets. While it can be argued that only the actual increase in the proportion of women measures the efficacy of regulation, a more ambitious target setting may also signal a change in corporate conduct and the achievement of an intended effect. Figure 6-2 presents the summary of the empirical results for the executive board in consideration of the hypotheses.

The **following section** discusses the empirical results in conjunction with the findings on the supervisory board. GDDR determinants at both corporate hierarchy levels are compared to critically debate GDDR efficacy from a more holistic point of view.

H_{6a}:	The efficacy of GDDR on the executive board is positively associated with a high level of public pressure.	**Supported**
H_{6b}:	The efficacy of GDDR on the executive board is negatively associated with a low level of public pressure.	**Not supported**
H_{7}:	The efficacy of GDDR on the executive board is positively associated with companies' capital market orientation.	**Not supported**
H_{8}:	The efficacy of GDDR on the executive board is associated with companies' age.	**Partially supported**
H_{9}:	The efficacy of GDDR on the executive board is associated with companies' reporting practice regarding gender diversity of the executive board before the implementation of GDDR.	**Supported**
H_{10}:	The efficacy of GDDR on the executive board is positively associated with the proportion of women on companies' supervisory board.	**Partially supported**
H_{11}:	The efficacy of GDDR on the executive board is positively associated with female chairmanship of companies' supervisory board.	**Partially supported**

Figure 6-2: Results for the determinants hypotheses on the executive board

6.3 Discussion

After the previous sections discussed the findings separately for each corporate hierarchy level, this section discusses the empirical results considering **both hierarchy levels** to gain further insights into determinants of GDDR efficacy. On the one hand, the empirical results reveal discrepancies in the determinants of GDDR efficacy between supervisory and executive boards. On the other hand, the determinants vary within the investigated hierarchy level depending on the GDDR efficacy proxy. Table 6-14 summarizes the results of the determinants analysis of GDDR efficacy on the supervisory (section 6.2.1) and the executive boards (section 6.2.2). The results are presented according to the investigated panel and hierarchy level in consideration of the hypotheses.

First, the finding that **high public pressure** determines GDDR efficacy holds true irrespective of the investigated hierarchy level and the used efficacy measure. However, the empirical results of both sub-studies suggest that the impact of high public pressure on the increase in the actual proportion of women (Panel A; $\Delta PoWoSB$ or $\Delta PoWoEB$ as dependent variable) is larger than on the level of self-set targets for the presence of female board members (Panel B; *TarWoSB* or *TarWoEB* as dependent variable). In line with the assumptions derived from theory (legitimacy theory, stakeholder theory, and institutional theory), the pressure of stakeholders seems to urge companies to incorporate societal expectations and, therefore, to increase gender diversity on corporate boards. Thus, the results of both sub-studies support the theoretical consideration of *Hombach/Sellhorn* (2019) that the efficacy of regulations based on targeted transparency mechanisms relies on public pressure. Moreover, the empirical results provide evidence for a higher actual increase in gender diversity. This result is in line with findings of prior research that find comparable reactions in response to the Spanish gender diversity regulation (*Peña-Martel et al.* (2022), p. 199). Aside from actual increases in board gender diversity, companies that face high public pressure react to public pressure and disclose higher gender diversity targets. By appointing more female managers, companies could demonstrate that they are aware of societal expectations, even if they are temporarily unable to increase gender diversity for various reasons (e.g., due to ongoing contracts or lack of female candidates). This result indicates that companies subject to high public pressure may aim to further increase gender diversity in later years after the introduction of GDDR.

Comparision of determinants of GDDR efficacy					
		Panel A		Panel B	
Hypotheses: The efficacy of GDDR...		**Supervisory board**	**Executive board**	**Supervisory board**	**Executive board**
H_{2a}/H_{6a}:	...is positively associated with a high level of public pressure	Supported	Supported	Supported	Partially supported
H_{2b}/H_{6b}:	...is negatively associated with a low level of public pressure	Not supported	Not supported	Supported	Not supported
H_3/H_7:	...is (positively) associated with companies' capital market orientation.	Not supported	Not supported	Supported	Partially supported
H_4/H_8:	...is associated with companies' age.	Not supported	Not supported	Not supported	Supported
H_5/H_9:	...is associated with companies' gender diversity reporting practice before the implementation of the GDDR.	Not supported	Supported	Not supported	Supported
H_{10}:	...on the executive board is positively associated with the proportion of women on companies' supervisory board.	n/a	Not supported	n/a	Supported
H_{11}:	...on the executive board is positively associated with female chairmanship of companies' supervisory board.	n/a	Supported	n/a	Not supported

Table 6-14: Comparison of determinants of GDDR efficacy

Second, the empirical results weakly support the negative association between **low public pressure** and GDDR efficacy. The assumed association is solely supported by the level of gender diversity target-setting for supervisory boards. Overall, low public pressure is therefore not identified as a determinant of GDDR efficacy. The mostly insignificant results indicate that companies subject to low public pressure do not appoint significantly fewer women to their boards than those subject to average or above-average public pressure. The results indicate that average or low public pressure does not lead to considerably different reactions from companies subject to GDDR than for companies experiencing high public pressure. In turn, this supports the notion that high public pressure especially shapes corporate behavior regarding gender diversity and, therefore, determines GDDR efficacy.

Third, companies' **capital market orientation** is associated with GDDR efficacy in terms of the level of self-set targets for the proportion of women (Panel B). Both sub-studies provide evidence that publicly listed companies disclose more ambitious targets for the presence of female board members. This finding aligns with the hypothesis derived from theory (institutional theory. stakeholder theory). However, the empirical results cannot deliver insights into companies' intention to disclose a higher target for the proportion of women on corporate boards. It remains an empirical question whether companies only signal awareness of gender diversity issues to address stakeholders' expectations or whether companies are honestly interested in fostering gender diversity. However, companies' capital market orientation is not associated with the actual increase in the proportion of women (Panel A). The discrepancies in corporate actions (i.e., the appointment of more female board members) and corporate targets (i.e., targets for more gender-diverse boards) suggest that publicly listed companies use disclosure primarily to meet societal demands.

Fourth, the empirical results of both sub-studies predominantly suggest that the **age of a company** is no determinant of GDDR efficacy. Nevertheless, the multivariate regression for the executive board sub-study provides weak evidence that older companies set more ambitious targets for the proportion of women. This indicates that the positive association (derived from institutional theory) outweighs the potential negative effects of the old boys' network phenomenon (section 4.2.2). However, as stated with respect to companies' capital market orientation, the underlying intentions of the disclosure of higher gender diversity targets are doubtful. On the one hand, it may reflect the true intention of the company to increase the proportion of women in the future. On the other hand, companies can also use the disclosure of ambitious targets to pretend a shift in their appointment behavior.

Fifth, the empirical results provide evidence that the disclosure of quantified **targets for the proportion of women before GDDR was implemented** determines GDDR efficacy. The executive board sub-study suggests that companies that voluntarily set quantified targets regarding gender diversity increase gender diversity to a larger extent than companies that do not disclose targets beforehand (Panel A). Furthermore, the results indicate that these companies set higher targets for the presence of female board members on executive boards (Panel B). Accordingly, dealing with gender diversity issues in advance of the regulatory intervention seems to positively impact GDDR efficacy. The GDDR may increase companies' awareness of gender diversity issues due to the mandatory reporting obligations and, thus, nudge companies to actually increase the proportion of female board members. On the contrary, the findings do not provide evidence that these companies have already realized gender equality on their corporate boards before the implementation of GDDR. However, the results of the supervisory board subsample do not support these findings.

Finally, the results for the association between the proportion of women on the supervisory board and GDDR efficacy, as well as the association between supervisory board chairpersonship and GDDR efficacy, are solely **applicable to the executive board**. Therefore, the results are not discussed in detail again. Nevertheless, the results indicate that the gender of the chairpersons on a higher corporate level may affect the appointing decision on a lower corporate level within a two-tier corporate governance system.

In summary, high public pressure and the voluntary target-setting practices of companies are identified as determinants of GDDR efficacy. The other variables impact GDDR efficacy solely on a particular corporate hierarchy level or in terms of higher gender diversity targets. Overall, the multivariate analyses show that a **multitude of determinants** influences companies' appointment decisions and target-setting behaviors in response to GDDR. The following chapter analyzes the possible consequences of changed corporate board compositions on the financial reporting quality.

7 GDDR and financial reporting quality

This chapter analyzes the association between increased gender diversity on the supervisory board in the context of GDDR and financial reporting quality (RQ3). Section 7.1 describes the research design, including the identification strategies, the dependent and independent variables, and the analyzed sample. Section 7.2 presents the results of the multivariate regression analysis. Lastly, Section 7.3 discusses the results.

7.1 Research design

7.1.1 Identification strategies

The association between increased gender diversity on the supervisory board in the context of GDDR and financial reporting quality is analyzed based on a balanced panel data set. The dependent variable (a proxy for financial reporting quality) is continuously scaled. The independent variables are either continuously or binary scaled. Therefore, a **multivariate panel regression model** with fixed effects is appropriate for examining the relationship between a continuous dependent variable and independent variables. The assumptions of OLS regressions are already discussed in section 6.1.1 and, therefore, are not repeated in this chapter.

The results presented in section 5.2.3.1 reveal that companies that are subject to GDDR increase gender diversity on the supervisory board after the implementation of the regulation. Moreover, the results of the descriptive analysis show that the presence of female supervisory board members of companies affected by GDDR reach an average proportion of approx. 30% in 2021 (Figure 5-12). Thus, six years after GDDR came into force, the companies achieved the level of gender diversity stipulated by the mandatory gender quota. Consequently, the descriptive results indicate that companies subject to GDDR considerably increase the presence of female supervisory board members and, thus, alter the **composition of their supervisory board**. However, the descriptive results do not indicate which motives drive the increase in gender diversity on the supervisory board among companies affected by GDDR – whether it is primarily to maintain an optimal supervisory board composition or to respond to external pressure resulting from GDDR.

Furthermore, the determinants analysis identified several variables that influence the efficacy of GDDR (section 6.3). It indicates that **high public pressure** is an important variable determining the increase in the proportion of women on the supervisory board (section 6.2.1.5). Against the backdrop of theory and prior literature, the results suggest that companies facing high public pressure address societal expectations more frequently and appoint more female supervisory board members. To this end, as explained in the hypotheses development (section 4.2.3), it can be suspected that companies subject to high public pressure alter the supervisory board composition in the light of high public pressure and do not maintain an optimal board composition. An altered supervisory board composition in the context of GDDR that changes the ex-ante optimal supervisory board composition may affect the monitoring abilities of the supervisory board (section 4.2.3). To identify whether altered supervisory board composition in the context of GDDR affects financial reporting quality, the study implements **two identification strategies**.

The **first identification strategy** examines the general association between altered supervisory board composition in the context of GDDR and financial reporting quality. The study measures the increase in female supervisory board members to analyze potential consequences of more gender-diverse supervisory boards after the implementation of GDDR (hypothesis H_{12} (section 4.2.3)). Companies whose supervisory board consists of no or solely a marginal proportion of women may be more affected by GDDR than companies that have already reached a certain level of gender diversity. Similarly, *García Lara et al.* (2022) argue in the context of a mandatory gender quota regulation that companies with corporate board composition exhibiting a larger distance to the stipulated mandatory gender quota are more affected by the regulation (*García Lara et al.* (2022), pp. 4–5). Thus, the first identification strategy differentiates two groups, depending on whether a company is potentially greatly or less greatly affected by GDDR. The first group consists of companies that increase the presence of women on the supervisory board from a marginal proportion to a higher proportion during the sample period (treatment group). The second group comprises companies that do not considerably alter the gender diversity on the supervisory board during the sample period (control group). Thus, the control group consists of companies exhibiting a constantly low or high proportion of female board members. The differentiation of a treatment and control group allows to investigate to which extent GDDR shape gender diversity in supervisory boards. Hypothesis H_{12} postulates that the increase in gender diversity on the supervisory board (treatment group) is negatively associated with financial reporting quality.

The **second identification strategy** considers companies' potential incentives to increase the proportion of female supervisory board members in the context of GDDR. To this end, the level of public pressure in the context of altered supervisory board composition is considered. Companies that face high public pressure may increase gender diversity on the supervisory board to address societal expectations and not to achieve an optimal board composition. In order to identify potential influences of high public pressure on companies' incentives to increase the gender diversity of the supervisory board, the second identification strategy differentiates two groups of companies regarding their public visibility. Similar to the first identification strategy, the second identification strategy singles out companies that exhibit an increased gender diversity on the supervisory board. The first group consists of companies that increase gender diversity on the supervisory board and are subject to high public pressure (treatment group). The second group comprises companies that increase gender diversity on the supervisory board without facing high public pressure (control group). This differentiation strategy allows to investigate companies' incentives to increase the presence of female supervisory board members. Considering theory, the results of prior research as well as the findings of the determinants analysis (section 6.2.1.5), it can be suspected that increased gender diversity on the supervisory board in the context of high public pressure is negatively associated with financial reporting quality.

In summary, both identification strategies investigate the association between increased gender diversity on the supervisory board in the context of GDDR and financial reporting quality. The first identification strategy investigates the general association of increased gender diversity on the supervisory board and financial reporting quality. The second identification strategy adds to the first identification strategy and incorporates findings of the determinants analysis (section 6.3). The next section explains the variables included in the regression models.

7.1.2 Variables

Financial reporting quality measures

In order to examine the association between increased gender diversity of the supervisory board in the context of GDDR and financial reporting quality, this study performs a multivariate panel regression analysis. Therefore, a **quantifiable measurement of financial reporting quality** is required. Both identification strategies use a proxy for financial reporting quality as the dependent variable in the respective multivariate regression models.

Accounting literature provides a variety of definitions and measures for financial reporting quality.[149] The **quality of earnings** is a key element that determines the financial reporting quality and, therefore, is one of the most established proxies for financial reporting quality in prior research. Following *Ball/Shivakumar* (2005), financial reporting should be useful to investors and all other stakeholders that contract with the company (*Ball/Shivakumar* (2005), p. 126). Thus, financial reporting aims to provide decision-useful information that reflects the company's financial performance and condition.

However, managers can behave opportunistically and undertake actions to maximize their compensation (section 4.1.1) and thereby affect financial reporting quality. When managers use accounting policy choices to alter financial statements, to conceal company's economic performance, or to influence contractual outcomes relying on the reported earnings, such behavior is referred to as earnings management (*Healy/Wahlen* (1999), p. 368). Hence, earnings management impairs the decision-usefulness of financial reports, as it distorts company's financial performance. Within the two-tier corporate governance system, the **supervisory board is responsible for reviewing the accuracy of financial reports**, detecting earnings management, and ensuring a true and fair view of financial performance (section 2.2.1).

The majority of accounting literature uses the **concept of accruals** to identify earnings management (*Dechow et al.* (2010), p. 348). Since accruals are well-established in literature (in the context of board gender diversity: e.g., *García Lara et al.* (2022); *Hoang et al.* (2017); *Srinidhi et al.* (2011)), this study uses accruals as a proxy for financial reporting quality.[150] Accruals can be briefly defined as the recognition of earnings in a financial period, while the corresponding cash flows may be recognized in a different period (*Dechow/Dichev* (2002), p. 36). Prior research provides a bunch of concepts to measure accruals (*McNichols* (2002), p. 62).

[149] For a discussion of financial reporting quality, cf. *Hagemann* (2017), pp. 13–25.

[150] Accounting literature provides further proxies for financial reporting quality. Alternative proxies are earnings persistence, earnings smoothness, earnings predictability, asymmetric timeliness, time loss recognition, and target beating (*Dechow et al.* (2010), p. 346.)

The **total accruals** are calculated based on the measure developed by *Francis/Wang* (2008).[151] Equation 7.1 presents the formula for the calculation of total accruals. Instead of calculating total accruals based on the balance sheet and the income statement alone, the method additionally uses information from the cash flow statement. The earnings component is operationalized by earnings before extraordinary items.[152] For the cash flow component, cash flows from operating activities are used.

$$(7.1) \qquad TACC_{i,t} = \frac{EBEI_{i,t} - CFO_{i,t}}{TA_{i,t-1}}$$

where,

$TACC_{i,t}$	is the total accruals for company *i* in year *t*,
$EBEI_{i,t}$	is earnings before extraordinary items for company *i* in year *t*,
$CFO_{i,t}$	is the cash flow from operating activities for company *i* in year *t*,
$TA_{i,t}$	is the total assets for company *i* in year *t*,
i	is an item in the company index, and
t	is an item in the period index (years).

Accruals can be divided into two main components: non-discretionary (or normal) and discretionary (or abnormal) accruals (*Dechow et al.* (2010), p. 358; also: *Hagemann* (2017), p. 21; *Rave* (2022), p. 183). Non-discretionary accruals arise when accounting standards are applied neutrally, reflecting the fundamental performance of a company without any managerial discretion (*Dechow et al.* (2010), p. 358; *Healy* (1985), p. 89). **Discretionary accruals** occur when managers use their judgment within the flexibility allowed by accounting standards, influencing reported earnings (*Healy* (1985), p. 89). This discretionary component may indicate earnings management, where accruals deviate from the expected non-discretionary accruals. Consequently, discretionary accruals suggests lower earnings quality and distorted financial reporting (*Dechow et al.* (2010), p. 358).

Total accruals need to be separated into their two components to determine the discretionary accruals. Following *Francis/Wang* (2008), the discretionary accruals of a company are the difference between total accruals and the predicted accruals of a company (equation (7.2); *Francis/Wang* (2008), pp. 167–168). Larger discretionary accruals imply greater earnings management and therefore lower financial reporting quality (*Francis/Wang* (2008), p. 167).

151 The measurement concept of *Francis/Wang* (2008) is adapted from the work of *DeFond/Park* (2001) which relies on *DeAngelo* (1986). *García Lara et al.* (2022) also use the *Francis/Wang* (2008) model to investigate the impact of a gender diversity regulation on financial reporting quality in a single country setting with a comparable sample size.

152 Since the disclosure of extraordinary items is prohibited both under the German regulations of the HGB and international standards (i.e. IFRS), net income is used instead of earnings before extraordinary items.

$$(7.2) \quad DACC_{i,t} = TACC_{i,t} - PACC_{i,t}$$

where,

$DACC_{i,t}$ is the discretionary accruals for company *i* in year *t*,

$PACC_{i,t}$ is the predicted accruals (as defined in equation 7.3) for company *i* in year *t*, and

all other variables as defined above.

Many calculation methods estimate the predicted accruals of a company based on the comparison with the total accruals of a matched company portfolio (e.g., *Jones* (1991); *Kothari et al.* (2005)).[153] In contrast, the model provided by *Francis/Wang* (2008) uses the **company as its own benchmark** to calculate the predicted accruals (*Francis/Wang* (2008), p. 168). This calculation method is beneficial for this study for two reasons. First, using matched company portfolios (e.g., at the industry-year level) can cause problems due to company-specific characteristics (e.g., differences in size or the company's investment cycle) (*García Lara et al.* (2022), p. 8). Calculating predicted accruals using a company as its own benchmark mitigates this problem. Second, estimating predicted accruals based on an industry-year level requires a sufficiently large number of portfolio companies for each industry to predict reliable total accruals (*Francis/Wang* (2008), p. 168). By contrast, the calculation method of *Francis/Wang* (2008) allows the estimation of predicted accruals for small samples (*García Lara et al.* (2022), p. 8; *Hoang et al.* (2017), p. 150). Due to the sample size analyzed in the study at hand, the calculation method of *Francis/Wang* (2008) provides more reliable results compared to calculation methods relying on matched company portfolios.

In detail, the **predicted accruals** are computed as the difference between company's previous year ratio of current accruals over sales revenues and its prior year ratio of depreciation expenses over gross property, plant, and equipment (*Francis/Wang* (2008), p. 168). The predicted accruals are scaled by the total assets of the prior year (*Francis/Wang* (2008), p. 169). Equation 7.3 illustrates the calculation of predicted accruals.

$$(7.3) \quad PACC_{i,t} = \frac{\left\{\left[Rev_{i,t} * \left(\frac{CACC_{i,t-1}}{Rev_{i,t-1}}\right)\right] - \left[PPE_{i,t} * \left(\frac{Dep_{i,t-1}}{PPE_{i,t-1}}\right)\right]\right\}}{TA_{i,t-1}}$$

where,

[153] These alternative calculation methods estimate the expected total accruals of a company based on a industry-year comparison. To reliably calculate the expected total accruals of a company, a sufficient number of company observations for each industry and year is required. For detailed description of the calculation of different alternative methods to estimate the discretionary accruals of a company, cf. *Hagemann* (2017), pp. 145–149, or *Rave* (2022), pp. 182–187.

$PACC_{i,t}$	is the predicted accruals for company *i* in year *t*,
$CACC_{i,t}$	is the current accruals (as defined in equation 7.3) for company *i* in year *t*,
$Rev_{i,t}$	is the sales revenue for company *i* in year *t*,
$PPE_{i,t}$	is the gross property, plant, and equipment for company *i* in year *t*,
$Dep_{i,t}$	is the depreciation expenses for company *i* in year *t*, and

all other variables as defined above.

The calculation of the predicted accruals requires the company's current accruals. **Current accruals** are measured as the change in non-cash working capital (*Francis/Wang* (2008), p. 169). Specifically, current accruals are defined as the difference between the delta in current assets and the change in cash and short-term investments, less the difference between the delta in current liabilities, less the change in short-term debt (equation 7.4, *Francis/Wang* (2008), p. 169).

$$(7.4)\quad CACC_{i,t} = (\Delta CA_{i,t} - \Delta Cash_{i,t}) - (\Delta CL_{i,t} - \Delta STD_{i,t})$$

where,

$CACC_{i,t}$	is the current accruals for company *i* in year *t*,
$\Delta CA_{i,t}$	is the change in current assets for company *i* in year *t*,
$\Delta Cash_{i,t}$	is the change in cash and short-term investments for company *i* in year *t*,
$\Delta CL_{i,t}$	is the change in current liabilities for company *i* in year *t*,
$\Delta STD_{i,t}$	is the change in short-term debt for company *i* in year *t*, and

all other variables as defined above.

This study uses figures stated in cash flow statements, income statements, and balance sheets at the fiscal year-end to calculate the proxy for financial reporting quality. Following prior literature, all values required to compute the discretionary accruals are winsorized at the 1 and 99 percentiles (*García Lara et al.* (2022), p. 9) to mitigate biased results caused by extreme observations. Moreover, the study uses the absolute amount of discretionary accruals (**unsigned discretionary accruals**). Signed discretionary accruals indicate whether the use of managerial discretion results in increased or decreased earnings (*Francis/Wang* (2008), p. 168). However, this study aims to measure financial reporting quality based on the accuracy and reliability of reported earnings. It is not of central importance whether managerial discretion is used to increase or decrease earnings quality. Thus, unsigned discretionary accruals are appropriate to estimate the financial reporting quality of a company (similar: *García Lara et al.* (2022)). Larger values of discretionary accruals suggest lower earnings quality (*García Lara et al.* (2022), p. 9; *Srinidhi et al.* (2011), p. 1616).[154]

In order to calculate the accruals of a company, **financial data** for sample companies is collected from the BvD Dafne database. Missing figures are hand-collected from annual reports. Financial data from three consecutive years is needed to calculate discretionary accruals (*Francis/Wang* (2008), p. 169). Since the study analyzes whether the GDDR (enacted in 2015; section 2.2.3.1) affects financial reporting quality, financial data over a period of nine years (between 2013 and 2021) is needed.

Independent variables

The **first identification** strategy captures the increase in gender diversity on the supervisory board in the context of GDDR. The variable of interest (*SB Div incr*) is a dummy variable that takes the value of one, if the proportion of women on the supervisory board increases from less than or equal to 16.67%[155] to more than 16.67% during the sample period, and zero otherwise. If the dummy variable is coded as one, it indicates that the gender diversity of the supervisory board is affected by GDDR. If the dummy variable is coded as zero, it suggests that the gender diversity of the supervisory board is not or solely marginally affected by GDDR. The development of gender diversity on the supervisory boards is hand-collected, as stated in section 5.1.1.

The **second identification** strategy uses two independent variables to examine the association between increased gender diversity on supervisory boards in the context of GDDR and financial reporting quality. To capture companies that increase gender diversity on the supervisory board during the sample period, the first step is identical to the first identification strategy. An increase in gender diversity is defined as an increase in the proportion of women on the supervisory board from less than or equal to 16.67% to more than 16.67% during the sample period. In the second step, companies that increase gender diversity on the supervisory board are further clustered into two groups based on public pressure. The first group of companies increases gender diversity on the supervisory board and is subject to high public pressure (treatment). The second group of companies increases gender diversity on the supervisory board and is not subject to high public pressure (no

---

154 Within the German two-tier corporate governance system, the supervisory board is required to monitor and control the executive board (section 2.2.1). As stated in the hypotheses development (section 4.2.3), the study assumes that a changed supervisory board composition in response to the GDDR affects financial reporting quality, because the optimal supervisory board composition is altered. However, the GDDR targets also the executive board. It cannot be discarded, that the GDDR change the composition of the executive board and, therefore, alter the decision-making quality. A poorer decision-making (e.g., investment decisions) can also result in higher accruals (*García Lara et al.* (2022), p. 9). However, as the gender diversity on the executive board increased to a smaller extent (section 5.2.3.2), it can be assumed that the changes do not considerably drive the change in accruals.

155 The average supervisory board of companies affected by the GDDR consists of 12 members (Table 5-3 (section 5.1.3)). The presence of two female board member corresponds to a mathematical proportion of 16.67%. Thus, the dummy variable captures companies with no, one, or two female supervisory board members, on average. Similarly, *García Lara et al.* (2022) define companies as greatly affected by the mandatory gender quota if they have to appoint two or more female board members to fulfill the mandatory gender quota (*García Lara et al.* (2022), p. 8).

treatment). In accordance with the determinants analysis (section 6.1.2), public pressure is proxied by media attention. To ensure a sufficient number of observations in each group, high public pressure is defined as the upper 50%-percentile in German and English news counts.[156] To sum up, the variables of interest in the second identification strategy are two dummy variables. The first dummy variable (*SB Div incr treat*) takes the value of one if the company increases gender diversity on the supervisory board and is subject to high public pressure and zero otherwise. The second dummy variable (*SB Div incr notreat*) takes the value of one if the company increases gender diversity on the supervisory board and is not subject to high public pressure.

Control variables

Prior literature investigating the association between corporate board composition and financial reporting quality suggests that further variables are associated with financial reporting quality. The following variables **derived from theory and prior literature** are included as control variables in the multivariate regressions: companies' capital market orientation, company size, leverage, growth, profitability, loss indicator, and type of auditor (*García Lara et al.* (2022); *García Lara et al.* (2017); *Gull et al.* (2018); *Srinidhi et al.* (2011); *Hoang et al.* (2017); *Krishnan/Parsons* (2008); *Schumann et al.* (2024); *Panzer/Müller* (2015)). These control variables are included in both regression models of the two identification strategies.

Prior literature indicates that incentives to manage financial reporting differ with respect to companies' **capital market orientation** (*Burgstahler et al.* (2006), p. 1013). Since most gender diversity regulations predominantly regulate publicly listed companies, most studies investigating the association of gender diversity regulation and financial reporting quality analyze solely listed companies (e.g., *García Lara et al.* (2022); *Srinidhi et al.* (2011)). However, private companies are supposed to manage earnings to a larger extent than public companies (*Burgstahler et al.* (2006), pp. 1003–1004). Thus, *listed* is assumed to be negatively associated with financial reporting quality. *Listed* is a dummy variable that takes the value of one if the company is listed on a regulated market and zero otherwise.

Institutional theory suggests that larger companies have greater institutional monitoring and, therefore, face greater pressure to meet societal expectations (*Srinidhi et al.* (2011), p. 1617). Prior literature predominantly supports these theoretical considerations and found **company size** to be positively associated with financial reporting quality (*García Lara et al.* (2017), p. 660; *García Lara et al.* (2022), p. 12; *Panzer/Müller* (2015), p. 15; *Srinidhi et al.* (2011), p. 1623). However, other studies provide mixed results for the association of firm size and financial reporting quality in a gender diversity context (*Gull et al.* (2018), p. 270; *Schumann et al.* (2024), p. 156). Similar to section 6.1.2, company size (*firm size*) is measured as the natural logarithm of total assets (e.g., *Srinidhi et al.* (2011), p. 1617).

[156] Note that a different threshold for classifying high and low public pressure is used in analyzing the association between increased gender diversity in the context of GDDR and financial reporting. Using the thresholds from the determinant analysis would yield an extremely small number of observations for the variables of interest, making inferential statistical analysis unfeasible.

Findings of prior literature suggest that **leverage** may be positively or negatively associated with financial reporting quality (*Francis/Wang* (2008), p. 171; *García Lara et al.* (2022), p. 12; *Gull et al.* (2018), p. 270; *Panzer/Müller* (2015), p. 13). On the one hand, companies with greater leverage are supposed to face improved external monitoring (e.g., by creditors) and, thereby, are incentivized to reduce earnings management (*Panzer/Müller* (2015), p. 13). On the other hand, more indebted companies have a greater likelihood of bankruptcy, which could incentivize them to increase earnings management (*Francis/Wang* (2008), p. 171). Similar to section 6.1.2, *leverage* is defined as the ratio of total debt divided by total assets (e.g., *Francis/Wang* (2008), p. 170).

The company's **growth** is supposed to be associated with the financial reporting quality for two reasons. First, prior literature argues that growth is positively associated with the level of discretionary accruals because fast-growing companies are incentivized to conceal poor financial performance (*García Lara et al.* (2017), p. 655; *Schumann et al.* (2024), p. 150). Second, from a mathematical perspective, growth can affect the current accruals if the relation between sales and gross property, plant, and equipment is non-linear (*Francis/Wang* (2008), p. 171). However, prior literature provides mixed results for the direction of the association (*García Lara et al.* (2022), p. 12; *Srinidhi et al.* (2011), p. 1630; *Panzer/Müller* (2015), p. 15). Contrary to section 6.1.2, *growth* is measured as the yearly change in total sales revenues (e.g., *Francis/Wang* (2008), p. 171).

Profitability is found to be an important driver of discretionary accruals (*Kothari et al.* (2005)) and, therefore, of financial reporting quality. On the one hand, managers of poor-performing companies may use earnings management to inflate reported earnings, resulting in reduced financial reporting quality (*García Lara et al.* (2017), p. 655). On the other hand, well-performing companies have fewer incentives to inflate earnings through earnings management than poor-performing companies (*Srinidhi et al.* (2011), p. 1620). Thus, higher profitability of companies is positively associated with financial reporting quality. Profitability is measured as earnings before interest and taxes over total assets (e.g., *García Lara et al.* (2022), p. 10).

Prior literature has found that reported company losses are positively associated with financial reporting quality (*García Lara et al.* (2022), p. 15; *Gull et al.* (2018), p. 268; *Panzer/Müller* (2015), p. 16; *Srinidhi et al.* (2011), p. 1632). Managers of loss-making companies can exert less discretion over accruals (*Gull et al.* (2018), p. 261). Consequently, managers of companies with negative financial performance have less discretion for earnings management (*Srinidhi et al.* (2011), p. 1632). Thus, a positive association between **loss** and financial reporting quality is assumed. *Loss* is a dummy variable that takes the value of one if the company has reported a loss in the fiscal year and zero otherwise (e.g., *Panzer/Müller* (2015), p. 13).

In addition, the **choice of the auditor** influences the earnings quality of a company (*Gull et al.* (2018), p. 270; *Lawrence et al.* (2011), p. 261). Larger (Big 4) auditors are assumed to detect earnings management more frequently and to provide better audit quality (*Francis/Wang* (2008), p. 183; *Srinidhi et al.* (2011), p. 1620). Besides the greater financial and personnel resources of larger auditors compared to small auditors (*Lawrence et al.* (2011), p. 260), it is assumed that larger auditors provide better audit quality to minimize litigation risks and to protect their reputation (*Panzer/Müller* (2015), p. 13; *Srinidhi et al.* (2011), p. 1614). Accordingly, prior literature indicates that an audit by a large auditor is positively associated with financial reporting quality. *Big 4 auditor* is a dummy variable that takes the value of one if a company is audited by a Big 4 auditor in the fiscal year and zero otherwise (e.g., *Srinidhi et al.* (2011), p. 1619).

BvD Dafne provides the **data for the control variables**. Missing values were hand-collected from annual reports. Following prior literature, industry and year fixed effects are included in all regression models to control for industry- and year-invariant effects (*García Lara et al.* (2022), p. 9; *Srinidhi et al.* (2011), p. 1622).

Both identification strategies are performed separately to analyze the association between GDDR and a company's financial reporting quality. Equations 7.5 and 7.6 present the **multivariate regression model** for each identification strategy and the corresponding independent variables.

$$(7.5)\quad FRQ_{i.t} = \beta_0 + \beta_1 * SB\ Div\ incr_i + \sum\gamma_n * Controls_{i.t} + \sum\delta_n * FE + \varepsilon_{i,t}$$

and

$$(7.6)\quad FRQ_{i,t} = \beta_0 + \beta_1 * SB\ Div\ incr\ treat_i + \beta_2 * SB\ Div\ incr\ notreat_i + \sum\gamma_n * Controls_{i,t} + \sum\delta_n * FE + \varepsilon_{i,t}$$

where,

$SB\ Div\ incr_{i,t}$	is a dummy variable that takes the value of one, if the proportion of women on the supervisory board increases from less than or equal to 16.67% to more than 16.67% during the sample period, and zero otherwise,
$SB\ Div\ incr\ treat_i$	is a dummy variable that takes the value of one, if the proportion of women on the supervisory board increases from less than or equal to 16.67% to more than 16.67% during the sample and is subject to high public pressure, and zero otherwise,
$SB\ Div\ incr\ notreat_i$	is a dummy variable that takes the value of one, if the proportion of women on the supervisory board increases from less than or equal to 16.67% to more than 16.67% during the sample and is not subject to high public pressure, and zero otherwise,
$\sum Controls_{i,t}$	are the control variables as previously defined,[157]

[157] For an overview of the control variables and their calculation, cf. Appendix 10.

$\sum FE$ are industry and year fixed effects,

$\varepsilon_{i,t}$ is the error term for company *i* in year *t*, and

all other variables as defined above.

7.1.3 Sample adjustments

To analyze the association between GDDR and financial reporting quality, adjustments to the base sample from the determinants analysis of GDDR efficacy (section 6.1.3) are necessary. This analysis focuses on supervisory boards affected by GDDR. Thus, 63 companies subject to the mandatory gender quota on the supervisory board are not the object of investigation and are removed from the sample. Table 7-1 summarizes the sample selection process. The sample used to investigate the association between GDDR and financial reporting quality **is the same as for the sub-study on the supervisory board in the determinants analysis** of the efficacy of GDDR (section 6.1.3, Table 6-1).

Sample adjustments		
	Number of companies	Company years
Base sample for the analysis of determinants of GDDR efficacy	**143**	**1,001**
Less companies subject to the mandatory gender quota	-63	-441
Final sample for the analysis of the association between GDDR and financial reporting quality	**80**	**560**

Table 7-1: Sample adjustments for the analysis of the association between GDDR and financial reporting quality

7.2 Results

This section presents the results of the analysis investigating the association between GDDR and financial reporting quality to address the **third research question** (RQ3). First, the section provides the descriptive statistics of the variables included in the regression models. Second, bivariate correlation analysis presents the correlation of each pair of variables. Third, the section presents the results of the multivariate regressions analyzing the association between increased gender diversity in the context of GDDR and financial reporting quality. Lastly, multivariate regression models are tested in terms of sensitivity and robustness.

7.2.1 Descriptive statistics

Table 7-2 presents the descriptive statistics for the variables included in the multivariate regression models of both identification strategies. Similar to sections 6.2.1.1 and 6.2.2.1, the table reports the sample size, mean, standard deviation (std. dev.), 25% percentile (Q25), median, and 75% percentile (Q75) for the continuous variables. For the dummy variables included in the regression models, Table 7-2 reports the proportion of company-year observations that exhibit certain characteristics. Although **existing research** has not examined the influence of GDDR on financial reporting quality, the results are compared with studies that have investigated the impact of other regulatory interventions.

FRQ is the dependent variable in the regression models. The variable is measured by unsigned discretionary accruals that serve as a proxy for financial reporting quality. Higher discretionary accruals (higher FRQ) indicate lower financial reporting quality. The mean of FRQ is 0.06. It implies that, on average, 6% of the total assets of a company are discretionary accruals. The median exhibits a comparable value of 0.05. However, the descriptive statistics suggest variances in the level of discretionary accruals among sample companies. While the discretionary accruals account for 2% of the total assets of companies of the 25% percentile (Q25; 0.02), companies of the 75% percentile (Q75; 0.09) exhibit a considerably higher value of 9%. Prior literature that measures discretionary accruals based on the *Francis/Wang* (2008) model finds slightly larger (0.124 (*García-Meca et al.* (2015), p. 10)) or similar mean values for unsigned discretionary accruals (0.06 (*Hoang et al.* (2017), p. 154)). While *García Lara et al.* (2022) report discretionary accruals for Norwegian companies, *Hoang et al.* (2017) investigate Vietnamese companies. Varying accounting method choices among countries or contextual factors (e.g., quality of audits) determining the financial reporting quality can cause differences in the observed level of signed discretionary accruals.

Descriptive statistics for the (continuous) variables for the analysis of financial reporting quality						
Variables[a]	**n**	**Mean**	**Std. dev.**	**Q25**	**Median**	**Q75**
FRQ	560	0.06	0.06	0.02	0.05	0.09
Firm size	560	2.92	4.30	0.66	1.63	3.09
Leverage	560	0.57	0.21	0.45	0.57	0.70
Growth	560	0.08	0.22	-0.01	0.06	0.14
Profitability	560	0.06	0.07	0.02	0.05	0.09
Descriptive statistics for the (binary) variables for the analysis of financial reporting quality						
Variables[a]	**n**	**# of company-years (% of company-years)**				
SB Div incr	560	217 (39%)				
SB Div incr treat	560	128 (23%)				
SB Div incr notreat	560	89 (16%)				
Listed	560	301 (54%)				
Loss	560	102 (18%)				
Big 4 auditor	560	405 (72%)				

[a]FRQ is the unsigned discretionary accruals calculated using the model provided by *Francis/Wang (2008)*. Firm size is the total assets of the company in € billion. Leverage is the ratio of total liabilities over the total assets. Growth is measured as the difference of sales revenues and sales revenues of the prior year scaled by sales revenues of the prior year. Profitablility is measured as earnings before interests and taxes over total assets. SB Div incr is a dummy variable that takes the value of one, if the proportion of women on the supervisory board increases from less than or equal to 16.67% to more than 16.67% during the sample period and zero otherwise. SB Div incr treat is a dummy variable that takes the value of one, if the proportion of women on the supervisory board increases from less than or equal to 16.67% to more than 16.67% during the sample and is subject to high public pressure and zero otherwise. SB Div incr notreat is a dummy variable that takes the value of one, if the proportion of women on the supervisory board increases from less than or equal to 16.67% to more than 16.67% during the sample and is not subject to high public pressure and zero otherwise. All continious variables are winsorized at the 1st and 99th percentiles.

Table 7-2: Descriptive statistics for financial reporting quality variables

Because the sample is identical to that analyzed in the GDDR efficacy analysis on the supervisory board, the descriptive statistics for the variables **firm size** and **leverage** are already discussed in section 6.2.1.1. With a mean of €2.92 billion, the analyzed companies have a comparable size to those analyzed in comparable studies (*García Lara et al.* (2022), p. 10; *Hoang et al.* (2017), p. 152). Furthermore, the sample's mean leverage of 57% (0.57) is consistent with prior studies, such as those measuring discretionary accruals using the *Francis/Wang* (2008) model (mean = 0.562 (*García Lara et al.* (2022), p. 10)) or analyzing a German sample (mean = 0.644. (*Panzer/Müller* (2015), p. 13)).

Contrary to section 6.2.1.1, **growth rates** are measured based on the change in sales revenues due to the calculation method of accruals (7.1.2). On average, sample companies grow by 8% yearly (0.08 (mean)). The magnitude of the standard deviation (0.22) indicates that the growth ratios differ substantially among sample companies. The spread between the 25% percentile (-0.01 (Q25)) and the 75% (0.14 (Q75)) supports this indication. While the companies of the 25% percentile shrink, on average, by 1% per year, the companies of the 75% percentile grow by 14% per year. For German companies, prior literature reports comparable growth ratios and also suggests that the growth rates vary considerably within the analyzed sample (0.060 (mean); 0.146 (std. dev.), *Panzer/Müller* (2015), p. 14).

Profitability is measured as earnings before interests and taxes over total assets. The mean value of 0.06 indicates that companies included in the sample gain 6% profit scaled by total assets. Furthermore, the standard deviation of 0.07 suggests that the profitability of sample companies is not homogeneous. However, on average, the companies in the 25% percentile report a positive financial result of 2% measured by total assets (0.02 (Q25)). Moreover, companies in the 75% percentile achieve a positive financial result of 9% relative to total assets (0.09 (Q75)). Prior literature supports the results of varying profitability but reports slightly lower values ((0.029 (mean); 0.14 (std. dev.), *García Lara et al.* (2022), p. 10) and (0.04 (mean); 0.09 (std. dev.), *Srinidhi et al.* (2011), p. 1626)).

39% of the sample companies **increase gender diversity on the supervisory board** during the sample period from less or equal to 16.67% to more than 16.67% (SB Div incr). Thus, before the implementation of GDDR, 39% of the supervisory boards had two or fewer female members. During the sample period, these boards increased the number of female members to more than three. As descriptive results in section 5.2.3.1 indicate, companies affected by GDDR considerably increased the share of female supervisory board members between 2014 and 2021 (Figure 5-13, section 5.2.3.1). However, the supervisory boards of the remaining companies (61%) do not necessarily consist of less than 16.67% female board members. If a company's supervisory board consistently had more or less than 16.67% female members throughout the entire sample period, it is not included in the variable.

The study identified high public pressure as an important determinant of GDDR efficacy (section 6.3). In line with this finding, the descriptive results presented in Table 7-2 show that 23% of the companies **increased gender diversity** on the supervisory board **while subject to high public pressure** (SB Div incr treat). By contrast, only 16% of the companies increased the presence of women on the supervisory board while not affected by high public pressure (SB Div incr notreat). These findings indicate that companies subject to high public pressure increase the proportion of female supervisory board members more frequently. However, 16% of the companies altered their supervisory board composition in terms of gender diversity without facing high public pressure. Thus, it can be assumed that the companies increase gender diversity on the supervisory board for different reasons.

The **capital market orientation** of companies (listed) included in the sample is already discussed in section 6.2.1.1. Slightly more than half (54%) of the companies are listed on a regulated market. The remaining 46% of the sample are private companies.

Companies report a **financial loss** in 18% of the company-years. Hence, in most of the years (82%), the companies are profitable. This result is in line with the descriptive results of profitability that indicate that companies make a profit on average (mean = 0.06, profitability). Some studies find higher proportions of company-year observations reporting a loss (33% (*García Lara et al.* (2022), p. 10)). However, *Panzer/Müller* (2015) find a slightly smaller value for a German sample (12% (*Panzer/Müller* (2015), p. 13)).

The majority of companies (72%) in the sample are audited by **Big 4 auditors**. Following theoretical consideration and findings of prior literature, the audit by Big 4 auditors is positively associated with earnings quality and, therefore, financial reporting quality. Prior research that investigates earnings quality or financial reporting quality finds even higher values for financial reports audited by large auditors (89% (*Panzer/Müller* (2015), p. 13), 92% (*Gull et al.* (2018), p. 263)). Prior research analyzes samples consisting of listed companies (*García Lara et al.* (2022); *Gull et al.* (2018)). The different sample characteristics of prior studies may explain the higher proportion of reports audited Big 4 auditors, as listed companies are more frequently audited by Big 4 auditors. Thus, the lower number of reports audited by Big 4 auditors in the sample seems plausible.

7.2.2 Correlation analysis

Similar to the **bivariate analysis** in section 6.2.1.2, Table 7-3 reports Spearman's rank correlation coefficients for the variables of the financial reporting quality analysis. It presents the correlation coefficients and significance levels (p-values in parentheses) for the dependent, GDDR, and control variables. Significant pairwise coefficients of the dependent variable (*FRQ*) and GDDR or control variables are printed in bold. Since unsigned discretionary accruals are used as a proxy for *FRQ*, positive correlation coefficients indicate a negative association with *FRQ* and vice versa.

Firm size (-0.0771) and *loss* (-0.1509) are **negatively and statistically significantly correlated** with *FRQ*. For *firm size*, the coefficient suggests a weak correlation at the 10% level that is very close to zero.[158] The correlation coefficient of *firm size* indicates that larger companies tend to have lower unsigned discretionary accruals and, hence, exhibit better financial reporting quality than smaller companies. By contrast, *loss* indicates a strong statistically significant correlation at the 1% level. The variable *loss* suggests that companies reporting a negative financial result have better financial reporting quality compared to profitable companies. Furthermore, for *leverage*, the correlation analysis provides a negative coefficient but not at a statistically significant level.

[158] A coefficient between 0 and 0.5 indicates a weak correlation, a coefficient between 0.5 and 0.7 a moderate correlation, and a coefficient between 0.7 and 1 a strong correlation (*Kobelt/Steinhausen* (2006), p. 122).

Correlation matrix for the financial reporting quality analysis											
Variables[a]	FRQ	SB Div Incr	SB Div Incr treat	SB Div Incr notreat	Listed	Firm size	Leverage	Growth	Profitability	Loss	Big 4 auditor
FRQ	-										
SB Div Incr	0.0369 (0.4192)	-									
SB Div Incr treat	0.0363 (0.4273)	-	-								
SB Div Incr notreat	0.0078 (0.8699)	-	-0.2365 *** (0.0000)	-							
Listed	0.0647 (0.1571)	0.2747 *** (0.0000)	0.5058 *** (0.0000)	-0.2158 *** (0.0000)	-						
Firm size	**-0.0771 *** **(0.0917)**	0.0365 (0.4252)	0.0989 ** (0.0302)	-0.0653 (0.1535)	0.0337 (0.4607)	-					
Leverage	-0.0651 (0.1544)	-0.2212 *** (0.0000)	-0.3233 *** (0.0000)	0.0769 * (0.0922)	-0.4306 *** (0.0000)	0.2150 *** (0.0000)	-				
Growth	**0.1619 ***** **(0.0004)**	0.1122 ** (0.0140)	0.1147 ** (0.0119)	0.0177 (0.6989)	0.2024 *** (0.0000)	-0.1205 *** (0.0082)	-0.1266 *** (0.0055)	-			
Profitability	**0.1160 **** **(0.0110)**	0.1737 *** (0.0001)	0.1547 *** (0.0007)	0.0536 (0.2412)	0.3173 *** (0.0000)	-0.0545 (0.2331)	-0.1756 *** (0.0001)	0.0418 (0.3604)	-		
Loss	**-0.1509 ***** **(0.0009)**	-0.1264 *** (0.0049)	-0.0816 * (0.0682)	-0.0748 * (0.0930)	-0.2133 *** (0.0000)	-0.0268 (0.5580)	0.2167 *** (0.0000)	-0.2099 *** (0.0000)	-0.3756 *** (0.0000)	-	
Big 4 auditor	**0.1068 **** **(0.0193)**	0.2757 *** (0.0000)	0.2399 *** (0.0000)	0.0918 ** (0.0396)	0.2424 *** (0.0000)	0.2626 *** (0.0000)	-0.1365 *** (0.0028)	0.0787 * (0.0849)	0.0962 ** (0.0351)	-0.1333 *** (0.0045)	-

[a]The table reports Spearman correlation coefficients for a pairwise correlation of the FRQ variables. Respective p-values are presented below the coefficients in parentheses.
*, **, and *** indicate statistical significance at the 10%, 5%, and 1% levels, respectively.

Table 7-3: Correlation matrix for variables in the financial reporting quality analysis

Growth (0.1619), *profitability* (0.1160), and *Big 4 auditor* (0.1068) are **positively and statistically significantly correlated** with *FRQ*. The coefficients of all three variables indicate a weak correlation to *FRQ*. While the coefficient of *growth* is strongly statistically significant at the 1% level, the coefficients of *profitability* and *Big 4 auditor* show moderate statistical significance at the 5% level. In economic terms, the correlation analysis suggests that companies with higher growth rates (*growth*), more positive financial results (*profitability*), and audited by a large auditor (*Big 4 auditor*) show higher unsigned discretionary accruals. Thus, these companies have a weaker financial reporting quality. The coefficient direction of *growth* and *profitability* is in line with prior research. In contrast to the expectations, the coefficient Big 4 auditor positively correlates with *FRQ*. However, since the correlation analysis solely indicates pairwise coefficients, the correlation may vary in the multivariate regression.

However, not all variables which are positively correlated with *FRQ* are statistically significant. The coefficients of *SB Div incr* (0.0369), *SB Div incr treat* (0.0363), *SB Div incr notreat* (0.0078), and *listed* (0.0647) are positive, **statistically insignificant**, and close to zero. Thus, the correlation coefficients of these variables indicate no correlation with *FRQ*.

Furthermore, Table 7-3 shows that the control variable *listed* (0.5058) is **positively and strongly statistically significantly correlated** with *SB Div Incr treat*. Expressed in economic terms, the result indicates that listed companies more frequently increase gender diversity on the supervisory board while they face high public pressure. However, the results of a bivariate analysis provide solely a first impression of potential associations. As presented in the correlation analysis in the context of the determinants analysis on the supervisory board (section 6.2.1.2, Table 6-4), listed companies exhibit a moderate and statistically significant correlation to high public pressure. This correlation is reasonable as companies listed on a regulated market are more in the focus of society and, thus, face a higher level of public pressure (institutional theory, section 4.1.2.3). However, strong correlations between independent and control variables indicate multicollinearity issues. The collinear variables *listed* and *SB Div Incr treat* are therefore included in separate regression models to address multicollinearity issues. The correlation analysis only provides a first indication of the bivariate correlation between financial reporting quality and influencing factors. However, the financial reporting quality can depend on several variables simultaneously.

7.2.3 Multivariate analyses

This section examines **hypothesis H_{12}** based on two identification strategies to analyze whether GDDR affects the financial reporting quality of companies (RQ3). The regression models include financial reporting quality as the dependent variable, independent variables that capture the impact of GDDR, and control variables that are found to be related to financial reporting quality (section 7.1.2). The regression model results show the association between financial reporting quality and further variables included in the model. The level of unsigned discretionary accruals is used as a proxy for financial reporting quality. Thus, higher values of unsigned discretionary accruals imply lower financial reporting quality. Accordingly, positive (negative) coefficients indicate a negative (positive) association with financial reporting quality.

First identification strategy

Table 7-4 aggregates the results for the first identification strategy that examines the impact of altered supervisory board composition in the context of GDDR. The multivariate regression analysis comprises **two different models**. Model 1 includes all independent and control variables but does not consider industry and year fixed effects. In addition to the full set of variables of the first identification strategy, Model 2 includes industry and year fixed effects.

Both models (Model 1 and Model 2) are **statistically significant** (F-stat). Moreover, Table 7-4 presents the adjusted R^2, indicating the total variance each model explains. Model 1 exhibits a small adjusted R^2 (6.19%). Thus, Model 1 explains solely a marginal proportion of the total variance in the financial reporting quality. The adjusted R^2 of Model 2 is considerably higher (21.29%). The higher adjusted R^2 indicates that the inclusion of fixed effects structures enhances the explanatory power of the multivariate regression model. Prior literature that also investigates the association between gender diversity regulations on the supervisory board and financial reporting quality reports similar (e.g., around 26% (*García-Meca et al.* (2015), p. 12)) or smaller adjusted R^2 (e.g., between 11% and 15% (*Panzer/Müller* (2015), p. 15)). Moreover, the maximum VIFs support the results of the bivariate correlation analysis and do not indicate multicollinearity issues in both models.

The results of **Model 1** (full regression model without fixed effects) indicate a negative and statistically significant association between *SB Div incr* (-0.010) and *FRQ*. However, the statistical significance is marginal (at the 10% level). Furthermore, the control variables *growth* (0.042) and *Big 4 auditor* (0.016) and *profitability* (0.089) show a positive and statistically significant relationship with *FRQ*. By contrast, the coefficients of *firm size* (-0.005) and *loss* (-0.013) are negatively and statistically significant at the 5% level. The other control variables do not exhibit a statistically significant association with *FRQ*. However, the results are not discussed in detail due to the marginal explanatory power of Model 1 (adjusted R^2 of 6.19%).

Model 2 includes industry and year fixed effects. Considering industry fixed effects is reasonable because time-invariant industry-specific factors may affect the financial reporting quality. For this reason, other methods to determine discretionary accruals (e.g., the modified *Jones* (1991) model) estimate the discretionary accruals of a company based on an industry-year comparison. To address structural differences in the level of discretionary accruals within industries, industry fixed effects are included in the model. Furthermore, year fixed effects should be considered because accounting methods (e.g., regulations for the depreciation and amortization of assets) change over time and may affect the accruals of companies. To examine the financial reporting quality and not changes in accounting methods, Model 2 includes year fixed effects. Including industry and year fixed effects increases the explanatory power of the model (adjusted R^2 of 21.29%).

Multivariate panel regression models for the association between GDDR and financial reporting quality				
Identification strategy 1 FRQ as dependent variable				
Variables	**Hypothesis**	**Expected sign**	**Model 1**	**Model 2**
SB Div incr	H_{12}	(+)	-0.010* (-1.83)	0.004 (0.54)
Listed		(+)	0.005 (0.82)	-0.001 (-0.10)
Firm size		(-)	-0.005** (-1.97)	-0.005* (-1.72)
Leverage		(+/-)	0.018 (1.24)	0.019 (1.20)
Growth		(+/-)	0.042*** (3.39)	0.044*** (3.29)
Profitability		(+/-)	0.089* (1.76)	0.126** (2.36)
Loss		(-)	-0.013** (-2.31)	-0.019*** (-2.90)
Big 4 auditor		(-)	0.016*** (2.87)	0.014** (2.16)
Constant			0.100*** (3.29)	0.108*** (2.60)
Control variables			YES	YES
Fixed effects: Year, Industry			NO	YES
N			560	560
Adj. R^2			6.19%	21.29%
F-stat			5.61***	6.84***
Max. VIF			1.41	1.41

The table reports the results (OLS coefficients, t-statistics in parentheses) of the multivariate panel regression of the first identification strategy for Model 1 (full model without fixed effects), and Model 2 (full model with fixed effects). The expected directions are presented next to the variables.
*, **, and *** indicate significance at the 10%, 5%, and 1% level, respectively.

Table 7-4: Multivariate panel regression models (first identification strategy) for the association between GDDR and financial reporting quality

Contrary to Model 1, Model 2 does not indicate a statistically significant relationship between *SB Div Incr* (0.004) and *FRQ*. Moreover, the coefficient is close to zero. The insignificant coefficient indicates that companies that increase the proportion of women on the supervisory board during the sample period do not exhibit statistically significant higher or lower discretionary accruals and, therefore, **no higher or lower financial reporting quality**. However, some coefficients of the control variables indicate a statistically significant relationship with *FRQ*. *Growth* (0.044), *profitability* (0.126), and *Big 4 auditor* (0.014) are positively and statistically significantly associated with *FRQ*. *Growth* is strongly statistically significant at the 1% level, whereas *profitability* and *Big 4 auditor* exhibit a moderate statistical significance at the 5% level. In economic terms, companies that exhibit higher growth rates (*growth*) report, on average, 4.4% more discretionary accruals than companies with lower growth rates. *Profitability* and *Big 4 auditor* can be interpreted in a similar way. Moreover, the coefficient of *firm size* (-0.005) is negative and marginally statistically significant at the 10% level. *Loss* (-0.019) is negatively and strongly statistically significantly associated with *FRQ* at the 1% level. Thus, companies reporting a negative financial result exhibit 1.9% lower discretionary accruals, measured by total assets, than those reporting a positive financial result. Accordingly, companies reporting a loss have higher financial reporting quality. The coefficients of *firm size*, *growth*, *profitability*, and *loss* exhibit the expected direction. However, contrary to the expected association, *Big 4 auditor* shows a positive relationship with *FRQ*. This means that companies audited by large auditors (*Big 4 auditor*) report, on average, higher discretionary accruals. Thus, the results do not support the findings of prior research, which indicate a higher financial reporting quality for companies audited by a Big 4 auditor (e.g., *Francis/Wang* (2008), p. 183).

Second identification strategy

Table 7-5 reports the results of the second identification strategy. In contrast to the first identification strategy, the second identification strategy considers **the level of public pressure** in the context of increased gender diversity on the supervisory board. The second identification strategy includes four different multivariate regression models. Similar to Model 1 of the first identification strategy, Model 3 includes all variables without controlling for industry and year fixed effects. Model 4 includes the full model and considers industry and year fixed effects.

The F-stats indicate that the models of the second identification strategy are statistically significant and can explain the variance of financial reporting quality. Furthermore, Table 7-5 reports the **adjusted R^2** for each multivariate regression model. Model 3 shows an adjusted R^2 (6.10%), indicating low explanatory power. The result is similar to Model 1 of the first identification strategy. Fixed effects structures considerably enhance the explained proportion of the total variance. For the full regression with industry and year fixed effects (Model 4), the adjusted R^2 exhibits a value of 22.03%. Model 4 and Model 5 address multicollinearity issues and exclude pairwise collinear variables. Excluding these variables does not affect the explanatory power of the regression model. Model 4 reports an adjusted R^2 of 22.03% and Model 5 of 22.01%. As stated for the first identification strategy, these values are similar or higher compared to prior literature. Lastly, a maximum VIF of 1.67 (Model 3 and Model 4) suggests that the models have no multicollinearity issues.

Model 3 is the full model without fixed effects. The coefficient of *SB Div incr treat* (-0.007) is statistically insignificant and close to zero. Thus, Model 3 does not suggest a relationship between *SB Div incr treat* and *FRQ*. However, the other variable of interest, *SB Div incr no treat* (-0.013), indicates a negative and moderate statistically significant association with *FRQ*. Moreover, some control variables are associated with *FRQ*. *Firm size* (-0.005) suggests a negative and moderate statistically significant association at the 5% level. *Loss* (-0.014) is negatively and statistically significantly related to *FRQ* at the 5% level. On the contrary, the variables *growth* (0.042) and *Big 4 auditor* (0.016) are positively and strongly statistically significantly related to *FRQ* at the 1% level. *Profitability* (0.089) is positively associated with *FRQ* but at a low statistical significance level (10% level). Similar to the first identification strategy (Model 1), the results of Model 3 are not further discussed due to the low explanatory power of the model (adjusted R^2 of 6.10%).

Multivariate panel regression models for the association between GDDR and financial reporting quality

Identification strategy 2
FRQ as dependent variable

Variables	Hypothesis	Expected sign	Model 3	Model 4	Model 5	Model 6
SB Div incr treat	H_{12}	(+)	-0.007 (-0.90)	0.017* (1.78)	0.014* (1.40)	-
SB Div incr notreat	H_{12}	(+)	-0.013** (-1.85)	-0.007 (-1.01)	-0.006 (-0.84)	-0.011 (-1.48)
Listed		(+)	0.003 (0.48)	-0.011 (-0.97)	-	-0.004 (-0.30)
Firm size		(-)	-0.005** (-2.08)	-0.006* (-1.92)	-0.006* (-1.94)	-0.006* (-1.93)
Leverage		(+/-)	0.020 (1.29)	0.018 (1.16)	0.023 (1.46)	0.014 (0.94)
Growth		(+/-)	0.042*** (3.34)	0.043*** (3.20)	0.042*** (3.14)	0.043*** (3.25)
Profitability		(+/-)	0.089* (1.76)	0.131** (2.49)	0.128** (2.45)	0.126** (2.37)
Loss		(-)	-0.014** (-2.36)	-0.022*** (-3.12)	-0.021*** (-2.92)	-0.020*** (-3.00)
Big 4 auditor		(-)	0.016*** (2.90)	0.015** (2.24)	0.013** (2.04)	0.017*** (2.66)
Constant			0.104*** (3.44)	0.122*** (2.93)	0.116*** (2.81)	0.123*** (2.97)
Control variables			YES	YES	YES	YES
Fixed effects: Year, Industry			NO	YES	YES	YES
N			560	560	560	560
Adj. R^2			6.10%	22.03%	22.01%	21.54%
F-stat			5.04***	6.78***	7.49***	7.06***
Max. VIF			1.67	1.67	1.26	1.45

The table reports the results (OLS coefficients, t-statistics in parentheses) of the multivariate panel regression of the second identification strategy for Model 3 (full model without fixed effects), Model 4 (full model with fixed effects), Model 5 (SB Div incr treat), and Model 6 (listed). The expected directions are presented next to the variables.
*, **, and *** indicate significance at the 10%, 5%, and 1% level, respectively.

Table 7-5: Multivariate panel regression models (second identification strategy) for the association between GDDR and financial reporting quality

Model 4 is the full model, including industry and year fixed effects. Contrary to Model 3, the results indicate no statistically significant association between *SB Div incr notreat* (-0.007) and *FRQ*. However, Model 4 suggests a positive and statistically significant relationship between *SB Div incr treat* (0.017) and *FRQ*. The relationship is statistically significant at the 10% level. Expressed in economic terms, companies that increase the gender diversity of the supervisory board and face high public pressure report on average 1.7% higher discretionary accruals than companies that increase gender diversity on the supervisory board without being subject to high public pressure or companies that do not alter the gender diversity on the supervisory board at all. Setting this in relation to the mean total assets of the analyzed sample (€2.92 billion), companies that increase the gender diversity on the supervisory board while subject to high public pressure (*SB Div incr treat*) exhibit €49.64 million more discretionary accruals.[159] Furthermore, some control variables in Model 4 indicate a statistically significant association with *FRQ*. *Firm size* (-0.006) and *loss* (-0.022) are negatively and statistically significantly related to *FRQ* at the 10% (*firm size*) or 1% level (*loss*). Moreover, *growth* (0.043) and *profitability* (0.131) are positively and statistically significantly associated with *FRQ* at the 1% level (*growth*) and 5% level (*profitability*). *Big 4 auditor* (0.015) also suggests a positive and statistically significant relationship to *FRQ* but at the 5% level.

Model 5 and Model 6 address multicollinearity issues. Compared to Model 4, the adjusted R^2 values remain nearly unchanged (at least 21.54% (Model 6)). Accordingly, excluding collinear variables does not affect the explanatory power of the full model with all variables. The coefficients of Model 5 (without *listed*) are comparable to those of Model 4. The directions of the coefficients remain the same for all variables. The variables of interest (*SB Div incr treat* and *SB Div incr notreat*) show marginal changes in terms of magnitude but not in statistical significance. *SB Div incr notreat* (-0.006) is still negatively associated with *FRQ* but remains statistically insignificant. By contrast, the coefficient of *SB Div incr treat* (0.014) suggests a positive and statistically significant relationship with *FRQ*. The statistical significance of most control variables in Model 5 is unchanged compared to Model 4. Model 6 (without *SB Div incr treat*) reports similar results to Model 4. Only the statistical significance of *Big 4 auditor* (0.017) increases from the 5% to the 1% level. Apart from marginal changes in the magnitude of the coefficients, the coefficients are similar in terms of direction and statistical significance.

7.2.4 Sensitivity analyses and robustness tests

The multivariate regression models performed in both identification strategies are tested for their robustness against alternative variable calculations and sensitivity to changes in the proxies used. The results of the robustness tests performed in the determinants analysis (sections 6.2.1.4 and 6.2.2.4) suggest that the measurement of high public pressure may rely on the used news count database. Thus, the regression for the second identification strategy is performed when the **treatment component** (public pressure) of *SB Div incr treat* and *SB Div incr notreat* is alternatively measured on the basis of either German or English news counts instead of a combined measurement. Since the empirical model of the first identification strategy does not consider public pressure, the robustness test cannot be applied to that model.

Table 7-6 presents the results of the alternative public pressure measurement.

---

159 The value of the discretionary component of total accruals is calculated as *mean firm size* * *unsigned discretionary accruals*, e.g., €2.92 billion * 0.017 = €49.64 million (similar *Rave* (2022), pp. 198–199).

Robustness tests for the association between GDDR and financial reporting quality				
Variables	**Hypothesis**	**Expected sign**	**German news counts**	**English news counts**
SB Div incr treat	H_{12}	(+)	0.016* (1.72)	0.017* (1.74)
SB Div incr notreat	H_{12}	(+)	-0.010 (-1.30)	-0.009 (-1.14)
Listed		(+)	-0.010 (-0.93)	-0.012 (-1.03)
Firm size		(-)	-0.006** (-2.11)	-0.005* (-1.69)
Leverage		(+/-)	0.018 (1.14)	0.017 (1.10)
Growth		(+/-)	0.043*** (3.18)	0.044*** (3.26)
Profitability		(+/-)	0.128** (2.45)	0.137*** (2.58)
Loss		(-)	-0.021*** (-3.06)	-0.022*** (-3.12)
Big 4 auditor		(-)	0.016** (2.37)	0.014** (2.19)
Constant			0.129*** (3.10)	0.113*** (2.71)
Control variables			YES	YES
Fixed effects: Year, Industry			YES	YES
N			560	560
Adj. R^2			22.02%	22.01%
F-stat			6.78***	6.77***
Max. VIF			1.55	1.55

The table reports the results (OLS coefficients, t-statistics in parentheses) of the multivariate panel regression model of the second identification strategy when considering either German or English news counts for the treatment component (public pressure) of SB Div incr treat and SB Div incr notreat. The expected directions are presented next to the variables.
*, **, and *** indicate significance at the 10%, 5%, and 1% level, respectively.

Table 7-6: Robustness tests for the association between GDDR and financial reporting quality

The multivariate regression models do not change when considering either **German** (adjusted R^2 = 22.02%) **or English news counts** (adjusted R^2 = 22.01%). Furthermore, the coefficients of the variables of interest (*SB Div incr treat* and *SB Div incr notreat*) do not change in statistical significance and vary solely marginally in magnitude depending on the used news count database. The same holds true for the association between control variables and the dependent variable. The coefficient of *firm size* (-0.005) is the only one that decreases in statistical significance from the 5% to the 10% level when assessing the treatment component based on English news counts. Hence, the empirical results of the second identification strategy are robust against changes in the news counts database for the treatment component.

To test whether the models are sensitive to changes in the proxies, multiple sensitivity analyses are performed. First, it is tested whether the chosen threshold indicating an increased gender diversity on the supervisory board may drive the results. For this purpose, instead of the sharp threshold of 16.67% an **alternative threshold** is chosen to determine the independent dummy variables (*SB Div incr* for the first identification strategy, *SB Div incr treat* and *SB Div incr notreat* for the second identification strategy). In order to analyze the sensitivity of the results, an increased gender diversity on the supervisory board is assumed if companies increase the proportion of women from less or equal to 16.67% to equal to or more than 30%. For companies affected by GDDR, the average supervisory board size of 12 members (median (Table 5-3)) means the alternative threshold implies an increase in the proportion of female supervisory board members from two or less to four or more. Thus, the alternative threshold requires a higher increase in the proportion of female supervisory board members to indicate increased gender diversity.

Table 7-7 reports the results of both identification strategies with the alternative threshold. The variable of interest (*SB Div incr*) employed in the **first identification strategy** becomes statistically significant at the 5% level when using the alternative proxy. Thus, *SB Div incr* (0.015) suggests a positive association with *FRQ*. This result indicates that companies increasing gender diversity on the supervisory board from 16.67% or less to 30% or more exhibit poorer financial reporting quality. The alternative threshold does not change the statistical significance and magnitude of most control variables. Only the statistical significance of *firm size* (-0.006) increases from a 10% level to a 5% level. Due to the changes in statistical significance and magnitude of the independent variable (*SB Div incr*), the results suggest that the first identification is sensitive to the alternative threshold. However, using the alternative threshold leads to a change of the independent variable that is in line with the assumptions of hypothesis H_{12}. Thus, considering only companies that increase the gender diversity on supervisory boards to a larger extent indicates that a negative association between *SB Div incr* and financial reporting quality is evident. From a methodological perspective, it has to be considered that the requirements of the alternative threshold reduced the number of observations included in the dummy variable but lower the statistical power. Nevertheless, untabulated results suggest that the number of observations (168 observations) is still sufficient to meet the OLS regression assumptions.

The results of the sensitivity analyses suggest that the multivariate regression model of the **second identification strategy** is insensitive to the alternative threshold. The variables of interest *SB Div incr treat* (0.019) and *SB Div incr notreat* (0.011) reveal no changes in statistical significance and solely marginal changes in coefficients' magnitude. However, the coefficient of *SB Div incr notreat* changes from a negative to a positive direction but remains statistically insignificant. Furthermore, all control variables are unchanged in statistical significance and magnitude.

Multivariate panel regression models for the association between GDDR and financial reporting quality				
Sensitivity analysis Alternative threshold (<= 16.67% to >= 30%) for increased gender diversity on supervisory boards				
Variables	**Hypothesis**	**Expected sign**	**First identification strategy**	**Second identification strategy**
SB Div incr	H_{12}	(+)	0.015** (2.05)	-
SB Div incr treat	H_{12}	(+)	-	0.019* (1.79)
SB Div incr notreat	H_{12}	(+)	-	0.011 (1.31)
Listed		(+)	-0.004 (-0.38)	-0.006 (-0.59)
Firm size		(-)	-0.006** (-2.12)	-0.006** (-2.10)
Leverage		(+/-)	0.019 (1.20)	0.019 (1.21)
Growth		(+/-)	0.043*** (3.22)	0.043*** (3.22)
Profitability		(+/-)	0.127** (2.40)	0.129*** (2.44)
Loss		(-)	-0.020*** (-2.99)	-0.020*** (-2.97)
Big 4 auditor		(-)	0.013** (2.07)	0.013** (2.09)
Constant			0.121*** (3.15)	0.121*** (3.14)
Control variables			YES	YES
Fixed effects: Year, Industry			YES	YES
N			560	560
Adj. R^2			21.95%	21.86%
F-stat			7.44***	6.65***
Max. VIF			1.43	1.55

The table reports the results (OLS coefficients, t-statistics in parentheses) of the multivariate panel regression models with an alternative threshold for increased gender diversity on supervisory boards for the first and second identification strategy. The expected directions are presented next to the variables.
*, **, and *** indicate significance at the 10%, 5%, and 1% level, respectively.

Table 7-7: Multivariate regression models of both identification strategies using an alternative threshold

Moreover, the sensitivity analyses investigate how alternative proxies for control variables influence the results of the multivariate regression models of both identification strategies. First, the natural logarithm of sales revenues or number of employees is used as a proxy for **company size** instead of the natural logarithm of total assets. The results of the first identification strategy are mostly insensitive using alternative *firm size* proxies. While *firm size* (-0.005) is marginally statistically significantly associated with the dependent variable when using the natural logarithm of total assets, the association is statistically insignificant when using the natural logarithm of sales revenues (*firm size* (0.003)) and number of employees (*firm size* (-0.003)). Moreover, the coefficient of *Big 4 auditor* becomes statistically insignificant (*firm size* measured by the natural logarithm of sales revenues) or decreases in statistical significance (*firm size* measured by the natural logarithm of employees). Overall, the results of the first identification strategy are insensitive to alternative proxies of company size. The same holds true for the results of the second identification strategy. Similar to the first identification strategy, *firm size* and *Big 4 auditor* are the only variables that change statistical significance for both alternative company size proxies. *Firm size* suggests a statistically insignificant association with the dependent variable when measured by the natural logarithm of sales revenues (*firm size* (0.001)) or employees (*firm size* (-0.003)). Similar to the first identification strategy, *Big 4 auditor* becomes statistically insignificant when considering the natural logarithm of sales revenues (*Big 4 auditor* (0.009)) and less statistically significant when considering the natural logarithm of employees (*Big 4 auditor* (0.012)). Additionally, *listed* (-0.018) indicates a negative and marginally statistically significant relationship with *FRQ* when the number of employees is employed as a proxy for company size. In summary, the results of both identification strategies are mostly insensitive to a changed proxy of company size.

Second, alternative proxies for companies' **growth rates** (*growth*) are used. Instead of measuring the *growth* based on the change in sales revenues, *growth* is measured by changes in total assets and number of employees. The empirical results of the first identification strategy are mostly insensitive to changes in the growth proxy. The statistical significance of *firm size* (-0.006) increases slightly from the 10% to the 5% level when measuring growth rates based on the change in the number of employees. Moreover, *profitability* (0.096) becomes slightly less statistically significant when measuring the growth rates by changes in total assets. By contrast, the relationship between *profitability* (0.111) and *FRQ* is statistically significant at the 1% level when growth rates are measured based on the change in the number of employees. For the second identification strategy, all control variables remain stable in statistical significance and magnitude when alternative proxies for growth rates are utilized. However, the alternative proxies for growth rates affect the results of one variable of interest (*SB Div Incr treat*). The coefficient of *SB Div incr treat* (0.015) is statistically insignificant and slightly lower in magnitude when measuring the growth rates based on changes in total assets. Thus, the results indicate that the association between *SB Div incr treat* and the dependent variable shows some sensitivity to changes in the proxy of growth rates. As explained in section 7.1.2, the change in total assets may affect the results as the calculation of *FRQ* relies mainly on the changes in sales revenues. Therefore, the alternative growth rates proxy may influence the association between *SB Div incr treat* and *FRQ*. However, considering the adjusted R^2 values of the models using alternative proxies, they indicate a slightly lower explanatory power of the model (21.13% for the model measuring *growth* based on changes in total assets, 20.89% for the model measuring *growth* based on changes in employees). The lower explanatory power of the alternative models, combined with the methodological reasons for using changes in sales revenues as a proxy for *growth* (section 7.1.2), indicates that the initial model should be preferred.

Lastly, both identification strategies are performed based on alternative clustered **industry fixed effects**. Instead of NACE codes, SIC codes are used. For the first identification strategy, the results mostly remain unchanged. The adjusted R^2 value of the regression model using SIC codes (adjusted R^2 = 21.81%) is slightly higher than that of the regression model using NACE codes (adjusted R^2 = 21.29%). Furthermore, Big 4 auditor (0.019) is the only variable that changes statistical significance (from the 5% to the 1% level). All other variables remain constant in statistical significance and vary solely marginally in magnitude. The results of the second identification strategy reveal similar results. The explanatory power of the model with SIC code clustered industry fixed effects (adjusted R^2 = 22.66%) is slightly higher than that with NACE code clustered industry fixed effects (adjusted R^2 = 22.03%). The control variable *listed* (0.016) becomes marginally statistically significant at the 10% level, and *firm size* (-0.006) increases in statistical significance from the 10% level to the 5% level. Furthermore, similar to the first identification strategy, the positive relationship between *Big 4 auditor* (0.019) and *FRQ* suggests a slightly increased statistical significance from the 10% level to the 5% level. The coefficients of all other variables included in the model do not change in statistical significance and vary only marginally in magnitude when using industry fixed effects based on SIC codes. Thus, the results indicate that both identification strategies are mostly insensitive to changed industry fixed effects. The next section discusses the results of the multivariate regression models in order to answer the third research question (RQ3).

7.3 Discussion

This chapter investigated the association between GDDR and financial reporting quality (RQ3). Since GDDR intends to foster gender diversity on the supervisory board, companies need to change their supervisory board composition to increase the proportion of women. However, the **composition of the supervisory board** is crucial for financial reporting quality because the supervisory board, as the controlling body of the executive board, monitors and controls the accuracy of financial statements (*Campbell/Mínguez-Vera* (2008), p. 435; *Du Plessis/Saenger* (2017b), p. 148).

To this end, two identification strategies were developed to analyze the association between increased gender diversity on the supervisory board in the context of GDDR and financial reporting quality (H_{12}). The empirical results are discussed against the **backdrop of theory and compared to findings of prior research** that investigate the association between gender diversity regulation and financial reporting quality. Similar to the discussion of the second research question (RQ2), prior research is scarce since no study has yet investigated the consequences of GDDR. Nevertheless, prior studies analyzed the association between increased gender diversity on the supervisory board and financial reporting quality in the context of voluntary regulations or mandatory gender quotas. However, **differences in the results** of this study and prior literature might occur due to differences in characteristics of gender diversity regulations (e.g., GDDR and mandatory gender quota). Further differences in results might arise from different samples (e.g., Germany vs. Norway) or different sample periods (e.g., 2015-2021 vs. 2002-2010). Irrespective of diverging results which may occur due to the differences in research designs and analyzed gender diversity regulations, prior research provides valuable insights. The findings of prior studies contribute to an enhanced understanding of the association between increased board gender in the context of GDDR and financial reporting quality.

Principal-agent theory suggests a negative association between increased gender diversity on the supervisory board in the context of GDDR and financial reporting quality. Shareholders appoint the optimal composition of supervisory board members under given conditions to avoid opportunistic behavior of managers. Thus, a company's current nexus of contracts on the supervisory board is assumed to be optimal. The implementation of GDDR changes the given conditions and may change appointment decisions. Thus, the ex-ante optimal composition of the supervisory board is altered. Consequently, with respect to the theoretical assumption that shareholders appoint a composition of supervisory board members that respect their interests and ensure the highest financial reporting quality, the optimal supervisory board composition is affected. Hence, the altered, non-optimal composition of supervisory board members is assumed to influence the financial reporting quality negatively. The results of the first identification strategy provide no evidence for the negative association between increased gender diversity on the supervisory board in the context of GDDR and financial reporting quality. However, sensitivity analyses reveal that the impact of altered supervisory board composition and financial reporting quality depends on the extent of the increase in gender diversity (section 7.2.4). The empirical results suggest that companies increasing the proportion of female supervisory board members to a large extent exhibit poorer financial reporting quality.

Prior research suggests a **negative association between the implementation of mandatory gender quotas and financial reporting quality** (*García Lara et al.* (2022)). In more detail, *García Lara et al.* (2022) find that companies which are more affected by the mandatory gender quota exhibit poorer financial reporting quality than companies that have to increase board gender diversity to a smaller extent (*García Lara et al.* (2022), p. 12). The results of the first identification strategy partially support the findings of prior studies. While the initial model does not suggest a negative association between increased gender diversity and financial reporting quality, the sensitivity analyses find evidence for this association. However, the type of gender diversity regulations may determine the association between increased gender diversity and financial reporting quality. *García Lara et al.* (2022) investigate the setting of a mandatory gender quota (section 3.3.2), where the analyzed companies are forced by law to increase the presence of female board members and alter the composition of the corporate board. By contrast, companies affected by GDDR are not stipulated by law to change the composition of the supervisory board.

In the context of GDDR, companies may change the composition of supervisory boards for two reasons. On the one hand, companies may appoint more female supervisory board members irrespective of GDDR. Accordingly, these companies maintain an optimal supervisory board composition since they voluntarily appoint more women. Resource dependence theory suggests that women can add beneficial attributes to the supervisory boards which, inter alia, enhance the monitoring abilities of supervisory boards. Furthermore, prior studies that investigate voluntary settings report higher financial reporting quality for more gender-diverse corporate boards (*Hoang et al.* (2017), p. 155; *Panzer/Müller* (2015), p. 15). On the other hand, companies may appoint more female supervisory board members and alter the composition of the supervisory board due to external pressure created by GDDR. Under these conditions, companies alter appointment decisions to **address external pressure**, resulting in a non-optimal supervisory board composition. In these cases, the impact of altered supervisory board composition on financial reporting quality might be similar to the impact in the context of a mandatory gender quota. However, the results of the first identification strategy do not provide insights into companies' incentives to increase gender diversity on the supervisory board. Thus, it cannot be ruled out that increased gender diversity on the supervisory board is not predominantly triggered by GDDR.

The second identification strategy addresses potential diverging incentives to appoint more female supervisory board members. Theories (institutional theory, stakeholder theory) suggest that companies subject to **high public pressure** may appoint more female board members to meet societal expectations, resulting in a less than optimal composition of the supervisory board. The findings of the determinants analyses support the theoretical assumption that high public pressure is positively associated with increased gender diversity on the supervisory board in the context of GDDR (section 6.2.1.5). Moreover, as stated above, prior literature reveals that the extent to which gender diversity regulations affect the board composition (i.e., the number of female board members a company needs to appoint to the board to meet the legal requirements) is associated with financial reporting quality (*García Lara et al.* (2022), p. 12). For this purpose, the second identification strategy considers a treatment component (public pressure) for companies that increase gender diversity on the supervisory board. The results of the multivariate regression analysis support this assumption of an association between the implementation of GDDR and financial reporting quality. Companies that increase the proportion of women on the supervisory board and are greatly affected by GDDR show a lower financial reporting quality than companies increasing gender diversity on the supervisory board without facing high public pressure. Thus, the empirical results support the findings of *García Lara et al.* (2022). Consequently, hypothesis H_{12} is partially supported.

Comparing the results with the findings of the determinants analysis of GDDR efficacy (section 6.3) underpins the importance of high public pressure in the context of GDDR. First, the level of public pressure determines the efficacy of GDDR. Companies subject to high public pressure increase the proportion of women on targeted hierarchy levels to a larger extent. Second, increased gender diversity on the supervisory board, in conjunction with high public pressure, is negatively associated with financial reporting quality. Thus, the findings suggest that high public pressure incentivizes companies to appoint more female supervisory board members to meet external expectations. Furthermore, these results **support the theoretical considerations** of *Hombach/Sellhorn* (2019), who suggest the central importance of public pressure in the regulatory mechanisms of GDDR (section 2.1.2). Moreover, since this study uses media attention as a proxy for public pressure, the results suggest that information intermediaries contribute to effective GDDR.

Overall, the results of the multivariate regression analyses provide **partial support for hypothesis H_{12}**. On the one hand, increased gender diversity on the supervisory board in the context of GDDR is not generally negatively associated with financial reporting quality (first identification strategy). The association depends on the extent of increased supervisory board gender diversity. On the other hand, the results suggest that increased gender diversity on the supervisory board in the context of GDDR is negatively associated with financial reporting quality when considering companies' potential incentives. Thus, the results suggest a lower financial reporting quality for companies that increase gender diversity on the supervisory board when facing high public pressure. The empirical analyses address and answer the third research question (RQ3). Figure 7-1 summarizes the result of the financial reporting quality hypothesis H_{12}.

H_{12}:	Increased gender diversity on the supervisory board in the context of GDDR is negatively associated with financial reporting quality	**Partially supported**

Figure 7-1: Result for the financial reporting quality hypothesis

8 Conclusions

This study investigates whether GDDR shape the proportion of women on corporate boards, the determinants of its efficacy, and the consequences of altered supervisory board compositions. This chapter concludes this study. Section 8.1 summarizes the main findings of the empirical analysis. Section 8.2 discusses the implications and contribution of these results. Finally, based on the limitations of the study at hand, avenues for potential future research are drawn (section 8.3).

8.1 Main results

Gender diversity in corporate management positions has been a highly contentious topic in political and public debates for the last decades. Women remain largely underrepresented in upper corporate management positions worldwide. To address this issue, many national regulators introduced recommendations for gender diversity on corporate boards (e.g., in national corporate governance codes) aimed at increasing the participation of women at the top of corporate hierarchies. However, these voluntary policies have not achieved the desired level of female representation on corporate boards. Consequently, regulators have implemented mandatory gender quotas, requiring companies to appoint more women to their boards. On the one hand, these coercive gender diversity regulations effectively increase the proportion of women on corporate boards, as companies are compelled to comply under the threat of severe sanctions. On the other hand, such regulatory intervention affects companies' appointment decisions, resulting "*in a partial or complete loss of companies' discretionary freedoms*" (*Mensi-Klarbach et al.* (2021), p. 581). Therefore, companies often criticize mandatory gender quotas, expressing concerns that changes in board composition could negatively impact their performance. This situation presents a **dilemma for regulators**, who must balance the objective of promoting gender diversity in corporate management with the need to respect companies' appointment decision freedoms.

Against this backdrop, the German regulator has implemented **GDDR**, which blends the flexibility of voluntary policies with more binding regulations by requiring companies to disclose information on corporate gender diversity. However, since Germany is the first country to implement GDDR, the efficacy and consequences of this innovative regulatory approach are largely unknown. Because GDDR lacks the obligation to increase gender diversity at the targeted corporate hierarchy levels, the efficacy of GDDR is an empirical question.

A review of the limited empirical research on GDDR reveals a significant gap in the literature. To date, prior research has not investigated the efficacy and further consequences of GDDR. Therefore, this study pursued the following analyses to address the **research questions**:

- a descriptive analysis of the development of the proportion of women in management positions after the implementation of GDDR (RQ1a);
- a descriptive analysis of differences in reporting practices across companies affected by GDDR (RQ1b);
- an analysis of the determinants that are associated with the efficacy of GDDR on different corporate hierarchy levels (RQ2); and

- the association between increased gender diversity on boards in the context of GDDR and financial reporting quality (RQ3).

Two different **research methods** were employed to answer the research questions of this study. First, a content analysis was conducted to assess the proportion of women on each corporate hierarchy level (RQ1a) and to evaluate the reporting practice of companies affected by GDDR (RQ1b). Second, multivariate regression analyses were used to investigate the determinants of GDDR efficacy (RQ2) and the relationship between increased participation of women on corporate boards and financial reporting quality (RQ3).

A conceptual foundation was established to support the **empirical analyses**. Chapter 2 outlined different regulatory approaches aimed at promoting gender diversity and presented the theoretical mechanisms of GDDR. It also provided an in-depth explanation of the gender diversity regulation implemented in Germany. Chapter 3 reviewed the empirical research on gender diversity regulations and identified gaps in the literature. It highlighted descriptive studies on GDDR, empirical findings on the effectiveness of various gender diversity regulations, and the consequences of an increased proportion of women on corporate boards. Chapter 4 then developed the theoretical foundations and subsequently derived the hypotheses for the empirical analyses. These hypotheses were based on principal-agent theory, legitimacy theory, stakeholder theory, institutional theory, and resource dependence theory. Chapter 5 provided a detailed analysis of the development of the proportion of women on all corporate hierarchy levels targeted by GDDR and examined the disclosure practice of companies subject to GDDR. A content analysis was performed to analyze annual reports and corporate governance statements of 214 private and public companies affected by GDDR between 2014 and 2021. Based on the evaluation of the actual changes in gender diversity on corporate boards and the development of self-set targets disclosed by companies, chapter 6 empirically analyzed the determinants of GDDR efficacy. This was achieved through multivariate panel regression models applied in two sub-studies focusing on different corporate hierarchy levels to identify the similarities and differences in the determinants of GDDR efficacy. Chapter 7 explored the association between increased gender diversity on supervisory boards and companies' financial reporting quality within the context of GDDR. A multivariate panel regression analysis was conducted to determine whether companies that increased gender diversity on their supervisory boards to a large extent exhibited lower financial reporting quality.

Concerning the research questions mentioned above, the empirical analyses yielded the following **findings**:

First, the development of the composition of corporate boards and management levels revealed that the **proportion of women across all targeted corporate hierarchy levels increased** during the sample period, surpassing the levels of gender diversity before the implementation of GDDR. The increase in female participation is statistically significant for supervisory and executive boards as well as for the first management level below the executive board (RQ1a). For instance, the proportion of women on the executive board rose from an average of 9% in 2014 to 16% in 2021. Despite this overall increase in gender diversity, chairs of both supervisory and executive boards are only staffed on rare occasions by women (e.g., in 2021, 11 (5%) supervisory board chairs and six (3%) executive board chairs were held by women), indicating the persistence of a "second glass ceiling" (*Bozhinov et al.* (2019)) for female board members. Furthermore, the participation of women varies across corporate hierarchy levels. While over 30% of supervisory board members were female in 2021, only about 16% of executive board members were women in 2021. By contrast, the participation of women in management levels is higher than on the executive board, but the increase is less substantial and statistically less significant. Nonetheless, the statistically significant increase in gender diversity across most corporate hierarchy levels suggests that GDDR has successfully met its objective of increasing the proportion of women in management positions.

Second, despite the regulatory requirement to publish information, the content analysis revealed instances of non-compliance. Eight companies failed to provide the required reports altogether, and **22% of available corporate reports were either partially or entirely non-compliant** with the disclosure requirements of FüPoG I. Private companies (36%) were less compliant than public companies (10%), indicating that capital market orientation may influence adherence to reporting standards. The analysis further showed that 22% of the non-compliant reports mentioned none of FüPoG I requirements, while the remaining 78% lacked certain required information. This considerable proportion of unavailable or incomplete reports points to challenges in enforcing disclosure requirements. Additionally, the content analysis highlighted variations in how companies publish the information mandated by FüPoG I. While 87% of affected companies included gender diversity information in their management reports, 13% opted to publish a separate statement on their website. This variation in disclosure practices necessitates that users retrieve corporate gender diversity information from multiple sources.

Lastly, the reporting practice of self-set targets for the proportion of women on corporate hierarchy levels required by GDDR varies across corporate hierarchy levels (RQ1b). The self-set targets for supervisory boards (24% in 2021) were higher than those for executive boards (17% in 2021). However, most hierarchy levels, except the second management level, showed an upward trend in self-set targets over time. The sharp increases in these targets after 2017 suggest that the obligation to publish renewed targets after the first target achievement period seems to influence the level of self-set targets. Nevertheless, **half of the companies affected by GDDR set a target of zero** for female participation on the executive board, indicating companies frequently target gender-uniform executive boards. Moreover, many companies failed to meet their self-set targets across all hierarchy levels. Notably, 37% of companies on the executive board did not provide reasons for missing their self-set targets, thereby infringing reporting requirements. Among those companies that justify the reasons for missed targets at the respective hierarchy level, the results indicate a variety of reasons. As one of the most frequently stated reasons at all corporate hierarchy levels, companies referred to the qualifications of female candidates, which they claimed hindered the appointment of women to board and management positions.

The empirical analysis of the **determinants of GDDR efficacy** revealed both common and distinct determinants associated with the efficacy of GDDR across supervisory and executive boards (RQ2). At both corporate hierarchy levels, the level of public pressure determines GDDR efficacy. Consistent with the expectations derived from legitimacy theory, stakeholder theory, and institutional theory, companies exposed to high public pressure significantly increased the proportion of women to a larger extent and set higher targets for female participation compared to companies facing lower public pressure. While companies facing low public pressure reveal significantly lower self-set targets on supervisory boards, low public pressure is not negatively associated with target-setting on executive boards. The findings support the theoretical assumption by *Hombach/Sellhorn* (2019) that public pressure is crucial for effective targeted transparency regulations, such as GDDR. Additionally, since media attention was used as a proxy for public pressure, the findings suggest that information intermediaries like the media may play a significant role in providing information to stakeholders, thereby influencing the level of public pressure. Moreover, the analysis also found that capital market orientation influences the target-setting behavior of both supervisory and executive boards. Publicly listed companies set higher targets for female representation on both boards compared to private companies. This aligns with the expectations from institutional theory, which posits that publicly traded companies, being more visible in society, tend to set more ambitious gender diversity targets to demonstrate their commitment to these issues. However, this holds only for the target-setting behavior.

Furthermore, the study identified **hierarchy-level specific determinants of GDDR efficacy**. On the executive board, company age emerged as an influencing factor that determines the target-setting for the proportion of women. Older companies set higher targets for the presence of women on executive boards than younger companies. However, similar to capital market orientation, this determinant applies solely to the target-setting behavior. Additionally, pre-existing gender diversity targets before the implementation of GDDR influenced GDDR efficacy on the executive board. Companies that published quantified targets voluntarily before GDDR came into force increased the proportion of women more significantly than companies that did not. These companies also set significantly higher targets for the proportion of women on the executive board. Consequently, GDDR seems to nudge companies that voluntarily disclosed quantified targets to intensify their endeavors to promote gender diversity on their executive board. Moreover, in line with the expectations derived from the particularities of the German two-tier corporate governance system, gender diversity on supervisory boards determines GDDR efficacy on executive boards. A larger proportion of women on supervisory boards is associated with more ambitious targets for the participation of women on executive boards. This suggests that women at the top of the corporate hierarchy promote gender diversity at the lower level by setting higher gender diversity targets. Similarly, the presence of female supervisory board chairpersons is positively associated with actual increases in the proportion of women on executive boards, indicating that women in these powerful positions actively foster female participation on the executive board. Overall, the analysis suggests that public pressure is a determinant of GDDR efficacy across both hierarchy levels. Other determinants are hierarchy-level specific, highlighting the complexity of factors influencing gender diversity in corporate governance.

The study exploited the unique setting of the GDDR implemented in Germany to analyze the relationship between GDDR and companies' financial reporting quality (RQ3). The results of the first identification strategy provide no evidence that increased gender diversity on supervisory boards in the context of GDDR is associated with companies' financial reporting quality. However, the second identification strategy, which took into account the level of public pressure, offered a more nuanced view. The empirical results indicate that companies that increased the presence of female supervisory board members while facing high public pressure exhibit poorer financial reporting quality. This finding aligns with expectations derived from principal-agent theory, which posits that companies typically optimize their supervisory board composition in the absence of regulatory interventions. Any regulatory intervention that alters this optimal composition could lead to a suboptimal board structure. Consistent with this theoretical perspective, the study found that companies which **increased gender diversity** on their supervisory boards **in the context of high public pressure provide lower-quality financial reporting**. Prior research suggests that this decline in quality could be attributed to the characteristics of the newly appointed female supervisory board members. However, the findings do not support a general negative relationship between increased gender diversity and financial reporting quality, indicating that female board members do not inherently weaken financial reporting quality. Compared to prior studies investigating the impact of gender diversity regulations on financial reporting quality, this study supports the findings that mandatory increase (or increases in response to public pressure) is negatively associated with companies' financial reporting quality.

The results of this study provide **several implications** for regulators, users of corporate reports, preparers, auditors, and enforcement institutions, which are discussed in the following section.

8.2 Implications and contributions

The empirical results of this study reveal that the proportion of women increased across all affected corporate hierarchy levels following the implementation of GDDR. Hence, **regulators** (in the particular case of this study, the German Federal Government) can be confirmed that GDDR achieve the objective of increasing female participation in top management positions. Prior studies primarily focused on the development of the representation of women on supervisory and executive boards as well as on the target-setting on these hierarchy levels. This study expands the scope by examining gender diversity on management levels below the executive board. Additionally, this study delivers detailed insights into the reporting practices, including narrative explanations that justify missed self-set targets. The German regulator can utilize the descriptive findings of this study to monitor the development of female managers on management levels below the executive board. This information is important, as future executive board members are frequently recruited from these management levels. Additionally, the descriptive results and anecdotal evidence offer the regulator valuable insights into the challenges companies encounter in increasing the number of women on corporate boards or in upper management positions. This may help to identify structural obstacles in promoting corporate gender diversity. As this study is the first to analyze the determinants of GDDR efficacy, the results provide critical evidence that different factors influence regulatory efficacy. The results indicate that regulatory efficacy is affected by a combination of high public pressure and hierarchy-specific determinants. Since inconsistent regulatory efficacy across different companies is not desirable, the regulator may find this information useful for reassessing and potentially refining the regulatory approach to ensure more consistent and effective gender diversity regulation. Finally, the results of the financial reporting quality analysis indicate that GDDR may cause unintended consequences, such as lower financial reporting quality, that deviate from the regulation's primary objectives, potentially conflicting with the regulators' intentions. This may sensitize regulators to the fact that regulatory intervention affecting the composition of corporate boards may also be related to the outcomes (e.g., financial performance) of a company. Hence, regulators can use these findings to consider and incorporate potentially unintended consequences of GDDR when adjusting or enacting GDDR.

In general, **users of corporate disclosures**, including investors and other stakeholders, benefit from the implementation of GDDR. The mandatory disclosure requirements of GDDR provide more comprehensive information on corporate gender diversity, enabling users to better assess gender diversity in upper management positions. This leads to a reduction in information asymmetries regarding corporate gender diversity. Additionally, users can evaluate companies' gender diversity targets, allowing them to gauge a company's commitment to addressing gender diversity issues and promoting female participation in management positions. The findings of this study sensitize users to critically evaluate companies' reporting practices, as the descriptive results show that many companies do not fully comply with the disclosure requirements. Moreover, given that several companies fail to meet their self-set targets, users should carefully assess whether companies frequently miss these targets and whether they provide credible reasons for missing them. The findings of the determinants analysis indicate that companies appoint more female board members when they are subject to public pressure. This insight is valuable for investors, who may consider the extent to which a company's appointment decisions are influenced by such pressure in response to stakeholders' demands. Additionally, investors might take into account the findings of the financial reporting quality analysis to anticipate potential negative consequences of increased gender diversity on supervisory boards.

The empirical results also offer important implications for **preparers of corporate disclosures**. Companies subject to GDDR can use the findings of the descriptive results to identify areas for improvement in complying with disclosure requirements. Furthermore, the analysis of narrative explanations sheds light on the challenges other companies face in meeting their gender diversity targets, which could suggest areas for improvement in their own appointment processes. Companies affected by GDDR may utilize the findings of the determinants analysis to assess to which extent they are potentially affected by the implementation of GDDR. Based on the identified determinants, preparers may also anticipate the reactions of peer companies, thereby managing reputational risks. Moreover, the findings on financial reporting quality highlight the importance of carefully considering the composition of the supervisory board. Companies should weigh the decision to appoint more female board members to meet stakeholder demands for gender diversity against the possibility that such appointments might lead to a less optimal board composition, potentially affecting financial reporting quality.

Given the compliance issues identified by the content analysis, this study also presents important implications for **auditors and enforcement institutions**. First, some companies either fail to publish the information required by GDDR or are unable or unwilling to provide previously published reports. These findings suggest that enforcement institutions (i.e., the BaFin), who are responsible for verifying the existence of gender diversity disclosures under GDDR, should closely scrutinize the adequacy of these disclosures. Ensuring that the required information is appropriately disclosed is crucial to maintaining regulatory compliance. Second, the analysis shows that many reports frequently omit some of the information mandated by GDDR. Since auditors are currently not tasked with reviewing the content of gender diversity disclosures, regulators should consider expanding the scope of auditors' responsibilities to include the content review of these disclosures. This expanded duty could involve verifying the reasons provided by companies for missing their self-set targets. Without such a review, users of these disclosures are unable to assess the credibility of the justifications provided and must rely on the companies' statements without verification. Given that the mechanisms of GDDR are designed to function through the power of information and enhanced transparency, ensuring the completeness and reliability of the disclosed information is essential for regulatory efficacy. Therefore, integrating a review of the content into the audit process would strengthen the integrity of the GDDR and ensure that its objectives are realized.

In light of the results and implications, this study makes several significant **contributions to the literature**. First, it contributes to the stream of descriptive literature examining the development of corporate gender diversity and disclosure practices in the context of GDDR. Prior studies predominantly focused on the supervisory and executive board (Women-on-Board-Index (e.g., *FidAR e.V.* (2023)), Women Executive Barometer (e.g., *Sondergeld et al.* (2024)), and the annual information commissioned by German Federal Government[160] (e.g., *Deutscher BT/BR – DIP* (2023b), BT-Drs. 20/9850). This study extends the literature by exploring the development of gender diversity at management levels below the executive board in more detail. Additionally, this study contributes to the field by offering a detailed analysis of the achievement of self-set gender diversity targets and companies' narrative explanations for missed targets. Prior research has not covered the achievement of these self-set targets or the reasons for not meeting them. The descriptive analysis in this study offers valuable insights into challenges companies face when intending to appoint more female board members or managers. Second, this study is the first to investigate the determinants of GDDR efficacy, thereby deepening the understanding of the factors associated with the efficacy of GDDR. Given the critical role of companies' appointment decisions on upper corporate hierarchy levels, understanding the determinants of GDDR efficacy is of major importance. Moreover, the findings contribute to the theoretical framework proposed by *Hombach/Sellhorn* (2019) regarding the regulatory mechanisms of targeted transparency regulations by providing empirical evidence for the significance of public pressure and the role of information intermediaries.

[160] Note that the annual information of the German Federal Government include some scarce information on the proportion of women on management levels below the executive board, but do not provide any analysis (e.g., time trends) due to data availability issues (*Deutscher BT/BR – DIP* (2023b), BT-Drs. 20/9850, pp. 54-55).

Third, this study contributes to the literature on the efficacy of gender diversity regulations. While prior studies have mainly focused on the impact of voluntary policies and mandatory gender quotas on corporate board gender diversity, this study adds to the empirical findings by examining a different regulatory approach. Adding findings on another regulatory approach offers new insights into gender diversity regulations. Finally, this study directly contributes to the literature on the relationship between increased gender diversity on corporate boards within the context of gender diversity regulations and financial reporting quality. The only directly comparable study, conducted by *García Lara et al.* (2022), explicitly examined the impact of increased board gender diversity under a mandatory gender quota on financial reporting quality. This study, by contrast, provides valuable insights from a regulatory approach that does not mandate increases in corporate board gender diversity, thereby offering a broader perspective on the effects of different regulatory strategies.

8.3 Limitations and outlook

Empirical research is inherently subject to certain **limitations**, and this study is no exception. Accordingly, this study has drawbacks due to the empirical research setting and methodological design. First, **generalizability** may be limited by the focus on large private and public German companies. It is questionable whether these findings are applicable to other settings. The findings may be determined by the particularities of the two-tier corporate governance system (e.g., *Mensi-Klarbach et al.* (2021)). Therefore, how GDDR shapes gender diversity on corporate management levels, its determinants, and its consequences may differ in other corporate governance systems. Additionally, the findings may be most relevant to countries with cultural influences and regulatory traditions similar to Germany (e.g., *Seierstad et al.* (2017b)). However, the findings of this study might not be transferable to countries with other cultural backgrounds. Moreover, the sample of the analyzed companies is limited to 214 companies because of the time-intensive manual data collection (e.g., also *Hannen* (2017), p. 224). This study focused on the largest private and public companies impacted by GDDR; the effects of GDDR on smaller companies may differ substantially. For instance, smaller private companies, which are less prominent and visible in society, might not experience a comparable level of public pressure. Given that high public pressure was identified as a determinant of GDDR efficacy, the regulatory approach may be less effective for these smaller companies.

Moreover, the impact of GDDR has been analyzed for the first seven years of its implementation (between 2015 and 2021), covering the early stages of the regulation's application (e.g., the second target achievement period for self-set gender diversity targets has not expired for most affected companies, cf. Appendix 3). Changes in the composition of corporate boards and management positions can be slow due to existing contractual commitments, so the results **might differ over a longer period**. Additionally, as GDDR introduced new requirements for corporate gender diversity reporting, preparers, stakeholders, auditors, and enforcement institutions might not have fully adapted to these requirements. Over time, these groups may incorporate and respond to this information more effectively, potentially leading to different findings in future studies. Despite these considerations, this study examines the largest available sample period with accessible reports to analyze whether GDDR shape corporate gender diversity.

The analysis of the extent to which the GDDR shaped gender diversity at both management levels below the executive board was constrained by **limited data availability**. The development of the proportion of women and the development of self-set targets for the proportion of women in management positions relied on a significantly smaller sample size compared to the corporate board subsamples. Companies that disclosed detailed, partially voluntary information on gender diversity at management levels below the executive board may react differently to GDDR than those that did not provide such information. For instance, companies with fewer female managers at these levels may have refrained from voluntarily disclosing these figures, potentially to avoid unfavorable comparisons with peer companies. Consequently, the impact of GDDR on corporate gender diversity may be less pronounced in these companies, leading to potentially different results. Furthermore, some companies disclosed reports that were non-compliant with GDDR requirements, omitting some required information. For example, certain companies that failed to meet their self-set gender diversity targets by the end of the target achievement period did not provide reasons for these failures. As a result, only narrative explanations from reports that included justifications for missed targets were evaluated. The reasons for missing these targets may differ for companies that did not provide explanations, introducing a potential bias in the analysis.

This study employed proxies to measure GDDR efficacy and its determinants. In the determinants analysis presented in chapter 6, two different proxies were utilized to capture GDDR efficacy as accurately as possible. Given that previous research defined the efficacy of gender diversity regulation as "*a higher amount of what is demanded, namely a higher share of women*" (*Gregorič et al.* (2017), p. 275), the **chosen proxies** seem appropriate. Additionally, media attention is used as a proxy for public pressure as a potential determinant of GDDR efficacy. However, public attention can manifest in forms other than broad media coverage, such as pressure from powerful stakeholders, raising questions about whether this proxy fully captures the breadth of public pressure. If the proxy does not comprehensively cover public pressure, this noisy environment could weaken the power of the statistical tests (*Nienhaus* (2015), pp. 206–207). Nonetheless, the determinants analysis found statistically significant associations between public pressure and GDDR efficacy at different corporate hierarchy levels, emphasizing the media's importance as a source of public pressure.

Moreover, the determinants analysis includes only selected determinants derived from theories and prior research. It is possible that other **unexamined factors** also influence GDDR efficacy. Such factors were not included in the analysis because they were not identified in the theoretical foundation. Regression models are limited to measurable variables (*Proppe* (2009), pp. 254–255), meaning that not all potential determinants can be analyzed. For instance, companies' appointment processes and institutionalized application procedures could influence candidate selection and the participation of women. However, companies generally do not provide information on appointment decisions and processes, limiting their inclusion in the analysis.

Regarding the analysis of the association between increased gender diversity in the context of GDDR and financial reporting quality in chapter 7, it is important to recognize certain assumptions underlying the **concept of accruals**. For instance, higher discretionary accruals of companies that increase gender diversity on the supervisory board while facing high public pressure do not necessarily imply that female supervisory board members have poorer monitoring abilities. Companies facing high public pressure may also experience intensified pressure from investors to meet financial performance expectations, leading managers to engage in more earnings management. Additionally, this study focuses on the relationship between changes in supervisory board composition and financial reporting quality, which simplifies a complex reality. Other factors, such as accounting method choices, also influence financial reporting quality (*Dechow et al.* (2010), p. 379). Moreover, the calculation of the model used in this study to estimate discretionary accruals relies on companies functioning as their own benchmark. Alternative methods for calculating discretionary accruals, such as industry-year comparisons, could not be applied due to the small sample size and insufficient observations in each industry. Therefore, the chosen method was deemed the most reliable for this context (*García Lara et al.* (2022), p. 8). Despite general criticism of the measurement of discretionary accruals as a proxy for financial reporting quality, the accruals concept can provide insights into the potentially unintended consequences of increased gender diversity on corporate boards in the context of GDDR.

While the determinants analysis and the analysis of the association between increased gender diversity on supervisory boards and financial reporting quality yielded statistically significant results, **a cause-effect relation cannot be assumed**. Due to the characteristics of GDDR, no control group was available for comparison in these analyses, meaning that the influence of other relevant variables (omitted variables) cannot be entirely ruled out. Additionally, the issue of **reverse causality** may arise when the dependent variable could influence the independent variables (*Proppe* (2009), p. 255). In this study, it cannot be excluded that companies that significantly increase the proportion of women on their boards attract more media attention because of their higher gender diversity. Consequently, the empirical analysis only provides insights into associations between variables, without allowing for definitive conclusions regarding causality (*Auer/Rottmann* (2020), p. 421).

From the limitations of this study and the sparsely researched field of GDDR, several **areas for future research** emerge. Expanding the sample to include smaller companies (e.g., private companies subject to one-third co-determination or public companies not listed on the German prime standard) could offer valuable insights. Future research could investigate whether GDDR are effective in promoting gender diversity in smaller companies, which may experience less public pressure. Such research could enhance the understanding of the impact of GDDR and contribute to a broader comprehension of targeted transparency regulations.

While this study analyzed the determinants of GDDR efficacy, it did not explore **why companies respond differently** to the implementation of the regulation. Since the information required by GDDR alters the information available to stakeholders, it may also impact the information available to the disclosing companies themselves (*Hombach/Sellhorn* (2019)). Although the results indicate that external information channels influence GDDR efficacy, it remains unclear whether internal information channels within companies also affect their appointment decisions regarding gender diversity. Conducting interviews with companies could provide valuable insights into the reasons behind their decisions to increase gender diversity in management positions, thereby deepening the understanding of the regulatory mechanisms underlying GDDR.

In 2021, the German regulator revised the GDDR, tightened the reporting requirements, and enhanced enforcement through the enactment of FüPoG II. A future study could examine whether these **regulatory changes** have altered GDDR efficacy and assess if the findings align with the results of the study at hand. Additionally, empirical research could explore how more standardized reporting requirements and more rigorous auditing impact the effectiveness of this regulatory intervention. Moreover, if other countries adopt comparable GDDR (e.g., by the sustainability report required by the CSRD (see section 2.2.5)), future research could leverage these different contexts to investigate how variations in corporate governance systems, cultural factors, and regulatory traditions influence GDDR efficacy. This could reveal whether country-specific factors influence GDDR efficacy and whether the company-specific determinants identified in this study are applicable across different settings.

The empirical findings of this study indicate that companies have increased gender diversity in corporate management positions following the implementation of GDDR. Therefore, it can be concluded that the regulation was effective and contributed to higher gender diversity. However, these companies display varying reporting practices and encounter different challenges in achieving targeted female representation. Several influencing factors determine GDDR efficacy. However, increased gender diversity on supervisory boards in response to high public pressure can be negatively associated with financial reporting quality. Looking ahead, it will be interesting to observe whether the trend towards more gender-diverse corporate management positions will persist and potentially accelerate due to the enactment of FüPoG II. Widening the perspective beyond regulatory action, it also remains to be seen how public pressure (e.g., through public debates and media attention) influences the developments towards gender equality in leadership positions. Moving forward, the constant increase of women in the labor force, as well as the continuous state of change in the social role of men and women, may not only increase public pressure but also raise the bar for mandatory quotas or self-set targets beyond 30%. On the one hand, without mandatory gender quotas, companies retain the discretion to respond to stakeholders' demands for greater female participation in management positions. On the other hand, regulators must decide whether the observed increase in corporate gender diversity is adequate to fulfill the **constitutional mandate for gender equality** as outlined in the German Basic Law, or if there is a need to expand the application of mandatory gender quotas or to raise the targeted participation of women beyond 30% to ensure this objective is met.

Appendix

Appendix 1: Content analysis catalog for GDDR

Structure of the content analysis catalog for GDDR	
A) General information	
A.1	**Company name** [text]
A.2	**Fiscal year end** [date]
A.3	**Year** [year]
A.4	**Parity co-determination** [0/1]
A.5	**Legal form** [name]
A.6	**Index** [DAX/MDAX/SDAX/(n/a)]
B) Disclosures	
B.1	**Location of the corporate governance statement** [management report/website]
B.2	**Seperate section for information required by the GDDR** [0/1]
B.3	**Visualization of information**
B.3.1	Table [0/1]
B.3.2	Figure [0/1]
C) Information on gender diversity	
C.1	**Supervisory board**
C.1.1	Information about the actual composition
C.1.1.1	Total number of members [number]
C.1.1.2	Number of female members [number]
C.1.1.3	Total number of members (shareholder representatives) [number]
C.1.1.4	Number of female members (shareholder representatives) [number]
C.1.1.5	Total number of members (employee representatives) [number]
C.1.1.6	Number of female members (employee representatives) [number]
C.1.1.7	Gender of the chairperson (w/m) [0/1]
C.1.1.8	if female: Name of the chairperson [text]
C.1.2	Information required by GDDR
C.1.2.1	Self-set target [0/1]
C.1.2.2	Level of self-set target (%) [number]
C.1.2.3	Level of self-set target (absolute number of women) [number]
C.1.2.4	Target achievement period [date]
C.1.2.5	Final target achievement [0/1]
C.1.2.6	Explanation for missed targets [0/1]
C.1.2.7	Justification for missed targets [text]

(Table is continued on the next page)

C.2	**Executive board**
C.2.1	Information about the actual composition
C.2.1.1	Total number of members [number]
C.2.1.2	Number of female members [number]
C.2.1.3	Gender of the chairperson (w/m) [0/1]
C.2.1.4	if female: Name of the chairperson [text]
C.2.2	Information required by the GDDR
C.2.2.1	Self-set target [0/1]
C.2.2.2	Level of self-set target (%) [number]
C.2.2.3	Level of self-set target (absolute number of women) [number]
C.2.2.4	Target achievement period [date]
C.2.2.5	Final target achievement [0/1]
C.2.2.6	Explanation for missed targets [0/1]
C.2.2.7	Justification for missed targets [text]
C.3	**First management level**
C.3.1	Information about the actual composition
C.3.1.1	Information on the management level [0/1]
C.3.1.2	Total number of members [number]
C.3.1.3	Number of female members [number]
C.3.1.4	Proportion of female managers [number]
C.3.2	Information required by the GDDR
C.3.2.1	Self-set target [0/1]
C.3.2.2	Level of self-set target (%) [number]
C.3.2.3	Level of self-set target (absolute number of women) [number]
C.3.2.4	Target achievement period [date]
C.3.2.5	Final target achievement [0/1]
C.3.2.6	Explanation for missed targets [0/1]
C.3.2.7	Justification for missed targets [text]
C.4	**Second management level**
C.4.1	Information about the actual composition
C.4.1.1	Information on the management level [0/1]
C.4.1.2	Total number of members [number]
C.4.1.3	Number of female members [number]
C.4.1.4	Proportion of female managers [number]
C.4.2	Information required by the GDDR
C.4.2.1	Self-set target [0/1]

(Table is continued on the next page)

C.4.2.2	Level of self-set target (%) [number]
C.4.2.3	Level of self-set target (absolute number of women) [number]
C.4.2.4	Target achievement period [date]
C.4.2.5	Final target achievement [0/1]
C.4.2.6	Explanation for missed targets [0/1]
C.4.2.7	Justification for missed targets [text]

Table A-1: Content analysis catalog for GDDR

Appendix 2: The development in the proportion of women on supervisory boards by representatives

Sample	Group of representatives	Proportion of women on supervisory boards							
		2014	2015	2016	2017	2018	2019	2020	2021
Full sample (n = 1,712)	All members	20.31%	22.60%	25.06%	27.32%	29.32%	30.18%	31.17%	32.45%
	Shareholder representatives	16.67%	19.81%	22.42%	25.00%	27.28%	28.40%	29.17%	30.59%
	Employee representatives	23.06%	23.89%	26.10%	27.93%	29.35%	29.77%	31.18%	32.07%
Type of regulatory intervention									
Quota companies (n = 523)	All members	22.36%	24.82%	28.77%	31.23%	33.92%	34.90%	35.65%	36.23%
	Shareholder representatives	19.96%	23.42%	27.38%	29.86%	32.49%	33.07%	33.27%	34.62%
	Employee representatives	24.80%	26.27%	30.22%	32.67%	35.42%	36.79%	38.10%	37.91%
GDDR companies (n = 1,189)	All members	19.13%	21.32%	22.93%	25.07%	26.58%	27.39%	28.47%	30.19%
	Shareholder representatives	14.97%	17.98%	19.92%	22.53%	24.54%	25.95%	26.98%	28.45%
	Employee representatives	21.93%	22.31%	23.40%	24.80%	25.23%	25.00%	26.40%	28.06%
Capital market orientation									
Private companies (n = 800)	All members	20.33%	22.52%	23.98%	26.30%	27.44%	28.01%	28.83%	30.74%
	Shareholder representatives	16.01%	18.84%	20.68%	23.56%	25.28%	26.62%	27.43%	29.07%
	Employee representatives	21.81%	22.66%	23.77%	25.25%	25.39%	24.89%	26.02%	27.77%
Public companies (n = 912)	All members	20.30%	22.68%	26.23%	28.44%	31.34%	32.51%	33.66%	34.28%
	Shareholder representatives	17.30%	20.72%	24.05%	26.34%	29.13%	30.03%	30.76%	31.97%
	Employee representatives	24.72%	25.52%	29.21%	31.48%	34.48%	36.05%	37.77%	37.59%

Table A-2: The development of the proportion of women on supervisory boards by representatives

Appendix 3: Target achievement period ends of self-set targets by hierarchy levels

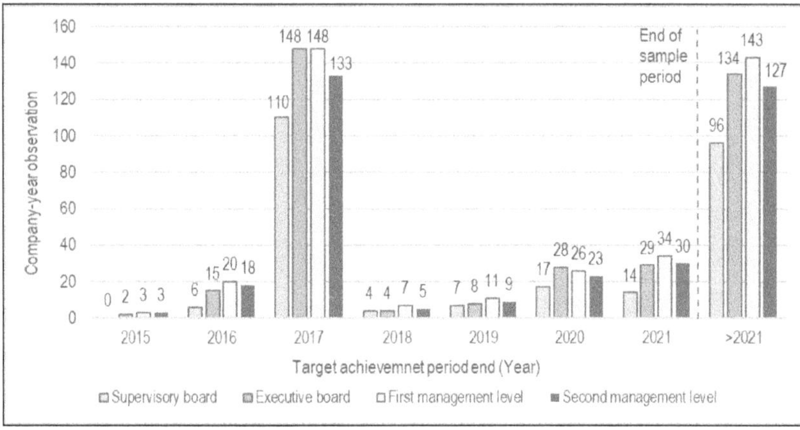

Figure A-1: Target achievement period ends of self-set targets by hierarchy levels

Appendix 4: Control variables for the determinants of GDDR efficacy on the supervisory board

Control variables for the determinants of GDDR efficacy on the supervisory board		
Vairbale	**Name**	**Calculation**
Board size	$SB\ size_{i,t}$	The number of Supervisory Board members of company *i* in year *t*.
Company size	$Firm\ size_{i,t-1}$	Natrual logarithm of the absolute value of total assets in € billion company *i* in year *t-1*.
Pre-existing female board members	$Pre\text{-}law\ WoSB_{i,2014}$	Dummy variable that takes the value of one if the Supervisory Board consists of at least one female member in 2014, and zero otherwise.
Leverage	$Leverage_{i,t-1}$	$Leverage_{i,t-1} = (Total\ liabilities_{i,t-1}) / (Total\ assets_{i,t-1})$
Growth rates	$Growth_{i,t-1}$	$Growth_{i,t-1} = (Total\ assets_{i,t-1} - Total\ assets_{i,2014}) / (Total\ assets_{i,2014})$

Table A-3: Control variables for the determinants of GDDR efficacy on the supervisory board

Appendix 5: Control variables for the determinants of GDDR efficacy on the executive board

Control variables for the determinants of GDDR efficacy on the executive board		
Vairbale	**Name**	**Calculation**
Board size	$EB\ size_{i,t}$	The number of executive board members of company *i* in year *t*.
Company size	$Firm\ size_{i,t-1}$	Natrual logarithm of the absolute value of total assets in € billion company *i* in year *t-1*.
Pre-existing female board members	$Pre\text{-}law\ WoEB_{i,2014}$	Dummy variable that takes the value of one if the executive board consists of at least one female member in 2014, and zero otherwise.
Leverage	$Leverage_{i,t-1}$	$Leverage_{i,t-1} = (Total\ liabilities_{i,t-1}) / (Total\ assets_{i,t-1})$
Growth rates	$Growth_{i,t-1}$	$Growth_{i,t-1} = (Total\ assets_{i,t-1} - Total\ assets_{i,2014}) / (Total\ assets_{i,2014})$

Table A-4: Control variables for the determinants of GDDR efficacy on the executive board

Appendix 6: Correlation matrix for the supervisory board sub-study (Panel A)

Correlation matrix for variables on the supervisory board (Panel A)											
Variables[a]	ΔPoWoSB	High pressure	Low pressure	Listed	Firm age	Pre-law TarWoSB	SB size	Pre-law WoSB	Firm size	Leverage	Growth
ΔPoWoSB	-										
High pressure	**0.2375 ***** **(0.0000)**	-									
Low pressure	**-0.0732 *** **(0.0824)**	-0.1499 *** (0.0000)	-								
Listed	**0.0762 *** **(0.0715)**	0.3302 *** (0.0000)	-0.3927 *** (0.0000)	-							
Firm age	-0.0021 (0.9613)	-0.1047 ** (0.0131)	-0.1464 *** (0.0005)	0.1462 *** (0.0005)	-						
Pre-law TarWoSB	**0.0958 **** **(0.0235)**	0.3579 *** (0.0000)	-0.3086 *** (0.0000)	0.7975 *** (0.0000)	0.0851 ** (0.0440)	-					
SB size	-0.0280 (0.5088)	-0.2383 *** (0.0000)	0.3319 *** (0.0000)	-0.8837 *** (0.0000)	-0.0871 ** (0.0393)	-0.6914 *** (0.0000)	-				
Pre-law WoSB	**-0.1765 ***** **(0.0000)**	-0.1017 ** (0.0190)	0.1615 *** (0.0000)	-0.4785 *** (0.0000)	-0.1326 *** (0.0017)	-0.4595 *** (0.0000)	0.5137 *** (0.0000)	-			
Firm size	**0.1858 ***** **(0.0000)**	0.2303 *** (0.0000)	-0.0673 (0.1117)	0.0152 (0.7190)	0.0271 (0.5227)	0.0164 (0.6980)	0.1028 ** (0.0150)	0.0492 (0.2451)	-		
Leverage	**-0.1687 ***** **(0.0001)**	-0.0629 (0.1369)	0.2586 *** (0.0000)	-0.4237 *** (0.0000)	-0.2461 *** (0.0000)	-0.3905 *** (0.0000)	0.4052 *** (0.0000)	0.2465 *** (0.0000)	0.2309 *** (0.0000)	-	
Growth	**0.2274 ***** **(0.0000)**	0.2343 *** (0.0000)	-0.1553 *** (0.0002)	0.4167 *** (0.0000)	0.0754 * (0.0747)	0.3570 *** (0.0000)	-0.3735 *** (0.0000)	-0.2275 *** (0.0000)	0.0490 (0.2468)	-0.1510 *** (0.0003)	-

[a]The table reports Spearman correlation coefficients for a pairwise correlation of the GDDR efficacy measures on the supervisory board and determinant variables. Respective p-values are presented below the coefficients in parentheses.
*, **, and *** indicate statistical significance at the 10%, 5%, and 1% levels, respectively.

Table A-5: Correlation matrix for the supervisory board sub-study (Panel A)

Appendix 7: Correlation matrix for the supervisory board sub-study (Panel B)

Correlation matrix for variables on the supervisory board (Panel B)											
Variables[a]	TarWoSB	High pressure	Low pressure	Listed	Firm age	Pre-law TarWoSB	SB size	Pre-law WoSB	Firm size	Leverage	Growth
TarWoSB	-										
High pressure	**0.1819 ***** **(0.0000)**	-									
Low pressure	-0.0180 (0.6722)	-0.1499 *** (0.0000)	-								
Listed	-0.0366 (0.3867)	0.3302 *** (0.0000)	-0.3927 *** (0.0000)	-							
Firm age	-0.0647 (0.1263)	-0.1047 ** (0.0131)	-0.1464 *** (0.0005)	0.1462 *** (0.0005)	-						
Pre-law TarWoSB	**-0.0898 **** **(0.0337)**	0.3579 *** (0.0000)	-0.3086 *** (0.0000)	0.7975 *** (0.0000)	0.0851 ** (0.0440)	-					
SB size	**0.1017 **** **(0.0161)**	-0.2383 *** (0.0000)	0.3319 *** (0.0000)	-0.8837 *** (0.0000)	-0.0871 ** (0.0393)	-0.6914 *** (0.0000)	-				
Pre-law WoSB	**0.2804 ***** **(0.0000)**	-0.1017 ** (0.0190)	0.1615 *** (0.0000)	-0.4785 *** (0.0000)	-0.1326 *** (0.0017)	-0.4595 *** (0.0000)	0.5137 *** (0.0000)	-			
Firm size	0.0188 (0.6567)	0.2303 *** (0.0000)	-0.0673 (0.1117)	0.0152 (0.7190)	0.0271 (0.5227)	0.0164 (0.6980)	0.1028 ** (0.0150)	0.0492 (0.2451)	-		
Leverage	-0.0391 (0.3558)	-0.0629 (0.1369)	0.2586 *** (0.0000)	-0.4237 *** (0.0000)	-0.2461 *** (0.0000)	-0.3905 *** (0.0000)	0.4052 *** (0.0000)	0.2465 *** (0.0000)	0.2309 *** (0.0000)	-	
Growth	-0.0331 (0.4341)	0.2343 *** (0.0000)	-0.1553 *** (0.0002)	0.4167 *** (0.0000)	0.0754 * (0.0747)	0.3570 *** (0.0000)	-0.3735 *** (0.0000)	-0.2275 *** (0.0000)	0.0490 (0.2468)	-0.1510 *** (0.0003)	-

[a]The table reports Spearman correlation coefficients for a pairwise correlation of the GDDR efficacy measures on the supervisory board and determinant variables. Respective p-values are presented below the coefficients in parentheses.

*, **, and *** indicate statistical significance at the 10%, 5%, and 1% levels, respectively.

Table A-6: Correlation matrix for the supervisory board sub-study (Panel B)

Appendix 8: Correlation matrix for the executive board sub-study (Panel A)

Correlation matrix on the executive board (Panel A)													
Variables[a]	ΔPoWoEB	High pressure	Low pressure	Listed	Firm age	Pre-law TarWoEB	WoSB	SB chair	EB size	Pre-law WoEB	Firm size	Leverage	Growth
ΔPoWoEB	-												
High pressure	**0.1866 ***** **(0.0000)**	-											
Low pressure	**-0.0650 **** **(0.0493)**	-0.1985 *** (0.0000)	-										
Listed	**0.0853 ***** **(0.0098)**	0.2701 *** (0.0000)	-0.6776 *** (0.0000)	-									
Firm age	**0.0616 *** **(0.0634)**	0.2141 *** (0.0000)	-0.2103 *** (0.0000)	0.2173 *** (0.0000)	-								
Pre-law TarWoEB	**0.1522 ***** **(0.0000)**	0.2558 *** (0.0000)	-0.1799 *** (0.0000)	0.3305 *** (0.0000)	0.1201 *** (0.0003)	-							
WoSB	0.0025 (0.9406)	0.2150 *** (0.0000)	0.0299 (0.3675)	-0.0315 (0.3417)	-0.0458 (0.1673)	0.0481 (0.1468)	-						
SB chair	0.0412 (0.2141)	-0.0391 (0.2293)	0.0038 (0.8686)	-0.0476 (0.1611)	0.0002 (0.9961)	-0.0286 (0.3988)	0.1296 *** (0.0001)	-					
EB size	**0.1159 ***** **(0.0005)**	0.4539 *** (0.0000)	-0.1914 *** (0.0000)	0.2633 *** (0.0000)	0.2843 *** (0.0000)	0.1900 *** (0.0000)	0.1451 *** (0.0000)	-0.0197 (0.5555)	-				
Pre-law WoEB	**-0.2996 ***** **(0.0000)**	0.2982 *** (0.0000)	0.1228 *** (0.0003)	-0.1145 *** (0.0007)	0.0969 *** (0.0034)	0.1350 *** (0.0001)	0.2193 *** (0.0000)	0.0204 (0.5282)	0.2780 *** (0.0000)	-			
Firm size	**0.1826 ***** **(0.0000)**	0.5928 *** (0.0000)	-0.2685 *** (0.0000)	0.3112 *** (0.0000)	0.1966 *** (0.0000)	0.2267 *** (0.0000)	0.1803 *** (0.0000)	0.0334 (0.3155)	0.5224 *** (0.0000)	0.1195 *** (0.0003)	-		
Leverage	-0.0025 (0.9388)	0.2241 *** (0.0000)	0.1486 *** (0.0000)	-0.2029 *** (0.0000)	-0.0636 * (0.0551)	-0.0422 (0.2033)	0.1599 *** (0.0000)	-0.0311 (0.3503)	0.1559 *** (0.0000)	0.1562 *** (0.0000)	0.3119 *** (0.0000)	-	
Growth	**0.1470 ***** **(0.0000)**	0.0016 (0.9613)	-0.1543 *** (0.0000)	0.2502 *** (0.0000)	0.0549 * (0.0982)	0.0675 ** (0.0417)	0.0550 * (0.0974)	-0.0498 (0.1337)	0.0289 (0.3843)	-0.1189 *** (0.0003)	-0.0197 (0.5528)	-0.1314 *** (0.0001)	-

[a]The table reports Spearman correlation coefficients for a pairwise correlation of the GDDR efficacy measures on the executive board and determinant variables. Respective p-values are presented below the coefficients in parentheses.
*, **, and *** indicate statistical significance at the 10%, 5%, and 1% levels, respectively.

Table A-7: Correlation matrix for the executive board sub-study (Panel A)

Appendix 9: Correlation matrix for the executive board sub-study (Panel A)

Correlation matrix on the executive board (Panel B)													
Variables[a]	TarWoEB	High pressure	Low pressure	Listed	Firm age	Pre-law TarWoEB	WoSB	SB chair	EB size	Pre-law WoEB	Firm size	Leverage	Growth
TarWoEB	-												
High pressure	**0.2281 ***** **(0.0000)**	-											
Low pressure	**0.1059 ***** **(0.0016)**	-0.1985 *** (0.0000)	-										
Listed	**-0.0963 ***** **(0.0039)**	0.2701 *** (0.0000)	-0.6676 *** (0.0000)	-									
Firm age	**0.0805 **** **(0.0152)**	0.2141 *** (0.0000)	-0.2103 *** (0.0000)	0.2173 *** (0.0000)	-								
Pre-law TarWoEB	**0.1020 ***** **(0.0023)**	0.2558 *** (0.0000)	-0.1799 *** (0.0000)	0.3305 *** (0.0000)	0.1201 *** (0.0003)	-							
WoSB	**0.2615 ***** **(0.0000)**	0.2150 *** (0.0000)	0.0299 (0.3675)	-0.0315 (0.3417)	-0.0458 (0.1673)	0.0481 (0.1468)	-						
SB chair	0.0553 (0.1013)	-0.0391 (0.2293)	0.0038 (0.8686)	-0.0476 (0.1611)	0.0002 (0.9961)	-0.0286 (0.3988)	0.1296 *** (0.0001)	-					
EB size	**0.1311 ***** **(0.0001)**	0.4539 *** (0.0000)	-0.1914 *** (0.0000)	0.2633 *** (0.0000)	0.2843 *** (0.0000)	0.1900 *** (0.0000)	0.1451 *** (0.0000)	-0.0197 (0.5555)	-				
Pre-law WoEB	**0.4620 ***** **(0.0000)**	0.2982 *** (0.0000)	0.1228 *** (0.0003)	-0.1145 *** (0.0007)	0.0969 *** (0.0034)	0.1350 *** (0.0001)	0.2193 *** (0.0000)	0.0204 (0.5282)	0.2780 *** (0.0000)	-			
Firm size	**0.1444 ***** **(0.0000)**	0.5928 *** (0.0000)	-0.2685 *** (0.0000)	0.3112 *** (0.0000)	0.1966 *** (0.0000)	0.2267 *** (0.0000)	0.1803 *** (0.0000)	0.0334 (0.3155)	0.5224 *** (0.0000)	0.1195 *** (0.0003)	-		
Leverage	**0.0941 ***** **(0.0045)**	0.2241 *** (0.0000)	0.1486 *** (0.0000)	-0.2029 *** (0.0000)	-0.0636 (0.0551)	-0.0422 (0.2033)	0.1599 *** (0.0000)	-0.0311 (0.3503)	0.1559 *** (0.0000)	0.1562 *** (0.0000)	0.3119 *** (0.0000)	-	
Growth	-0.0069 (0.8351)	0.0016 (0.9613)	-0.1543 *** (0.0000)	0.2502 *** (0.0000)	0.0549 * (0.0982)	0.0675 ** (0.0417)	0.0550 * (0.0974)	-0.0498 (0.1337)	0.0289 (0.3843)	-0.1189 *** (0.0003)	-0.0197 (0.5528)	-0.1314 *** (0.0001)	-

aThe table reports Spearman correlation coefficients for a pairwise correlation of the GDDR efficacy measures on the executive board and determinant variables. Respective p-values are presented below the coefficients in parentheses.
*, **, and *** indicate statistical significance at the 10%, 5%, and 1% levels, respectively.

Table A-8: Correlation matrix for the executive board sub-study (Panel B)

Appendix 10: Control variables for the financial reporting quality analysis

Control variables for the financial reporting quality analysis		
Vairbale	**Name**	**Calculation**
Capital market orientation	*Listed* $_{i,t}$	Dummy variable that takes the value of one if company *i* is listed on a regulated market in year *t* and zero otherwise.
Company size	*Firm size* $_{i,t-1}$	Natrual logarithm of the absolute value of total assets in € billion company *i* in year *t-1*.
Leverage	*Leverage* $_{i,t-1}$	*Leverage* $_{i,t-1}$ = (*Total liabilities* $_{i,t-1}$) / (*Total assets* $_{i,t-1}$)
Growth rates	*Growth* $_{i,t}$	$Growth_{i,t-1}$ = (Sales $revenues_{i,t-1}$ - Sales $revenues_{i,t-1}$) / (Sales $revenues_{i,t-1}$)
Profitability	*Profitability* $_{i,t}$	$Profitability_{i,t-1}$ = (Earnings before interest and $taxes_{i,t}$) / (*Total assets* $_{i,t}$)
Loss	*Loss* $_{i,t}$	Dummy variable that takes the value of one if company *i* has reported a loss in the year *t* and zero otherwise.
Auditor	*Big 4 auditor* $_{i,t-1}$	Dummy variable that takes the value of one if company *i* is audited by a Big 4 auditor in year *t* and zero otherwise.

Table A-9: Control variables for the financial reporting quality analysis

List of cited annual reports

A

Aurubis AG (2018): Annual Report 2017, Germany 2018.

B

Bilfinger SE (2018): Annual Report 2017, Germany 2018.

Brenntag AG (2016): Annual Report 2015, Germany 2016.

C

Capgemini Deutschland GmbH (2019): Annual Report as at 31 December 2017 and Management Report, Germany 2019.

D

Deutsche Börse AG (2022): Annual Report 2021, Germany 2022.

DIC Asset AG (2018): Annual Report 2017, Germany 2018.

G

GEA Group AG (2022): Annual Report 2021, Germany 2022.

H

HUGO BOSS AG (2018): Annual Report 2017, Germany 2018.

M

Morphosys AG (2018): Annual Report 2017, Germany 2018.

P

Phillips GmbH (2018): Annual and Consolidated Financial Statements for the Financial Year from 01.01.2017 to 31.12.2017, Germany 2018.

S

Sartorius AG (2018): Annual Report 2017, Germany 2018.

Siemens AG (2018): Annual Report 2017, Germany 2018.

Software AG (2018): Annual Report 2017, Germany 2018.

V

Vaillant GmbH (2019): Annual Financial Statements for the Financial Year from 01.01.2018 to 31.12.2018, Germany 2019.

W

Wabco Holding GmbH (2018): Consolidated Financial Statement for the Financial Year from 01.01.2017 to 31.12.2017, Germany 2018.

Wacker Neuson SE (2021): Annual Report 2020, Germany 2021.

List of cited laws, regulations, and standards

National laws, regulations, and standards

Germany

AktG	German Corporation Act as of September 6, 1965 (BGBl. I p. 1089), last amended by Article 61 Amendment Act dated December 11, 2023 (BGBl. 2023 I No. 354).
BT-Drucksache 16/5279	Motion to Introduce a Quota for Supervisory Boards of Publicly Listed Companies – Bundestag printed matter 16/5279 of May 9, 2007.
BT-Drucksache 16/12108	Motion to Introduce a Quota for Supervisory Boards of Publicly Listed Companies – Bundestag printed matter 16/12108 of March 4, 2009.
BT-Drucksache 18/1878	Draft Law on Gender-Equitable Composition of Supervisory Boards, Committees, and Leadership Levels (Leadership Law) – Bundestag printed matter 18/1887 of June 25, 2014.
BT-Drucksache 18/3784	Draft Law for the Equal Participation of Women and Men in Leadership Positions in the Private and Public Sector – Bundestag printed matter 18/3784 of January 20, 2015.
BT-Drucksache 18/4227	Draft Law for the Equal Participation of Women and Men in Leadership Positions in the Private and Public Sector – Bundestag printed matter 18/4227 of June 4, 2015.
BT-Drucksache 19/26689	Draft Law to Supplement and Amend the Regulations for the Equal Participation of Women in Leadership Positions in the Private and Public Sector – Bundestag printed matter 19/26689 of February 15, 2021.
BT-Drucksache 20/6498	Draft Law for the Labeling of Food Products with the Type of Animal Husbandry from Which the Food Is Derived (Animal Husbandry Labeling Act – TierHaltKennzG) – Bundestag printed matter 20/6498 of April 21, 2023.
BT-Drucksache 20/12787	Draft Law for the Implementation of Directive (EU) 2022/2464 of the European Parliament and of the Council of 14 December 2022 – Bundestag printed matter 20/12787 of September 9, 2024.
CSR-Richtlinie-Umsetzungsgesetz	German Act of to Strengthen Non-Financial Reporting by Companies in Their Management and Consolidated Management Reports, as of April 11, 2017 (BGBl. I 2017, No. 20).

DrittelbG	German Act of One-Third Participation as of May 18, 2004 (BGBl. I 2004, No. 25), last amended by Article 21 Amendment Act dated August 7, 2021 (BGBl. 2021 I No. 51).
DRS No. 20	German Accounting Standard No. 20, Group Management Report as of November 02, 2012, last amended on June 16, 2023.
EGAtkG	German Introductory Act of the Stock Corporation Act as of September 6, 1965 (BGBl. I 1965, No. 48), last amended by Article 14 Amendment Act dated December 11, 2023 (BGBl. 2023 I No. 354).
GCGC	German Corporate Governance Code as of April 28, 2022, Announcement in the Federal Gazette on June 27, 2022.
GG	Basic Law for the Federal Republic of Germany as of May 23,1949 (BGBl. 1949, No. 1), last amended by Article 1 Amendment Act dated December 12, 2022 (BGBl. 2022 I No. 54).
GmbHG	German Law on Limited Liability Companies as of April 20, 1892 (RGBl. 1897, p. 477), last amended by Article 9 Amendment Act dated February 22, 2023 (BGBl. 2023 I No. 51).
HGB	German Commercial Code as of May 10, 1897 (RGBl. 1897, pp. 219-436), last amended by Article 2 Amendment Act dated April 11, 2024 (BGBl. 2024 I No. 120).
MitbestG	German Co-Determination Act as of May 4, 1967 (BGBl. 1967 I, No. 51), last amended by Article 17 Amendment Act dated August 7, 2021 (BGBl. 2021 I No. 51).
MontanMitbestG	German Iron and Steel Co-Determination Act as of May 21, 1951 (BGBl. 1951 I, No. 24), last amended by Article 14 Amendment Act dated August 7, 2021 (BGBl. 2021 I No. 51).
MontanMitbestGErgG	German Supple-mentary Act to the Iron and Steel Co-Determination Act as of August 7, 1956 (BGBl. 1956 I, No. 38), last amended by Article 15 Amendment Act dated August 7, 2021 (BGBl. 2021 I No. 51).

SEAG	German Act Implementing Council Regulation (EC) No. 2157/2001 of October 8, 2001 on the Statute for European Company (SE) as of December 22, 2004 (BGBl. 2004 I, No. 73), last amended by Article 8 Amendment Act dated June 19, 2023 (BGBl. 2023 I No. 54).

International laws, regulations, and standards

Corporate Social Responsibility Directive	Directive (EU) 2022/2464 of the European Parliament and of the Council of 14 December, 2022 amending Regulation (EU) No 537/2014, Directive 2004/109/EC, Directive 2006/43/EC and Directive 2013/34/EU, as regards corporate sustainability reporting.
European Gender Diversity Directive	Directive (EU) 2022/2381 of the European Parliament and of the Council of 23 November, 2022 on improving the gender balance among directors of listed companies and related measures.
European regulation	Regulation (EC) No 1606/2002 of the European Parliament and of the Council of 19 July, 2002 on the application of international accounting standards.
European Sustainability Reporting Standards	Commission delegated Regulation (EU) 2023/2772 of 31 July, 2023 supplementing Directive 2013/34/EU of the European Parliament and of the Council as regards sustainability reporting standards.
NACE Implementation	Regulation (EEC) No. 3037/90 of October 9, 1990 on the statistical classification of economic activities in the European Community
Non-Financial Reporting Directive	Directive 2014/95/EU of the European Parliament and of the Council of 22 October, 2014 amending Directive 2013/34/EU as regards disclosure of non-financial and diversity information by certain large undertakings and groups.

Bibliography

A

Abbott, K./Snidal, D. (2000): Hard and Soft Law in International Governance, in: International Organization, Vol. 54, No. 3, 2000, pp. 421-456.

Abbott, L./Parker, S./Presley, T. (2012): Female Board Presence and the Likelihood of Financial Restatement, in: Accounting Horizons, Vol. 26, No. 4, 2012, pp. 607-629.

Ackermann, F./Eden, C. (2011): Strategic Management of Stakeholders: Theory and Practice, in: Long Range Planning, Vol. 44, No. 3, 2011, pp. 179-196.

Adams, R./de Haan, J./Terjesen, S./van Ees, H. (2015): Board Diversity: Moving the Field Forward, in: Corporate Governance: An International Review, Vol. 23, No. 2, 2015, pp. 77-82.

Adams, R./Ferreira, D. (2009): Women in the boardroom and their impact on governance and performance, in: Journal of Financial Economics, Vol. 94, No. 2, 2009, pp. 291-309.

Agresti, A. (2010): Analysis of ordinal categorical data, 2nd edition, Hoboken et al. 2010.

Agresti, A. (2013): Categorical data analysis, 3rd edition, Hoboken et al. 2013.

Aguilera, R./Cuervo-Cazurra, A. (2009): Codes of Good Governance, in: Corporate Governance: An International Review, Vol. 17, No. 3, 2009, pp. 376-387.

Aguilera, R./Jackson, G. (2003): The Cross-National Diversity of Corporate Governance: Dimensions and Determinants, in: The Academy of Management Review, Vol. 28, No. 3, 2003, pp. 447-465.

Ahern, K./Dittmar, A. (2012): The Changing of the Boards: The Impact on Firm Valuation of Mandated Female Board Representation, in: The Quarterly Journal of Economics, Vol. 127, No. 1, 2012, pp. 137-197.

Akerlof, G. (1970): The Market for "Lemons": Quality Uncertainty and the Market Mechanism, in: Contemporary Accounting Research, Vol. 84, No. 3, 1970, pp. 488-500.

Alemann, A. (2008): Die Demographisierung der Geschlechtergleichstellung in Wirtschaft und Gesellschaft: Ergebnisse einer Fallstudie zum Gleichstellungsgesetz für die deutsche Wirtschaft, in: Giesecke, D./Rehberg, K.-S. (eds.), Die Natur der Gesellschaft, Frankfurt am Main 2008, pp. 2643-2652.

Allemand, I./Bédard, J./Brullebaut, B./Deschênes, J. (2022): Role of Old Boys' Networks and Regulatory Approaches in Selection Processes for Female Directors, in: British Journal of Management, Vol. 33, No. 2, 2022, pp. 784-805.

Anca, C./Gabaldon, P. (2013): The Media Impact of Board Member Appointments in Spanish-Listed Companies: A Gender Perspective, in: Journal of Business Ethics, Vol. 122, No. 3, 2013, pp. 425-438.

Andreicovici, I./Hombach, K./Sellhorn, T. (2018): Firm Value Effects of Targeted Disclosure Regulation: The Role of Reputational Costs, URL: https://ssrn.com/abstract=3204505 (26.07.2024).

Arena, C./Cirillo, A./Mussolino, D./Pulcinelli, I./Saggese, S./Sarto, F. (2015): Women on board: evidence from a masculine industry, in: Corporate Governance, Vol. 15, No. 3, 2015, pp. 339-356.

Arndt, P./Wrohlich, K. (2019): Gender quotas in a European comparison: Tough sanctions most effective, in: DIW Weekly Report, Vol. 9, No. 38, 2019, pp. 338-344.

Arrow, K. (1985): The Economics of Agency, in: Pratt, J. W./Zeckhauser, R. J. (eds.), Principals and Agents: The Structure of Business, Boston 1985, pp. 37-51.

Arulampalam, W./Booth, A./Bryan, M. (2007): Is There a Glass Ceiling over Europe? Exploring the Gender Pay Gap across the Wage Distribution, in: Industrial and Labor Relations Review, Vol. 60, No. 2, 2007, pp. 163-186.

Ashforth, B./Gibbs, B. (1990): The Double-Edge of Organizational Legitimation, in: Organization Science, Vol. 1, No. 2, 1990, pp. 177-194.

Auer, B./Rottmann, H. (2020): Statistik und Ökonometrie für Wirtschaftswissenschaftler – Eine anwendungsorientierte Einführung, 4th edition, Wiesbaden 2020.

B

Backhaus, K./Erichson, B./Gensler, S./Weiber, R./Weiber, T. (2023): Multivariate Analysemethoden – Eine anwendungsorientierte Einführung, 17th edition, Wiesbaden 2023.

Backhaus, R. (2021): Die Quotengesetzgebung nach dem FüPoG II und die Kommanditgesellschaft auf Aktien, in: Die Aktiengesellschaft, Vol. 66, No. 18, 2021, pp. 653-660.

Bainbridge, S. (2000): Mandatory Disclosure: A Behavioral Analysis, in: University of Cincinnati Law Review, Vol. 68, No. 4, 2000, pp. 1023-1060.

Ball, R./Shivakumar, L. (2005): Earnings quality in UK private firms: comparative loss recognition timeliness, in: Journal of Accounting and Economics, Vol. 39, No. 1, 2005, pp. 83-128.

Bartel, R. (1990): Charakteristik, Methodik und wissenschaftsmethodische Probleme der Wirtschaftswissenschaften, in: Wirtschaftswissenschaftliches Studium, Vol. 19, No. 2, 1990, pp. 54-59.

Barth, D. (2009): Prognoseberichterstattung, Frankfurt am Main 2009.

Bayer, W./Hoffmann, T. (2015): Frauenquote und Zahl der betroffenen Unternehmen, in: Die Aktiengesellschaft, Vol. 60, No. 1-2, 2015, pp. R4-R7.

BDA/BDI (2014): Geschlechterquote: Richtiges Ziel, falscher Weg – Stellungnahme zum Referentenentwurf eines "Gesetzes zur gleichberechtigten Teilhabe von Frauen und Männern an Führungspositionen in der Privatwirtschaft und im öffentlichen Dienst".

Berens, W./Schmitting, W. (2004): Zum Verhältnis von Controlling, Interner Revision und Früherkennung vor dem Hintergrund der Corporate Governance, in: Freidank, C.-C. (ed.), Corporate Governance und Controlling, Berlin et al. 2004, pp. 51-76.

Berliner Erklärung (2024): Historie, URL: https://www.berlinererklaerung.de/historie (17.06.2024).

Betz, M./O'Connell, L./Shepard, J. (1989): Gender differences in proclivity for unethical behavior, in: Journal of Business Ethics, Vol. 8, No. 5, 1989, pp. 321-324.

Biddle, G./Hilary, G. (2006): Accounting Quality and Firm-Level Capital Investment, in: The Accounting Review, Vol. 81, No. 5, 2006, pp. 963-982.

Bilimoria, D. (2006): The relationship between women corporate directors and women corporate officers, in: Journal of Managerial Issues, Vol. 18, No. 1, 2006, pp. 47-61.

Boesso, G./Kumar, K. (2007): Drivers of corporate voluntary disclosure – A framework and empirical evidence from Italy and the United States, in: Accounting, Auditing & Accountability Journal, Vol. 20, No. 2, 2007, pp. 269-296.

Bøhren, Ø./Staubo, S. (2014): Does mandatory gender balance work? Changing organizational form to avoid board upheaval, in: Journal of Corporate Finance, Vol. 28, 2014, pp. 152-168.

Boone, A./Casares Field, L./Karpoff, J./Raheja, C. (2007): The determinants of corporate board size and composition: An empirical analysis, in: Journal of Financial Economics, Vol. 85, No. 1, 2007, pp. 66-101.

Bortz, J./Schuster, C. (2016): Statistik für Human- und Sozialwissenschaftler, 7th edition, Berlin et al. 2016.

Bouwman, M. (1984): Expert vs novice decision making in accounting: A summary, in: Accounting, Organizations and Society, Vol. 9, No. 3-4, 1984, pp. 325-327.

Boyd, B. (1990): Corporate linkages and organizational environment: A test of the resource dependence model, in: Strategic Management Journal, Vol. 11, No. 6, 1990, pp. 419-430.

Bozhinov, V./Joecks, J./Scharfenkamp, K. (2021): Gender spillovers from supervisory boards to management boards, in: Managerial and Decision Economics, Vol. 42, No. 5, 2021, pp. 1317-1331.

Bozhinov, V./Koch, C./Schank, T. (2019): The Second Glass Ceiling: Women's Role in Supervisory Boards of German Firms, in: Schmalenbach Business Review, Vol. 71, No. 3, 2019, pp. 385-411.

Brass, D. (1985): Men's and Women's Networks: A Study of Interaction Patterns and Influence In an Organization, in: Academy of Management Journal, Vol. 28, No. 2, 1985, pp. 327-343.

Breid, V. (1995): Aussagefähigkeit agencytheoretischer Ansätze im Hinblick auf die Verhaltenssteuerung von Entscheidungsträgern, in: Zeitschrift für betriebswirtschaftliche Forschung, Vol. 47, No. 9, 1995, pp. 821-854.

Bundesministerium für Ernährung und Landwirtschaft (BMEL) (2023): Weg frei: Die Tierhaltungskennzeichnung kommt, URL: https://www.bmel.de/DE/themen/tiere/tierschutz/tierhaltungskennzeichnung/tierhaltungskennzeichnung.html (31.08.2024).

Bundesministerium für Familie, Senioren, Frauen und Jugend (BMFSFJ) and Bundesministerium der Justiz und für Verbraucherschutz (BMJ) (2014a): Referentenentwurf des Bundesministeriums für Familie, Senioren, Frauen und Jugend und des Bundesministeriums der Justiz und für Verbraucherschutz – Entwurf eines Gesetzes für die gleichberechtigte Teilhabe von Frauen und Männern an Führungspositionen in der Privatwirtschaft und im öffentlichen Dienst (31.08.2024).

Bundesministerium für Familie, Senioren, Frauen und Jugend (BMFSFJ) and Bundesministerium der Justiz und für Verbraucherschutz (BMJ) (2014b): Referentenentwurf des Bundesministeriums für Familie, Senioren, Frauen und Jugend und des Bundesministeriums der Justiz und für Verbraucherschutz – Entwurf eines Gesetzes für die gleichberechtigte Teilhabe von Frauen und Männern an Führungspositionen in der Privatwirtschaft und im öffentlichen Dienst (31.08.2024).

Bundesministerium für Familie, Senioren, Frauen und Jugend (BMFSFJ) and Bundesministerium der Justiz und für Verbraucherschutz (BMJ) (2014c): Referentenentwurf des Bundesministeriums für Familie, Senioren, Frauen und Jugend und des Bundesministeriums der Justiz und für Verbraucherschutz – Entwurf eines Gesetzes für die gleichberechtigte Teilhabe von Frauen und Männern an Führungspositionen in der Privatwirtschaft und im öffentlichen Dienst (31.08.2024).

Bundesministerium für Familie, Senioren, Frauen und Jugend (BMFSFJ) (2011a): Frauen in Führungspositionen – Status Quo und Zielsetzungen der 30 DAX-Unternehmen, URL: https://www.bmfsfj.de/resource/blob/76392/0125e67650c41b54a0d978e699f818a3/frauen-in-fuehrungspositionen-status-quo-und-zielsetzungen-data.pdf (31.08.2024).

Bundesministerium für Familie, Senioren, Frauen und Jugend (BMFSFJ) (2011b): Kristina Schröder fordert Flexi-Quote für Frauen in Führungspositionen, URL: https://www.bmfsfj.de/bmfsfj/aktuelles/alle-meldungen/kristina-schroeder-fordert-flexi-quote-fuer-frauen-in-fuehrungspositionen-82240 (31.08.2024).

Bundesministerium für Familie, Senioren, Frauen und Jugend (BMFSFJ) (2017): Gesetz für die gleichberechtigte Teilhabe von Frauen und Männern an Führungspositionen in der Privatwirtschaft und im öffentlichen Dienst, URL: https://www.bmfsfj.de/bmfsfj/service/gesetze/gesetz-fuer-die-gleichberechtigte-teilhabe-von-frauen-und-maennern-an-fuehrungspositionen-in-der-privatwirtschaft-und-im-oeffentlichen-dienst-119350 (31.08.2024).

Büning, H./Trenkler, G. (1994): Nichtparametrische statistische Methoden, 2nd edition, Berlin et al. 1994.

Burgstahler, D./Hail, L./Leuz, C. (2006): The Importance of Reporting Incentives: Earnings Management in European Private and Public Firms, in: The Accounting Review, Vol. 81, No. 5, 2006, pp. 983-1016.

Bürk, T./Wentz, K. (2022): Die vorstandsrechtlichen Neuregelungen des zweiten Führungspositionen-Gesetzes (FüPoG II), in: Der Konzern, Vol. 20, No. 5, 2022, pp. 177-187.

Busse von Colbe, W./Fülbier, R. (2013): Accounting and the Business Economics Tradition in Germany, in: Biondi, Y./Zamboni, S. (eds.), Accounting and business economics, New York 2013, pp. 39-68.

C

Campbell, K./Mínguez-Vera, A. (2008): Gender Diversity in the Boardroom and Firm Financial Performance, in: Journal of Business Ethics, Vol. 83, No. 3, 2008, pp. 435-451.

CDU/CSU and FDP (2009): Wachstum. Bildung. Zusammenhalt., 2009, URL: https://archiv.cdu.de/system/tdf/media/dokumente/091026-koalitionsvertrag-cducsu-fdp_0.pdf?file=1 (01.09.2024).

CDU/CSU and SPD (2013): Deutschlands Zukunft gestalten, 2013, URL: https://archiv.cdu.de/sites/default/files/media/dokumente/koalitionsvertrag.pdf (01.09.2024).

Chang, W./Dambra, M./Schonberger, B./Suk, I. (2023): Does Sensationalism Affect Executive Compensation? Evidence from Pay Ratio Disclosure Reform, in: Journal of Accounting Research, Vol. 61, No. 1, 2023, pp. 187-242.

Chapple, L./Humphrey, J. E. (2014): Does Board Gender Diversity Have a Financial Impact? Evidence Using Stock Portfolio Performance, in: Journal of Business Ethics, Vol. 122, No. 4, 2014, pp. 709-723.

Chen, J./Roberts, R. (2010): Toward a More Coherent Understanding of the Organization–Society Relationship: A Theoretical Consideration for Social and Environmental Accounting Research, in: Journal of Business Ethics, Vol. 97, No. 4, 2010, pp. 651-665.

Choudhury, B. (2016): Social Disclosure, in: Berkeley Business Law Journal, Vol. 13, No. 1, 2016, pp. 183-216.

Clarkson, M. (1995): A Stakeholder Framework for Analyzing and Evaluating Corporate Social Performance, in: The Academy of Management Review, Vol. 20, No. 1, 1995, pp. 92-117.

Contrafatto, M. (2014): The institutionalization of social and environmental reporting: An Italian narrative, in: Accounting, Organizations and Society, Vol. 39, No. 6, 2014, pp. 414-432.

Core, J. E./Guay, W./Larcker, D. F. (2003): Executive equity compensation and incentives: a survey, in: Economic Policy Review, Vol. 9, No. 1, 2003, pp. 27-50.

Cormier, D./Magnan, M./van Velthoven, B. (2005): Environmental disclosure quality in large German companies: Economic incentives, public pressures or institutional conditions?, in: European Accounting Review, Vol. 14, No. 1, 2005, pp. 3-39.

Cotter, D./Hermsen, J./Ovadia, S./Vanneman, R. (2001): The Glass Ceiling Effect, in: Social Forces, Vol. 80, No. 2, 2001, pp. 655-682.

Cromme, G. (2005): Corporate Governance in Germany and the German Corporate Governance Code, in: Corporate Governance: An International Review, Vol. 13, No. 3, 2005, pp. 362-367.

Cumming, D./Leung, T./Rui, O. (2015): Gender Diversity and Securities Fraud, in: Academy of Management Journal, Vol. 58, No. 5, 2015, pp. 1572-1593.

Cuomo, F./Mallin, C./Zattoni, A. (2016): Corporate Governance Codes: A Review and Research Agenda, in: Corporate Governance: An International Review, Vol. 24, No. 3, 2016, pp. 222-241.

D

Das, P. (2023): Ökonometrie in Theorie und Praxis – Analyse von Querschnitt-, Zeitreihen- und Paneldaten mit Stata 15.1, Singapore 2023.

Davies, A. (1999): A strategic approach to corporate governance, Aldershot 1999.

DeAngelo, L. (1986): Accounting Numbers as Market Valuation Substitutes: A Study of Management Buyouts of Public Stockholders, in: The Accounting Review, Vol. 61, No. 3, 1986, pp. 400-420.

Dechow, P./Dichev, I. (2002): The Quality of Accruals and Earnings: The Role of Accrual Estimation Errors, in: The Accounting Review, Vol. 77, No. s-1, 2002, pp. 35-59.

Dechow, P./Ge, W./Schrand, C. (2010): Understanding earnings quality: A review of the proxies, their determinants and their consequences, in: Journal of Accounting and Economics, Vol. 50, No. 2-3, 2010, pp. 344-401.

Deegan, C. (2002): Introduction – The legitimising effect of social and environmental disclosures - a theoretical foundation, in: Accounting, Auditing & Accountability Journal, Vol. 15, No. 3, 2002, pp. 282-311.

Deegan, C./Unermann, J. (2011): Financial Accounting Theory, 2nd edition, London et al. 2011.

DeFond, M./Park, C. (2001): The Reversal of Abnormal Accruals and the Market Valuation of Earnings Surprises, in: The Accounting Review, Vol. 76, No. 3, 2001, pp. 375-404.

Deutscher BT/BR – DIP (2014): BT-Plenarprotokoll 18/46, Stenografischer Bericht vom 03. Juli 2014, URL: https://dserver.bundestag.de/btp/18/18046.pdf (30.08.2024).

Deutscher BT/BR – DIP (2015a): BR-Plenarprotokoll 932, Stenografischer Bericht vom 27. März 2015, URL: https://dserver.bundestag.de/btp/18/18083.pdf (30.08.2024).

Deutscher BT/BR – DIP (2015b): BT-Plenarprotokoll 18/83, Stenografischer Bericht vom 30. Januar 2015, URL: https://dserver.bundestag.de/btp/18/18083.pdf (30.08.2024).

Deutscher BT/BR – DIP (2015c): BT-Plenarprotokoll 18/92, Stenpgrafischer Bericht vom 06. März 2015, URL: https://dserver.bundestag.de/btp/18/18092.pdf (30.08.2024).

Deutscher BT/BR – DIP (2017a): BT-Drs. 18/11500, Erste jährliche Information der Bundesregierung über die Entwicklung des Frauen- und Männeranteils an Führungsebenen und in Gremien der Privatwirtschaft und des öffentlichen Dienstes, URL: https://dserver.bundestag.de/btd/18/115/1811500.pdf (31.08.2024).

Deutscher BT/BR – DIP (2017b): BT-Drs. 18/13333, Bericht der Bundesregierung über den Frauen- und Männeranteil an Führungsebenen und in Gremien der Privatwirtschaft und des öffentlichen Dienstes, URL: https://dserver.bundestag.de/btd/18/133/1813333.pdf (31.08.2024).

Deutscher BT/BR – DIP (2020a): BT-Drs. 19/20361, Dritte Jährliche Information der Bundesregierung über die Entwicklung des Frauen- und Männeranteils an Führungsebenen und in Gremien der Privatwirtschaft und des öffentlichen Dienstes, URL: https://dserver.bundestag.de/btd/19/203/1920361.pdf (31.08.2024).

Deutscher BT/BR – DIP (2020b): BT-Drs. 19/20362, Vierte Jährliche Information der Bundesregierung über die Entwicklung des Frauen- und Männeranteils an Führungsebenen und in Gremien der Privatwirtschaft und des öffentlichen Dienstes, URL: https://dserver.bundestag.de/btd/19/203/1920362.pdf (31.08.2024).

Deutscher BT/BR – DIP (2020c): BT-Drs. 19/24615, Evaluationsgutachten über die Wirksamkeit des Gesetzes für die gleichberechtigte Teilhabe von Frauen und Männern an Führungspositionen in der Privatwirtschaft und im öffentlichen Dienst sowie über den Erfüllungsaufwand und Stellungnahme der Bundesregierung, URL: https://dserver.bundestag.de/btd/19/246/1924615.pdf (31.08.2024).

Deutscher BT/BR – DIP (2021): BT-Drs. 19/32704, Fünfte Jährliche Information der Bundesregierung über die Entwicklung des Frauen- und Männeranteils an Führungsebenen und in Gremien der Privatwirtschaft und des öffentlichen Dienstes, URL: https://dserver.bundestag.de/btd/19/327/1932704.pdf (31.08.2024).

Deutscher BT/BR – DIP (2023a): BT-Drs. 20/5340, Sechste Jährliche Information der Bundesregierung über die Entwicklung des Frauenanteils an Führungsebenen und in Gremien der Privatwirtschaft und des öffentlichen Dienstes, URL: https://dserver.bundestag.de/btd/20/053/2005340.pdf (31.08.2024).

Deutscher BT/BR – DIP (2023b): BT-Drs. 20/9850, Siebte Jährliche Information der Bundesregierung über die Entwicklung des Frauenanteils in Führungsebenen und in Gremien der Privatwirtschaft und des öffentlichen Dienstes des Bundes sowie der Unternehmen mit unmittelbarer Mehrheitsbeteiligung des Bundes, URL: https://dserver.bundestag.de/btd/20/098/2009850.pdf (31.08.2024).

Deutscher Frauenrat (2014): Stellungsnahme des Deutschen Frauenrates zum Referentenentwurf des Bundesministerium für Familie, Senioren, Frauen und Ju- gend und des Bundesministeriums der Justiz und für Verbraucherschutz, URL: https://www.bmfsfj.de/resource/blob/119392/2623945edd79f31316fa430138f0c2d7/deutscher-frauenrat-data.pdf (22.06.2024).

Deutscher Juristinnenbund (djb) (2024): Aktionärinnen fordern Gleichberechtigung, URL: https://www.djb.de/frauen-in-fuehrungspositionen (31.08.2024).

Dhir, A. (2015): Challenging Boardroom Homogeneity – Corporate Law, Governance, and Diversity, Cambridge 2015.

DiMaggio, P./Powell, W. (1983): The Iron Cage Revisited: Institutional Isomorphism and Collective Rationality in Organizational Fields, in: American Sociological Review, Vol. 48, No. 2, 1983, pp. 147-160.

DIW Berlin (2024): German Institute for Economic Research, URL: https://www.diw.de/en/diw_01.c.618953.en/the_institute.html (31.08.2024).

Doldor, E. (2016): Gender Diversity on UK Boards: Exploring Resistance to Quotas, in: Gröschl, S./Takagi, J. (eds.), Diversity Quotas, Diversity Perspectives, London et al. 2016, pp. 153-166.

Doldor, E. (2017): The Merits and Shortcomings of a Voluntary Approach, in: Seierstad, C./Gabaldon, P./Mensi-Klarbach, H. (eds.), Gender Diversity in the Boardroom, Cham 2017, pp. 13-44.

Donaldson, T./Preston, L. (1995): The Stakeholder Theory of the Corporation: Concepts, Evidence, and Implications, in: The Academy of Management Review, Vol. 20, No. 1, 1995, pp. 65-91.

Döring, N. (2023): Forschungsmethoden und Evaluation in den Sozial- und Humanwissenschaften, 6th edition, Berlin 2023.

Dowling, J./Pfeffer, J. (1975): Organizational Legitimacy: Social Values and Organizational Behavior, in: The Pacific Sociological Review, Vol. 18, No. 1, 1975, pp. 122-136.

dpa (2014): Ministerien bereiten umfassende Frauenquote vor, URL: https://www.zeit.de/politik/deutschland/2014-06/frauenquote-ministerien-entwurf (30.07.2024).

Du Plessis, J./Großfeld, B./Saenger, I./Sandrock, O. (2017): An Overview of German Business or Enterprise Law and the One-Tier and Two-Tier Board Systems Contrasted, in: Du Plessis, J. J./Großfeld, B./Luttermann, C./Saenger, I./Sandrock, O./Casper, M. (eds.), German Corporate Governance in International and European Context, 3rd edition, Berlin 2017, pp. 1-16.

Du Plessis, J./Saenger, I. (2017a): The General Meeting and the Management Board as Company Organs, in: Du Plessis, J. J./Großfeld, B./Luttermann, C./Saenger, I./Sandrock, O./Casper, M. (eds.), German Corporate Governance in International and European Context, 3rd edition, Berlin 2017, pp. 63-104.

Du Plessis, J./Saenger, I. (2017b): The Supervisory Board as Company Organ, in: Du Plessis, J. J./Großfeld, B./Luttermann, C./Saenger, I./Sandrock, O./Casper, M. (eds.), German Corporate Governance in International and European Context, 3rd edition, Berlin 2017, pp. 105-166.

Dyck, A./Volchkova, N./Zingales, L. (2008): The Corporate Governance Role of the Media: Evidence from Russia, in: The Journal of Finance, Vol. 63, No. 3, 2008, pp. 1093-1135.

E

Eesley, C./Lenox, M. (2006): Firm responses to secondary stakeholder action, in: Strategic Management Journal, Vol. 27, No. 8, 2006, pp. 765-781.

Eid, M./Gollwitzer, M./Schmitt, M. (2017): Statistik und Forschungsmethoden, 5th edition, Weinheim 2017.

Eisenhardt, K. (1989): Agency Theory: An Assessment and Review, in: The Academy of Management Review, Vol. 14, No. 1, 1989, pp. 57-74.

Eng, L./Mak, Y. (2003): Corporate governance and voluntary disclosure, in: Journal of Accounting and Public Policy, Vol. 22, No. 4, 2003, pp. 325-345.

Erlei, M./Leschke, M./Sauerland, D. (2016): Institutionenökonomik, 3rd edition, Stuttgart 2016.

Estlund, C. (2011): Just the Facts: The Case for Workplace Transparency, in: Stanford Law Review, Vol. 63, No. 2, 2011, pp. 351-408.

European Commission (2020): Questions and Answers: Gender Equality Strategy 2020-2025,
URL: https://ec.europa.eu/commission/presscorner/api/files/document/print/en/qanda_20_357/QANDA_20_357_EN.pdf (29.07.2024).

F

Fama, E./Jensen, M. (1983): Separation of Ownership and Control, in: The Journal of Law and Economics, Vol. 26, No. 2, 1983, pp. 327-350.

Fang, L./Peress, J. (2009): Media Coverage and the Cross-section of Stock Returns, in: The Journal of Finance, Vol. 64, No. 5, 2009, pp. 2023-2052.

Farrell, K. A./Hersch, P. L. (2005): Additions to corporate boards: the effect of gender, in: Journal of Corporate Finance, Vol. 11, No. 1-2, 2005, pp. 85-106.

Fauver, L./Fuerst, M. (2006): Does good corporate governance include employee representation? Evidence from German corporate boards, in: Journal of Financial Economics, Vol. 82, No. 3, 2006, pp. 673-710.

Ferrari, G./Ferraro, V./Profeta, P./Pronzato, C. (2022): Do Board Gender Quotas Matter? Selection, Performance, and Stock Market Effects, in: Management Science, Vol. 68, No. 8, 2022, pp. 5618-5643.

Ferreira, D. (2015): Board Diversity: Should We Trust Research to Inform Policy?, in: Corporate Governance: An International Review, Vol. 23, No. 2, 2015, pp. 108-111.

FidAR e.V. (2011): Women-on-Board-Index 160, URL: https://wob-index.de/webmedia/documents/wob160/2011-3/110630_Studie_WoB-Index_IV_end.pdf (01.09.2024).

FidAR e.V. (2012): Women-on-Board-Index 160, URL: https://wob-index.de/webmedia/documents/wob160/2012-2/120614_Studie_WoB-Index_VI_5.pdf (01.09.2024).

FidAR e.V. (2013): Women-on-Board-Index 160, URL: https://wob-index.de/webmedia/documents/wob160/2013-3/131130_Studie_WoB-Index_IXX_end.pdf (01.09.2024).

FidAR e.V. (2014a): FidAR Stellungnahme zum Referentenentwurf, URL: https://www.fidar.de/presse-aktuelles/die-quote-gesetze/ansicht/artikel/fidar-stellungnahme-zum-referentenentwurf.html (01.09.2024).

FidAR e.V. (2014b): Women-on-Board-Index 160, URL: https://wob-index.de/webmedia/documents/wob160/2014-3/140930_Studie_WoB-Index_XXIII_end.pdf (01.09.2024).

FidAR e.V. (2015): Women-on-Board-Index 160, URL: https://wob-index.de/webmedia/documents/wob160/2015-2/150611_Studie_WoB-Index_XX_end.pdf (01.09.2024).

FidAR e.V. (2016): Woman-on-Board-Index 160, URL: https://wob-index.de/webmedia/documents/wob160/2016-2/160915_Studie_WoB-Index_160_VI_end.pdf (01.09.2024).

FidAR e.V. (2017): Women-on-Board-Index 185, URL: https://wob-index.de/webmedia/documents/wob185/2017/170114_Studie_WoB-Index_185_Gestaltung_end.pdf (01.09.2024).

FidAR e.V. (2018): Women-on-Board-Index 185, URL: https://wob-index.de/webmedia/documents/wob185/2018/180114_Studie_WoB-Index_185_II_end.pdf (01.09.2024).

FidAR e.V. (2019): Woman-on-Board-Index 185, URL: https://wob-index.de/webmedia/documents/wob185/2019/190114_Studie_WoB-Index_185_III.pdf (01.09.2024).

FidAR e.V. (2020): Women-on-Board-Index 185, URL: https://wob-index.de/webmedia/documents/wob185/2020/epaper/ (01.09.2024).

FidAR e.V. (2021): Women-on-Board-Index 185, URL: https://www.yumpu.com/de/document/read/65758037/fidar-women-on-board-index-185 (01.09.2024).

FidAR e.V. (2022): Women-on-Board-Index 185, URL: https://www.yumpu.com/de/document/read/67040096/women-on-board-index-185 (01.09.2024).

FidAR e.V. (2023): Women-on-Board-Index 185, URL: https://www.yumpu.com/de/document/read/68336895/women-on-board-index-wobindex-2023 (01.09.2024).

Fink, C./Kajüter, P. (2021a): Teil A, in: Fink, C./Kajüter, P. (eds.), Lageberichterstattung, 2nd edition, Stuttgart 2021, pp. 1-72.

Fink, C./Kajüter, P. (2021b): Teil B, in: Fink, C./Kajüter, P. (eds.), Lageberichterstattung, 2nd edition, Stuttgart 2021, pp. 73-442.

Fink, C./Schmidt, R. (2015): Neue Entwicklungen in der Lageberichterstattung, in: Der Betrieb, Vol. 68, No. 38, 2015, pp. 2157-2165.

Fisher, R. (1935): The Design of Experiments, Edinburgh 1935.

Fiss, P./Zajac, E. (2006): The Symbolic Management of Strategic Change: Sensegiving Via Framing and Decoupling, in: Academy of Management Journal, Vol. 49, No. 6, 2006, pp. 1173-1193.

Francis, B./Hasan, I./Park, J./Wu, Q. (2015): Gender Differences in Financial Reporting Decision Making: Evidence from Accounting Conservatism, in: Contemporary Accounting Research, Vol. 32, No. 3, 2015, pp. 1285-1318.

Francis, J./Wang, D. (2008): The Joint Effect of Investor Protection and Big 4 Audits on Earnings Quality around the World, in: Contemporary Accounting Research, Vol. 25, No. 1, 2008, pp. 157-191.

Frank, U. (2003): Einige Gründe für eine Wiederbelebung der Wissenschaftstheorie, in: Die Betriebswirtschaft, Vol. 63, No. 3, 2003, pp. 278-292.

Freeman, R./Harrison, J./Wicks, A./Parmar, B./Colle, S. (2010): Stakeholder Theory – The State of the Art, Cambridge 2010.

Freeman, R./Reed, D. (1983): Stockholders and Stakeholders: A New Perspective on Corporate Governance, in: California Management Review, Vol. 25, No. 3, 1983, pp. 88-106.

Freisinger, G.M. (2011): "Die Nullen müssen weg", URL: https://www.manager-magazin.de/unternehmen/karriere/a-772213.html (01.09.2024).

Fromholzer, F./Simons, C. (2015): Die Festlegung von Zielgrößen für den Frauenanteil in Aufsichtsrat, Geschäftsleitung und Führungspositionen, in: Die Aktiengesellschaft, Vol. 60, No. 13, 2015, pp. 457-467.

Fülbier, R./Sellhorn, T. (2023): Understanding and improving the language of business: How accounting and corporate reporting research can better serve business and society, in: Journal of Business Economics, Vol. 93, No. 6, 2023, pp. 1089-1124.

Fülbier, R. U. (2004): Wissenschaftstheorie und Betriebswirtschaftslehre, in: WiSt - Wirtschaftswissenschaftliches Studium, Vol. 33, No. 5, 2004, pp. 266-271.

Fung, A./Graham, M./Weil, D. (2007): Full Disclosure – The Perils and Promise of Transparency, Cambridge 2007.

G

Gabaldon, P./Giménez, D. (2017): Gender Diversity on Boards in Spain: A Non-mandatory Quota, in: Seierstad, C./Gabaldon, P./Mensi-Klarbach, H. (eds.), Gender Diversity in the Boardroom, Cham 2017, pp. 47-74.

Gabaldon, P./Mensi-Klarbach, H./Seierstad, C. (2017): Gender Diversity in the Boardroom: The Multiple Versions of Quota Laws in Europe, in: Seierstad, C./Gabaldon, P./Mensi-Klarbach, H. (eds.), Gender Diversity in the Boardroom, Cham 2017, pp. 233-253.

García Lara, J./García Osma, B./Mora, A./Scapin, M. (2017): The monitoring role of female directors over accounting quality, in: Journal of Corporate Finance, Vol. 45, 2017, pp. 651-668.

García Lara, J./Penalva, J./Scapin, M. (2022): Financial reporting quality effects of imposing (gender) quotas on boards of directors, in: Journal of Accounting and Public Policy, Vol. 41, No. 2, 2022, 106921.

García-Meca, E./García-Sánchez, I.-M./Martínez-Ferrero, J. (2015): Board diversity and its effects on bank performance: An international analysis, in: Journal of Banking & Finance, Vol. 53, 2015, pp. 202-214.

Gathmann, F./Teevs, C. (2011): Zwei Ministerinnen im Quotenkampf, URL: https://www.spiegel.de/politik/deutschland/schroeder-gegen-von-der-leyen-zwei-ministerinnen-im-quotenkampf-a-792261.html (30.07.2024).

Gerum, E./Brühl, K./Debus, M./Martin, C./Schlepper, S./Stieglitz, N. (2007): Das deutsche Corporate Governance-System – Eine empirische Untersuchung, Stuttgart 2007.

Göbel, E. (2021): Neue Institutionenökonomik – Grundlagen, Ansätze und Kritik, München 2021.

Goette, W. (2019): §161 Erklärung zum Corporate Governance Kodex, in: Goette, W./Habersack, M. (eds.), Münchener Kommentar zum Aktiengesetz, 5th edition, München 2019, Rn. 1-121.

Goldin, C. (2014): A Grand Gender Convergence: Its Last Chapter, in: American Economic Review, Vol. 104, No. 4, 2014, pp. 1091-1119.

Gould, J. A./Kulik, C. T./Sardeshmukh, S. R. (2018): Trickle-down effect: The impact of female board members on executive gender diversity, in: Human Resource Management, Vol. 57, No. 4, 2018, pp. 931-945.

Graf-Vlachy, L./Oliver, A./Banfield, R./König, A./Bundy, J. (2020): Media Coverage of Firms: Background, Integration, and Directions for Future Research, in: Journal of Management, Vol. 46, No. 1, 2020, pp. 36-69.

Gray, R./Kouhy, R./Lavers, S. (1995): Corporate social and environmental reporting, in: Accounting, Auditing & Accountability Journal, Vol. 8, No. 2, 1995, pp. 47-77.

Gray, R./Owen, D./Adams, C. (1996): Accounting and Accountability: Changes and Challenges in Corporate Social and Environmental Reporting, London 1996.

Greenwood, R./Raynard, M./Kodeih, F./Micelotta, E./Lounsbury, M. (2011): Institutional Complexity and Organizational Responses, in: The Academy of Management Annals, Vol. 5, No. 1, 2011, pp. 317-371.

Gregorič, A./Oxelheim, L./Randøy, T./Thomsen, S. (2017): Resistance to Change in the Corporate Elite: Female Directors' Appointments onto Nordic Boards, in: Journal of Business Ethics, Vol. 141, No. 2, 2017, pp. 267-287.

Gregory-Smith, I./Main, B. G. M./O'Reilly III, C. A. (2014): Appointments, Pay and Performance in UK Boardrooms by Gender, in: The Economic Journal, Vol. 124, No. 574, 2014, pp. F109-F128.

Grochla, E. (1978): Einführung in die Organisationstheorie, Stuttgart 1978.

Groll, T. (2011): Vorerst keine Frauenquote, URL: https://www.zeit.de/karriere/beruf/2011-10/frauenquote-selbstverpflichtung-unternehmen/komplettansicht (29.07.2024).

Grosvold, J./Brammer, S./Rayton, B. (2007): Board diversity in the United Kingdom and Norway: an exploratory analysis, in: Business Ethics: A European Review, Vol. 16, No. 4, 2007, pp. 344-357.

Grunewald, B./Müller, H.-F. (2023a): § 10 Die Kommanditgesellschaft auf Aktien (KGaA), in: Grunewald, B./Müller, H.-F. (eds.), Gesellschaftsrecht, 12th edition, Tübingen 2023, pp. 324-327.

Grunewald, B./Müller, H.-F. (2023b): § 11 Die Europäische Aktiengesellschaft (SE), in: Grunewald, B./Müller, H.-F. (eds.), Gesellschaftsrecht, 12th edition, Tübingen 2023, pp. 328-329.

Gul, F. A./Srinidhi, B./Ng, A. C. (2011): Does board gender diversity improve the informativeness of stock prices?, in: Journal of Accounting and Economics, Vol. 51, No. 3, 2011, pp. 314-338.

Gull, A./Nekhili, M./Nagati, H./Chtioui, T. (2018): Beyond gender diversity: How specific attributes of female directors affect earnings management, in: The British Accounting Review, Vol. 50, No. 3, 2018, pp. 255-274.

H

Habersack, M. (2019a): § 111 Aufgaben und Rechte des Aufsichtsrats, in: Goette, W./Habersack, M. (eds.), Münchener Kommentar zum Aktiengesetz, 5th edition, München 2019, Rn. 1-163.

Habersack, M. (2019b): § 95 Zahl der Aufsichtsratsmitglieder, in: Goette, W./Habersack, M. (eds.), Münchener Kommentar zum Aktiengesetz, 5th edition, München 2019, Rn. 1-27.

Habersack, M. (2019c): § 96 Zusammensetzung des Aufsichtsrats, in: Goette, W./Habersack, M. (eds.), Münchener Kommentar zum Aktiengesetz, 5th edition, München 2019, Rn. 1-63.

Habersack, M./Kersten, J. (2014): Chancengleiche Teilhabe an Führungspositionen in der Privatwirtschaft - Gesellschaftsrechtliche Dimensionen und verfassungsrechtliche Anforderungen, in: Betriebs-Berater, Vol. 69, No. 47, 2014, pp. 2819-2830.

Hagemann, G. (2017): Financial Reporting Quality in Emerging Economies, Frankfurt am Main 2017.

Hall, R. (1996): Organizations – Structures, Processes, and Outcomes, 6th edition, Englewood Cliffs 1996.

Hannen, S. (2017): Is Integrated Reporting a useful format for investors?, Frankfurt am Main 2017.

Hargarten, S./Seidler, H. (2016): Praxisprobleme der Anwendung des § 264 Abs. 3 HGB, in: Betriebs-Berater, Vol. 71, No. 46, 2016, pp. 2795-2798.

Hart, O./Holmström, B. (1987): The theory of contracts, in: Bewley, T. F. (ed.), Advances in Economic Theory, Cambridge 1987, pp. 71-156.

Hasnas, J. (1998): The Normative Theories of Business Ethics: A Guide for the Perplexed, in: Business Ethics Quarterly, Vol. 8, No. 1, 1998, pp. 19-42.

Hayghe, H. (1999): Developments in women's labor force participation, in: Monthly Labor Review, Vol. 122, No. 12, 1999, p. 41.

Healy, P. (1985): The effect of bonus schemes on accounting decisions, in: Journal of Accounting and Economics, Vol. 7, No. 1-3, 1985, pp. 85-107.

Healy, P./Wahlen, J. (1999): A Review of the Earnings Management Literature and Its Implications for Standard Setting, in: Accounting Horizons, Vol. 13, No. 4, 1999, pp. 365-383.

Healy, P. M./Serafeim, G. (2020): Voluntary, Self-Regulatory, and Mandatory Disclosure of Oil and Gas Company Payments to Foreign Governments, in: Accounting Horizons, Vol. 34, No. 1, 2020, pp. 111-129.

Heard, J./Bolce, W. (1981): The political significance of corporate social reporting in the United States of America, in: Accounting, Organizations and Society, Vol. 6, No. 3, 1981, pp. 247-254.

Heidemann, J./Landherr, A./Müller, A.-L. (2013): Berichterstattung über Frauen in Führungspositionen — eine Analyse der DAX 30-Unternehmen, in: Schmalenbachs Zeitschrift für betriebswirtschaftliche Forschung, Vol. 65, No. 5, 2013, pp. 488-512.

Henning, P. (2011): Neue Empfehlung zur Zusammensetzung des Aufsichtsrats, in: Der Aufsichtsrat, Vol. 8, No. 4, 2011, pp. 52-53.

Herb, A. (2015): Gesetz für die gleichberechtigte Teilhabe an Führungspositionen - Umsetzung in der Praxis, in: Der Betrieb, Vol. 68, No. 17, 2015, pp. 964-970.

Hermalin, B./Weisbach, M. (2006): A Framework for Assessing Corporate Governance Reform,
URL: https://www.nber.org/system/files/working_papers/w12050/w12050.pdf (30.07.2024).

Hess, D. (2008): The Three Pillars of Corporate Social Reporting as New Governance Regulation: Disclosure, Dialogue, and Development, in: Business Ethics Quarterly, Vol. 18, No. 4, 2008, pp. 447-482.

Hill, C./Jones, T. (1992): Stakeholder-Agency Theory, in: Journal of Management Studies, Vol. 29, No. 2, 1992, pp. 131-154.

Hillman, A./Cannella, A./Paetzold, R. (2000): The Resource Dependence Role of Corporate Directors: Strategic Adaptation of Board Composition in Response to Environmental Change, in: Journal of Management Studies, Vol. 37, No. 2, 2000, pp. 235-256.

Hillman, A./Dalziel, T. (2003): Boards of Directors and Firm Performance: Integrating Agency and Resource Dependence Perspectives, in: The Academy of Management Review, Vol. 28, No. 3, 2003, pp. 383-396.

Hillman, A./Withers, M./Collins, B. (2009): Resource Dependence Theory: A Review, in: Journal of Management, Vol. 35, No. 6, 2009, pp. 1404-1427.

Hillman, A. J./Shropshire, C./Cannella Jr., A. A. (2007): Organizational Predictors of Women on Corporate Boards, in: Academy of Management Journal, Vol. 50, No. 4, 2007, pp. 941-952.

Hirsch, R./Slack, J./Smith, R. (1982): Techniques of trend analysis for monthly water quality data, in: Water Resources Research, Vol. 18, No. 1, 1982, pp. 107-121.

Hoang, T./Abeysekera, I./Ma, S. (2017): The Effect of Board Diversity on Earnings Quality: An Empirical Study of Listed Firms in Vietnam, in: Australian Accounting Review, Vol. 27, No. 2, 2017, pp. 146-163.

Hohenstatt, K.-S./Willemsen, H./Naber, S. (2014): Zum geplanten Gesetz zur gleichberechtigten Teilhabe an Führungspositionen – Gut gemeint – aber auch gut gemacht?, in: ZIP: Zeitschift für Wirtschaftsrecht, Vol. 35, No. 46, 2014, pp. 2220-2226.

Holst, E./Kirsch, A. (2016a): Corporate Boards of Large Companies: More Momentum Needed for Gender Parity, in: DIW Economic Bulletin, Vol. 6, No. 3, 2016, pp. 13-25.

Holst, E./Kirsch, A. (2016b): Financial Sector: Share of Women on Corporate Boards Increases Slightly but Men Still Call the Shots, in: DIW Economic Bulletin, Vol. 6, No. 3, 2016, pp. 27-38.

Holst, E./Wrohlich, K. (2017): Top decision-making bodies in large companies: gender quota shows initial impact on supervisory boards; executive board remains a male bastion, in: DIW Economic Bulletin, Vol. 7, No. 1-2, 2017, pp. 3-15.

Holst, E./Wrohlich, K. (2018): Top-decision making bodies of large businesses: gender quota for supervisory boards is effective – development is almost at a standstill for executive boards, in: DIW Weekly Report, Vol. 8, No. 3, 2018, pp. 17-31.

Holst, E./Wrohlich, K. (2019): Increasing number of women on supervisory boards of major companies in Germany: executive boards still dominated by men, in: DIW Weekly Report, Vol. 9, No. 3, 2019, pp. 18-32.

Hombach, K./Sellhorn, T. (2019): Shaping Corporate Actions Through Targeted Transparency Regulation: A Framework and Review of Extant Evidence, in: Schmalenbach Business Review, Vol. 71, No. 2, 2019, pp. 137-168.

Horsch, A. (2004): Agency und Versicherungsintermediation, in: Wirtschaftswissenschaftliches Studium, Vol. 33, No. 9, 2004, pp. 531-536.

Hughes, M./Paxton, P./Krook, M. (2017): Gender Quotas for Legislatures and Corporate Boards, in: Annual Review of Sociology, Vol. 43, No. 1, 2017, pp. 331-352.

I

Ingram, P./Simons, T. (1995): Institutional and Resource Dependence Determinants of Responsiveness to Work-Family Issues, in: Academy of Management Journal, Vol. 38, No. 5, 1995, pp. 1466-1482.

J

Jensen, M./Meckling, W. (1976): Theory of the firm: managerial behavior, agency costs and ownership structure, in: Journal of Financial Economics, Vol. 3, No. 4, 1976, pp. 305-360.

Joecks, J./Pull, K./Vetter, K. (2013): Gender Diversity in the Boardroom and Firm Performance: What Exactly Constitutes a "Critical Mass?", in: Journal of Business Ethics, Vol. 118, No. 1, 2013, pp. 61-72.

Jones, J. (1991): Earnings Management During Import Relief Investigations, in: Journal of Accounting Research, Vol. 29, No. 2, 1991, p. 193.

Jost, P.-J. (2001): Die Prinzipal-Agenten-Theorie in der Betriebswirtschaftslehre, Stuttgart 2001.

Junker, C./Schmidt-Pfitzner, J. (2015): Quoten und Zielgrößen für Frauen (und Männer) in Führungspositionen - Die neue Gesetzeslage und Handlungsempfehlungen, in: Neue Zeitschrift für Gesellschaftsrecht, Vol. 16, No. 24, 2015, pp. 929-938.

K

Kajüter, P. (2020): § 289f Erklärung zur Unternehmensführung, in: Schmidt, K./Ebke, W. F. (eds.), Münchener Kommentar zum Handelsgesetzbuch, 4th edition, München 2020, Rn. 1-43.

Kajüter, P. (2024): Der Regierungsentwurf zum CSRD-Umsetzungsgesetz, in: Zeitschrift für Internationale Rechnungslegung, Vol. 19, No. 9, 2024, pp. 401-406.

Kallmeyer, H. (1983): Rechte und Pflichten des Aufsichtsrats in der Kommanditgesellschaft auf Aktien, in: Zeitschrift für Unternehmens- und Gesellschaftsrecht, Vol. 12, No. 1, 1983,57-75.

Kanter, R. (1977a): Men and women of the corporation, New York 1977.

Kanter, R. (1977b): Some Effects of Proportions on Group Life: Skewed Sex Ratios and Responses to Token Women, in: American Journal of Sociology, Vol. 82, No. 5, 1977, pp. 965-990.

Kaplan, S./Pany, K./Samuels, J./Zhang, J. (2009): An Examination of the Association Between Gender and Reporting Intentions for Fraudulent Financial Reporting, in: Journal of Business Ethics, Vol. 87, No. 1, 2009, pp. 15-30.

Kaspereit, T./Lopatta, K./Onnen, D. (2017): Shareholder Value Implications of Compliance with the German Corporate Governance Code, in: Managerial and Decision Economics, Vol. 38, No. 2, 2017, pp. 166-177.

Kassarjian, H. (1977): Content Analysis in Consumer Research, in: Journal of Consumer Research, Vol. 4, No. 1, 1977, pp. 8-18.

Katz, D./Kahn, R. (1966): The social psychology of organizations, New York 1966.

Kendall, M. (1975): Rank correlation methods, 2nd edition, London et al. 1975.

Khor, A. (2003): Social contract theory, legitimacy theory and corporate social and environmental disclosure policies: constructing a theoretical framework, Nottingham 2003.

Kieser, A./Walgenbach, P. (2010): Organisation, 6th edition, Stuttgart 2010.

King, B./Soule, S. (2007): Social Movements as Extra-Institutional Entrepreneurs: The Effect of Protests on Stock Price Returns, in: Administrative Science Quarterly, Vol. 52, No. 3, 2007, pp. 413-442.

Kirsch, A. (2017): Women's Access to Boards in Germany — Regulation and Symbolic Change, in: Seierstad, C./Gabaldon, P./Mensi-Klarbach, H. (eds.), Gender Diversity in the Boardroom, Cham 2017, pp. 205-232.

Kirsch, A. (2018): The gender composition of corporate boards: A review and research agenda, in: The Leadership Quarterly, Vol. 29, No. 2, 2018, pp. 346-364.

Kirsch, A./Sondergeld, V./Thompson, P./Wrohlich, K. (2023a): Corporate reporting provides insight into companies' commitment to gender equality, in: DIW Weekly Report, Vol. 13, No. 3-4, 2023, pp. 32-39.

Kirsch, A./Sondergeld, V./Wrohlich, K. (2022a): Markedly more women on executive boards of large companies; inclusion requirement seemingly already having an effect, in: DIW Weekly Report, Vol. 12, No. 3-4, 2022, pp. 20-31.

Kirsch, A./Sondergeld, V./Wrohlich, K. (2022b): While gender quotas for top positions in the private sector differ across EU countries, they are effective overall, in: DIW Weekly Report, Vol. 12, No. 3-4, 2022, pp. 32-39.

Kirsch, A./Sondergeld, V./Wrohlich, K. (2023b): Number of women on boards of large companies keeps growing: momentum from inclusion requirement, however, is waning, in: DIW Weekly Report, Vol. 13, No. 3-4, 2023, pp. 20-31.

Kirsch, A./Wrohlich, K. (2020a): More women on supervisory boards: increasing indications that the effect of the gender quota extends to executive boards, in: DIW Weekly Report, Vol. 10, No. 4-5, 2020, pp. 44-49.

Kirsch, A./Wrohlich, K. (2020b): Proportion of women on top-decision making bodies of large companies increasing, except on supervisory boards in the financial sector, in: DIW Weekly Report, Vol. 10, No. 4-5, 2020, pp. 32-42.

Kirsch, A./Wrohlich, K. (2021a): Gender diversity benefits supervisory board work of many companies, in: DIW Weekly Report, Vol. 11, No. 3-4, 2021, pp. 32-38.

Kirsch, A./Wrohlich, K. (2021b): Number of women on boards of large firms increasing slowly; legal requirements could provide momentum, in: DIW Weekly Report, Vol. 11, No. 3-4, 2021, pp. 20-31.

Klettner, A./Clarke, T./Boersma, M. (2016): Strategic and Regulatory Approaches to Increasing Women in Leadership: Multilevel Targets and Mandatory Quotas as Levers for Cultural Change, in: Journal of Business Ethics, Vol. 133, No. 3, 2016, pp. 395-419.

Kobelt, H./Steinhausen, D. (2006): Wirtschaftsstatistik für Studium und Praxis, 7th edition, Stuttgart 2006.

Koch, J. (2023): § 42. Die Societas Europaea (SE; Europäische Aktiengesellschaft), in: Koch, J. (ed.), Gesellschaftsrecht, 13th edition, München 2023, pp. 453-461.

Kocher, D. (2022): Vorstandsquote und Mandatspause nach dem FüPoG II, in: Der Betrieb, Vol. 75, No. 3, 2022, pp. 104-108.

Kogut, B./Colomer, J./Belinky, M. (2014): Structural equality at the top of the corporation: Mandated quotas for women directors, in: Strategic Management Journal, Vol. 35, No. 6, 2014, pp. 891-902.

Kolb, S./Meyer, Y. C. (2016): Gesetz für einen gleichberechtigten Zugang von Frauen zu Führungspositionen, in: Unternehmenssteuern und Bilanzen, Vol. 14, No. 13, 2016, pp. 492-499.

Kornmeier, M. (2007): Wissenschaftstheorie und wissenschaftliches Arbeiten – Eine Einführung für Wirtschaftswissenschaftler, Heidelberg 2007.

Kothari, S./Leone, A./Wasley, C. (2005): Performance matched discretionary accrual measures, in: Journal of Accounting and Economics, Vol. 39, No. 1, 2005, pp. 163-197.

Krieger, G. (2012): Corporate Governance und Corporate Governance Kodex in Deutschland, in: Zeitschrift für Unternehmens- und Gesellschaftsrecht, Vol. 41, No. 2-3, 2012, pp. 202-227.

Krishnan, G./Parsons, L. (2008): Getting to the Bottom Line: An Exploration of Gender and Earnings Quality, in: Journal of Business Ethics, Vol. 78, No. 1-2, 2008, pp. 65-76.

L

Labelle, R./Francoeur, C./Lakhal, F. (2015): To Regulate Or Not To Regulate? Early Evidence on the Means Used Around the World to Promote Gender Diversity in the Boardroom, in: Gender, Work & Organization, Vol. 22, No. 4, 2015, pp. 339-363.

Lai, K./Srinidhi, B./Gul, F./Tsui, J. (2017): Board Gender Diversity, Auditor Fees, and Auditor Choice, in: Contemporary Accounting Research, Vol. 34, No. 3, 2017, pp. 1681-1714.

Lanfermann, G./Baumüller, J. (2024): Anwendungsfragen zur Nachhaltigkeitsberichterstattung im Konzern nach der CSRD – Teil 8: Der RegE zum CSRD-Umsetzungsgesetz (UmsG) – wichtige Änderungen und (verbleibende) Zweifelsfragen im Konzern, in: Der Konzern, **[Jahrgang fehlt!]**, No. 10, 2024, pp. 383-388.

Larrinaga-González, C. (2007): Sustainability Reporting – Insights from Neoinstitutional Theory, in: Unerman, J./Bebbington, J./O'Dwyer, B. (eds.), Sustainability Accounting and Accountability, London 2007, pp. 150-167.

Latham, G./Locke, E. (2013): Goal Setting Theory: The Current State, in: Latham, G. P./Locke, E. A. (eds.), New Developments in Goal Setting and Task Performance, New York 2013, pp. 623-630.

Lawrence, A./Minutti-Meza, M./Zhang, P. (2011): Can Big 4 versus Non-Big 4 Differences in Audit-Quality Proxies Be Attributed to Client Characteristics?, in: The Accounting Review, Vol. 86, No. 1, 2011, pp. 259-286.

Leuz, C. (2010): Different approaches to corporate reporting regulation: How jurisdictions differ and why, in: Accounting and Business Research, Vol. 40, No. 3, 2010, pp. 229-256.

Lindblom, C. (2010): The implications of organizational legitimacy for corporate social performance and disclosure – Critical perspectives on accounting conference, in: Gray, R./Bebbington, J./Gray, S. (eds.), Social and environmental accounting, London 2010, pp. 51-63.

Lingnau, V. (1995): Kritischer Rationalismus und Betriebswirtschaftslehre, in: Wirtschaftswissenschaftliches Studium, Vol. 24, No. 3, 1995, pp. 124-129.

Liu, B./McConnell, J. (2013): The role of the media in corporate governance: Do the media influence managers' capital allocation decisions?, in: Journal of Financial Economics, Vol. 110, No. 1, 2013, pp. 1-17.

Locke, E. (1968): Toward a theory of task motivation and incentives, in: Organizational Behavior and Human Performance, Vol. 3, No. 2, 1968, pp. 157-189.

Lombardo, E./Verge, T. (2022): Early to Act, Late to Achieve, in: Engeli, I./Mazur, A. (eds.), Gender equality and policy implementation in the corporate world, Oxford 2022, pp. 267-286.

Lorenzen, P. (1974): Konstruktive Wissenschaftstheorie, Frankfurt am Main 1974.

M

Mann, H. (1945): Nonparametric tests against trend, in: Econometrica: Journal of the econometric society, Vol. 13, No. 3, 1945, pp. 245-259.

Mateos de Cabo, R./Grau, P./Gimeno, R./Gabaldón, P. (2022): Shades of Power: Network Links with Gender Quotas and Corporate Governance Codes, in: British Journal of Management, Vol. 33, No. 2, 2022, pp. 703-723.

McHugh, M. (2013): The chi-square test of independence, in: Biochemia Medica, Vol. 23, No. 2, 2013, pp. 143-149.

McNichols, M. (2002): Discussion of the Quality of Accruals and Earnings: The Role of Accrual Estimation Errors, in: The Accounting Review, Vol. 77, No. s-1, 2002, pp. 61-69.

Meek, G./Roberts, C./Gray, S. (1995): Factors Influencing Voluntary Annual Report Disclosures By U.S., U.K. and Continental European Multinational Corporations, in: Journal of International Business Studies, Vol. 26, No. 3, 1995, pp. 555-572.

Meijer, A. (2013): Local Meanings of Targeted Transparency: Understanding the Fuzzy Effects of Disclosure Systems, in: Administrative Theory & Praxis, Vol. 35, No. 3, 2013, pp. 398-423.

Meinhövel, H. (2005): Grundlagen der Principal-Agent-Theorie, in: Horsch, A./Meinhövel, H./Paul, S. (eds.), Institutionenökonomie und Betriebswirtschaftslehre, München 2005, pp. 65-80.

Meinhövel, M./Schaumann, K. (2021): Wie analysieren Kapitalgeber einen IFRS-Konzernabschluss?, in: Kapitalmarktorientierte Rechnungslegung, Vol. 21, No. 1, 2021, pp. 31-38.

Mensi-Klarbach, H./Leixnering, S./Schiffinger, M. (2021): The Carrot or the Stick: Self-Regulation for Gender-Diverse Boards via Codes of Good Governance, in: Journal of Business Ethics, Vol. 170, No. 3, 2021, pp. 577-593.

Mensi-Klarbach, H./Seierstad, C. (2020): Gender Quotas on Corporate Boards: Similarities and Differences in Quota Scenarios, in: European Management Review, Vol. 17, No. 3, 2020, pp. 615-631.

Mensi-Klarbach, H./Seierstad, C./Gabaldon, P. (2017): Setting the Scene: Women on Boards: The Multiple Approaches Beyond Quotas, in: Seierstad, C./Gabaldon, P./Mensi-Klarbach, H. (eds.), Gender Diversity in the Boardroom, Cham 2017, pp. 1-12.

Meyer, J./Rowan, B. (1977): Institutionalized Organizations: Formal Structure as Myth and Ceremony, in: American Journal of Sociology, Vol. 83, No. 2, 1977, pp. 340-363.

Miller, T./Triana, M. (2009): Demographic Diversity in the Boardroom: Mediators of the Board Diversity-Firm Performance Relationship, in: Journal of Management Studies, Vol. 46, No. 5, 2009, pp. 755-786.

Mitchell, R./Agle, B./Wood, D. (1997): Toward a Theory of Stakeholder Identification and Salience: Defining the Principle of who and What Really Counts, in: The Academy of Management Review, Vol. 22, No. 4, 1997, pp. 853-886.

Morris, R. (1987): Signalling, Agency Theory and Accounting Policy Choice, in: Accounting and Business Research, Vol. 18, No. 69, 1987, pp. 47-56.

N

n.a. (2001): Chancengleichheit von Frauen und Männern in Beruf und Familie erhöhen – Interview mit Bundesministerin Dr. Christine Bergmann, in: Berufsbildung in Wissenschaft und Praxis, Vol. 29, No. 6, 2001, pp. 5-7.

Näsi, J./Näsi, S./Phillips, N./Zyglidopoulos, S. (1997): The Evolution of Corporate Social Responsiveness, in: Business & Society, Vol. 36, No. 3, 1997, pp. 296-321.

Nekhili, M./Gatfaoui, H. (2013): Are Demographic Attributes and Firm Characteristics Drivers of Gender Diversity? Investigating Women's Positions on French Boards of Directors, in: Journal of Business Ethics, Vol. 118, No. 2, 2013, pp. 227-249.

Neuendorf, K. (2017): The content analysis guidebook, 2nd edition, Los Angeles et al. 2017.

Newson, M./Deegan, C. (2002): Global expectations and their association with corporate social disclosure practices in Australia, Singapore, and South Korea, in: The International Journal of Accounting, Vol. 37, No. 2, 2002, pp. 183-213.

Nienhaus, M. (2015): Segment reporting under IFRS 8, Frankfurt am Main 2015.

O

O'Donovan, G. (2002): Environmental disclosures in the annual report, in: Accounting, Auditing & Accountability Journal, Vol. 15, No. 3, 2002, pp. 344-371.

P

Page, A./Sealy, R./Parker, A./Hauser, O. (2024): Regulation and the trickle-down effect of women in leadership roles, in: The Leadership Quarterly, Vol. 35, No. 5, 2024,101721.

Panzer, L./Müller, S. (2015): Earnings quality and gender diversity on German supervisory boards: an empirical analysis, in: Problems and Perspectives in Management, Vol. 13, No. 4, 2015, pp. 9-18.

Patten, D. (1992): Intra-industry environmental disclosures in response to the Alaskan oil spill: A note on legitimacy theory, in: Accounting, Organizations and Society, Vol. 17, No. 5, 1992, pp. 471-475.

Pearce, J./Zahra, S. (1992): Board composition from a strategic contingency perspective, in: Journal of Management Studies, Vol. 29, No. 4, 1992, pp. 411-438.

Pearson, K. (1900): X. On the criterion that a given system of deviations from the probable in the case of a correlated system of variables is such that it can be reasonably supposed …, in: The London, Edinburgh, and Dublin Philosophical Magazine and Journal of Science, Vol. 50, No. 302, 1900, pp. 157-175.

Peña-Martel, D./Pérez-Alemán, J./Santana-Martín, D. J. (2022): Media visibility and board gender diversity, in: Business Ethics, the Environment & Responsibility, Vol. 31, No. 1, 2022, pp. 192-208.

Peng, M. (2004): Outside directors and firm performance during institutional transitions, in: Strategic Management Journal, Vol. 25, No. 5, 2004, pp. 453-471.

Perrault, E. (2015): Why Does Board Gender Diversity Matter and How Do We Get There? The Role of Shareholder Activism in Deinstitutionalizing Old Boys' Networks, in: Journal of Business Ethics, Vol. 128, No. 1, 2015, pp. 149-165.

Pfaff D. /Zweifel, P. (1998): Die Principal-Agent Theorie – Ein fruchtbarer Beitrag der Wirtschaftstheorie zur Praxis, in: Wirtschaftswissenschaftliches Studium, Vol. 27, No. 4, 1998, pp. 184-190.

Pfarr, H. M. (2001): Ein Gesetz zur Gleichstellung der Geschlechter in der Privatwirtschaft, Düsseldorf 2001.

Pfeffer, J. (1972a): Merger as a Response to Organizational Interdependence, in: Administrative Science Quarterly, Vol. 17, No. 3, 1972, pp. 382-394.

Pfeffer, J. (1972b): Size and Composition of Corporate Boards of Directors: The Organization and its Environment, in: Administrative Science Quarterly, Vol. 17, No. 2, 1972, pp. 218-228.

Pfeffer, J. (1973): Size, Composition, and Function of Hospital Boards of Directors: A Study of Organization-Environment Linkage, in: Administrative Science Quarterly, Vol. 18, No. 3, 1973, pp. 349-364.

Pfeffer, J./Salancik, G. (1978): The external control of organizations – A resource dependence perspective, New York et al. 1978.

Poletti-Hughes, J./Dimungu-Hewage, D. (2023): The Effectiveness of Gender Diversity Reforms and the Impact of a Familial Culture: A Spillover Effect on Board Independence, in: British Journal of Management, Vol. 34, No. 3, 2023, pp. 1316-1339.

Popper, K. (1934): Logik der Forschung – Zur Erkenntnistheorie der modernen Naturwissenschaft, Wien 1934.

Popper, K. (2005): Logik der Forschung, 11th edition, Tübingen 2005.

Post, C./Byron, K. (2015): Women on Boards and Firm Financial Performance: A Meta-Analysis, in: Academy of Management Journal, Vol. 58, No. 5, 2015, pp. 1546-1571.

Powell, M./Ansic, D. (1997): Gender differences in risk behaviour in financial decision-making: An experimental analysis, in: Journal of Economic Psychology, Vol. 18, No. 6, 1997, pp. 605-628.

Proppe, D. (2009): Endogenität und Instrumentenschätzer, in: Klapper, D./Konradt, U./Walter, A./Wolf, J. (eds.), Methodik der empirischen Forschung, 3rd edition, Wiesbaden 2009, pp. 253-266.

R

Raffée, H./Abel, B. (1979): Aufgaben und aktuelle Tendenzen der Wissenschaftstheorie in den Wirtschaftswissenschaften, in: Raffée, H./Abel, B. (eds.), Wissenschaftstheoretische Grundfragen der Wirtschaftswissenschaften, München 1979, pp. 1-10.

Rahaman, A./Lawrence, S./Roper, J. (2004): Social and environmental reporting at the VRA: institutionalised legitimacy or legitimation crisis?, in: Critical Perspectives on Accounting, Vol. 15, No. 1, 2004, pp. 35-56.

Ramanathan, K. (1976): Toward a Theory of Corporate Social Accounting, in: The Accounting Review, Vol. 51, No. 3, 1976, pp. 516-528.

Ramsey, J. (1969): Tests for Specification Errors in Classical Linear Least-Squares Regression Analysis, in: Journal of the Royal Statistical Society Series B: Statistical Methodology, Vol. 31, No. 2, 1969, pp. 350-371.

Rave, C. (2022): Business Combinations under Common Control, Berlin 2022.

Rhode, D./Packel, A. (2014): Diversity on Corporate Boards: How Much Difference Does Difference Make?, in: Delaware Journal of Corporate Law, Vol. 39, No. 2, 2014, pp. 377-426.

Richter, R./Furubotn, E. (2010): Neue Institutionenökonomik – Eine Einführung und kritische Würdigung, 4th edition, Tübingen 2010.

Rimmelspacher, D./Kliem, B. (2021): FüPoG II: Geänderte Angaben zur Frauenförderung in der Erklärung zur Unternehmensführung, in: Die Wirtschaftsprüfung, Vol. 74, No. 23, 2021, pp. 1460-1466.

Röhm-Kottmann, M./Gundel, A. (2015): Frauenquote und Zielgrößen für den Frauenanteil – Berichtspflichten in der Erklärung zur Unternehmensführung, in: Die Wirtschaftsprüfung, Vol. 68, No. 21, 2015, pp. 1110-1115.

Rothenburg, V./Moench, L. (2023): Führungspositionen-Richtlinie: Strengere Vorgaben für deutsche börsennotierte Unternehmen?, in: Die Aktiengesellschaft, Vol. 68, No. 7, 2023, pp. 217-219.

Rotsch, F./Weninger, H. (2015): Geschlechterquote - Umsetzungsfragen in der Praxis, in: Der Konzern, Vol. 13, No. 7-8, 2015, pp. 298-306.

Ruhnke, K./Schmidt, M. (2017): Veröffentlichungs- und Prüfungspflichten im Zusammenhang mit der Erklärung zur Unternehmensführung und der nichtfinanziellen Erklärung, in: Der Betrieb, Vol. 70, No. 44, 2017, pp. 2557-2563.

S

Sandrock, O. (2017): The Impact of European Developments on German Codetermination and German Corporate Law, in: Du Plessis, J. J./Großfeld, B./Luttermann, C./Saenger, I./Sandrock, O./Casper, M. (eds.), German Corporate Governance in International and European Context, 3rd edition, Berlin 2017, pp. 243-328.

Sattelberger, T. (2011): Praxisbeispiel Telekom: Die Frauenquote – Qual der Entscheidung und der schwierige Weg vor uns, in: Krell, G./Ortlieb, R./Sieben, B. (eds.), Chancengleichheit durch Personalpolitik, 6th edition, Wiesbaden 2011, pp. 429-435.

Schanz, G. (1988): Methodologie für Betriebswirte, 2nd edition, Stuttgart 1988.

Schipper, K. (1989): Earnings Management, in: Accounting Horizons, Vol. 3, No. 4, 1989, pp. 91-102.

Schulz, S./Ruf, C. (2015): Zweifelsfragen der neuen Regelungen über die Geschlechterquote im Aufsichtsrat, in: Betriebs-Berater, Vol. 70, No. 20, 2015, pp. 1155-1163.

Schulze, P. (2007): Beschreibende Statistik, 6th edition, München et al. 2007.

Schumann, F./Thun, T./Dauth, T./Zülch, H. (2024): Does top management team diversity affect accounting quality? Empirical evidence from Germany, in: Journal of Management and Governance, Vol. 28, No. 1, 2024, pp. 137-175.

Schweitzer, M. (1978): Wissenschaftsziele und Auffassungen in der Betriebswirtschaftslehre: Eine Einführung, in: Schweitzer, M. (ed.), Auffassungen und Wissenschaftsziele der Betriebswirtschaftslehre, Darmstadt 1978, pp. 1-14.

Seibt, C. (2015): § 76 Leitung der Aktiengesellschaft, in: Schmidt, K./Lutter, M. (eds.), Aktiengesetz Kommentar, 3rd edition, Köln 2015, Rn. 1-49.

Seibt, C. (2021): Frauen in Leitungsorganen und Führungspositionen – RegE zum Zweiten Führungspositionen-Gesetz, in: Der Betrieb, Vol. 74, No. 9, 2021, pp. 438-447.

Seidler, H. (2016): Fehlende, unvollständige oder falsche Angaben eines Unternehmens zur Frauenquote: Pflichten des Abschlussprüfers?, in: Betriebs-Berater, Vol. 71, No. 16, 2016, pp. 939-942.

Seierstad, C./Gabaldon, P./Mensi-Klarbach, H. (2017a): Gender Diversity in the Boardroom – Volume 2: Multiple Approaches Beyond Quotas, Cham 2017.

Seierstad, C./Huse, M. (2017): Gender Quotas on Corporate Boards in Norway: Ten Years Later and Lessons Learned, in: Seierstad, C./Gabaldon, P./Mensi-Klarbach, H. (eds.), Gender Diversity in the Boardroom, Cham 2017, pp. 11-45.

Seierstad, C./Warner-Søderholm, G./Torchia, M. /Huse, M. (2017b): Increasing the Number of Women on Boards: The Role of Actors and Processes, in: Journal of Business Ethics, Vol. 141, No. 2, 2017, pp. 289-315.

Shocker, A./Sethi, S. (1973): An Approach to Incorporating Societal Preferences in Developing Corporate Action Strategies, in: California Management Review, Vol. 15, No. 4, 1973, pp. 97-105.

Shubham /Charan, P./Murty, L. (2018): Secondary stakeholder pressures and organizational adoption of sustainable operations practices: The mediating role of primary stakeholders, in: Business Strategy and the Environment, Vol. 27, No. 7, 2018, pp. 910-923.

Singh, V./Terjesen, S./Vinnicombe, S. (2008): Newly appointed directors in the boardroom, in: European Management Journal, Vol. 26, No. 1, 2008, pp. 48-58.

Sojo, V. E./Wood, R. E./Wood, S. A./Wheeler, M. A. (2016): Reporting requirements, targets, and quotas for women in leadership, in: The Leadership Quarterly, Vol. 27, No. 3, 2016, pp. 519-536.

Sondergeld, V./Wrohlich, K. (2021): Mindestbeteiligung von Frauen in Vorständen: Einige Unternehmen sind neuem Gesetz bereits zuvorgekommen, in: DIW aktuell, No. 65, 2021, URL: https://www.diw.de/de/diw_01.c.819614.de/publikationen/diw_aktuell/2021_0065/mindestbeteiligung_von_frauen_in_vorstaenden__einige_unternehmen_sind_neuem_gesetz_bereits_zuvorgekommen.html (01.09.2024).

Sondergeld, V./Wrohlich, K./Kirsch, A. (2024): Share of women on the executive boards of large companies has increased, but generally is at most one woman, in: DIW Weekly Report, Vol. 14, No. 3, 2024, pp. 18-28.

SPD and Bündnis 90/Die GRÜNEN (1998): Aufbruch und Erneuerung - Deutschlands Weg ins 21. Jahrhundert, 1998, URL: https://library.fes.de/pdf-files/bibliothek/downl/koalitionsvertrag1998.pdf (01.09.2024).

Spence, M. (1973): Job Market Signaling, in: The Quarterly Journal of Economics, Vol. 87, No. 3, 1973, pp. 355-374.

Spindler, G. (2019): § 76 Leitung der Aktiengesellschaft, in: Goette, W./Habersack, M. (eds.), Münchener Kommentar zum Aktiengesetz, 5th edition, München 2019, Rn. 1–159.

Spindler, G. (2023): § 76 Leitung einer Aktiengesellschaft, in: Goette, W./Habersack, M. (eds.), Münchener Kommentar zum Aktiengesetz, 6th edition, München 2023, Rn. 1-223.

Spremann, K. (1990): Asymmetrische Information, in: Zeitschrift für Betriebswirtschaft, Vol. 60, No. 5-6, 1990, pp. 561-586.

Srinidhi, B./Gul, F./Tsui, J. (2011): Female Directors and Earnings Quality, in: Contemporary Accounting Research, Vol. 28, No. 5, 2011, pp. 1610-1644.

Statistische Bundesamt (2024): Teilhabe von Frauen am Erwerbsleben, URL: https://www.destatis.de/DE/Themen/Arbeit/Arbeitsmarkt/Qualitaet-Arbeit/Dimension-1/teilhabe-frauen-erwerbsleben.html (31.08.2024).

Stevenson, B./Wolfers, J. (2009): The Paradox of Declining Female Happiness, in: American Economic Journal: Economic Policy, Vol. 1, No. 2, 2009, pp. 190-225.

Stiglitz, J. (1975): The Theory of "Screening," Education, and the Distribution of Income, in: American Economic Review, Vol. 65, No. 3, 1975, pp. 283-300.

Stoney, C./Winstanley, D. (2001): Stakeholding: Confusion or Utopia? Mapping the Conceptual Terrain, in: Journal of Management Studies, Vol. 38, No. 5, 2001, pp. 603-626.

Suchman, M. (1995): Managing Legitimacy: Strategic and Institutional Approaches, in: The Academy of Management Review, Vol. 20, No. 3, 1995, pp. 571-610.

Sun, J./Liu, G./Lan, G. (2011): Does Female Directorship on Independent Audit Committees Constrain Earnings Management?, in: Journal of Business Ethics, Vol. 99, No. 3, 2011, pp. 369-382.

T

Teichmann, C./Rüb, C. (2015): Die gesetzliche Geschlechterquote in der Privatwirtschaft, in: Betriebs-Berater, Vol. 70, No. 16, 2015, pp. 898-906.

Teigen, M. (2012): Gender quotas on corporate boards: On the diffusion of disinct national policy reform, in: Engelstad, F./Teigen, M. (eds.), Firms, Boards and Gender Quotas: Comparative Perspectives, Bingley 2012, pp. 115-146.

Teigen, M. (2022): From Shockwave to Ripple?, in: Engeli, I./Mazur, A. (eds.), Gender equality and policy implementation in the corporate world, Oxford 2022, pp. 197-217.

Terjesen, S./Aguilera, R. V./Lorenz, R. (2015): Legislating a Woman's Seat on the Board: Institutional Factors Driving Gender Quotas for Boards of Directors, in: Journal of Business Ethics, Vol. 128, No. 2, 2015, pp. 233-251.

Terjesen, S./Sealy, R. (2016): Board Gender Quotas: Exploring Ethical Tensions From A Multi-Theoretical Perspective, in: Business Ethics Quarterly, Vol. 26, No. 1, 2016, pp. 23-65.

Terjesen, S./Sealy, R./Singh, V. (2009): Women Directors on Corporate Boards: A Review and Research Agenda, in: Corporate Governance: An International Review, Vol. 17, No. 3, 2009, pp. 320-337.

Terjesen, S./Trombetta, L. (2017): Gender Diversity on Boards in the United States, Australia, and Isreal, in: Seierstad, C./Gabaldon, P./Mensi-Klarbach, H. (eds.), Gender Diversity in the Boardroom, Cham 2017, pp. 235-260.

Thiruvadi, S./Huang, H.-W. (2011): Audit committee gender differences and earnings management, in: Gender in Management: An International Journal, Vol. 26, No. 7, 2011, pp. 483-498.

Torchia, M. /Calabrò, A./Huse, M. (2011): Women Directors on Corporate Boards: From Tokenism to Critical Mass, in: Journal of Business Ethics, Vol. 102, No. 2, 2011, pp. 299-317.

U

Ullmann, A. (1985): Data in Search of a Theory: A Critical Examination of the Relationships Among Social Performance, Social Disclosure, and Economic Performance of U.S. Firms, in: The Academy of Management Review, Vol. 10, No. 3, 1985, pp. 540-557.

Useem, M./Karabel, J. (1986): Pathways to Top Corporate Management, in: American Sociological Review, Vol. 51, No. 2, 1986, pp. 184-200.

V

van der Laan, G./van Ees, H./van Witteloostuijn, A. (2008): Corporate Social and Financial Performance: An Extended Stakeholder Theory, and Empirical Test with Accounting Measures, in: Journal of Business Ethics, Vol. 79, No. 3, 2008, pp. 299-310.

van der Laan Smith, J./Adhikari, A./Tondkar, R. (2005): Exploring differences in social disclosures internationally: A stakeholder perspective, in: Journal of Accounting and Public Policy, Vol. 24, No. 2, 2005, pp. 123-151.

Vasi, I./King, B. (2012): Social Movements, Risk Perceptions, and Economic Outcomes, in: American Sociological Review, Vol. 77, No. 4, 2012, pp. 573-596.

Velte, P. (2024): Diversity Reporting im Spannungsfeld zwischen Nachhaltigkeits- und Corporate-Governance-Berichterstattung, in: Zeitschrift für Corporate Governance, Vol. 19, No. 2, 2024, pp. 84-93.

Verband deutscher Unternehmerinnen (VdU) (2014): Stellungnahme, URL: https://www.bmfsfj.de/resource/blob/119432/854ea9b3918cba2d3cf1efdc4a93f852/vdu-data.pdf (22.06.2024).

Vereinigung Schweizerischer Unternehmen in Deutschland (VSUD) (2014): Referentenentwurf eines Gesetzes für die gleichberechtigte Teilhabe von Frauen und Männern an Führungspositionen in der Privatwirtschaft und im öffentlichen Dienst, URL: https://www.bmfsfj.de/resource/blob/119436/c8383891c5cb4523caea704747e7afb7/vsud-data.pdf (22.06.2024).

W

Wang, M./Kelan, E. (2013): The Gender Quota and Female Leadership: Effects of the Norwegian Gender Quota on Board Chairs and CEOs, in: Journal of Business Ethics, Vol. 117, No. 3, 2013, pp. 449-466.

Wasmann, D./Rothenburg, V. (2015): Praktische Tipps zum Umgang mit der Frauenquote, in: Der Betrieb, Vol. 68, No. 6, 2015, pp. 291-296.

Weil, D./Fung, A./Graham, M./Fagotto, E. (2006): The Effectiveness of Regulatory Disclosure Policies, in: Journal of Policy Analysis and Management, Vol. 25, No. 1, 2006, pp. 155-181.

Weil, D./Graham, M./Fung, A. (2013): Science and regulation. Targeting transparency, in: Science, Vol. 340, No. 6139, 2013, pp. 1410-1411.

Werder, A./Bartz, J. (2012): Corporate Governance Report 2012: Kodexregime und Kodexinhalt im Urteil der Praxis, in: Der Betrieb, Vol. 65, No. 16, 2012, pp. 869-878.

Werder, A./Bartz, J. (2013): Corporate Governance Report 2013: Abweichungskultur und Unabhängigkeit im Lichte der Akzeptanz und Anwendung des aktuellen DCGK, in: Der Betrieb, Vol. 66, No. 17, 2013, pp. 885-895.

Werder, A./Bartz, J. (2014): Corporate Governance Report 2014: Erklärte Akzeptanz des Kodex und tatsächliche Anwendung bei Vorstandsvergütung und Unabhängigkeit des Aufsichtsrats, in: Der Betrieb, Vol. 67, No. 17, 2014, pp. 905-914.

Werder, A./Böhme, J. (2011a): Corporate Governance Report 2011 – Zur tatsächlichen Anwendung ausgewählter Kodexbestimmungen für Hauptversammlung und Aufsichtsrat (Teil I), in: Der Betrieb, Vol. 64, No. 23, 2011, pp. 1285-1290.

Werder, A./Böhme, J. (2011b): Corporate Governance Report 2011 – Zur tatsächlichen Anwendung ausgewählter Kodexbestimmungen für Hauptversammlung und Aufsichtsrat (Teil II), in: Der Betrieb, Vol. 63, No. 24, 2011, pp. 1345-1353.

Werder, A./Danilov, K. (2018): Corporate Governance Report 2018: Kodexakzeptanz und Kodexanwendung, in: Der Betrieb, Vol. 71, No. 34, 2018, pp. 1997-2008.

Werder, A./Danilov, K./Schwarz, P. (2021): Corporate Governance Report 2021: Akzeptanz und Anwendung des neuen Kodex, in: Der Betrieb, Vol. 74, No. 37, 2021, pp. 2097-2110.

Werder, A./Pissarczyk, A./Böhme, J. (2011): Grössere Kodexskepsis im General Standard? – Ergebnisse einer empirischen Untersuchung aktueller Ablehnungsbegründungen, in: Die Aktiengesellschaft, Vol. 56, No. 13, 2011, pp. 492-502.

Werder, A./Talaulicar, T. (2005): Kodex Report 2005: Die Akzeptanz der Empfehlungen und Anregungen des Deutschen Corporate Governance Kodex, in: Der Betrieb, Vol. 58, No. 16, 2005, pp. 841-846.

Werder, A./Talaulicar, T. (2006): Kodex Report 2006: Die Akzeptanz der Empfehlungen und Anregungen des Deutschen Corporate Governance Kodex, in: Der Betrieb, Vol. 59, No. 16, 2006, pp. 849-856.

Werder, A./Talaulicar, T. (2007): Kodex Report 2007: Die Akzeptanz der Empfehlungen und Anregungen des Deutschen Corporate Governance Kodex, in: Der Betrieb, Vol. 60, No. 16, 2007, pp. 869-875.

Werder, A./Talaulicar, T. (2008): Kodex Report 2008: Die Akzeptanz der Empfehlungen und Anregungen des Deutschen Corporate Governance Kodex, in: Der Betrieb, Vol. 61, No. 16, 2008, pp. 825-832.

Werder, A./Talaulicar, T. (2009): Kodex Report 2009: Die Akzeptanz der Empfehlungen und Anregungen des Deutschen Corporate Governance Kodex, in: Der Betrieb, Vol. 62, No. 14, 2009, pp. 689-696.

Werder, A./Talaulicar, T. (2010): Kodex Report 2010: Die Akzeptanz der Empfehlungen und Anregungen des Deutschen Corporate Governance Kodex, in: Der Betrieb, Vol. 63, No. 16, 2010, pp. 853-861.

Werder, A./Talaulicar, T./Kolat, G. (2003): Kodex Report 2003: Die Akzeptanz der Empfehlungen des Deutschen Corporate Governance Kodex, in: Der Betrieb, Vol. 56, No. 35, 2003, pp. 1857-1863.

Werder, A./Talaulicar, T./Kolat, G. (2004): Kodex Report 2004 - Die Akzeptanz der Empfehlungen und Anregungen des Deutschen Corporate Governance Kodex, in: Der Betrieb, Vol. 57, No. 25, 2004, pp. 1377-1382.

Werder, A./Talaulicar, T./Kolat, G. (2005): Compliance with the German Corporate Governance Code: an empirical analysis of the compliance statements by German listed companies, in: Corporate Governance: An International Review, Vol. 13, No. 2, 2005, pp. 178-187.

Werder, A./Turkali, J. (2015): Corporate Governance Report 2015: Kodexakzeptanz und Kodexanwendung, in: Der Betrieb, Vol. 68, No. 21, 2015, pp. 1357-1367.

Westphal, J. D./Stern, I. (2006): The Other Pathway to the Boardroom: Interpersonal Influence Behavior as a Substitute for Elite Credentials and Majority Status in Obtaining Board Appointments, in: Administrative Science Quarterly, Vol. 51, No. 2, 2006, pp. 169-204.

Westphal, J. D./Zajac, E. (1995): Who Shall Govern? CEO/Board Power, Demographic Similarity, and New Director Selection, in: Administrative Science Quarterly, Vol. 40, No. 1, 1995, pp. 60-83.

Williamson, O. (2000): The New Institutional Economics: Taking Stock, Looking Ahead, in: Journal of Economic Literature, Vol. 38, No. 3, 2000, pp. 595-613.

Wilsing, H.-U. (2012): Corporate Governance in Deutschland und Europa, in: Zeitschrift für Unternehmens- und Gesellschaftsrecht, Vol. 41, No. 2-3, 2012,291-308.

Winter, M./Marx, E./De Decker, N. (2015): Zielgrößen für den Frauenanteil in Führungspositionen bei mitbestimmten Unternehmen, in: Der Betrieb, Vol. 68, No. 23, 2015, pp. 1331-1335.

Wood, R. E./Whelan, J./Sojo, V./Wong, M. (2013): Goals, Goal Orientations, Strategies, and Performance, in: Latham, G. P./Locke, E. A. (eds.), New Developments in Goal Setting and Task Performance, New York 2013, pp. 90-114.

Woodward, D./Edwards, P./Birkin, F. (1996): Organizational Legitimacy and Stakeholder Information Provision 1, in: British Journal of Management, Vol. 7, No. 4, 1996, pp. 329-347.

Wooldridge, J. (2010): Econometric analysis of cross section and panel data, Cambridge, Massachusetts et al. 2010.

Wooldridge, J. (2020): Introductory econometrics – A modern approach, 7th edition, Boston, MA 2020.

World Economic Forum (2022): Global Gender Gap Report 2022, URL: https://www3.weforum.org/docs/WEF_GGGR_2022.pdf (30.07.2024).

Z

Zalata, A./Ntim, C./Choudhry, T./Hassanein, A./Elzahar, H. (2019): Female directors and managerial opportunism: Monitoring versus advisory female directors, in: The Leadership Quarterly, Vol. 30, No. 5, 2019, 101309.

Zeger, S./Liang, K.-Y. (1986): Longitudinal Data Analysis for Discrete and Continuous Outcomes, in: Biometrics, Vol. 42, No. 1, 1986, p. 121.

Zenou, E./Allemand, I./Brullebaut, B. (2017): Gender Diversity on French Boards: Example of a Success from a Hard Law, in: Seierstad, C./Gabaldon, P./Mensi-Klarbach, H. (eds.), Gender Diversity in the Boardroom, Cham 2017, pp. 103-124.

Zhang, L. (2012): Board demographic diversity, independence, and corporate social performance, in: Corporate Governance: The International Journal of Business in Society, Vol. 12, No. 5, 2012, pp. 686-700.

Zucker, L. (1977): The Role of Institutionalization in Cultural Persistence, in: American Sociological Review, Vol. 42, No. 5, 1977, pp. 726-743.

www.ingramcontent.com/pod-product-compliance
Ingram Content Group UK Ltd.
Pitfield, Milton Keynes, MK11 3LW, UK
UKHW020834290926
15470UKWH00004B/1340

9 783631 940891